Takeovers

IVAN FALLON and JAMES SRODES

Takeovers

Pan Books
London, Sydney and Auckland

First published in Great Britain 1987 by Hamish Hamilton Ltd
This edition published 1988 by Pan Books Ltd,
Cavaye Place, London SW10 9PG

9 8 7 6 5 4 3 2 1

ISBN 0 330 29870 4

Printed and bound in Great Britain by
Cox & Wyman Ltd

This book is dedicated to Sue Fallon
and Cecile Srodes

Contents

List of Illustrations

Authors' Acknowledgements

We began this book in 1983 and finished it in April 1987, during which time the takeover boom changed considerably. Over these years, we have conducted hundreds of interviews and built up large files of tapes, notes, clippings and other material. Some of the events described in this book are so dramatic they sometimes read like a novel. We should state emphatically that, unlikely as they sometimes appear, they are never fiction. Events and meetings described here are supported by documents, eye witness accounts – or have been witnessed by one or both of us.

We would like to thank all those, many of them the leading characters in the takeover world, who gave us so freely of their time. We would also like to thank our colleagues in the press, whose coverage of the takeover boom we have drawn on, from such papers as *The Times*, *Sunday Times*, *Financial Times*, *Sunday Telegraph*, *Observer*, *Economist*, *Wall Street Journal*, *Washington Post*, *Acquisitions Monthly* and others. We also owe a debt of gratitude to those academic studies we have quoted, which include those by McKinsey, Kidder Peabody, the Institute of Fiscal Studies, the London Business School, Professor Porter of Harvard, Michael Jensen of Harvard and Geoff Meeks of Cambridge, among many others.

We are also grateful for access to a number of books, including *Two Tycoons* by Charles Gordon (Hamish Hamilton), *The Strategy of Takeovers* by Anthony Vice (McGraw Hill), *Merger Mania* by William Davis (Constable), *The Leyland Papers* by Graham Turner (Eyre & Spottiswoode), *New Anatomy of Britain* by Anthony Sampson (Hodder & Stoughton), *Return to Go* by James Slater (Weidenfeld & Nicolson), *Slater Walker* by Charles Raw (Andre Deutsch), *My Life with Tiny* by Richard Hall (Faber & Faber), *Tycoons* by William Kay (Piatkus), *Merger Mania* by Ivan Boesky (Bodley Head) and many others.

Finally we are both immensely grateful to those individuals who kept us on track. At the Washington end of the operation, Maryse Rhein, Lauren Chambliss and Irene Saunders Goldstein were invaluable. At the London end, we could not have survived without Sue Fallon, in a dual role as researcher and manuscript editor, and Denise Heywood.

We also freely acknowledge our debt to Vivienne Schuster and Jane Cushman, our agents in London and New York, and Penelope Hoare, our editor.

Ivan Fallon
James Srodes

A Glossary of Merger Buzzwords

ARBITRAGEUR: A market trader who buys shares in takeover targets, usually after a bid is announced, where he believes there will be a higher bid. As Ivan Boesky, the leading arbitrageur during the recent bid cycle, describes it, the arbitrageur 'takes on risk that the rest of the market will not accept'. Arbitrageurs have helped fuel the boom by providing liquidity to the market. Although arbitrage in its classic sense – equating the price of a commodity, currency or stock in one market with that in another – is an old and respected practice, it is relatively new in the corporate world, and still largely confined to Wall Street. Much discredited since the disgrace of Boesky, but it still goes on.

BEAR HUG: A variety of takeover strategy that seeks to hurry target company managements to recommend acceptance of a tender offer in a short period of time. The tactic involves sending target management a letter (later made public) offering to buy shares at a substantially higher than market price with a sternly worded reminder that the board and management have a fiduciary responsibility to act in the interest of shareholders. Entirely an American practice, which is now out of use because of Williams Act time extension rules (see *Saturday Night Special*, below).

CROWN JEWELS: The most attractive assets of a company. A Crown Jewels lock-up, such as that deployed by SCM in defending itself against Hanson, involves agreeing to sell these assets to a third party at a low price before the bid goes through, thus making the company much less interestig to the predator.

DAWN RAID: A practice which had a brief vogue in London in the early 1980s, whereby a predator's brokers swept into the market the instant it opened and bought up a large block of shares before the opposition had a chance to react. Robert Maxwell acquired his initial holding in British Printing with a dawn raid. Since the Malaysian government took over Guthrie Corporation the rules have changed – and so have the attitudes of the big institutions who will not accept a dawn raid offer now.

GOLDEN PARACHUTE: A generous compensation contract awarded by management to themselves in anticipation of a takeover.

GREENMAIL: 'Green' as in money and 'mail' as in 'blackmail'. The raider buys a significant stake in the target company in a fashion sufficiently menacing to convince it that a takeover is on the way – and might win. This may or may not be the actual intention. The target company is persuaded to buy back its own shares usually at a high premium – and a promise from the raider not to bid again.

HOSTILE TAKEOVER: A bid the management of the target company does not like.

LEVERAGED BUY-OUT: The purchase, usually by management, of a company, using its own assets as collateral for loans provided by banks or insurance companies. The new use of junk bonds has made leveraged buy-outs a common form of hostile device for takeovers as well as for defenders.

JUNK BONDS: More technically, 'high yield' bonds or loan stock. The term 'junk' comes from the dominant high yield bond issued prior to 1978 when the market was almost entirely made up of original issue investment grade bonds that had fallen on hard times and become more speculative – and high yielding. Only about 1,000 American corporations are judged to support so-called 'investment quality' (or A-rated) bonds as measured by Standard & Poor, Moody's or other reputable rating services, but it is unfair to describe every other company's bonds as unsafe or 'junk'. As devised by Drexel Burnham's mergers and acquisitions department in 1983, there has been in the US an explosion in mass-marketed, high interest yielding debt securities put on the market to finance frequently hostile takeover bids. Critics fear that, in many cases, the bidders can never make the assets earn the interest on the junk bonds they have taken on – particularly if there is a downturn in the economy. For a variety of reasons junk bonds have not become a part of the British bid scene.

PAC-MAN DEFENCE: After the video game in which the pursued little cursor survives by attempting to gobble up his bigger enemies.

POISON PILL: A defence technique where a company issues to its shareholders a special preferred dividend stock which is convertible, after a takeover, into the acquiror's shares; the successful bidder thus faces the prospect of heavy dilution. In a wider sense, it also applies to a defensive manouevre in which the target company takes on an enormous debt burden, and either distributes it to shareholders or uses it to buy up stock, thereby making itself much less attractive. Again, not used in Britain.

PROXY BATTLE: A battle between a company and some of its own shareholders. It starts with a group of dissident shareholders soliticiting proxies in order to force through a shareholder resolution.

SATURDAY NIGHT SPECIAL: A surprise tender offer with a 7–10 day expiration period. So called because the strategy often involves announcing it over the weekend, thus denying the rival management time to respond. Now out of use because of new state takeover laws and SEC rule changes.

SEC – SECURITIES & EXCHANGE COMMISSION: The US government agency that regulates securities trading. It has civil enforcement powers only and must seek criminal prosecutions through the US Justice Department.

SCORCHED EARTH POLICY: Extreme defensive tactics by a defending company; taking on heavy debt or selling off the key assets to save itself.

SHARK REPELLENT: Special provisions in a company's charter or bylaws designed to deter bidders.

TENDER OFFER: A cash offer to the shares of a public company for the shareholders' stock. In Britain a tender offer must be one price for 'any or all' shares, but in the US a tender offer may be made for any percentage of the outstanding stock.

WHITE KNIGHT: A friendly bidder, willing to offer more for a target's shares than an existing hostile bidder. A variation is the 'grey knight' who offers to buy the shares of the bidding company as an aid to the defence.

YUPPIE SCAM: The name given to the Wall Street insider trading scandal after a host of smart young lawyers, bankers, brokers and arbitrageurs were found to be in a dealing ring.

Preface

When we began this book in 1983, it was with the intention of examining the issues raised by the recent spate of takeovers, and of attempting to answer, in the light of the biggest takeover boom the world had ever seen, the basic question: are takeovers good or bad? Do they improve the efficiency of industry, provide better products and services, more and safer jobs, help the community – or are they damaging in all or some of these areas? Do they result in a more efficient use of capital? Or in asset stripping and financial rape?

Between us we had followed as financial journalists, often on a day to day basis, the big bids of recent years on both sides of the Atlantic. We had interviewed and come to know personally many of the key participants: the raiders, the defenders, the bankers, the brokers and the other individuals who live off the industry of taking over companies. Early in our researches there was little real debate on the merits or otherwise of the great changes we could see already taking place. But we never had any doubt that changes would come. What we failed to anticipate, however, was the sudden acceleration of forces in these past few years.

We never, for example, expected Ivan Boesky, the once-mythic 'king of the arbs', either to rise to the heights that he did – or to be thrown down so abruptly. Boesky gave us many interviews, not always very informative, but he answered our questions in his own fashion. Even while he did so, he talked on three phones at once, his mind half on the interview, half on his next deal. We were aware when we started

1

that insider trading was an integral part of the takeover scene but it never occurred to us that it would become quite so central, so organised and so pervasive – and be quite so dramatically exposed. We certainly never expected Boesky's demise to lead all the way back to London and Guinness, and result, for reasons which had nothing to do with insider trading but which had a lot to do with other dubious activities, in the destruction of so many careers.

Towards the end, it began to seem as if we might have no-one left to write about, so fast were the resignations pouring in and, in the case of Wall Street, the handcuffs going on. We never got to talk to Dennis Levine of Drexel Burnham, but some of the other fallen heroes of Wall Street gave us considerable help: Martin Siegel, for instance, the golden boy of Kidder Peabody who later replaced Levine at Drexel Burnham. Siegel earned more than $2m a year, was widely regarded as one of the brightest, if not *the* brightest and most personable of the mergers and acquisitions stars on Wall Street, and seemed to have everything going for him – and yet... Who could ever have believed that, at the end of both 1983 and 1984, this star of the business should meet Boesky for what both men called a 'tally up'? 'Now what did you do for me this year?' Boesky would say. And Siegel would give him an analysis of his leaks over the past twelve months.* In two years Boesky paid him $575,000 cash, delivered in suitcases by courier in a public place. It was Siegel who told Ivan Boesky that Carnation was about to get a takeover. It did – from the Swiss group Nestlé and Boesky made a profit of $28.3m on that deal alone.

In London we followed particularly closely the great mega-bids which opened and closed together: the battles for Distillers and for Imperial Group. We spent many hours talking to the raiders involved: James Gulliver and Ernest Saunders bidding for Distillers, Lord Hanson and Sir Hector Laing bidding for Imperial Group. Saunders of Guinness was always going to be a central character in this book – but we admit freely that we had little inkling of the context in which we would eventually write about him. Nor did he – he willingly co-operated with us, and gave us his last interview after the Department of Trade inspectors had appeared, but before the full revelations of what had been happening at Guinness had become public knowledge.

As this book has developed, the bid scene has changed out of all recognition. It has been a period of totally unprecedented boom, followed by a time of shock and revelation which has deeply shaken both Wall Street and London. In this context, it is in one respect unfortunate that the Ivan Boesky and other insider trading scandals

Wall Street Journal, 17 February, 1987.

occurred when they did. That is not to diminish any of the guilt they bear; but it is ironic that the once legendary 'king of the arbs' has been turned into a common scapegoat onto whom both Wall Street and the City of London financial communities have loaded their collective guilt. This is part of what we came to call the Boesky Effect: a collective hypocrisy which obscures the far wider impact.

Perhaps it is unavoidable that, as the complex international web of illegal double dealing unwinds, the public impression is created that Boesky and his confederate Dennis Levine were sinister masterminds and all the others accused (and still to be accused) were more or less culpable stooges in their schemes. It is also perhaps equally unavoidable to make the same mistake in considering the Guinness affair, which (as far as we know) had nothing to do with insider trading, yet had a great deal to do with bending or breaking the rules in the single-minded pursuit of a goal. That false premise leads to a series of false conclusions on the part of the lay public as well as the government and industry experts who are charged with protecting the interests that all of us have in credible capital markets.

The mistaken conclusions are that the Boesky ring operated undetected and unsuspected; and that Guinness was the first company to embark on a major share support operation to help it win a takeover bid. The impression given by those mistaken assumptions is that everything was fine until these bad men came along, and that life will return to normal once they are well out of harm's way. The temptation that faces us in these days of sorting out these huge scandals is to take the easy way: there is an urge simply to ensure that the short-cuts Boesky, Guinness and others used are closed off and that the problem is therefore solved. This, of course, is no solution at all.

The illegal insider trading ring that Boesky joined with Dennis Levine, and the abuses that emerged from the Guinness takeover of Distillers, are only symptoms of a more serious viral infection that has attacked first Wall Street, then the City of London and after that many of the other capital markets of the world. Boesky himself called it 'Merger Mania' in his book on the frenzy. Others have likened the current period of hostile, leveraged raids on the stock prices of corporations to earlier epochs of mass madness such as the eighteenth century's South Sea Bubble or the pre-Crash Wall Street margin frenzy of the 1920s. That infection has not gone away with the collapse of the hostile takeover boom; it is simply dormant.

Although there are marked similarities in the development of the merger boom in the United States and in Britain, there are marked differences, too. London, for a variety of reasons, avoided some of the most seriously worrying features, notably the rise of frightening new financing devices such as 'junk bonds' which have been so widely used on Wall Street and which were highly leveraged and collateralised against the capital assets of the target company itself. The British takeover scene also avoided the enormous shrinking of the equity, risk-capital, base which accompanied the boom in America, and which caused serious concern in the responsible areas of Washington, such as the office of the Fed chairman Paul Volcker.

But similarly worrying trends appear in both markets: for one, insider trading, which we found just as prevalent in London as in New York, even if it is not quite so highly organised; for another, the great pressure the investment and merchant banks bring on their clients to make often pointless bids – and earn fees for the banks; for a third, the absurdly high level of reward – in June 1986 a publication called the *Wall Street Letter* estimated that over 100 people in Wall Street earned more than $3m in 1985, and most of them made it from the mergers and acquisitions field.

This question of remuneration is not just one of envy or of 'two nations' – the financial community and everyone else. It is a serious point. When James Gulliver lost the battle for Distillers, he had to write off over £30m of costs – almost a year's profits. But if he had won, he would have had to pick up three sets of costs: his own (which had a success trigger, so they would have been higher); those of the loser Distillers; and also those of Guinness which cleverly managed to persuade Distillers to pick up its costs, win or lose. The total would have been around £170m, which is more than the total capital expenditure of Distillers in any year of its existence. Yet even these figures were small by comparison with those on Wall Street: Ivan Boesky in 1985 earned $100m personally and Michael Milken, the Drexel Burnham king-pin who basically invented the 'junk bond', accumulated a personal fortune of $500m almost without moving outside his office in California.

By contrast there was considerable publicity in Britain when Sir Ralph Halpern, the chairman of the Burton group, became the first man to earn (perfectly legitimately) more than £1m – publicly. Private estimates in the City of London suggest there were several hundred who earned more than that in the boom period of 1985/6.

In 1986 the director of the Institute of Fiscal Studies estimated that the major contested bids of the previous twelve months had cost £500m in expenses, a figure, he went on to observe, which was many times the cost of all management education and training in Britain.

*

The high earnings of the financial advisers is just one of the side effects of a takeover boom which has caught the public imagination in a way few financial events ever have in the past. They are, however, a factor in explaining the momentum and scale of the activity. Takeovers are nothing new: they have been around as long as the joint stock company. Nor are takeover booms a modern phenomenon: there was one in the United States 100 years ago, and it witnessed battles which in many ways were as bitter and hard fought as today's bids. Yet there is a great deal that is new and unexplained about the avalanche of hostile takeover bids which has hit New York and London, and spilled on into other countries: Canada, Australia and Hong Kong to name a few. The scale of it has been truly astonishing – £9bn worth of bids were completed in London in 1985, and that figure was passed in the first half of 1986 alone. Just five years ago, the running average for takeover activity was £1bn a year. In the United States during President Reagan's tenure of office, merger and acquisition activity has run at almost two-and-a-half times the level seen in the mid-and-late 1970s. In a dozen years it has risen from $13bn to over $180bn, and in ten years there has been $398bn worth of mergers and acquisitions business. In the past decade some 23,000 mergers have taken place including the swallowing up of 82 of the *Fortune* 500.

Scale however is only a part of it. Major industries, such as oil in the United States and retailing in Britain, have changed in a manner for which there is no precedent. The media and the drinks industries are among those which will never be the same again after this past few years. In advertising, a London company, Saatchi & Saatchi, which did not even exist 16 years ago, has become the biggest in the world through a series of acquisitions which have had a chain reaction along Madison Avenue. The City of London has changed beyond recognition in just a few years after a series of acquisitions and mergers completed on the back of its Big Bang de-regulation.

Takeovers have obtruded into all our lives as never before. It was a partial takeover bid for a small company called Westland Helicopters which in 1986 cost Mrs Thatcher two of her cabinet ministers and prompted from her the remark, made to an aide, that 'by six this evening I may no longer be prime minister'.* The Labour leader Neil Kinnock let her off the hook in the Commons that same afternoon, and she survived, but the Westland incident was to have a lasting effect on her government, crucially affecting decisions, such as the proposed sale of Land Rover to General Motors which came afterwards.

*Simon Jenkins, *Sunday Times*, December 1986.

The high earnings of the takeover specialists in the financial capitals of the United States and Britain cannot, however, compete with the glamour image of the real stars of the show: the takeover bidders themselves.

In the US the central characters are as well known today as many film stars: Boone Pickens, Carl Icahn, Ron Perelman, Sir James Goldsmith, Saul Steinberg, Rupert Murdoch. In Britain there is a similar cast of names which equally generates excitement: Lord Hanson, the printer and publisher Robert Maxwell, James Gulliver of Argyll, Stanley Kalms of Dixons – and, not so long ago, Ernest Saunders of Guinness. Goldsmith, through some of the most daring bids seen in Wall Street, has made himself over a billion dollars in five years. Murdoch, equally adventurous, is now probably ahead of him. In Britain Maxwell is moving up into the same league of personal wealth. Hanson and his American partner Sir Gordon White have been more successful in corporate terms than either man – they now run a group capitalised at over £6bn, although their own stakes are worth more modest amounts.

These men are part of a seminal change taking place in the capital markets of the western world. A whole new culture has come into being, reflected even in the language of the takeover game. Phrases such as 'greenmail', 'lock-ups', 'poison pills' and 'shark repellent' are now terms familiar in circles well removed from the robust world of Wall Street where they began. Changes have altered the whole shape and thrust of commercial activity, some of it for the better but some of it also for the worse. Not only are the acquisitions and mergers specialists the kings of the investment banks, but every decent-sized company now runs its own corporate finance division, in effect its own mini-merchant banking operations. There is scarcely a major company which has not now got a shopping list of potential targets to bid for; and which has not, at the same time, put into place the beginnings of a defence in case someone else bids for it. What a decade ago seemed to be the unchallenged order of corporate hierarchy has changed almost overnight. Few names in the *Fortune* Top 500 American corporations or the *Times* 500 companies in Britain can feel safe. 'It is generally recognised now that in the western capitalist hemisphere there are probably only two companies that are bid-proof by virtue of size: General Motors and IBM,' Trevor Swete of Hill Samuel recently remarked. Others add that they are not even sure about *them*.

There are those who argue that the justification for merger activity is that companies and industries become old and inefficient, and the takeover process can often bring about a new modern structure which otherwise might have evolved too late. There is considerable truth in that, and there is no doubt that a healthy level of takeover activity acts as the equivalent of the wolf on the edge of the caribou pack, keeping the herd healthy. There is also plenty of evidence that some of the best companies on either side of the Atlantic could not have come into being without the benefit of takeover activity.

But in many cases it can spell wholesale closures and destruction: the predator discovers he has made a mistake, he runs out of money, or he cynically overrides some of the wider social issues involved. Today in Britain no-one is keen to become the type of social villain that John Bentley and Jim Slater became in the era of asset stripping in the late 1960s, and takeovers have on the whole been more positive and healthier than they were in the last takeover boom when some of the actors were described by the late Patrick Hutber as 'appalling little men, in back-rooms in the City, shuffling bits of paper between each other'. Today's break-up is more likely to involve the sale of whole subsidiaries, often to the management. In the US, the leveraged buy-out, the management takeover of a subsidiary or even a whole company financed by high priced debt (usually junk bonds), has become one of the most active parts of the whole scene. In the list of high earning Wall Streeters, the names of Jerome Kohlberg, Henry Kravis and George Roberts, general partners of New York's leading leveraged buy-out specialists, Kohlberg Kravis & Roberts, ranked in the top five earners with $50m apiece in 1985.

There are wider issues to consider. The relationship of the company to society is changing, and its sensible development may be being challenged by the takeover boom. In America, especially, there is much public pressure on the corporation to be a force for social good – through long-term research, product development and exploration, minority hiring, cultural event sponsorship, environmental repairs and a host of other objectives.

Against this is the corporate raider, still largely an American phenomenon, but beginning to emerge in Britain too. In alliance with a new breed of activist pension adviser, the raider has been the catalyst for an incredible wave of corporate mergers, restructurings and manouevrings which have sent hundreds of millions of dollars washing through Wall Street. In the process, billions of dollars of corporate capital have been paid over to these raiders and the companies themselves have been borrowing (through the infamous junk bond) billions more to stay on track. In Britain the same trends, although less marked, can be observed – as with John Elliott's £1.8bn bid for Allied-Breweries. To assess the full implications of a raider making a bid for a much larger company, financed largely through borrowings, the bid was referred to the Monopolies Commission. And among the principal voices heard against it was that of the Bank of England which pointed to the American experience with some misgivings. 'The Bank told us that in the US since 1983 takeover activity has resulted in a net exchange of over $150bn of equity for debt. Such a trend could be a source of instability for many major industrial groups,' said the commission report. The Bank went on to make the point, true of even small businesses, that a takeover financed largely on borrowings would pre-empt a large part of the cash flow just for debt servicing, and add to the already considerable pressures on management 'to maximise profits and cash generation in the short term by reducing the expenditure on research, development of new products and investment in new methods and equipment'. The Bank added gloomily that 'the competitiveness of British industry would suffer'.

As yet, there is little sign of this; in fact there is some evidence to suggest the opposite may be true. But the danger is real enough. In the United States voices have increasingly been heard making a similar point: the threat of the corporate raider and the pressure from the institutional investors have increasingly been seen as not consistent with the long-term development of the company as either socially responsive or competitive in the longer term. The example set out in this book in the Phillips chapter shows how an entire town was dependent on a paternalistic oil company, and how it changed overnight with the appearance of T. Boone Pickens.

On the other hand Pickens himself has argued forcefully and persuasively that Big Oil had become what he calls the 'Good Ol' Boys' club', and that he, the outsider, made it think about the real owners, the shareholders, for the first time in two generations.

And what of the more measured takeovers, properly financed, and made by big, well-run companies? There have now been a series of academic studies done on the results of takeovers in both the United States and Britain which show a remarkably similar pattern. By and large, the shareholders of the target firm *do* receive more money for their shares than they paid for them initially. It would be unthinkable if it were otherwise. But what is truly astonishing is that the shareholders (the real owners, if one subscribes to that view) of the pursuing corporations rarely see any gain in *their* share prices as a result of a takeover.

Studies of hundreds of takeovers in the United States over the past decade show that only one third of the mergers have enriched the winning side; one third have been pretty much a wash; while one third of all modern M&A activity ends up *costing* the backing investors substantial sums. Those findings are a fairly precise summary of the British studies too.

Why then do companies make bids? The answer is the central theme of this book.

Pressure from the financial sector, anxious to keep its fee income going, is a part, though probably only a minor part, of the answer. Growth, measured in profits, sales and market share, is another factor – takeovers can often cut a dozen years of slow progress off an impatient management's planned progress. There is the desire to diversify, particularly for a one-product company, such as a tobacco firm or a whisky distiller. There are all sorts of grander rationalisations produced: the need to get bigger to take on the international competition, the desire to get into a foreign market, or to give an ambitious and able management new challenges on a less efficient company, or more simply because there is 'synergy' between the two groups which will turn two and two into five.

These are often post-rationalisations more than reasons. They ignore basic human fundamentals: the ambitions of individuals to make a mark, to win prestige and respect, or at least to become better known. They ignore also the excitement for the bidders stretched to their limit and beyond, playing giant games of strategy and tactics, of controlling the situation through intense media interest, advertising, circulars and stock market activity. Individual bidders have mentioned to us during our researches that they only feel fully alive when they are deep into a hostile bid, the teams fully tuned up and running, working day and night, through the weekends, seeing their every move in the papers day after day, becoming for this two or three month period the men everyone wants most to talk to. For the most aggressive raiders, making a bid is like climbing a mountain – unless it is a big bid, beyond the bidder's normal reach, there is no challenge. The adrenalin only flows when the peak is higher than anything reached before. The England Test cricketer Phil Edmonds found himself caught up in a small takeover battle in the autumn of 1986 when Sears Holdings bid for Blacks where he had a shareholding. Asked about it by Michael Parkinson on *Desert Island Discs*, Edmonds talked about the adrenalin boost he got from being involved, adding that he got the same charge out of it as he did when 'bowling to Alan Border' (the Australian captain and one of the greatest batsmen in the world).

This book, then, has more to say about personality than about institutions. It attempts to examine the broader issues raised by takeover mania, not in an academic or theoretical sense, but in the way mergers have actually arisen in the real market places. As this book developed, it struck us both more and more forcefully how the personalities of the individuals create the major events. It also struck us how arbitrarily and unscientifically decisions are often taken. The best practitioners of the takeover art rely on their own instincts far more than they do on detailed financial assessments and advice. An example: when Sir Gordon White of Hanson Trust was bidding for SCM, he had two reports prepared on its value. Cross-examined in court later, White admitted he had barely skimmed those reports. So how did he value the company? 'Gut feeling,' replied White bluntly. And his gut was right. The financial advice he got put a top price on SCM of $750m. White ended up paying nearly $1bn – and within a year had recouped all of that, and still retained the more profitable two-thirds of the company, conservatively valued at $1.7bn. And nobody seemed to have lost out.

In this book we have attempted to capture some of the excitement and tension takeover bids create among those involved. Most of the personalities are known to us personally and we are grateful for the time they have spent reliving what in some cases were painful memories. We have not attempted to write about every bid in detail, but have chosen those which in our view encapsulated the central themes, strategies, confrontations and principles.

We frankly admit that the answers to the question: 'Are *takeovers* good or bad?' has proved almost impossible to find. But our answers may be close to the question: 'Are *businessmen* good or bad?'

Ivan Fallon
James Srodes
April, 1987.

• CHAPTER ONE •

Giants of Times Past

In Britain, the biggest completed takeover of 1985 was the acquisition – for £615m cash – of House of Fraser by the Egyptian Fayed brothers. It was, however, small by comparison with the unfinished battles then raging, which made 1986 the busiest ever year in takeover history. It was also small compared to what was happening in the United States, where there had been three bids of more than $5bn in 1985: Royal Dutch/Shell for its own American subsidiary Shell Oil, Philip Morris's takeover of General Foods, and General Motors' acquisition of Hughes Aircraft, just a part of the empire left by the late billionaire recluse, Howard Hughes. Although 1984 had seen even bigger American bids – Chevron Corp's $13.3bn acquisition of Gulf Corp is still the big daddy of bids, followed by Texaco's $10.1bn takeover of Getty Oil – the level of activity through 1985 and 1986 continued to rise. Data bases in the US recorded more than 3000 completed transactions valued at $1m or more in 1985.

1985 had already seen all records broken in Britain: according to the magazine *Acquisitions Monthly*, there had been 968 takeovers worth £9.8bn. But in the first nine months of 1986 alone that figure more than doubled: the takeover roll stood at £20.2bn, 20 times the average total for an entire year in the early 1980s. The takeover boom was sounding as it had never done before.

Statistics of this kind are often mind-numbing. It takes a leap of imagination to grasp the fact that behind each and every takeover are hundreds, often thousands, of human beings: management, workers, customers, competitors and of course the legion of accountants, lawyers, bankers, stockbrokers, advertising agents and so forth, all of whom are affected – as indeed are the families of all of them.

Merger mania has created a low-key but growing level of disquiet on both sides of the Atlantic. But in Britain the level of protest, even from the Labour party, was markedly more subdued than it had been in the Heath era of the early 1970s when 'asset stripping' had been one of the 'dirty' slogans thrown at the City.

To some extent the subdued level of protest in Britain reflected the decline of the trade unions since the late 1970s, and the revival of interest in the City and investment. But it was also a reflection of the care the bidders, notably Lord Hanson and Sir Owen Green of BTR, gave to avoiding wholesale closures and redundancies which had accompanied the big takeovers of the late 1960s and early 1970s. Takeovers still often resulted in company break-ups, but the style had changed. When Hanson divided up the UDS stores chain and sold off the constituent parts – Richard Shops and John Collier for example – they went as going concerns, and in some cases to the management. There were some marches and sit-ins, but nothing approaching the scale of the public protest which, for instance, built up around Arnold Weinstock's decision in 1968 to close the AEI factory in Woolwich, South East London, with the loss of 500 jobs. In the 1980s the big closures and redundancies were happening in the public sector – in coal, steel, shipbuilding, the motor industry or the mines where hundreds of thousands of jobs had been lost. The 5500 *News International* printers, sacked after going on strike before the Murdoch papers moved to Wapping, created far more publicity than the £20bn of takeovers that happened in Britain in 1986.

Takeovers have always attracted a degree of stigma, both from the right, who fear the loss of competition, and from the left, who dislike too much power held in too few hands (unless it is in the hands of the state). But there is an astonishing degree of ambivalence on all sides. The view that takeovers are bad where they create a monopoly is as old as the concept of the corporation itself. In the nineteenth century, the growth of corporations and the explosion of economy-rocking monopoly attempts that followed the Civil War in the United States caused public outrage, although in the beginning at least much of it was directed at the concept that management and shareholders should be shielded from risk in the event of insolvency, through being incorporated as a limited company. 'The modern corporation is a legal individual without an ass to kick or a soul to save,' said John Ise, an early radical Populist from Kansas in the 1880s.

What the Morgans, the Rockefellers and the others tried to do in those palmy days was to gain monopoly positions and their mergers and stock trades were usually directed towards that end. 'Trusts' were what they called the combinations that, for example, led to small petroleum producers being coerced into the Standard Oil Trust; E. H. Harriman combined railroads; there was a meat trust, several attempts at grain trusts and various shipping combines. By 1880 John Davison Rockefeller controlled 95 per cent of the oil produced in America. The public outcry soon led to Washington enacting a series of anti-monopoly laws which coincided with the brief period of prosperity which lasted from the end of the depression of 1893 until the next recession of 1904.

It was 1911 before the Standard Oil Trust was finally broken up by the US Department of Justice; it was divided into 39 different and theoretically competitive companies, several of which are still among the biggest companies in the world: Exxon and Chevron for example. On hearing the decision of the Supreme Court, Rockefeller humorously sent an obituary to his old partners: 'Dearly beloved, we must obey the Supreme Court. Our splendid, happy family must scatter.'

A number of the old Rockefeller companies would emerge again, both as bidders and as targets, in the merger boom of the 1980s. So too would another creation of this monopoly era. J. P. Morgan, the man known as the Jupiter of Wall Street, was the great centraliser in a centralising age. In 1901 Morgan effectively eliminated the last element of competition in the steel industry by creating the United States Steel Company, which took over all the competition including Carnegie (who received $300m in bonds, the basis for his great foundation) and became the biggest business organisation the world had ever seen.

Ironically, that very company, now fallen upon hard times, was to get a bid from one of the new stable of predators, Carl Icahn, in the autumn of 1986. The latest takeover boom has reached to the very heart of the American economy.

In Britain, as in the United States, the life of many companies has also come full circle in the recent takeover boom. Before the First World War, Imperial Tobacco had been born from a series of mergers and takeovers, and through the 1960s and 1970s was one of the most aggressive bidders itself as it tried to diversify away from the declining business of tobacco. It made a number of disastrous mistakes, notably the purchase of Howard Johnson in the United States – and in 1985 it became a target company. Some of the modern-day giants – Distillers,

Unilever, Royal Dutch/Shell and Imperial Chemical Industries – are the products of mergers and acquisitions activity between the wars. Some of these very companies, thought so huge and powerful when they were put together, were among the targets, or potential targets, of the latest boom.

The second great period of merger activity in the US coincided with the boom period between 1925 and 1930. This time the objective was to control the production cycle from raw material to finished product – just as Henry Ford constructed his famous River Rouge plant where iron ore could be unloaded from barges at one end and gleaming black Model-T Fords would issue forth at the other.

The 1929 Crash and Depression put an end to massive conglomeration until well after the Second World War. But with the 1930s came a new type of activity: the defensive merger. There was too much capacity for the shrinking markets of the world, and the best way to eliminate it was to take over the opposition and close him down. No-one talked about takeover mania. The 'in' word at the time was 'rationalisation', and it often took place with government support.

Only after the war did the type of aggressive, or hostile, takeover that we recognise today begin to develop with any great force. In Britain government-imposed dividend restraint held down share prices on the stock market, and by the early 1950s a new breed of bidder soon discovered that asset values were often well above market capitalisation. It was particularly apparent in the property and stores sector, which attracted many raiders.

The best known and most daring of them was Charles Clore, described by the former financial journalist William Davis as 'the tycoon extraordinary, the gambler who took on the Establishment and invariably came out on the right side'. Clore's bid for the footwear group Freeman, Hardy and Willis is still relished by takeover connoisseurs in the City.

Years after his death, Clore's takeovers have acquired a mythology of their own. He was, as Charles Gordon in his book *Two Tycoons* describes him, 'the true initiator of the takeover as we know it today, the first begetter of the conglomerate, the entrepreneur with a finger in every pie'.

Yet by the standards of today's Wall Street raiders, the methods of the Clore era were almost gentlemanly. Davis described how he operated:

Months, sometimes years, before making a bid he started buying shares in the market. He did so gradually, so as not to arouse suspicions. And he operated through a nominee name – a device which enabled buyers to hide their true identity. It gave him a useful starting base, acquired at an average level well below the bid price. And if the offer flopped the other side's efforts to justify rejection to shareholders boosted the value of his holding to a point where he could sell at a useful gain.

Such methods are illegal today – a shareholding has to be declared within a few days of it going above five per cent, regardless of the number of names it is held through. And, even then, the City did not like such methods and imposed its own form of voluntary code. But as Davis, who was a City editor at the time, says: 'In the fifties, however, any reasonably thick-skinned operator could use [these methods] over and over again.' It is also ironic to speculate that of all the major companies currently deemed to be takeover favourites, Sears Holdings, the vehicle created by Charles Clore (the name came from his takeover of J. Sears and Co, the True-Form Boot company, and had nothing to do with Sears Roebuck with which Americans often confuse it) is among the favourites.

There were others around at the time of course: Sir Isaac Wolfson who built the Great Universal Stores empire; Lord Fraser of whom we shall hear more in the next chapter; Max Joseph who created Grand Metropolitan; Sir Jules Thorn of Thorn Electrical; and the property developer Jack Cotton. But Clore's is the name that will inevitably be associated with the takeover bid.

Curiously, the hostile bid remained a stranger to the United States until well into the 1970s, although in Britain it had become part of the scene 20 years earlier. In 1958 the City was shaken by what came to be called the Aluminium War: a battle for control of the British Aluminium Company, then trying to tie up a deal with the American group Alcoa, and the joint bidders Tube Investments and the American group Reynolds Metals.

It was a bid battle which established the reputation of a small merchant bank which until then was regarded as an upstart, the post-war creation of a German refugee, with little time for the City's traditions: S. G. Warburg. Warburg won convincingly for its clients TI-Reynolds by going into the market and buying every share they could find. Few would guess that two decades later Warburgs would be the leading merchant bank in the City.

It was this bid, plus Charles Clore's most ambitious foray yet, a bid for the brewery Watney Mann (which was repulsed), that inspired the City's first tentative takeover code in 1959, the precursor of today's much more elaborate Takeover Panel. In the light of the events since, and given the enormous growth of takeover activity, that decision must be one of the most important the City has ever taken. The United States had gone a different direction over 20 years earlier by creating the Securities and Exchange Commission. If the City had not at that point set up its own self-regulated takeover code, however ineffective at the beginning, it would have found it impossible to resist an SEC once the Labour government came to power in October 1964, and would have had even less chance in the anti-City mood that prevailed so strongly when Labour got back in again in 1974.

'The code reflected growing public awareness of the importance of mergers and takeovers,' wrote Tony Vice in his book *The Strategy of Takeovers*, 'coupled with the belief in the City and industry that control by statute (in the way that President Roosevelt had created the Securities and Exchange Commission) was probably impracticable and certainly undesirable.'

The repercussions of the Aluminium War ran on for some years. Together with Clore's bids, the City establishment had suffered a significant defeat, and was forced to rethink its whole attitude to the hostile bid. 'The Aluminium War helped to change both the City scene and the takeover game,' wrote William Davis in his book *Merger Mania*. 'The City began to shake off the club image, and to recognise the need for a competitive spirit.'

From the 1960s on, the Clore-style raid was hijacked by the City establishment and has been regarded as a perfectly respectable tool ever since. The most conservative of merchant banks developed their corporate finance departments, and soon the takeover experts had become the new stars of the City. It was performance that counted above all else – winning, with whatever tactics, and using whatever methods a bank could legally employ. Every major bid battle seemed to bring a new addition to the Takeover Code, as bright young merchant bankers found holes through which they could pass effortlessly. If a merchant bank showed itself queasy, reluctant, or simply unimaginative at finding ways around the code, the aggressive bidders soon went somewhere else. The pecking order in the City altered as rapidly as it did in industry.

Even Britain's biggest companies joined in the new bid spree. Perhaps the most seminal battle of all was that between ICI, Britain's biggest industrial concern and commonly referred to in journalists' shorthand as 'the bellwether of British industry', and its nearest rival Courtaulds. It was an imaginative, bold leap on the part of the then

ICI chairman, Paul Chambers, who first tried to arrange an agreed merger and, when that failed, launched what was for many years the biggest bid ever made in Britain - £200m. In the end the bid failed, but only just. Today, the winning board would probably give a party. 25 years ago, more traditional values still held: the Courtaulds board celebrated by going to church, filing solemnly into a City church to the great amusement of the journalistic community. Within a short time, the Courtaulds management, now led by Frank (later Lord) Kearton, showed a different side to their character, as they went on an astonishing bid spree themselves, taking them right through the 1960s and through most of the textile industry as well. Kearton was determined that his company would never be vulnerable again. That fear, too, would become a recurrent theme of the next 20 years, and is particularly apparent today.

The ICI-Courtaulds battle had another result. Until then the government had played no active role in takeover battles, which had been settled privately by shareholders and the City. But here for the first time was a takeover involving a major chunk of British industry, with hundreds of thousands of employees, and millions of pounds worth of exports - and the government had no power to intervene even if it wanted to. The Monopolies Commission only had powers to step in after the takeover had gone through, and then only if it was seen to be operating in a way which appeared to be against the public interest. It was obviously an unsatisfactory position, and the Labour party had some fun at the Conservative government's expense. The country was confronted with the spectacle, said Douglas Jay, later President of the Board of Trade (which had responsibility for the City, the Monopolies Commission and competition policy) 'of two giant companies, supposed to be models of enlightened private enterprise, suddenly grappling in a financial fight to the finish in which either short-term profits or megalomania will decide the issue, with the national interest nowhere considered'.

Jay himself changed that when he became a minister, but the involvement of government in the takeover arena developed in an even more unexpected and almost schizophrenic way in the years of the Wilson government. Labour created a new body, the Industrial Reorganisation Corporation, which was equipped with £150m of government money which it was to use to encourage mergers in the hope of improving Britain's competitive position with the rest of the world. British industry, the argument went - and it was largely true - was hopelessly inefficient, too fragmented and too small to take on the

American giants (the Japanese had not yet emerged). Answer: encourage it to get bigger and more efficient through mergers and takeovers. Britain still had effectively full employment, so no-one worried too much about the redundancies that would necessarily be created by this policy. There was much talk of a new industrial revolution, sponsored by the new body. The IRC, in the words of Harold Wilson at the time, would 'drag Britain kicking and screaming into the twentieth century'.

The IRC attracted some able men: Frank Kearton, the hero of the ICI-Courtaulds battle, became its part-time chairman, and Ronald Grierson, one of the brightest and ablest of Sir Sigmund Warburg's stars, became the chief executive (he was later succeeded by Charles Villiers, an even more eminent banker). Urged on by George Brown, in charge of the short-lived Department of Economic Affairs, the IRC had an active life. It became centrally involved in the biggest takeover boom Britain had yet seen, a period essentially of large industrial takeovers very different from the ones of the 1980s.

Its philosophy, particularly when contrasted with the attitude of the Labour party today, to the merger boom now sounds as if it came from another world. Certainly the modern Labour party does not like to be reminded of it, and Anthony Wedgwood Benn, the overseer of so much of it, would probably wish to pretend it never existed.

The IRC's first annual report set out the philosophy of the day:

> In the industries where structural change is urgently needed, the companies face a clear choice. They can themselves take steps to create stronger units; they can be taken over from within the industry or from outside it; or they can wither away. To discharge its statutory duty, the IRC continues to seek out the companies willing to take the first of these choices. The hope is that rationalisation can be by agreement, but if this proves impossible, IRC will not flinch from exercising its collective judgment in supporting positive action.

The organisation left no doubt of its intention to intervene directly in the bid arena if necessary – and quickly did so. These were still the days of the 'white hot technological revolution' and the spearhead of it was to be the IRC. One early example of direct involvement was in the scientific instrument industry: the government, inspired by Wedgwood Benn, wanted bigger units in this fragmented industry. John Davis of Rank Organisation had a similar concept and bid for Cambridge Instruments, having first carefully briefed the IRC people of his intentions. The IRC, however, was not impressed with Rank. But when a rival group, George Kent, put forward a counter-proposal which the government body enthusiastically endorsed, Rank then raised its bid, and one of the strangest bid battles of all got under way. Encouraged by Charles Villiers at the IRC, Kent again topped the Rank bid and the IRC came out into the open with a statement that the Kent offer had its full support. Davis at Rank made a still higher offer, and the IRC then entered the market off its own bat, buying not just Cambridge Instrument shares, but shares in the bidding company George Kent as well, in an effort to boost its share price and keep up the value of the bid. It won the day, but the repercussions were considerable.

The City complained loudly that the government, through the IRC, had completely altered the rules. From now on, it was argued, no-one would dare to make a bid without first getting IRC approval. 'When the situation recurs,' wrote the *Spectator*, 'will not the IRC-backed bidder get what he wants at the price he cares to name? The queue of those anxious to ingratiate themselves with the IRC will stretch from Pall Mall to Threadneedle Street.' The state had become involved more deeply and directly in private enterprise than it had ever done before in Britain – and ever has since.

There were more takeover battles in a similar vein. The ball bearing industry was 'rationalised' under direct and often overpowering pressure from the IRC. So was Britain's computer industry. But its major and lasting efforts came in more important industries: electrical engineering and in motors.

If Clore had been the leading figure of the 1950s, the principal player in the late 1960s was Arnold Weinstock. In 1967 and 1968 Weinstock completed two of the largest and most spectacular bids of the age, first the hostile takeover of AEI, and then a merger with the larger English Electric. Weinstock's background and style ideally suited the mood of the time. He was a statistician by training – he took a degree at Cambridge after first studying at the London School of Economics.

He married the daughter of the TV and radio manufacturer, Michael Sobell, and three years later went to work for him. The young Weinstock transformed the Sobell business, and then did a reverse takeover of the much bigger but ailing group GEC. Within two years he emerged as managing director there. The changes he brought about are now part of legend, head office staff was cut from 2000 to 200, 35 regional headquarters were closed, unprofitable product lines sold off or shut down, and new and rigorous financial targets were set. Profits trebled in the five years before 1967, but even so GEC was tiny in comparison to the American and European companies – and the

Japanese were a rapidly growing threat. Increasingly it made sense to put Britain's three big electrical companies, GEC, AEI and English Electric, together.

The first target, AEI, rejected all Weinstock's early overtures, but in 1967, backed by the IRC, Weinstock launched his bid. It was a long and bloody battle, even by modern standards, but Weinstock won. AEI had brought into play many of the defensive techniques that would later become a standard part of the arsenal of a defending merchant bank: it had spent £200,000 on advertising, a huge sum for the day; it had produced a forecast of sharply increased profits (it later turned in a large loss); it had even produced a new chairman elect, in the rounded shape of Lord Beeching, the man who had rationalised the British Rail network. And there was a primitive form of what came to be known in the Wall Street of the 1980s as the 'scorched earth' policy: it sold its minority stake in British Lighting Industries to Thorn, a move that rankles to this day with Weinstock. It even sold its head office to a property group, Land Securities, which showed a handsome profit on it within a year.

Immediately afterwards, Weinstock began talks with the chairman of English Electric, Lord Nelson. But before they had got very far, English Electric received a bid from another quarter: the much smaller Plessey, with assets a third the size, stepped into the arena, thus establishing a long rivalry between GEC and Plessey, which ran all the way into 1985, nearly 20 years later, when Weinstock finally made his own bid for Plessey – only to have it thrown out by the Monopolies Commission.

Weinstock won English Electric with the support of its board, the government and the City, which now regarded him as the hero of the day. Still in his early 40s, he ran a company which employed more than 200,000 people with sales of over £1bn, a giant of the day. He was, according to Davis, seen in Whitehall and the City alike as 'the vanguard of a new type of British tycoon'.

The City and Whitehall favoured rationalisation of Britain's key industries, and Weinstock seemed just the man to do it. He quickly showed how tough he could be as he closed factories and shed labour – 20,000 workers went in the first two years after the merger. His takeovers were widely hailed as the most important Britain had seen for more than 50 years, and a key part in the task of preparing Britain for the tougher competition that everyone could now see looming.

Today, GEC is still one of Britain's biggest companies, but its reputation and that of Weinstock has faded. Britain's share of exports in electrical and electronics goods has declined, while the Japanese, European and American firms have made huge inroads into the domestic market. GEC has almost retired from the manufacture of domestic appliances, of TVs and radios and has concentrated on the heavier end. Now, like AEI and English Electric 20 years ago, it has acquired the reputation of a sleeping giant which is itself vulnerable to takeover. Again the cycle has come full circle, in this case in a single generation.

There was another major government-inspired takeover of the time which also created a group employing more than 200,000 people: Donald Stokes of Leyland, Britain's largest bus and truck group, took over BMC to form the ill-fated British Leyland Motor Corporation. It is often forgotten with what high hopes it came into existence in 1968: it ranked second only to Volkswagen as the largest motor manufacturer in the world outside the US. It was Britain's fifth largest company, and the second biggest industrial group after ICI. It had no less than 250,000 shareholders. As Graham Turner wrote in his book *The Leyland Papers*, 'The superlatives flowed and the optimism overflowed: Britain now had a car giant fit to face the world.'

Harold Wilson and Wedgwood Been had both personally become involved in making this merger happen, marking the high water mark in government involvement in the takeover market. Why were they so keen on the merger? 'There were basically two reasons,' said Tony Vice in his book. 'One was that at that stage the Labour Cabinet was convinced of the great benefits of mergers to be achieved through economies in production, finance, and marketing; above all, ministers were seized with the need for British companies to merge in order to be able to compete with their larger European and US counterparts.'

Stokes was heavily applauded when he gave his own rationalisation for the merger. 'A company cannot survive in international markets without size, without marketing and service outlets, and without the advantages of scale for research and development,' he said. There was scarcely an industrialist in Britain at the time who, faced with competition from the big international companies, did not support that view.

The buzz phrase of the time was 'economies of scale', promoted by the influential Labour economist Professor Kaldor and others. Again it is easy to forget the climate of the day. A Labour government was actively promoting takeovers and mergers, knowing full well that redundancies would follow as sure as night follows day. Harold Wilson had continually voiced his view that the big motor groups were vastly overmanned. Graham Turner tells the story in his book of how Wilson, besieged in his hotel by a group of communist-led shop

21

stewards from BMC, finally decided to find out what they wanted. 'The stewards asked would he receive a delegation of twelve: Wilson proposed three and they settled on six. As the men marched into the room, he counted them: there were twelve. "Yes," he said, "that's one of your troubles at BMC, isn't it?-You always have twelve men where six will do."'

Today, after a government investment of over £3bn, what is left of British Leyland has about 51,000 employees – and is still losing money. Its share of the British market has shrunk from over 50 per cent to less than 20 per cent. And what remains of it, now called Rover Group, is increasingly dependent on its joint developments with the Japanese. The disastrous decline of the British motor industry had probably very little to do with this merger – most studies cite labour relations and poor management as the primary causes – but the industry would probably be in better shape today if it hadn't happened.

It was, however, one of the last of this particular run of mergers and takeovers, which had run its course by the end of the 1960s. For one thing there had been a change of government in Britain, and Edward Heath killed off the IRC in October 1970.

Its supporters could claim that its job was already done, and that the overpowering need to prepare British industry for international competition had been achieved. Fred Catherwood, then the director general of the National Economic Development Council, which is designed to improve the performance of British industry and includes the government, the trade unions and industry on its board, named five industries in which it was 'desperately necessary to get mergers in order to keep our end up in international competition'. They were the motor industry, which had now got British Leyland; computers, now merged under the banner of International Computers (now part of Standard Telephones and Cables); electrical engineering, which had been solved by GEC's takeovers; and shipbuilding and steel, both of which were nationalised.

The performance of four of the five industries since has been little short of catastrophic, and between them they have shed over 300,000 jobs since their mergers. The one exception is the electrical sector, and even that has not been an unqualified success.

While all this was happening a new style of takeover came to Britain from the United States. The third American merger wave was based on the management theory that a primary manufacturer should seek out some enterprise that provided counter-cyclical balance to his revenue lines. It didn't matter what the product lines were. It was known as the 'conglomerate' bid, and for a brief few years was the new fashion, its arch-priest a Dallas-based entrepreneur called Jimmy Ling. Ling combined the aeroplane-maker Chance-Vought with Temco, a ball-bearing maker, into Ling-Temco-Vought (or LTV as it now is).

In the decade that followed at least 70 per cent of the conglomerations of the 1960s were broken up. By the early 1970s 'gigantomania', as one official in the Nixon administration referred to it, was out of fashion even in the US. John Mitchell, Nixon's attorney general, was adopting a tougher line on allowing takeovers, and in one notable speech cited autos and razor blades as two industries dominated by giants which were dependent on foreign competition for technical innovations. By then, too, in the United States the conglomerate takeovers, notably Jimmy Ling's, were running into both financial problems and heavy criticism.

In Britain, the concept of the conglomerate was embraced in particular by one man, but developed in an entirely different direction from that pioneered by Ling. The era of Jim Slater had arrived.

The hangover of this era is still felt today. Slater brought an entire new philosophy which he soon spread from London to the other markets he moved into: Australia, Singapore, Hong Kong and to a lesser extent Canada. It would burn brightly for a few years, and then splutter out, leaving behind many unpleasant memories and a great deal of financial pain. But it also left behind, often still in embryo form, some of the major characteristics of the takeover boom of the 1980s.

It started glamorously. Slater himself was a personable 6ft 3in accountant, who had become something of a star in the motor industry. At 35, he had been the youngest man on the board of Leyland Motor; Donald Stokes, in the days before the merger with British Motors, had picked him out as a future chairman. Largely because of worries about his health – he was a self-confessed hypochondriac – he left the motor industry, and in 1963 started a small investment advisory business. Soon he had a partner. Slater afterwards described their meeting in his book *Return to Go*:

In September 1963 I first met Peter Walker, who was at that time shadow minister of Transport. We had both been featured in a series of articles entitled 'The Under Forties'. Peter had formed a dining club of those who were featured, and I met him as a result. He subsequently asked me to dine with him at his house at Walton-on-Thames, which was a few minutes away from my house in Esher. I well remember how during the dinner, when I complimented him upon the wine, he immediately turned to his personal assistant who was dining with us and said, 'Tim, make a note to send a case of this wine to Mr Slater in the morning!' I thought this was a wonderful gesture, but it was only when I received the invoice a week later that I realized that perhaps I had found a potential partner.'

The history from that point is briefly summarised by Slater himself: 'In the subsequent seven years an obscure £1.5m company called H. Lotery & Co Ltd was developed and expanded by me to a stage when its market capitalisation was in excess of £200m.'

That however hugely understates the influence, both beneficial and malevolent, of the Slater years. In September 1976 *The Times* called Slater 'the most remarkable phenomenon of the British financial scene in the 1960s and 1970s'. The investigative journalist Charles Raw, no friend to Slater nor Walker, subtitled his book on Slater Walker 'An investigation of a financial phenomenon' and wrote of it in his foreword:

> Its influence went further than the financial world. One forgets, perhaps, today [the book was published in 1977] just how closely Slater Walker was identified with the New Tories then emerging under Heath – of whom Walker was such an important member. They accepted the Slater Walker style of capitalism: indeed it was their answer to Harold Wilson's and Tony Benn's 'technological revolution'.

Anthony Sampson in his book *New Anatomy of Britain* wrote that Slater, like Walker, was 'the very paragon of the new Heath-type Tory – self-made, hard-working, unsentimental, competitive'. The Conservative government of 1970–74 was even labelled the 'Slater Walker' government. Both Slater and Walker had similar backgrounds to the new-style Tory: grammar school boys, from middle-class families, who had got to the top on their own wits and abilities. That described Edward Heath himself. It also described Margaret Thatcher, although she was never identified with the Slater era. Peregrine Worsthorne in the *Sunday Telegraph* wrote of the new Tories as the Mr Efficiencies, the meritocrats who would change the face of British industry, hacking away the deadwood, revolutionising the ingrained and old-fashioned habits of management, producing from the industrial mess a new and invigorating Britain.

Slater himself, in his book *Return to Go*, described the philosophy of the company:

> The object of Slater Walker from the beginning was to inject better

management into a range of existing companies. Clearly it must be of advantage to the economy to have dead assets liberated from basically hopeless ventures, and channelled instead into other enterprises that might be more successful.

Slater saw his own company doing what the IRC was attempting to achieve at the time.

The financial predator acted as a catalyst in stimulating fear within the fat and lazy managements, thereby making them more active. In some cases companies were bought by predators and then resold into stronger hands. In a sense, fear of the predator was an essential discipline for many boards, as without it they would have tended to rest upon the laurels of their predecessors.

This is very little different from the statements of Carl Icahn or Boone Pickens today, although neither is probably conscious of Slater's prior claim to this philosophy. For that is what it is: if takeovers genuinely did result in greater efficiency, if the mere threat of one spurred poor management to greater efforts, and weeded out poor performers whilst rewarding the efficient, then there would be little argument against them.

Unfortunately Slater never proved the point. He made some of the most dazzling takeover bids of the time, sometimes handling two or three at once. He first of all conglomerated; then, when that became unfashionable, changed course abruptly and became an investment bank, spinning off a series of satellite companies, into which he then fed acquisitions and financial services. He lurked somewhere behind almost every bid of the day, building share stakes secretly through a series of nominee companies, using different brokers and different names, and then injecting them into one or other of his satellite companies.

In the takeover world, these were heady times. 'At one time to be a Slater associate was akin in the City to being a companion to Alexander the Great,' wrote the *Sunday Telegraph* in October 1975.* 'He spun off golden whizz-kids by the dozen, seemingly able to pluck anyone out of the back office and transform them with an injection of a loan, a fat parcel of shares and a shell company into instant millionaires.'

In the seven years from 1967 to 1972 Slater had built up a group which controlled South Africa's tenth largest industrial company; his associates in Canada were capitalised at £75m; he had quoted companies in France, Belgium, Holland and Germany; and he was preparing a major move into the United States. His following in the

*Ivan Fallon.

stock markets was such that every time he took a stake in a company the shares automatically soared. In the first 18 months, the average rise in the shares of overseas companies he bought into rose by 1000 per cent.

The other side of the picture, however, was the growing public dislike for his activities and those of his satellites which, after 1972, took the term 'asset stripping'. There is no better description of this technique than that which appeared in *Fortune* magazine in June 1973, written by John Ball.

Spot an asset situation, move in on it, cash some of the assets, and use the profit to bankroll the next deal. It was a mode of operation relatively new to staid British business. Its success, indeed, depended on a certain claret-grouse-and-port-induced somnolence in British boardrooms – failure to earn a reasonable return on capital employed, and indifference to the fact that many corporate assets, notably real estate, had a current value much higher than the figure in the balance sheet.

It was when this technique, particularly when used by one of the brasher whizz-kids, John Bentley of Barclay & Son – a Slater satellite – resulted in wholescale redundancies, some of them taking place in front of the TV cameras, that Slater began a transformation from City hero to public villain. However he still talked confidently of building the biggest investment bank in the world, and many believed he could do it. 'Slater of course started as the great industrial renovator,' wrote the late Patrick Hutber, the legendary City editor of the *Sunday Telegraph*. 'But he quickly found his true role to be that of an investment banker, someone who I think is cleverer with money than anyone else in the world.'

Abruptly in 1973 everything began to fall apart. Slater agreed his biggest deal yet, a merger with the merchant bank Hill Samuel. Mounting opposition from the City establishment and from Slater's growing number of doubters killed it. Then came the Yom Kippur War and a miners' strike in Britain which was to bring down the Heath government; the City of London was plunged into its worst banking crisis in 50 years. Share prices collapsed faster than they had even in 1929, and property fell even faster. Slater reacted rapidly but too late, desperately scrambling to get into cash. By 1975 the full emptiness of his empire lay exposed and, with it, his promise of revolution in British management. Once when I* criticised him, he wrote to me angrily. 'You and I have a fundamental difference of philosophy. You criticise

*Ivan Fallon.

26

me for not having a long-term view. But a long-term view is merely an excuse for a short-term mistake.'

Years later, when he came to publish his book, he wrote:

I agree that I was too inclined to take a short-term view of everything. I did have hair-trigger reactions in market terms and tended to act almost instantly. In retrospect, a number of moves that were right and expedient in the short term were wrong in the long term. As a result of this tendency of mine we were constantly changing tack and failed to establish a real identity in later years.

Pursued from Singapore by the relentless Lee Kuan Yew, who talked ominously of stamping out forever Slater's form of 'freebooting capitalism', and with his empire collapsing around him, Slater stunned the City in October 1975 by suddenly announcing his resignation. His friend Jimmy Goldsmith replaced him as a short-term measure, basically to give the remnants of the group a decent burial, and to protect his own investment in the company. It was the Bank of England which had to pick up the tab: some £60m or so, although it eventually got most of it back.

Slater himself was a ruined man. In his book, written two years later, he said: 'I have been the subject of very considerable criticism, and the Singapore authorities have made an attempt to extradite me [it failed, but his deputy, Dick Tarling, was extradited to Singapore and served four months in Changi jail]; my personal fortune of some £8m has gone and my net financial position is now a very substantial minus figure.' (Although Slater today lives a quiet, private life, he is again a millionaire.)

The takeover boom had by then long ended, but the reverberations went on for years. The industrial strategy of the IRC, partly revived by the Tories, was then desultorily pursued by the new Labour government after 1974 through the National Enterprise Board, set up to invest directly in key companies, rather than to encourage takeovers.

The Slater era had given takeovers a bad name. Many of them had gone wrong, notably Slater's own string of them, but also some of the bids he encouraged: the Bowater takeover of Ralli International, another Slater satellite, was far from a success, for example. Almost all the Slater whizz-kids collapsed in the chill financial climate of the mid-1970s, and for the rest of the 1970s there were few major takeovers in Britain, and even fewer hostile battles. The political, social and economic climates had all moved against it: the Labour government was now as opposed to the further concentration of industry, unless it was done through the state (as with shipbuilding in

1975 for instance) as it had been favourable to it ten years before; in social terms, the term 'asset stripper' had become an epithet thrown at predators with notable effect – few were brave enough to risk the type of stigma that had attached itself to John Bentley and Slater himself; and finally the stock market was so depressed, and economic activity at such a low level, that most companies were thinking more about their own survival than they were about expansion.

The fourth and current merger wave began in the United States in the 1980s with the revised business rationale now calling on managers to seek 'synergy' in their acquisitions – that is to seek out a match in demands of managerial skills. Those days, however, abruptly ended in 1982 when William Agee of Bendix bid for Martin Marietta and touched off the first all-out 'Pac-man' defence, which ended up with both firms owning a majority share interest in the other.

Again a period of prosperity was developing, inflation was dropping and assets were considered undervalued. Other forces were at work. Congress had changed some of the laws to make 'managements more accountable to the public', and the public were more than just shareholders; public interest suits against corporate boards, damage suits for injuries, environmental suits for pollution have since turned boardrooms into fortresses.

In Britain, many of the names that emerged in the 1980s were new. But several of the 1960s/70s breed of bidder had survived, battle-hardened and wiser having learned from Slater's failures as well as his successes. There were the two other Jameses: Goldsmith and Hanson, both of them former Slater associates who had learned some of their bid techniques, not to mention some important lessons, from Slater, and who now began to deploy them in the United States in ways that would make a major impact even on that huge market. There was Jeffrey Sterling, who had once moved in the Slater orbit and who in the 1980s was to emerge at the head of P&O, running major shipping, property and construction (Bovis) interests. And there was Nigel Broackes of Trafalgar House, who won a battle for Cunard in 1971, bought the London Ritz in 1976, failed to get either the Savoy or Rolls-Royce Motors, but did win Beaverbrook Newspapers, publishers of the *Daily* and *Sunday Express*, in 1977. There was Owen Green of BTR who had bought some of the assets that Slater had allegedly 'stripped' and used them as the base for one of the most successful companies in Britain today, including the takeover of Thomas Tilling and Dunlop.

There was also another man, already something of a legend, whose own orbit had often touched that of Slater, and who had an unexpected but important part to play in the development of takeover history. That man was Tiny Rowland.

• CHAPTER TWO •

The Battle of Harrods

Just before eight on the morning of 31 October, 1984, a tall broad-shouldered man, in his late 60s, arrived at the entrance of an anonymous apartment block in London's Park Lane. A glass door slid silently back, permitting him to step in off the street. But another, heavier, armour-plated door prevented access to the lobby. From inside, two security men, immaculately attired in dark jackets and striped trousers, watched him warily. Although he was expected, he still had to announce himself formally and go through the well-rehearsed ritual, without which no-one got to the lifts in this building. The visitor did not object; he had just walked from his own apartment in a similar block around the corner. This was an area of London where many rich and powerful people lived or stayed, many of them foreigners. The visitor was as rich and powerful as most – and also as security conscious. The men he had come to see were even richer. The next few months would decide if they were also more powerful.

'Mr Rowland for Mr Al Fayed,' said the visitor. A security man dialled a number, spoke briefly, then nodded. The inner door slid back and Roland 'Tiny' Rowland, chief executive and major shareholder of the Lonrho international trading group, stepped into the sanctum of the Fayeds, three Egyptian brothers, little known outside a select few banking parlours in the City of London at the time, but soon to be on the front pages of every newspaper in the western world.

Rowland had come for breakfast and what was to prove a fateful meeting. As he stepped into the lift, and climbed eight floors to apartment 46, Rowland must have felt bitter and despondent. His mission that morning marked the end of his long-held dream: to take over the House of Fraser stores group and, with it, the jewel in London's retailing crown, Harrods of Knightsbridge.

The door of apartment 46 was plain oak and, like everything else in the building, subdued but secure-looking. The lobby inside was spacious and the ante-room, its walls covered with eighteenth-century English watercolours, even more so. A plain oak door beyond opened only after a discreet knock and a low electronic buzz.

The room Rowland now entered was an astonishing one, even by the standards of the rest of the building. It was panelled in oak, bought by one of the younger Fayed brothers, Ali, from an English stately home that was being torn down, and now skilfully fashioned to line an elegant study. At the back, almost in an alcove, was a large desk. It was carefully placed to present to its user one of the most surprising views in London: the large picture window, the length of the room, looked out at tree-top level over Hyde Park, and the room seemed to be floating in a great forest, rather than stuck in the heart of one of the world's greatest cities; from inside, the only building visible was the Albert Hall in the distance. The gleam of the Serpentine could just be glimpsed through the trees; not even a murmur from the traffic below on Park Lane reached the room. It was the inner sanctum of the Fayeds – and a fitting place to transact the business Rowland had come to do.

Rowland that morning had gone there to make a deal that few thought he would agree to. His Lonrho group, which controlled mining, agricultural and industrial interests all over the world as well as casinos in London's Mayfair and the luxurious Princess Hotel in Acapulco, also owned 29.9 per cent of the shares in House of Fraser, Britain's largest department stores group. For seven years Rowland had fought savagely to take over the whole of House of Fraser, but had been blocked by a combination of the British financial establishment, which disliked him intensely, and the British government, which distrusted him. Rowland coveted Harrods as he had never before coveted anything in his 67 years of life.

But that morning he had come to sell his shares. And the man he hoped would buy them was the figure who now rose to greet him. Mohamed Al Fayed, the eldest of the three Fayed brothers (the prefix 'Al' simply stands for the elder), was 54, a distinguished-looking man of above medium height, his greying hair slightly receding. He looked more like a fit sea captain off duty than an international businessman. Usually, in this building – which he seldom left when he was in London – he wore a turtleneck sweater and casual trousers, tailored for him at Turnbull & Asser, the Jermyn Street store that he later bought. This morning, he wore a dark suit and tie, matching the immaculate dark suit of Rowland.

Al Fayed had fallen under the spell of Harrods. He compared it to another of his assets, the Paris Ritz – a legendary institution, built for another age, which was not quite what it once was, but which could be restored to its former greatness. No store in the world had anything approaching the same prestige. Harrods was deeply embedded in the mythology of London, a byword for quality and snob appeal. At that point the Al Fayed empire employed 13,000 people worldwide. House of Fraser employed 25,000.*

What happened in that room in Park Lane that morning between these two men was unique and remarkable. Most takeovers are fought between vast teams of people on each side, advisers and technocrats of all kinds, some of the teams exceeding 100 professionals. We will see in this book how Ernest Saunders of Guinness never moved without a professional opinion and, if he didn't like it, would seek another one. In the United States bids are run by lawyers from the outset, and worked out through the courts.

Both men were mentally prepared for the deal they were about to agree. For more than a year Rowland had been delicately dangling his 29.9 per cent stake in House of Fraser in front of Al Fayed, but Mohamed was far from convinced he would sell. It meant far too much to him, and Rowland was wont to tease others with assets he knew they wanted – at a much publicised meeting at Claridges with Robert Maxwell, the British publisher, he had talked about selling the *Observer* newspaper, but had pulled back at the last moment, as Maxwell always suspected he would.

Rowland and the Egyptian had talked semi-seriously about Harrods in the summer, and it had suited Rowland to keep the talks simmering. Neither man could later recall who had first broached the concept of a deal, but both tended to attribute it to the other. 'He offered me the shares,' said Al Fayed. Rowland, in a letter dated 3 July, 1984, to Al Fayed, said: 'I have thought very carefully about your idea of buying Lonrho's 29.9 per cent holding in House of Fraser,' implying that it was Al Fayed who had put it to him. The talks had sputtered on through the summer and autumn, with neither man believing they would ever come to anything.

---

*Lonrho, for the record, employed 150,000 people, mostly in its mines, plantations and farms in Africa and Princess hotels.

That morning, however, as Mohamed lead the way into a dining room laid for breakfast and Ali joined them, Rowland made a serious proposal. If Al Fayed would offer him 300p a share in cash and deliver it within 48 hours, he could have his House of Fraser shares. If the Fayeds missed the deadline, or quibbled about the price or terms, then there was no deal. The shares at the time traded on the stock market at 250p. Rowland had paid the equivalent of around 150p a share for Lonrho's 46.1m shares. The terms meant that the Fayeds would have to find £138m in cash in two days. Lonrho would make a profit of £70m. But the Fayeds would have nearly a third of House of Fraser – a perfect platform from which to launch a bid for the rest. Mohamed did not haggle. Rowland, who still wanted to keep Fayed on the hook, indicated he had one or two other interested parties. But Al Fayed, rightly, did not believe he could find anyone else to give him that type of cash in the time he wanted it.

The Egyptian did not even hesitate when Rowland made his offer. 'Fine,' he said. What bank did Rowland want the money paid into? Rowland wanted a banker's draft. That was no problem. Just let him know when and where. If Rowland wanted £138m in cash, he could have it, not in 48 hours, but in 24 if necessary. There must be no strings attached: he would give Rowland the cash, Rowland would give him the shares, and that would be that.

Al Fayed had only one purpose in buying the shares – he intended to take over the whole of House of Fraser. He had already lined up a merchant bank, Kleinwort Benson, to handle it for him. Early feelers had indicated that the board of Fraser, terrified of Rowland, might agree. Rowland himself had indicated several months before that he would only sell his shares if Al Fayed went the whole hog. 'We have had so much loyalty and support from Lonrho and Fraser shareholders over the past year or two that it would be impossible for us to sell the shares while neglecting the effect on their holdings, if Lonrho accepted an individual offer,' Rowland wrote to Al Fayed. 'It seems to me that the value of their shares would subsequently fall.' (This was to prove completely wrong.) Later in the same letter he wrote: 'The acceptable thing for us would be an offer to all the shareholders.'

That was the mood in which Al Fayed recalls agreeing to the deal that morning. From the way in which Rowland behaved – and he had known him, on and off, for a dozen years – he still believes that was how Rowland saw the deal, too. The Lonrho chief executive seemed to have reached the end of the road on this takeover battle, blocked again and again by the government, the establishment, and by those in the City who disliked him. The prospect of a £70m profit, a useful sum even for a company Lonrho's size, offered a handsome compensation for his disappointment.

Al Fayed's interests were private and family-owned – there should be no surprise that he could make a decision of this kind without legal advisers. But Rowland, although the biggest shareholder in Lonhro, was still an employee of a public company, and had to report to a board of directors. Rowland, however, was a businessman of the old school. He prided himself that he could agree a deal, however big, with a handshake, and the details could be thrashed out by the lawyers and accountants afterwards. When he bought the *Observer* over breakfast in Claridges, he and the seller, Robert Anderson of Atlantic Richfield, did not even discuss the purchase price.

So when Al Fayed and Rowland shook hands on their deal, neither was in any doubt that the other would deliver. There was no need for documents, nor signatures, even on the back of an envelope. The deal was done.

As Al Fayed conducted Rowland to the lift, all was smiles and goodwill. Rowland, inwardly, can hardly have felt cheerful. But at the same time he must have had a feeling of relief and release – Harrods had haunted him, occupied hours and weeks of his management time, and, by his own admission, held back the progress of Lonrho. Now he would have the cash and the time to do other things.

The next day, Thursday, was a day of considerable activity. The Fayeds quickly put together the cash they needed and lodged it with Kleinwort Benson, one of the City of London's leading merchant banks. They were already planning ahead to a bid for the whole group, and wanted to make it all at the same time. For that they would need over £450m in cash. Even that, however, did not make them pause. This again is an important point; later Rowland insisted time and again that the Fayeds did not have enough money of their own to bid for Fraser. Yet it was he who offered them Lonrho's shares in the full expectation he would receive cash, and it was he who encouraged them to bid for the rest, also presumably believing at that point that they had the necessary cash. Only later did he challenge this.

Within hours, the Fayeds had made arrangements with the Royal Bank of Scotland for the extra money they would need. Then Mohamed went to Fraser's headquarters in Victoria to meet the board, led by Professor Roland Smith, Tiny Rowland's arch enemy. Smith suspected they were merely fronting for Rowland, and were just another ruse in the long battle for control of the stores group. 'I met Mohamed Al Fayed for the first time at our Victoria offices on

Thursday,' said Professor Smith neutrally that weekend. 'He told me that the family was considering purchasing Lonrho's stake and wanted to know if the deal would have our support.'

Al Fayed told Smith he was prepared to bid for the whole company at the same price he was offering Lonrho. But there was a condition: the bid had to be recommended both by the Fraser board and by its merchant bank S. G. Warburg. Al Fayed met the board again that evening at Victoria and was told there would be no recommendation of the sort he wanted – at least not yet.

Back at his own office in Cheapside, near St Paul's in the City, Rowland unexpectedly received another bid – Sears Holdings, the vehicle built up by Sir Charles Clore, had decided it would have one final try at taking over Harrods. The offer Lonrho received, however, was well short of what it wanted. Unfortunately the Sears' chief executive, Geoffrey Maitland Smith, and his chairman, Leonard Sainer, who for many years had been Clore's right hand man, were both away. A senior director, Aubrey Hawkins, did his best, and within hours had put together an offer which matched the Fayed bid of 300p a share but would have meant swopping Sears shares for the Fraser stake. Rowland turned it down. He rang Mohamed Al Fayed again. The shares, he told him, were his if he could come up with a draft for £138m by 10.30 the next morning.

The Fayeds did. On the following day, the banker's draft was handed over in the City offices of the Royal Bank of Scotland in exchange for the Fraser shares. By 12.20 the draft had cleared and the stake was now in Egyptian hands.

It had taken two days to put the whole deal together, from Rowland's visit to 60 Park Lane to cash being paid over in return for the share certificates. It seemed an astonishingly tame ending to the most long-drawn-out and bitterest of disputes. The battle seemed to be over, at least as far as Tiny Rowland was concerned. He now owned only a nominal few hundred shares in House of Fraser and his successors were already making the most conciliatory noises to the Fraser board. But it wouldn't be long before the truth dawned on all those concerned: it was merely the beginning of the most vicious phase yet in the great battle for Harrods.

This battle had already involved just about every bank and broking house of any note in the City of London. Successive governments, both Labour and Conservative, had found themselves faced with the most embarrassing decisions. There were questions in the House, almost perpetual government enquiries and investigations, and continual front-page headlines. New Secretaries of State for Trade were greeted by their civil servants on their first day in office with the sight of the biggest file in the whole department, and warned they were about to be bombarded and abused by Tiny Rowland. The battle brought into play all the complex elements of the British takeover scene, and exposed, as no other takeover before or since, the flaws of government and City attitudes to opposed takeovers.

At one stage or another each one of the bodies with responsibility for controlling British corporate mergers had to give rulings; they were often conflicting. There were no fewer than three Monopolies Commission enquiries and three different rulings (if the commission's enquiry into a suggested takeover of House of Fraser by Boots several years before is counted, then there were four – easily a record). There were two Departments of Trade enquiries into Lonrho – also a record. There were literally hundreds of references to the City's own self-regulatory body, the Takeover Panel – again breaking all the records. There were countless other records too: Tiny Rowland later remarked that his own favourite cartoon about House of Fraser was a dispirited shareholder opening an envelope and remarking: 'If only I'd had as many dividends as I've had circulars.' There was another one, too, which tickled him: a boss turning to his junior and remarking: 'I'm putting you on the Lonrho inquiry, Hammersley – an excellent career with a substantial pension.' Millions were spent on newspaper advertisement campaigns, on legal fees, on advisers' fees and on much, much else.

Rowland often remarked, more ruefully than bitterly, that 'Lonrho was the most investigated company in the world's history.' His wife Josie, concerned by the drain on her husband's once considerable energies, commented: 'I think Lonrho was created in order to be investigated.'

The battle for Harrods exposed the gaps in the rules and the subjectiveness of the decision-making at government level. It also exposed the City behaving at times at its worst, closing its ranks to block out a man considered an outsider. For much of the history of this bid, Rowland is a man deserving of sympathy, striving within the rules for a perfectly reasonable objective. For the latter part, which dates from that breakfast meeting, we have an obsessive and bitter man, pursuing an objective that he himself had allowed to slip from his grasp. The history of the bid also exposes, as perhaps no other except Guinness does, the central role of the personalities which soon outweigh the issues, the money, or even the target itself.

In this case, of course, there was a worthy target. Although there are bigger department stores in the world – Macey's in New York is larger

– Harrods is unique, the Rolls-Royce of stores. It occupies its own four and a half-acre site and the five-floor buildings on Knightsbridge contain a total selling space of 15½ acres, or 675,000 square feet. From this huge space, Harrods sells 'the world's most comprehensive range of merchandise and special services'. Its customers are the rich and the famous from all over the world. At the height of a crucial Opec meeting in 1981, the store opened especially for Sheikh Yamani to do some much photographed shopping. The Queen keeps an account at Harrods, as do 150,000 others around the world. It sells everything from 450 types of cheese to 150 pianos and 8000 dresses. Jimmy Carter disembarked from Air Force One at Andrews Air Base near Washington clutching a Harrods bag after a trip to London. In 1975 Harrods received a midnight call from friends of the then Governor of California, Ronald Reagan, ordering a baby elephant; it was duly despatched, with a large label around its neck, addressed simply: 'Governor Reagan, California'.

Tiny Rowland had realised many years before that ownership of Harrods would give him automatic respectability and international acceptability. He once related an incident which perhaps sheds more light on his desire for Harrods than anything else. He had spent some weeks setting up a meeting with the new president of Mexico, Lopez Portillo. Rowland had done business in Mexico for many years, and owned a beautiful house overlooking Acapulco Bay where he spent every Christmas. But he had big plans for Mexico and Portillo was crucial to them. 'What does your company do?' asked the president. Rowland began reciting the many African mining and trading interests – he did not yet own the Princess Hotel at Acapulco – and the president lost interest. 'If I could have said "We own Harrods" then I wouldn't have had to go any further.'*

Over the years Harrods had been at the centre of a number of much publicised takeover battles. In 1959 the rival stores group Debenhams attempted to get hold of it, but after a struggle, hectic by the standards of the day, mild by the standards of recent battles, was beaten by a Scotsman called Hugh Fraser, later Lord Fraser of Allander. Fraser had expanded his family drapery business to the point where he owned a big department store in every major town in Britain. But he, too, was bitten by the Harrods bug. 'The department store wanted by everyone, but especially by Fraser, was of course Harrods, believed to be well out of everyone's reach,' wrote Charles Gordon in his book *The*

*Interview with the authors.

37

Two Tycoons. 'Hugh Fraser would never have admitted to being a commercial snob, but he coveted Harrods all his life and he got it.'

There was of course a great deal more to Harrods than status. It was also a highly profitable and still growing business. Its 230 departments attracted 50,000 customers a day; it had its own furniture depository and its own art gallery, its own bank, theatre, library and pet shop, it had seven restaurants and four bars. In the financial year to 31 January, 1985, Harrods' turnover was £270m, and its profits were averaging nearly £1m a week.

There was therefore nothing new about a man like Rowland wanting Harrods – or even a man like Mohamed Al Fayed. Wanting and having were two different things, however. And however much he might have coveted it – and his interest in Harrods really only began in the mid-1970s – neither Rowland nor Al Fayed would have got near to owning the store if it had not been for a flaw in the character of the man who at that stage headed the House of Fraser.

When Lord Fraser took over Harrods in 1959 he was 56, a tough, respected, third generation retailer who was still regarded as an outsider by the traditional customers of the Knightsbridge store. He soon killed fears that he was only interested in stripping the best out of Harrods and, under his ownership, the splendid store became even better.

But in 1966, only seven years after he had accomplished his life-long dream, he died. His heir was only 29, but already something of a legend in the retailing business. The young Sir Hugh Fraser had, under his father's hard tutelage, learned his trade the traditional way, by working as everything from counter jumper to buyer. He boasted that by the age of 21 he knew by heart the price and catalogue number of every item the group sold.

In his first few years as head of the House of Fraser there were doubts about both his ability and his determination to maintain the impetus his father had given to the group. But soon he showed he had the same ambition and the same hunger to expand. He took the group much more into the south of England through a series of takeovers, notably the Army and Navy stores group. As profits grew, the doubts turned to accolades in the financial press.

They were premature. As he approached 40, Fraser gradually let a darker side of his character take control. His first marriage broke up, then, a few years later, his second. He was often to be seen in the casinos in London's Mayfair until the early hours. He drank heavily. Then early in 1977 there surfaced a scandal which brought his private life out into the open.

In addition to House of Fraser, there was another Fraser family concern, a public company called Scottish & Universal Investment Trust, or Suits for short. Fraser's father had put his non-retailing interests into it, including Whyte & Mackay whisky, the *Glasgow Herald* newspaper and various other investments, the most important one being most of the family holding in House of Fraser itself: Suits in fact owned 27.5 per cent of House of Fraser. The young Sir Hugh decided that was too much to tie up in one asset and in October 1974 sold a block of 17.5 per cent in Fraser to Carter Hawley Hale, the Los Angeles-based stores group. It was one of his other actions at Suits however which hit the headlines in March 1977. The group had become involved in a property deal which had turned sour and as a result had to write off £4.23m which it had lent to another company. Shareholders were not told of the loan. But before the announcement of the write off – and the subsequent fall in the Suits share price – Sir Hugh sold 1.5m shares. He needed the money to meet his gambling debts – he was now playing up to four roulette tables simultaneously, and losing heavily. But when the details of the share sale became known, he was immediately accused of 'insider dealing' (not then a criminal offence) and subjected to an enquiry by the London Stock Exchange, a serious matter for a chairman of two public companies.

Fraser was more astonished than anyone to find himself the subject of so much enquiry and investigation. He was not even aware he had done anything wrong until the accusations surfaced. In the event he was cleared of the more serious charge of insider dealing but heavily criticised by the Stock Exchange for 'inefficiency and ignorance of financial affairs'. His reputation as a shrewd businessman had taken a beating.

Worse still, the details of his drinking and gambling had also become public knowledge, with Sir Hugh openly admitting and discussing them with anyone who cared to ask him. He was clearly a deeply troubled man, his wealth no shield against his inner anguish and the failure of his private life. Questions began to surface about his position as chairman of the House of Fraser.

It was at this point that Tiny Rowland made his entry. He was already the *bête noir* of the British establishment. He himself claimed that Prince Philip had personally crossed his name off Buckingham Palace invitation lists. Worshipped by his own shareholders, almost all of them private people – there were few institutions – his controversial image was only exceeded by the success he had made of Lonrho. He had excited extreme feelings of loyalty and dislike. At one point the former prime minister Edward Heath had classed Lonrho's activities as 'an unpleasant and unacceptable face of capitalism', a phrase that would haunt Rowland for the rest of his days.

More mystery surrounded Rowland than any other person in the City, much of it encouraged by Rowland himself. His friend Daniel K. Ludwig, the American shipowner, property man and listed by *Forbes* magazine – before he lost over $1bn in the Brazilian jungle – as the richest man in the United States, once told Rowland that the press, unable to discover anything about him, had made up details in the hope he would react and correct them. 'Never correct anything,' he cautioned Rowland. 'Let them print whatever they like. It all adds to the legend.'

Rowland had long decided there was nothing wrong with a bit of mystery; it worked to your advantage. It was a theme he would often develop. 'If I know who your father was, where you went to school, what you studied at university, who you've worked for, then I know all about you, I know how you will behave, how you will react. You become an open book to me.' He indicated clearly that he intended to keep the covers on his own book firmly closed. Only at rare relaxed times did he open them to allow a brief glimpse.

'My father fled with the Dalai Lama in 1910,' he once said.* It was the time of the Younghusband expedition, and the Chinese invasion. But Rowland would not be drawn. He never liked to talk about his father.

In fact, Rowland's father was a German trader called Furhop who spent much of his life in India. His family firm traded from Hamburg but had offices in Calcutta, Madras and Rangoon – and for a while in Tibet until a Chinese expeditionary force reached Lhasa, forcing the Dalai Lama to flee. Furhop married a girl whose Dutch family had settled in England and taken the name Carton. They had a daughter before she journeyed back east with him before the First World War. Tiny was born on 17 November, 1917, the fourth child, in a British internment camp in India, where his parents were detained. Mystery still surrounds his nickname Tiny – no-one, including his wife, ever calls him anything else – as he is neither exceptionally tall or small, but it seems to have been given to him by his Indian nurse or ayah. Today he signs all his letters 'Tiny' above the more formal 'R. W. Rowland' and encourages friends and colleagues to address him as 'Tiny'.

Later, when he bought the *Observer*, the staff, in a desperate effort to stop him, turned loose the paper's best investigative journalist to discover what they could of his background. Much of it in the end was fed to the *Sunday Times*, and was used by the reporter Charles Raw to force an interview with Rowland, who talked, almost for the first time, about his background – but he was very guarded. More of it eventually

*Interview with the authors.

found its way into a book *My Life With Tiny* written by Richard Hall, who once edited the *Times of Zambia*, owned by Lonrho, and later worked for the *Observer*. Hall spent some effort and time tracking down Rowland's background, but his book is far from definitive. It contained enough material to infuriate Rowland, however, and Lonrho engaged in long and acrimonious correspondence with the publishers, Faber & Faber, in the spring of 1987.

What emerges from the work that has been done on Rowland's background, and from our own studies including many conversations with Rowland himself when he would occasionally begin to reminisce, is a picture of a man who in his early years travelled widely, both in India and Africa. He once hinted he went to school in Rumania, and he does seem to have had some connection with that country. In the 1920s the family returned to Hamburg, then the most international of German cities, and by the early 1930s Tiny, along with many young people of his age, was involved with the Hitler Youth. His father, however, was from all accounts a staunch anti-Nazi, and Tiny claimed it lost him his business.

Tiny was went to a minor English school, Churchers, in Petersfield, Hampshire, for a brief time during which he acquired his impeccable upper-class English accent. He did well there, both at sports and academically, although he did not stay long. Before the war he returned to Germany, although it is not clear why. But it was during this period that he claims to have been imprisoned for his anti-Nazi views. The correspondence with Hall's publishers says that he 'escaped from that prison', although how is not stated. By the age of 17 he had started working in London for his mother's brother, who had a firm of shipping agents.

When war came, the young Furhop was 21. Both his brothers had returned to Germany to join the Wehrmacht, and, according to Rowland's own account, 'both died fighting for Germany' (one of war wounds after the war). Tiny was by now very much a man-about-town, with his good looks, fair hair, flashing smile and his love of fast cars, and decided to stay with his parents in Britain. Just after the outbreak of war, and his 22nd birthday, he changed his name to Rowland. There are two versions as to why he chose this name. His own is that it was after an uncle on his mother's side. Richard Hall, however, claims it was much more flippant than that. He took the W of his middle name Walter and installed it into his first name Roland to produce Rowland.

He served with the Royal Army Medical Corps in Scotland – he says he volunteered and was not called up, as others have implied – and spent much of his time on the most menial of jobs, mainly latrine duty.

At one stage he went absent without leave in order to visit his father and as a result was imprisoned in a military jail for 27 days in 1940. Later he was interned briefly; his father spent most of the war years in an Isle of Man internment camp. Rowland, born in one British internment camp in one world war, watched his mother die of cancer in another British internment camp in another world war. His father married again, and father and son, never close, saw little of each other, although Tiny does seem to have financially supported the elder Furhop. Discharged from the services before the end of the war, Rowland still had to take whatever jobs he was offered – and this may have been the time he briefly became a porter on Paddington Station, a story which has gone into legend and which he at times encouraged and at other times denied. (He has done both in our presence, always mischievously, loving the mystery of it.)

Although no-one has succeeded in getting at the full record of Rowland's war years, by all accounts they were the unhappiest and most humiliating time of his life. It may be, as both friends and critics of his suggest, that his dislike of authority dates from this period. After the war he began to make up for lost time, launching himself into a series of business ventures, avoiding high taxes by dealing in businesses and factories rather than goods and services – there were no capital taxes in Britain in those days. At one stage he was the biggest refrigerator maker in Britain, employing 4000 people in Sheffield, until disaster struck and, according to his own account, most of the fridges blew up in a heatwave. He was living in the old Berkeley Hotel, dealing in cars – always a great interest of his, and he was, by most accounts, a superb driver – frequenting the best restaurants, the best tailors, and already a wealthy man. But in 1949, the Inland Revenue ruled that selling businesses was liable to income tax and Rowland, after a year's battling, sold up and went to South Africa where he began dealing in mines. In one year there, he later claimed, he made £6m. In 1950 that was an immense amount of money.

In the early 1950s Rowland moved north to what was then Rhodesia and began farming at Gatooma, doubling up his acreage under the plough each year, but actually living a simple, hard physical life. It was there he was joined by his old partner from Britain Lionel Taylor, who brought with him his three-year-old daughter Josie. Rowland, always popular with children, doted on her, and she adored him. (Years later, when he was 49, they married, and they now have four children.) The business world was too tempting, however, and increasingly he found and did deals, usually involving mining companies, finding acquisitions for the Rio Tinto group, a large mining finance house. In the mid-1950s he opened an office in Salisbury and began building up a minor empire: importing Mercedes and other items, dealing in mines and mining companies.

It was in Salisbury in 1961 that the Honourable Angus Ogilvy, then an aide to the businessman Harley Drayton and his conglomerate British Electric Traction, found him. Ogilvy, later husband to Princess Alexandra, had been given the task of sorting out oddments of the sprawling BET group in Africa.

One of them was the London and Rhodesia Mining and Land Company (Lonrho), a shell company then employing 350 people, run from a new building in Salisbury. Ogilvy later described it as 'just a ranching company with a couple of tin-pot mines'. Ogilvy lunched at the Standard Bank in Salisbury and asked the manager if he had any ideas about whom he could get to run Lonrho with a view to injecting some life into it. Rowland, as it happened, was in the market for a shell company into which he could put the interest which now occupied him more and more: a concession to run a pipeline from the port of Beira, on the east coast of Portuguese Mozambique, to Umtali in Rhodesia to carry all the landlocked country's oil.

Rowland and Ogilvy hit it off instantly. Later Ogilvy described Rowland as a 'Cecil Rhodes . . . a genius . . . but with flaws'.* Rowland was not a colonial in the Rhodes sense, but the pipeline was an African dream. There would be many others: Rowland's plan to handle all the maize exports of the Central African Federation, one of its most valuable foreign exchange earners, by converting the railway tanker trucks that his own pipeline put out of business; or his proposals to purchase all of the output of Mozambique's sawmills; or the giant Kenana sugar estates he built in the Sudan on the junction of the Blue and White Nile rivers. He had dreams of a rival to Opec, based on Mexico and Nigeria. Later his plans for Harrods were equally grandiose. He once said that Harrods was just the first step in a major strategy which would involve the acquisition of the British end of Woolworth, followed by Carter Hawley Hale.†

The visionary, charming Rowland appealed greatly to Ogilvy, and a deal was done. Rowland was to have options on Lonrho shares, which over the next 20 years would become (through his own efforts) worth more than £150m. Lonrho in turn would build the pipeline, having first negotiated a deal with seven major companies, including Shell, BP and Mobil, to supply 100 per cent of Rhodesia's oil.

By the time Rowland became involved in Harrods, Lonrho had grown out of all recognition. Rowland had taken it into most countries

*Daily Mail, 17 May, 1973.
† Interviews with the authors.

in Africa where it had sugar, wheat and cattle ranching interests. It had lead, copper, gold and coal mines in South Africa; gold in Ghana; newspapers, trading companies and refineries all over Africa. In Britain its interests were still relatively small, but Rowland had embarked on a major stream of acquisitions which would eventually make Lonrho the sole importer of Volkswagen and Audi cars, owners of the Jack Barclay Rolls-Royce concessionaires, casinos, hotels and the Wankel rotary engine. Later, too, he would buy the Princess Hotel in Acapulco where Howard Hughes spent the last two years of his life at a cost of $33,000 a day.

But his reputation in the City of London, which had soared in the 1960s as Lonrho's share price multiplied 24-fold, never recovered from a ferocious internal battle in 1973. A boardroom split pitted Rowland and half his directors against the other half. It led to charge and counter charge, with revelations of loans for houses and of Cayman Islands accounts used for tax avoidance. Rowland won, but a great deal of dirt stuck to everyone concerned. Angus Ogilvy, caught in the middle, resigned too late to protect the Royal Family from embarrassment.

When Rowland started his stalking of Harrods, he was very much an outsider, a man careless of whom he turned into enemies, willing to take on the establishment, the City, or anybody else. He positively courted controversy and dispute, actually enjoying the cut and thrust of a good public battle. 'I need problems,' he often said. 'Life is dull without problems. I have to have them.' *

In the spring of 1977, Rowland decided to take on some of the problems of Sir Hugh Fraser. In doing so he almost certainly had mixed motives. It was true that he had an affinity for people in distress – he showed that many times in his life, not least by setting Jim Slater back on his feet after Slater Walker collapsed leaving Slater owing more than £1m. And he showed it much later when Sir Freddie Laker's airline went down and Rowland set Laker up in business again (not successfully this time – their joint People's Airline soon folded). But he was also aware that Fraser provided the key to ownership of a company which would allow Rowland to thumb his nose at the establishment.

Rowland did not know Sir Hugh. Nor did he know anything about his current troubles beyond what he had read in the papers. But he recognised a fellow outcast, and felt that Fraser would not object to a gesture of sympathy. On the day he read the full details of Fraser's censure, he rang him. How about dinner, he suggested. Fraser

*Interviews with the authors.

gratefully accepted and that evening the two men met at the Dorchester Hotel, which had one of the finest restaurants in London and was at that stage a favourite haunt of Rowland's. It was not long before Fraser fell under the charm of his host. The key relationship of all that was to follow was forged that evening. It would be a turbulent one, but without it the Battle of Harrods would never have begun. Here is yet another example, so common in takeover history, of human nature and human relationships proving stronger than capital profit, greater efficiency, economies of scale, synergy or all the other textbook concepts put forward to explain why takeovers happen. No university professor, asked to explain the logic of this bid, would know how to evaluate this central factor. If Sir Hugh Fraser had been unimpressed by Tiny that evening, or had ignored his charm, history would have been very different. There are a hundred similar stories to be told of how some of our greatest corporations of today have been put together – but they are not to be found in the textbooks nor the academic analyses.

Here we have a classic meeting of the talented, driving maverick, capable of great leaps of imagination and boldness, and the fourth-generation retailer, brought up to run the greatest store in the world, but now emotionally distraught, his career and reputation in ruins. Like that breakfast with Mohamed Al Fayed, this dinner was one of the seminal moments in the history of the world's greatest store.

Fraser later admitted that he came to admire Tiny 'more than anyone except my own father. Rowland is like a father to me.'*

Within a few days, Rowland persuaded Fraser to agree to the first part of his plan to own Harrods. Fraser wanted cash; Rowland would give it to him. Fraser was fed up with Suits, where the controversy had forced him to abandon his chief executive role: Lonrho would buy his shares.

The City institutions were at the time calling for Fraser to resign from Suits altogether and hand over the chair to someone else. It was a situation that suited Rowland perfectly. In mid-March he made his announcement: Sir Hugh Fraser had sold a 24 per cent stake in Suits to Lonrho, and Rowland himself would replace Sir Hugh as chairman. Tiny had taken his first step along the road to control Harrods: he now owned 24 per cent of a company which in turn owned 10 per cent of House of Fraser.

The move was greeted with a howl of protest from the City and was attacked in the House of Commons: it was a 'marriage of convenience between the unacceptable face of international capitalism in the form

*Interview with the authors.

of Tiny Rowland and the unacceptable face of Scottish capitalism in the form of Sir Hugh Fraser', stormed one Labour MP.

But the deal was done; and soon Rowland tightened his grip. By July, he owned 30 per cent of Suits after buying shares in the market. That put it beyond the reach of anyone else. Then, that autumn, came step two: for £41m, or 175p a share (50 per cent above the market price), he bought a 20 per cent stake in House of Fraser from Carter Hawley. He now had 30 per cent of Suits, which in turn owned 10 per cent of Fraser; and he owned 20 per cent of Fraser direct. He was closing in.

In April 1978, a year after that first dinner with Sir Hugh, Lonrho bid for the whole of Suits and straightaway ran into what was to be the first of many fights with the government. The bid was referred to the Monopolies Commission, usually the end of the line for bids, not because the commission almost always says no, but because few companies are prepared to go through the lengthy process of arguing a bid through. Rowland, by now installed as deputy chairman of House of Fraser as well as chairman of Suits, was not going to give up lightly, however. His was a long-term strategy. He would argue it all the way.

It was another year before the commission finally reported. The City had done its best to persuade it to turn Rowland down, arguing that giving him control of Suits meant giving him effective control of the House of Fraser. But in the spring of 1979 the commission delivered its unanimous verdict: Rowland could go ahead and bid if he wanted to. But the Monopolies reference had cost him a year, during which time the independent directors of Suits had been able to prepare their defences. Now Rowland had to offer £20m on top of the £40m he had offered originally.

It was at this crucial juncture that Sir Hugh suddenly wobbled. He had been subjected to a year of ferocious pressure from his own mother, from other members of the family and from the Scottish lobby which resented the sale of any Scottish business into non-Scottish hands. The House of Fraser and Suits were famous Scottish companies. Fraser was told he must not sell them to Tiny Rowland. Rowland had been preoccupied with other problems, notably in Africa and doing deals with Daniel K. Ludwig and Atlantic Richfield's Robert Anderson. His empire by now was enormous; he was wrestling with solutions to the problems over Rhodesian independence, backing Joshua Nkomo to seize power when the embattled regime of Ian Smith finally gave up. He was planning a new gold mine in the Orange Free State. He was developing his interests in Mexico.

In short, he had neglected Hugh Fraser and, away from his influence, Fraser listened to other voices. Fraser now turned against him; and, even with his higher bid, Rowland could not win without the Fraser support. After all his careful planning, he seemed to have lost.

Fraser had supported a bid worth £42m from Rowland all through 1978. In the spring of 1979 he now rejected a bid worth nearly £60m. There was no particular logic in it. But it was understandable in human terms. He and his family trusts still owned 9 per cent of the Suits shares, and there were enough shareholders opposed to Rowland to ensure that Lonrho could not win this time.

In the end, it was the Rowland charm that won the day. The two men again had dinner at the Dorchester. Rowland made a proposal. He would there and then agree to pay Sir Hugh more for his Suits holding. Fraser in turn would recommend a new and higher offer for the company. Then Rowland would personally drive him to London airport, put him on a plane, and get him out of the country until the whole affair was over.

Within hours Fraser had flown to Canada where his sister had a lakeside house – and no telephone. No-one could contact Sir Hugh again and attempt to change his mind for the third time. A few days later the remaining Suits directors threw in the towel.

Up to this point the battle for Harrods had been more reminiscent of the bid tactics of the 1960s than of the 1980s. The House of Fraser at this point was vulnerable and available, leaderless and demoralised. One cannot imagine any of the corporate raiders who were to dominate the scene five years later hesitating for more than an hour or two. But Rowland, for all his imaginative skills, was still emotionally back in the time when bid targets were stalked carefully and over a matter of years, and share stakes were carefully accumulated.

Just then the path was clear. Rowland had successfully been all the way through the most searching of Monopolies Commission enquiries, which had stilled some of the doubts in the City that he was hiding deep dark secrets from public view. He owned 29.99 per cent of House of Fraser, was its deputy chairman and, with Sir Hugh Fraser, still precariously hanging on as chairman, seemed to be in effective control. The City had believed that his company, which had a cash crisis in the early 1970s, would run into trouble again, but instead profits were rising strongly, fuelled by the gold and precious metals boom of the time – Lonrho's once unprofitable platinum mine in South Africa for instance had suddenly become a very attractive investment. Early in 1978 the British authorities, after five years of investigation by Department of Trade Inspectors, had finally informed him that there were no grounds for legal action or criminal proceedings to be taken against him or his company for events in the early 1970s which had caused the 'unacceptable face' row and subsequent enquiry.

Yet at this crucial time he hesitated. In 1976 Rowland boasted that by the early 1980s Lonrho would be among the five biggest companies in Britain, and possibly the number one. 'Just you watch us,' he had said.* It was a conversation he often returned to as his company grew through the 1970s.

Rowland might still have made it but for the emotional commitment he made to taking over House of Fraser and owning Harrods. It absorbed his own energies and that of his management, and caused him to miss the many other opportunities which began to open up. The 1970s were a dead period for the bidders. With the 1980s came the biggest takeover boom of all time, which allowed men such as Sir James Goldsmith, Robert Maxwell, Lord Hanson, Ernest Saunders and others to gallop past Rowland, now locked into his seven-year campaign. Times were changing rapidly and the takeover game was shifting beneath his feet without his knowing it. The raiders of the 1980s tended to go for quick kills, concentrating utterly on a single objective, reacting instantly to the slightest shift of tactics or sentiment in their own marketplace.

Rowland made the mistake of putting Fraser on the backburner, believing management control was effectively his.

For a while the fickle Hugh Fraser, now gambling more and more heavily, remained a loyal Rowland pawn. In June 1979 he would tell House of Fraser shareholders: 'I know that Lonrho at the present moment has no intention of taking its interest any further.' He was, he added, speaking for his friend Tiny Rowland in making that statement. It was greeted with hollow laughter. He did have the wit to add: 'Don't ask me how long is a moment.'

For the present, however, Rowland was not prepared to bid for it. It was, after all, a tidy mouthful, and his cash resources were limited. He had spent £60m buying Suits, and another £41m buying Carter Hawley's 20 per cent stake in Fraser. That meant a cash outlay of over £100m. Lonrho's annual profits were by now over £90m – they were just £160,000 when Rowland took command in 1961. But much of those profits were earned in African countries and were non-remittable. Although he would never admit it, Rowland was stretched.

Therefore he chose a form of guerrilla action, or 'creeping control'. From his position as its major shareholder, he put forward a series of boardroom proposals, each one aimed at giving Lonrho more control.

*Interview with the authors.

The body of the Fraser board was flatly opposed to him; so were their merchant bankers Warburgs, increasingly the most important and influential bank in the City. Each proposal was strongly resisted. Rowland was not making the headway he expected.

And during this period Rowland was again busy elsewhere in the world, spending days travelling through Africa and the Middle East in his Grumman private jet, getting his pipeline, which had been closed during the entire 13 years of the illegal regime in Rhodesia, back into action. He had become fascinated with the prospect of getting the Russians out of Southern Africa and had persuaded his American business friends to bring pressure on their influential friends in government. Daniel K. Ludwig he saw as particularly useful in this context, because from the very early days he had supported the political career of Ronald Reagan. Reagan had even flown down, along with a large grouping of the great and the good, for the official opening of Ludwig's Princess Hotel in Acapulco. Rowland would later relate how he could get through to Reagan in the White House through Ludwig, with Ludwig shouting at Reagan: 'What are you doing about Angola? I want to know what you're doing about Angola?', while Reagan parried with polite queries about Ludwig's health and that of his wife. 'When are you going to come down and see us at the White House?' Ludwig, almost a recluse, never went.

But while Tiny was working on his grand plans, once again other influences were at work on Sir Hugh Fraser. He had already changed sides twice. Now he changed again. Sir Hugh's mother, a powerful influence, insisted he should support the family firm and not Lonrho. So did his fellow directors. In April 1980, the guerrilla warfare turned into a full-scale battle over Lonrho's insistence that House of Fraser should increase its dividend. The simmering battle had at last come to a head. It would now rage ceaselessly for four years – and at the time of writing, in the spring of 1987, is still going on.

The Fraser board insisted it needed all its available cash to modernise its hopelessly out-of-date stores and to catch up with some of the retailing trends which had passed it by. Rowland, however, chose the lifting of dividend restraint under the new Thatcher government to ask for another 2p a share. In what became known as the 'tuppenny tiff', Sir Hugh Fraser backed his board and fell out with Rowland yet again. He resigned from Suits and openly declared he would stop Rowland getting control of Harrods. Rowland, however, was relentless. He proposed resolution after resolution, and took them to shareholders' meetings where he and his faithful aide, the Conservative MP Edward DuCann (now Lonrho chairman), argued the case in some of the most acrimonious public shareholders' meetings in Britain. Rowland proposed new men for the board, and was defeated. But the more he was blocked, the more determined he became. By now the battle of Harrods had moved off the financial pages onto the front pages. Rowland was not making much headway, but he was still determined to wear down his opponents. He had blocked all Fraser attempts to expand in other directions, using his shares to prevent the issue of any new ones. It was stalemate.

Hostile bidders often find themselves up against similar roadblocks. The art, at this stage, is to find a way around. Rowland, all his career, had looked for the weak point in the opposition. And the Harrods side had a major weakness: Sir Hugh himself. In the summer of 1980, Fraser's directors sought help from the merchant bankers Warburgs. Something clearly had to be done. The Lonrho criticisms had drawn attention to the poor performance of Fraser and under the existing regime that seemed unlikely to improve.

But again Rowland missed his chance.

In August 1980 Warburgs produced its counter-punch: a new deputy to Sir Hugh would in effect run the company. There would be a new executive committee, headed by the Warburgs nominee, which would take all key decisions. Rowland would be excluded from the committee, and would indeed be required to stand down as deputy chairman of the main board. Warburgs would also nominate another board member, equally powerful, and possibly a third. Without consulting Rowland, the Fraser directors, including Sir Hugh, agreed. Now the battle at last was being taken to Rowland.

Sir Hugh wrote to Rowland with the news. He and the rest of the board, he said, had held discussions with other shareholders and agreed to strengthen the board 'with people who have broad management experience and could represent the interests of all shareholders'.

We have conducted considerable research and had discussions with several people before concluding that Professor Roland Smith can play a vital role in House of Fraser [wrote Sir Hugh. Letter dated August 4, 1980.] Professor Smith has accepted an invitation in principle to become deputy chairman of House of Fraser and chairman of the executive committee we intend to form, subject to formal approval. Apart from his academic eminence he has played key roles, whether as chairman, director or, as in several cases, as a member of the executive committees, in a number of important companies. He is held in the very highest regard by major institutional investors as well as by the companies with whom he works.

Rowland, in Africa at the time, was outraged. Furiously, he telexed Fraser that 'under no circumstances can my colleagues and I agree'. But in effect he was given no choice. He was even more annoyed by an article which appeared in the *Sunday Times* the following Sunday with a large picture of the professor arriving at Harrods to be saluted by the doorman. This indicated, he stormed, that already Professor Smith, although only deputy chairman, 'was assuming effective power'. Smith, quoted in the article, did not mince his words. The Lonrho directors were not going to have any influence over the executive committee, he announced bluntly. Asked about his immediate task of reversing the Lonrho threat, he was even more direct. 'Term time in Manchester starts in October. I would like to see Lonrho off by then. I am not going to lose this battle.'*

In many ways Smith was an inspired choice for the job. An imposing 6ft 4in Mancunian, he had made something of a profession of non-executive directorships. He promised to abandon some of them in return for the £50,000 a year he was being paid at Fraser, a generous sum for a non-executive role – except that this was no ordinary role. Tough and jovial, Smith was every bit a verbal match for the witty, caustic Rowland. For the rest of the battle, the exchange between the two men became something to savour. Curiously, each appreciated the verbal ability of the other, and at times Rowland would murmur that he really 'liked that man'. Smith gave no hint that he reciprocated the affection.

The new committee under Smith quickly ran foul of Lonrho. In an attempt to raise the low return on assets, it proposed a sale and leaseback of its D. H. Evans store in Oxford Street – the sale of the freehold to an insurance company, then an agreement to rent it back (the rent to be reviewed every five years) for a century. Rowland condemned it as 'one of the worst deals ever done in the City of London', and called yet another extraordinary general meeting to vote against it.

It was during the build-up to this meeting that Sir Hugh Fraser's personal problems came to a head. In casinos all over Mayfair his cheques were suddenly bouncing. Casino owners who had happily taken several million off him over the years now found his cheques returned marked 'refer to drawer – insufficient funds'. Could Sir Hugh Fraser, once one of Britain's richest men, really have gone through such a huge fortune in so short a time – more than £50m of it?

* *Sunday Times*, 10 August, 1980.

The rumours spread rapidly – and soon reached Rowland. Lonrho owned casinos of its own – Crockfords and the International Sporting Club. And Rowland quickly acquired some of the returned cheques. His legal advisers told him that in Scotland default on a personal cheque was *prima facie* evidence of insolvency and thus disqualified Sir Hugh, under House of Fraser's articles of association, from being a director. He had suddenly acquired a powerful lever which he intended to apply.

When Rowland faced the Fraser board with it, Sir Hugh's fellow directors were shaken by the news, but at first stood by Sir Hugh. At a meeting on 20 January, Rowland insisted that Fraser was unfit to be chairman and must step down. He was over-ruled. But Warburgs were embarrassed by the revelations. It was not good for the reputation of the City's leading merchant bank to be seen backing a man who apparently could not meet his gambling debts. They had to find a replacement quickly and get Sir Hugh out of the way. But first they had to get through the special shareholders' meeting which Sir Hugh had to chair. Afterwards, things would change.

Rowland, however, had no intention of waiting. On the eve of the meeting he wrote a letter to Sir Hugh and had it hand-delivered to him in Glasgow. It was anything but gentle. Later Sir Hugh described it: 'He accused me of being bankrupt. I said I could write him a cheque for £250,000 – or was it £500,000? I can't remember now.'*

Rowland had, however, achieved his objective. The next day in Glasgow, although it marked yet another defeat for Rowland at the hands of Fraser shareholders who supported the Fraser board, was Sir Hugh's last public meeting as chairman. Warburgs had attempted to have Sir Hugh replaced as chairman six months before, but the Fraser board had stood by him. Now, however, the time for loyalty had gone.

The next few days featured some of the most bizarre events of what was already one of the most extraordinary takeover battles. Immediately after the Glasgow meeting, Warburgs and the Fraser directors began actively to seek Sir Hugh's resignation. His own vote of six million shares, plus the votes which still loyally supported him, had been crucial at the meeting, and without them Lonrho might well have won. But with the meeting successfully out of the way, the opposing forces closed in for the kill. Fraser was about to meet his corporate end. That afternoon a proposal was put to him that he should resign. Warburgs later denied the proposal had come from them; others said that a Warburgs director rang Fraser at home to

*The Times, 27 January, 1981.

request a meeting and then suggested that he took over the honorary and non-executive role of president.

Fraser was furious. He would only go if the board fired him, he insisted, which is what the other directors now decided to do, believing that in this one instance at least they had the support of Lonhro. Only days before, it was Rowland who had insisted that Fraser be fired, and the other directors who supported him. Again, however, they underestimated Rowland.

That evening Rowland had a call from a *Financial Times* journalist. Warburgs, said the journalist, had called a meeting to decide on the future of Sir Hugh in Rowland's absence. It was the first Rowland knew of it. Rowland had not talked to Fraser for some months, but now rang a friend of Sir Hugh's to ask him to pass on the news. Late that evening the friend rang back. Sir Hugh, he said, needed time to 'reflect on the news'. The next day Rowland was in Paris when he heard from his office that Sir Hugh wanted to talk to him. It was now Thursday mid-day. The Warburgs meeting, to which neither Rowland nor Fraser had been invited, was scheduled for the following day. Fraser was in Scotland, Rowland in Paris, but both agreed they must meet immediately. As Rowland himself later said:

> There was little time. We were again on the same side, for quite different reasons. Sir Hugh was probably going to lose the chairmanship of his family company, not just because of my attack on him, but because of the sudden expression of reservations by his board towards him, reservations which Warburgs were encouraging with an intent to install their own candidate, Professor Smith. Lonrho feared the onset of increasing control by Warburgs, which indeed subsequently came into effective operation. We, therefore, had urgent reasons to meet, in facing the common threat.*

Rowland boarded his plane and took off, but out over the North Sea the windshield shattered and his German pilot, Captain William Wilming, declared an emergency. At zero feet, the plane diverted to London Heathrow and just made it. Undaunted, Rowland radioed ahead for another plane, and flew on to Scotland. He was ten minutes late for dinner; but at 7.10 that evening, as if nothing untoward had happened, he kept the appointment in the Marine Hotel in Troon, on the Scottish west coast.

It was at that dinner that Rowland first learned the truth behind the bouncing casino cheques. Fraser was far from bankrupt. In an attempt

---

*Evidence to the Department of Trade Inspector dated 17 February, 1984.

to cure himself of his addiction, he had sought medical help. A scheme, common for habitual gamblers, was worked out. Sir Hugh would deliberately arrange his affairs so that he did not have access to large amounts of cash. He would also make sure that he had little or no credit at any casino. His banks would have instructions to bounce any cheques above a certain amount made out to any casino, although if re-submitted they would honour them. No-one had reckoned on the bounced cheques falling into Rowland's hands, and even less on him using them to attack Sir Hugh at a crucial board meeting.

That evening the old father/son relationship was rekindled. Rowland and Fraser were back on the same side, this time to stay. Between them they represented 34 per cent of the Fraser shares. Rowland now determined to stop the Warburgs plan to replace Sir Hugh as chairman.

Part of the doctrine of the business culture is that major financiers and world-class business executives are cut from some mould different from other men. This special breed, it is generally believed, are not susceptible to irrationality. They have some special immunity to emotional mood swings and other human frailties, and thus their decisions are based on hard reasoning and an ability to gather information that other mortals lack.

Of course the notion of the passionless, logical business tycoon falls apart as soon as it is examined. The very drive and dedication such men invest in gambling billions when millions would do, their eccentricities (Howard Hughes was only an exaggeration, not an exception), and their often troubled personal relationships all point toward personalities which have weaknesses as glaring as their strengths. Most of the men at the sharp end of the takeover boom are possessed of driving energy, a sense of commitment, and above all an ability to turn what seems to be a disadvantage into an advantage.

Rowland up to this point had made the mistake of becoming distracted from his primary target. But now he showed how rapidly he could react to a situation that was moving away from him. He was still a big hitter, and now he decided to go for the biggest hit of his life.

What was to prove the most crucial board meeting in the whole battle of Harrods took place on 28 January, 1981. It was only in the early morning before the meeting that Rowland arrived at his decision. He realised that unless he could produce something dramatic that morning, his new ally Sir Hugh Fraser was going to be ignominiously ejected, and Lonrho's chances of getting control would be considerably less. Early that morning he rang his bank, Standard

Chartered. He needed a line of credit, say £200m. He wanted to bid for House of Fraser that morning. Although the bank was not yet open for business, he got what he wanted.

Then he called a meeting of his own directors – a formality, since his fellow directors seldom, if ever, voted against him. But time was pressing. The House of Fraser board meeting was scheduled for 9.30 on the other side of London at the Barker store in Kensington. It would take a good half hour to get there. They needed a statement. But it had to be on Standard Chartered paper. Hastily a director put a single sheet of paper into a typewriter and clumsily – and with much mis-typing and accidental mis-spelling – wrote the heading:

'Standard Chartered Bank'

Underneath he wrote:

'Press statement'

A secretary rescued him to type the announcement that Lonrho was prepared to make a cash offer for the 70.01 per cent of the shares in House of Fraser it did not already own. The girl was still typing as Rowland and his fellow director Paul Spicer prepared to set off for the meeting. She caught them at the lift and pressed the single sheet of paper into Rowland's hand.

At the meeting itself, Fraser initially took the chair. He was visibly shaken and upset and opened with a long denunciation against his fellow directors, accusing them of treachery and betrayal. Almost everyone there, he said, owed their promotions either to him or his father. Two who didn't, the Lonrho directors, were the only ones supporting him. With the bitterness at its height, Rowland sprang his surprise. He passed Fraser a sheet of paper, saying he had an announcement to make which should come from the chair. Fraser read it aloud, and the room erupted. Lonrho was offering 150p a share, valuing Fraser at £230m. Rowland, however, was not finished. His bid, he exclaimed, was conditional on there being no changes in the Fraser board, which meant Sir Hugh must stay. Again the table exploded.

The calm American Phil Hawley stepped in to try to effect a compromise: how about Sir Hugh becoming non-executive chairman, and Professor Smith taking over as executive chairman? That was turned down by a majority of eleven to four. All morning long, with adjournments and breaks for legal advice, the meeting went on. For four years the Fraser directors had suspected and then had their suspicions confirmed that Rowland wanted control of their company. They were ready for almost anything. The prospect of him bidding had gone on so long that, by that meeting, no-one believed it would actually happen. Now Rowland had caught everyone on the hop.

But they could still exact their revenge on Sir Hugh – and they did. Later Rowland was to remark of that meeting: 'The sad spectacle occurred of Sir Hugh Fraser, who had succeeded his father in 1966, being dismissed from that position and rising from his seat in the middle of the meeting.' Professor Smith had been sitting expectantly on his right throughout the meeting. When the vote finally went against him, Sir Hugh stood and with a polite smile turned to him. 'I suppose you'd like to sit here?' Smith moved over, marking the first time for four generations that a Fraser was not head of the house.

A couple of days later, at dinner at the Berkeley Hotel where Rowland often dines at his favourite corner table, he described that meeting with great gusto and enjoyment, reliving the moments when he felt he had rattled Professor Smith and his deputy Ernest Sharp, chuckling uncontrollably at some of the exchanges. Far from being upset by the result, he was in excellent spirits, committed at last to a full-scale bid for the biggest department stores group in Britain. He mentioned again the promise he had once given – that Lonrho would be among the top five companies. 'Now you will see!' He outlined some of his plans: he would sell the credit side to Debenhams for £100m, redevelop a number of the sites, and possibly sell off many of the less profitable stores around the country. With Sir Hugh's 4 per cent stake pledged to him, he already had 34 per cent. Control was in his reach.

But if the opposition had underestimated Rowland before, Rowland now underestimated the opposition. More truthfully he underestimated the power of the City establishment which had come to dislike him more and more. Although there was never a concerted campaign as such (Rowland would contend otherwise), there is little doubt that the major powers in the City, influenced by Warburgs and its stockbrokers Cazenove (the latter probably the most influential and powerful firm of establishment stockbrokers in the City), now increased their efforts to thwart Lonrho.

Left to the marketplace, Rowland's bid would almost certainly have succeeded. He might have been forced to raise it, but that is part of the cut and thrust of every takeover. But even in Mrs Thatcher's free market Britain, the marketplace did not always work unfettered. Warburgs and the opposing House of Fraser board, plus their many friends, now lobbied for the one obstacle which would stop, or at least slow down, the Rowland juggernaut: a Monopolies Commission reference. And just as Rowland thought he had won, the bid was referred.

The Monopolies Commission is a curious animal in the British merger and acquisitions scene. Its members consist of at least one leading lawyer, and representatives from the various 'public interest' groups – a trade union leader, a member of a consumer organisation, a number of academics, an industrialist and so on. Except for the chairman they are all part-time, although there is a full-time back-up staff. The members of the Commission are required to consider the matters referred to them and to decide whether or not they operate 'against the public interest'. They have examined several of Britain's major industries – bread, cement, brewers, and even tampons and condoms – but their main task is to examine the mergers and acquisitions which might not be in 'the public interest'.

With this reference, Rowland was very unfortunate. He had already been through the Monopolies Commission with Suits; now he was back again with House of Fraser. A few years later, under the reign of Cecil Parkinson or Norman Tebbit, the bid would almost certainly not even have been referred: there was no threat to 'competition' in it. But at this stage competition policy, if it existed at all, bent to the winds of political lobbying – and the Fraser camp was very adept at that. It was a devastating blow. Rowland at least knew what to expect – he had been through enough enquiries already. He later remarked: 'Such inquiries take months to conclude and involve a great deal of the time of the senior management of the companies concerned and enormous expense, particularly in legal fees.'

The battle had been bitter and personal; it now became doubly so. Rowland announced his intention to fire Professor Smith the instant he won control. Smith and his colleagues, on the other hand, provided the commission with long and detailed evidence to show how unsuitable a person Rowland was to run their company. Details of Sir Hugh Fraser's gambling addiction were brought up; the Lonrho boardroom battle and the subsequent Department of Trade report were gone over. Warburgs wheeled in some powerful City institutional fund managers (notably Hugh Jenkins of the National Coal Board pension fund, one of the biggest in the country) who voiced their opposition. The Commission learned in great detail about what it later delicately referred to as 'the acrimonious nature of the disputes' between the two companies, adding that 'there was little agreement between the two parties as to the rights and wrongs' of them.

*

For the board of House of Fraser, its battle with Lonrho was by now pretty well a full-time affair. For Rowland, however, increasingly obsessed though he was with owning Harrods, it was still just one of his many interests. All the time he was battling for control of Fraser, he was pursuing another ambition, too: to own a major British newspaper. He had bid for *The Times* and *Sunday Times* when the Thomson Organisation sold them after nearly a year's closure of the two papers, but had been beaten by Rupert Murdoch. He was still in negotiation with Reed International, which owned the *Daily Mirror*. But for some years he had been discussing with his American friend Robert Anderson another deal – the purchase of the *Observer*, owned by Atlantic Richfield.

On 25 February, just two days before he learned his Fraser bid was to be referred, Rowland announced that he had bought the *Observer*. The deal had been carried out with such speed and secrecy that the editor, Donald Trelford, was only told late on the day of the announcement by a telephone call from Anderson who, after four years of ownership, had just been made chairman. Trelford assembled his editorial staff and told them that the *Observer* board had not even been given a hint of what was happening. 'Mr Anderson chaired his first board meeting here last week and gave us every assurance that all was well. He certainly didn't consult us or warn us about selling.' One Lonrho director sent shivers through the paper by saying what everyone feared: 'We always wanted a paper so we could really express the views of Africa and the Third World.' Already journalists were talking darkly about the *Observer*, widely read in Africa, being used as a mouthpiece to further Lonrho's ambitions there.

Yet again it was a move greeted by general amazement. 'Mr Tiny Rowland,' wrote the distinguished journalist Max Hastings in the *Evening Standard*, 'has reached into the bottomless pandora's box that he has made of Lonrho and produced another astonishment. While his great assault on Harrods is undecided, overnight he has made himself a press lord.'

Newspaper bids are, it was argued immediately after the *Observer* announcement, in a 'special category of public importance',* and therefore subject to government enquiry. There was a cry for an immediate Monopolies Commission enquiry, a campaign led by the *Observer* itself whose staff voiced open consternation at the thought of being part of the Lonrho empire.

Rowland, accustomed to keeping his own counsel, refused to let this

---

*Letter to *The Times*, 21 March, 1981.

particular argument go past without a riposte. He wrote to *The Times*, on 23 March, 1981.

The Beaverbrook family sold the *Express*, the *Sunday Express* and the London *Evening Standard* for £14 million to the multinational Trafalgar House, whose managing director took personal charge of the Express Group. Mr David Astor after 27 years as owner/editor sold the *Observer* to an American oil company with international interests. The *Standard* and the *Evening News* suddenly merged to give an evening monopoly to the New Standard. *The Times* and the *Sunday Times* passed from a Canadian multinational to an Australian multinational company.

All of these, he added, 'swam past' under Conservative and Labour governments. The *Observer* was losing money at a rate of £4m a year. Why should that purchase not go through, too?

Rowland, however, would not have an easy ride. He was not yet a press lord, as Hastings had prematurely elected him. John Biffen referred the *Observer* deal to the Monopolies Commission, as well, and Rowland found himself the first man in history to be fighting two Commission enquiries at once. He confessed to another deal he had in mind, if the *Observer* deal had gone through smoothly: he was about to buy the *Daily Mirror* for some £50m. But he wisely decided to postpone it – even he could not face three enquiries running simultaneously. Biffen never had any notion that, by referring both the House of Fraser and the *Observer* bids, he was opening up the way for Robert Maxwell to take the *Daily Mirror* (for twice the price Rowland had agreed) three years later.

By the end of 1981 Rowland had won one enquiry and lost the other. The Commission and the government allowed the *Observer* deal, albeit with heavy caveats relating to editorial control.

But he lost Harrods.

The Monopolies Commission decided that the proposed takeover would entail 'at least a very real and substantial risk that the efficiency of Fraser would deteriorate seriously'. John Biffen accepted the decision. The British papers the next day carried similar headlines. *'Tiny's hand is frozen.'* The grounds on which the bid was turned down were generally regarded as exceptionally weak – and, for almost the only time in his career, Rowland found himself transformed from social villain to folk hero. Unanimously the press took up his case, insisting, as the *Guardian* (normally no friend of Rowland) put it, that he had received 'a disgracefully raw deal'.

The Commission quoted some curious reasons for its conclusions. Since acquiring Whyte & Mackay whisky, the Lonrho-owned hotels, which previously had purchased only negligble amounts, had increased their purchases to half the total they sold; similarly they were now big purchasers of Lonrho-made linen. The leading City Editor of the time, Patrick Sergeant, wrote in his columns in the *Daily Mail*: 'I do not think I am alone in finding the Commission's arguments thin and their verdict poor.' The rest of the press condemned it. The *Financial Times* called it 'feeble', *The Times* thought it was 'odd', and the *Daily Telegraph*'s City Editor Andreas Whittam Smith reckoned the Commission had done 'more damage to its own reputation than to Lonrho'. One of the Commissioners, H. H. Hunt, wrote his own note of dissent: he thought the bid should have been allowed. The decision, viewed in the light of the manner in which the mega-bids for Distillers and Imperial Group were treated in the spring of 1986, becomes still more peculiar. It becomes more curious still when it is realised that, four years later, the Commission would again investigate the self-same issue – and this time give an entirely different decision.

But rightly or wrongly, however unpredictably and however clumsily, the Monopolies Commission had dealt Rowland a major setback from which he seemed most unlikely to recover in his battle for Harrods. True, the government had left a slight opening, indicating that 'in the light of new circumstances' it might consider lifting the undertakings it had forced Lonrho to give not to proceed with its bid. But there seemed little possibility of Lonrho ever getting through that opening.

The next three years were ones of unremitting war between the two sides. Lonhro made proposal after proposal aimed at harrying both the board of Fraser and the government. It called extraordinary general meetings, put up resolutions at annual meetings, attempted to get Harrods demerged, and many other new ploys. Gradually the battle faded from the front pages, the issues now so predictable, the rhetoric so well-known.

But the government remained embarrassed by it and there was much talk that 'the City must find a solution to it all'. The City tried. Countless schemes were put forward. Every retailer of any size at some point made Rowland an offer for his block of shares. British-American Tobacco made a bid, as did Sears. There were deals proposed whereby somebody else would bid for House of Fraser and then sell Harrods back to Rowland for an agreed price – £250–300m was talked about for the store alone, although Lonrho's first bid had only been worth

£240m for the whole company. At one memorable annual meeting Professor Smith turned on Rowland and told him to 'get your tanks off my lawn'. It was a spontaneous remark, but representative of the war mentality which prevailed.

Rowland, his early humour now giving way to grimness and bitterness, gradually adapted his tactics. Few other businessmen would have continued against the forces he now faced. Rowland, however, settled in with siege tactics, aimed at wearing the opposition down. That very nearly worked, too.

Lonrho was finding support from unexpected quarters. The merits of demerging Harrods were considerable, and there were many neutral observers who felt that Rowland had a good idea. Harrods, freed of the drain of the other Fraser stores, could be worth anything up to £300m – more than the whole group was capitalised at. There were tax and other problems, however. And the Fraser management continued to argue strongly that it was not worth it, that Rowland would merely snap up the demerged Harrods, and that Fraser without its flagship would just be a problem company. On 30 June 1983, Rowland had actually got 53 per cent of the votes cast in favour of a resolution to demerge Harrods, but again he had been outmanouevred – another resolution required a 75 per cent majority and the board claimed it over-ruled the first.

While the public battle was becoming more acrimonious, the most important player yet to appear on the stage was preparing for his entrance.

Towards the end of 1982 Mohamed Al Fayed was nearing the first stage of his meticulous restoration of the Ritz Hotel of which he was proud. The next step was to build up the clientele. He had an extra supply of 1983 Ritz diaries made up: small, simple, blue leather, with the coat of arms and the words 'Hotel Ritz, Paris' picked out in gold. Customers of the Ritz got them free. Others paid $30 for them. They were to be sent out to potential clients of the Ritz anywhere in the world. The Ritz staff assembled their list of addresses for the mail shot, using, among other lists, Al Fayed's own address book. Still in it, dating from the time Al Fayed was a Lonrho director, was the name and address of Tiny Rowland.

Rowland had not talked to any of the Fayed family for seven years. The diary, with his initials on it, came, he said afterwards, as 'a surprise'. Politely he wrote back, thanking Al Fayed and suggesting they meet when next he was in London. It was the spring of 1983 before they finally got together and after that met every three or four months, according to both men. Mostly they saw each other in 60 Park Lane.

The second DTI inquiry, headed by John Griffiths QC, finally dragged to an end in the autumn of 1984 after a year during which the inspector had followed through all the suspicions and gossip that came his way. Rowland upstaged him by producing a report of his own, almost identical in appearance, which slammed the inspector harder than Griffiths slammed him. Griffiths kept running down blind alleys, and in the end was told by the government to end his enquiry. He cleared Rowland and Lonrho.

By now Rowland had opened up still another front. His constant lobbying with the government had finally got him somewhere. The Monopolies Commission had been ordered, yet again, to investigate a Lonrho bid for House of Fraser. Its decision would over-rule all previous rulings. Rowland at last might be in the clear. Harrods could yet be his. He could still win, if only he could get it to change its mind. The Commission was now much more 'competition' oriented, and there seemed no reason why he should be turned down. Through the summer and autumn of 1984 his hopes began to rise. Then at the end of October, the day before that crucial breakfast meeting in Park Lane, came a blow he had not been expecting: the Commission would extend its enquiry for another three months. Rowland's impeccable intelligence sources indicated he was going to get another rejection. This time the Commission would go even further: it would urge the government to force Lonrho to dispose of its shares. According to Rowland, Sir Godfray Le Quesne said to Edward Ducann: 'Why don't you sell your shares?' It was one of Rowland's lowest moments. He could not understand why the government machine seemed to have one rule for him, one for everyone else. His mood swung violently between anger and the desire for revenge, and despair that his dream of owning Harrods should end in this way. Those close to him in those days said that this decision to extend the Monopolies Commission enquiry was the breaking point for him, the one time his determination wavered.

It was at that moment that Rowland turned to Mohamed Al Fayed. He knew that the Egyptian was interested in owning unique and prestige assets. What he did not know was that for a full two years Al Fayed had been watching events at House of Fraser far more closely than he pretended. He was far more interested in Harrods than Rowland ever guessed.

Rowland later alleged that it was the Al Fayeds who had organised the three-month extension of the Monopolies Commission probe, and had, in effect, laid an elaborate trap for him. The Al Fayeds strenuously deny that allegation, and say instead that they entered the deal in good faith, believing that Rowland was genuinely selling out and offering them the chance to buy the whole group. Over many conversations with the Fayeds, and particularly Mohamed,* they appear frank and remarkably open, and truly astonished and dismayed at the situation they found themselves in. 'I would never have done it, never have touched House of Fraser or Harrods or any of it, if I had known what would happen. My dignity, and the dignity of my family, is far more important to me than any of this,' said Mohamed.

It is possible that Rowland envisaged the sale as something of a holding operation: he would sell to the Fayeds, whom he might assume would be less likely than he was to face the whole panoply of a Monopolies Commission investigation, partly because they would not be willing to fight publicly, and lose their much-prized privacy. Then perhaps, when circumstances changed, he could buy back again.

But none of this was discussed at that breakfast meeting in October 1984. The deal done that morning, as least as far as the Fayeds were concerned, was final.

'He offered us the stock, we said fine, we'll take it – and goodbye.' Mohamed, relating the story, wipes his hands together expressively.

Rowland almost certainly underestimated the wealth of the Al Fayeds. He knew they were rich – he himself had referred to their wealth on several occasions: 'The Al Fayeds have huge joint interests,' he wrote to the Department of Trade inspector John Griffiths, 'and, if you make enquiries, you will hear that when in London they conduct all their business from their Park Lane apartment, and know and receive numerous visitors every day from the City. They are extremely well known, and have brought well over a thousand million pounds worth of business to this country.'† On several other occasions Rowland had deliberately drawn attention to the scale of the Al Fayeds' wealth.

He certainly seems to have believed they could find the initial £138m for his 29.99 per cent stake. He may not, on the other hand, have believed they could muster the cash for the whole of Fraser, although only a few months before he had indicated he would only sell to them *if* they made a bid for the lot. Rowland later spent months and several million pounds building a dossier on the wealth of the Fayeds, in an attempt to prove they did not have the money to pay for House of

*Conversations with the authors.
†Griffith's report.

63

Fraser. Yet when the time came the Fayeds produced over £500m without apparent effort.

Within hours of the sale of his 29.99 per cent, Rowland was already setting the scene for what lay ahead. The Fayeds announced, as part of their deal, that two of them, Mohamed and his polished and anglofied brother Ali, would join the Fraser board, replacing Rowland himself and Lonrho's ageing and (very) non-executive former chairman, Lord Duncan-Sandys, who would come off. The first hint that all might not be sweetness and light came in the *Observer* that weekend: Rowland and Duncan-Sandys might not resign. The journalist added that Lonrho was already thinking of buying back into the House of Fraser. 'Of course we might,' said Rowland. 'It would depend on the price. We are a trading company. That means we are buyers and sellers.'

Lonrho in fact was not at all a trading company in that sense, and was not in the habit of buying and selling share stakes. The Fraser share price had already risen sharply since the deal – so what was the point of selling out 29.99 per cent and then buying back again? It made no sense. Yet that *Observer* article was clearly written from an informed standpoint.

Within days Lonrho was in the market, buying Fraser shares again, pushing the price higher and sending ripples of unease through the Fayed camp. A week after selling out, Lonrho was once again one of the biggest shareholders, having spent £21m on buying a 4.5 per cent stake.

'There were many theories being advanced about what Britain's most mercurial and determined tycoon might be planning,' commented the *Financial Times*, reflecting the puzzlement that reigned in the City. One week Rowland had sold nearly 30 per cent of Fraser shares at 300p a share. The next week he was back in the market buying at around the same price. Why? Even some of his former supporters decided to call it a day. From the Bahamas, Jack Hayward, a millionaire businessman who rejoiced under the title 'Union Jack' Hayward because of his intense pro-Britishness, rang his London stockbrokers, Rowe and Pitman, and asked them to sell his one million shares. 'I simply said get as near 300p as you can,' said Hayward later. Afterwards he breathed a sigh of relief. 'Thank God, I'm out of it,' he said. 'It's such a trauma.' There were plenty of others willing to take the same view. Fraser shares had never been so high. Now there was a willing buyer in the market, snapping up all the stock he could lay hands on. Rowland had been prevented under his Monopolies Commission undertakings from going above 29.99 per cent for four years, and so had been out of the market. Now he could buy right back up to 29.99 per cent again – and seemed to be intent on doing so.

Hayward made over £2m on his investment so had nothing to complain about. Ashraf Marwan, the late president Nasser's son-in-law and a former head of Egyptian intelligence, also sold his shares in the market, making about £4m. In both cases Lonrho was the buyer. Both Hayward and Marwan had told the Griffiths enquiry that they had only bought after reading an article in the *Sunday Telegraph** called 'Slater's Tip'. It was a short piece but caused at least three people to invest more than £10m between them – and to end up with profits of around £8m. It appeared on 15 May, 1983 and read:

> Jim Slater passes on this idea for making money for free. It is called Tip-the Scales Investment Trust – and it cannot go wrong.
>
> What it does is this. It makes one investment: a million House of Fraser shares. Cost: £1.86m. It then turns up at the annual meeting in June and votes them in favour of the demerger of Harrods.
>
> This is enough to tip the balance in favour of Lonrho's resolution (at least it was this weekend).
>
> With Harrods demerged, the share price rises to, say, 250p; you sell and move on to the next tight takeover bid.

The investors had done rather better than that, getting 300p a share for their holdings.

There was a further reason for unease. 'Tiny told me on the phone he would resign from the Fraser board,' said Mohamed Al Fayed.† 'Then suddenly he wouldn't go.' A week after he sold his stake, Rowland gave an interview to the *Sunday Times*. 'We look on the Al Fayeds as good friends, but we're used to battle by circular. We see no reason why we should resign.' By now, however, the Al Fayeds were beginning to show that they too could fight.

The initial suspicions at House of Fraser were giving way to relief – the Fayeds were not, after all, just Lonrho puppets. Professor Smith and his colleagues made enquiries. The picture they found was extremely interesting. Although it was far from complete, there was evidence that these men were every bit as wealthy as was claimed for them. When the first oil crisis happened in 1973, the Fayeds were perfectly positioned for it. They had an oil trading business based in Dubai and were able to buy oil in large quantities at the official rate, selling it on

*Written by Ivan Fallon.
† Interview with the authors.

the spot market in a rapidly rising market. On one deal alone, according to Mohamed, they made $400m. The oil boom brushed off onto their other businesses too: they built and still manage the Trade Centre in Dubai, the biggest development in the country, and in all were agents for contracts running to well over $2bn. They moved into the US, buying a share in the Rockefeller Centre, and a stake in a small Texas bank. Oil trading was, however, by far the most profitable. Mohamed later would point with some scorn to the publicity surrounding the New York oil trader Marc Rich, reputed to be worth $2bn. That, he implied, was small beer – the really successful oil traders, he intimated, were hardly ever heard of. He and his brothers were in the business.

By 1984, after a second successful oil boom, the Al Fayeds were rich enough to take on Tiny Rowland. They liked London more and more, and in Park Lane they had built a penthouse on the roof, invisible from prying eyes, but probably one of the most elegant apartments in London, with a room, known to the family as the 'rotunda', which had a view over three-quarters of London. Mohamed had peopled it with Egyptian antiques, including two giant black Nubian figures, standing in the hallway acting as lampstands. He also had a house in Surrey, and they had bought the family seat of the Earls of Ross, Balnagown Castle, in Scotland and spent nearly £1m renovating it. They had also bought the Dorchester Hotel, and resold it to the Sultan of Brunei at the same price they paid for it. 'He wanted it, because his father used to stay there,' Mohamed explained.

Tiny Rowland, in his campaign against them, would try to paint an entirely different picture of the Fayeds and their background, but the picture that unfolded to Professor Smith and his board was one of an intensely private family, with substantial wealth and widespread business interests. In Paris, they had powerful friends, including the then mayor (and later prime minister) Jacques Chirac. Furthermore, the Fayeds were willing to commit themselves long-term to a business, as they were showing with the Ritz, where Mohamed was personally involved in the refurbishment in the finest detail, even to the furnishings in the bedroom suites, and the bath fittings. (Chirac later awarded him the Legion d'Honneur for his contribution to France.)

Smith much preferred the Fayeds to Rowland. They were proving very easy to get on with, very supportive; they liked what he was doing at Fraser, and indicated to him that they wanted him to continue doing it if and when they took control. Tiny Rowland, on the other hand, had said again and again that the first man to go when he won Fraser would be Professor Smith.

It was around this time that Rowland began to realise his mistake.

He had believed the Fayeds would never emerge from behind their intense privacy to fight him. He had not realised that they would build up their own press contacts and their own political lobby. And he had never thought for a moment that they would be welcome at the House of Fraser. Rowland himself was bad at all these things; and he believed the Fayeds, simply because they were rich foreigners operating in a country where being part of the establishment was so important, would be even worse.

Nor could Rowland believe that the Fayeds would so quickly grasp the politics and complexities of the House of Fraser boardroom. Mohamed, smiling, polite and private, gave little hint of the determination and the intelligence which had made him so wealthy. Only occasionally did the outsider get a flash of it – and then usually only when Mohamed was giving orders to one of his employees – or if he went against what Al Fayed wanted. For all his shrewdness and experience, Rowland simply did not know his man. Even when the Fayed camp publicly announced that it would support the Fraser board 'if necessary' to remove Rowland and Lord Duncan-Sandys from the board, he refused to believe it. 'I am totally unconcerned by what has been said. I am quite certain that the Fayeds would not dream of voting against us,' he said.*

But he had abandoned his power base by selling his shares and he abruptly realised that, if they wanted him off, the Fayeds would have him off. The Fayeds did – they were furious that he was breaking what they called a 'gentleman's agreement' that he would go. Now he was making statements such as: 'If I don't leave, I will have to be thrown off the board.'

The Fayeds did not want a public row, however, and told Smith to make Rowland resign – but leave him some dignity. A few days later Rowland retreated. Smith forced him to agree to go, allowing him to keep some face by staying on until the end of the year, which was only six weeks away.

In normal circumstances that would have been the end of the fight. In fact, a new phase was just beginning. The campaign to discredit the Fayeds now began in earnest. Rowland began to suggest in public that the Fayeds were not as rich as they claimed, that they could not have afforded the £138.2m they had paid for their holding, and that they were fronting for the Sultan of Brunei. Although publicly he could say, as he did in the *Observer* at the end of the year, 'Mohamed and Ali

*The Daily Telegraph, 18 November, 1984.

are close friends of mine,' privately he had files made up and showed them to journalists; he sent them along to the Department of Trade, trying to persuade the government not to clear the purchase of the 29.99 per cent stake – it still had to get permission from the Office of Fair Trading. He was also intent on laying the groundwork for stopping them getting permission for the next step – a bid for the whole company.

On 1 January, 1985 the Lonrho directors on the House of Fraser board had formally gone, and Mohamed Al Fayed and his brother Ali joined. The Fayed era had begun. First of all, however, they had to get full control and there were two main obstacles. There was Rowland, now openly insisting that he would make a bid again if the Monopolies Commission, due to report early in March, allowed him to; and, secondly, there was the government itself – Lonrho had faced formidable Monopolies Commission obstacles, and there was no reason to believe the Fayeds would not have to run through the same gamut.

Against that, however, there was one major factor in their favour: the government was so fed up with the whole saga of Harrods that it wanted it resolved soon. It is conceivable that, if Tiny Rowland had kept his nerve that much longer and had not so misread the situation at the end of 1984, he would have won. It is even more conceivable that, if Tiny Rowland had been even fractionally more conciliatory in his attitude to the authorities, they would have been forced by the merits of the situation to let him have Harrods. Now, however, there was an alternative, and increasingly that alternative looked a ready cure for a running sore which had infected half a dozen secretaries of state so far. There was also another factor: the pound sterling suddenly went into a spin early in the year, falling at one stage to just above parity with the dollar over one weekend when the press officer in Downing Street badly briefed the Sunday lobby journalists. 'This was very important to us,' said Mohamed afterwards, referring to the low level of sterling. He could use dollars to buy Fraser with a knock-out bid which the Fraser board would approve – and which might well get the government's support.

His merchant bankers, Kleinwort Benson, met Professor Smith at the end of February. Terms of a bid, which the board of Fraser would agree to after all those years of unacceptable bids, were now worked out in a matter of days. The board of Fraser met early in March on a Sunday afternoon to agree the deal. There was one moment of unease as a Scottish director asked the blunt question: 'I assume the Al Fayeds have got the money?' After a moment's silence John MacArthur of Kleinwort Benson, handling the bid for the Fayeds, spoke up. 'I'm in a large hole if they haven't,' he said. He had pledged Kleinwort's reputation on that fact, but was not concerned: the necessary £430m needed to buy out the other 70.01 per cent of House of Fraser appeared as readily as the first cash. With the fall in sterling, Mohamed agreed to offer £4 a share, £1 a share more than he had paid Rowland for his stake, and more than double the 150p a share which Rowland had originally offered, and with which he would have won the day but for the intervention of the Monopolies Commission. The new bid would value the House of Fraser at £615m, making it the biggest completed bid of 1985, but modest in the light of other retailing bids which soon followed – for instance the £1.8bn which Stanley Kalms of Dixons offered for Woolworth.

On Monday 4 March the bid was announced. To the watching City it seemed incredible that the battle could end here. Surely something or someone, notably Rowland, would intervene to wreck the peace? 'It may be too much to hope for,' remarked Lex in the *Financial Times* that morning, 'but it looks as if the longest running soap opera in the stock market ... is at last drawing to a close.'

There was, however, one key obstacle still to clear: the government. Rowland was convinced the Fayeds would falter at this hurdle. He was now confident that the Monopolies Commission would clear him this time round: the third enquiry into his bid hopes was now at last nearing completion. Professor Roland Smith agreed to handle the lobbying for the Fayeds. The man who had to decide was Norman Tebbit, at that stage still feeling his way in his new role as Secretary of State for Trade and Industry where he had replaced Cecil Parkinson. Both camps made their representations to him. Tebbit later was caustic about it in remarks to friends. Of the two Rolands, he said, he actually preferred Tiny to the professor, although he was not very taken with either one. But the Fayeds were prepared to invest hard dollars in Britain at a low time for sterling; the board of Fraser, the City establishment in the shape of Warburgs (holders of around 15 per cent in Fraser by now), Cazenove and Kleinwort, were in favour; and there seemed to him no reason at all to oppose it.

Rowland did his best to find him one. In mid-March he and Edward Du Cann turned up in Tebbit's office, armed with a large dossier on the Fayeds. Tebbit listened bemusedly to Rowland's bitter attack on the Egyptian brothers, whom Rowland himself had brought into the situation and had praised to the department's own inspector.

Later much of this material turned up in the *Observer*. It was strenuously denied and is the subject of several libel writs.

*

Four days later, on 7 March, 1985, Tiny Rowland at last received what he had wanted for seven years: official sanction to bid for the House of Fraser. The Monopolies Commission finally reported with a complete reversal of its own findings of December 1981. Now it concluded that a Lonrho takeover of House of Fraser 'may be expected not to operate against the public interest'. Rowland instantly urged that the Fayeds' bid be referred. 'We have had four years of investigations and had to provide roomfuls of information about our exact intentions if we take over House of Fraser,' he said. 'It would hardly be reasonable if the Al Fayeds got a go ahead just on a few hours conversation.' If they were referred, he added, he would bid again. That day's headline in the *Financial Times* read: 'Lonrho prepares for new offensive to win control of Fraser.' Rowland still needed Tebbit formally to release him from the undertakings he had already been forced to give not to bid, or procure a bid, for House of Fraser. But that was a mere formality.

There was one final frantic week left in the Battle of Harrods. As *The Times* wrote on 9 March: 'The future ownership of House of Fraser and the much prized Harrods is now in the Government's gift.' By the following Tuesday afternoon at the latest – and this was Saturday – Tebbit would have to decide whether or not to refer the Fayeds' bid. By Wednesday President Mubarrak of Egypt would be in No. 10 Downing Street to be wined and dined by Mrs Thatcher. Mohamed Al Fayed would also be there. It would be a big Egyptian evening. As Kenneth Fleet wrote in *The Times* that Saturday: 'I would like to be a fly on the wall if Mrs Thatcher has to explain to the president why the government had seen fit, that very morning, to baulk the bid for Fraser made by his distinguished fellow countrymen, his friends the Al Fayeds. It would not exactly strike a blow for better Anglo-Egyptian relations on which the prime minister is keen.'

That Sunday, the *Observer* came out with another attack upon the background of the Fayeds. The *Sunday Telegraph* on the other hand urged that the Fayeds should not have to go through a Monopolies Commission process. 'For everybody's sake – Fraser chairman Professor Smith's, his directors, management, staff, shareholders and suppliers, and for the sake of MMC chairman Sir Godfray Le Quesne and those of his overworked staff,' wrote the City editor Ian Watson, 'it is time for Norman Tebbit to conclude that enough is enough and let shareholders decide.'

In the event shareholders did decide – although they did not have an enormous choice. The Fayeds decided they would not wait for Tebbit. On the Monday before he was due to pronounce, they invaded the market. By lunchtime they had taken their stake from 29.9 per cent to 37.4 per cent. Tiny Rowland, again caught off guard, decided to sell the second tranche of shares he owned: 9.7m of them, for which Lonrho received £39.1m, to give it a further profit of £10m. His sale clinched the matter.

He had now sold to the Fayeds not once but twice.

Other holders, seeing no possibility of a counter-bid, followed suit. By the end of the trading day, the Fayed holding had swept past 50 per cent. In the end Tebbit waited until Thursday to make his pronouncement. He would not refer the Fayeds to the Monopolies Commission. He had, he said, given his ruling based on assurances from the Egyptian brothers that they would develop the group long-term; but he particularly placed the onus on the bankers, Kleinwort Benson, who effectively guaranteed the financial standing of the Fayed family. At the same time Tebbit, in the light of the Monopolies Commission decision, finally released Tiny Rowland from his undertaking not to bid for House of Fraser. By that stage it was a matter of academic interest.

Sipping the Fayed proprietary Ritz champagne later that day, Professor Roland Smith commented on his great adversary. 'It is a bit like arriving at the right platform to find your train has gone. After being in the public eye for several years the House of Fraser is now going off the air altogether.'

It was not quite as simple as that. The *Observer* continued to pursue the Rowland vendetta against the Fayeds. And Tiny Rowland refused to give up his dream. Two years later, in April 1987, yet another enquiry began.

There is a final ironic footnote to the Harrods takeover. Some time after it was all over, we asked Norman Tebbit what his attitude to Lonrho's bid had been. 'If only Tiny Rowland could have read my mind at that time, he would never have sold out,' he replied. 'I didn't care who owned Harrods or House of Fraser – I was interested only in takeovers on competition grounds, and there was no competition element involved.' In other words, if Rowland had kept his nerve and his resolve that much longer in the autumn of 1984, Harrods would probably be his today, and the Fayeds would be as private and unknown in Britain as they were before.

The Battle of Harrods was the only takeover bid to have spanned the two takeover eras of the 1970s and the 1980s. In many ways Tiny Rowland was the general still fighting the last war – tactically he was back in the 'Slater era', using the same strategies used and discredited then. Because he had shut himself off from much of the City, he was not open to creative new schemes which banks such as Morgan

Grenfell and Warburgs were offering to their clients, some of which were, in their turn, to be equally discredited. Rowland ran the bid very much by the seat of his pants. Even his offer was made on the spur of the moment, to be contrasted with, say, James Gulliver's careful build-up to another Scottish institution, Distillers, which he planned for two years. Running a hostile bid in the City of London in the 1980s requires considerable organisation and planning; the successful bidders, such as Lord Hanson or Sir Owen Green, use teams of top lawyers, top accountants, and one of the four or five front-line banks in c ·porate finance. They also use another discipline which Rowland scorned: public relations. As the bid boom of the 1980s wore on, the bidders and their advisers increasingly realised the importance of a good press. Many of the more seasoned bidders soon learned the value of advertising, too: in his bid for Distillers, Gulliver would employ Saatchi & Saatchi who came up with some slick ads which were so effective that the rival bidder, Guinness, eventually sued.

Rowland too ruled himself out of the 'leveraged' bid finance which would later creep in from the United States. Others at the time were watching the raids of Boone Pickens and Carl Icahn with enormous interest, debating the value of their tactics and financing. Men like Sir James Goldsmith, Lord Hanson and Rupert Murdoch decided that, rather than adapting American methods to Britain, it would be even better to use American methods in the United States – and made some spectacular bids there.

Tiny Rowland however never learned any of these lessons. He was too distracted, too busy fighting everyone, and there was no-one close to him who could advise him. Even so, he nearly made it, largely on the strength of his personality.

Yet the House of Fraser bid sets out the points we will allude to many times in this book. In takeover bids, men, however powerful and successful, expose their full obsessiveness, their unreasonableness and their personal weaknesses. Anyone who thinks that all takeover bids are the result of meticulous planning, that endless sums and permutations are put through computers, and that huge corporations enter a bid only when they have worked out exactly the benefits involved, and how much the target is worth, must think again. The bid arena is not like that, and never was. Like any place else, it is made up of people who in some senses may be extraordinary, but who emotionally are not a lot different from the rest of us. When Tiny Rowland was hurt, he bled like anyone else. When he won a victory, he celebrated like anyone else. The same is true of Mohamed Al Fayed, of James Gulliver – or of Ernest Saunders of Guinness.

CHAPTER THREE

Wall Street's Gunslingers

The battle for Harrods was in many ways a one off. There had been nothing like it before, and there will quite possibly be nothing like it again. As it deteriorated into years of hard slogging, and slanging, it had become isolated from the main trends which were developing. It lasted so long that it bridged the bid periods of the 1970s and the 1980s, and may now run on into the 1990s. Even the personalities seemed to have aged to the point where they came from a different generation. Tiny Rowland had entered it full of zest; he ended it an embittered old man, railing against the injustice of the government, the establishment, and Harrods' new owners. Sir Hugh Fraser died, aged 50. Only the Fayeds emerged with dignity, still not knowing what their offence had been.

To the new gunslingers on Wall Street, Tiny Rowland and his friends Robert Anderson and Daniel K. Ludwig were from another age. As we shall see in this book, takeover tactics and strategies can alter in the twinkling of an eye, and the real professionals are those who either anticipate the trends, or actually set them. Some of the runners from the day when Rowland was a big figure on the takeover scene were still in the race, and could show the newcomers that experience and stamina counted: Sir James Goldsmith and Lord Hanson to name two. Goldsmith in particular found he was in his element in the takeover scene of the 1980s.

There were new pacemakers now, moving on those industries which had faltered, fallen from grace or had just simply thrown up a gap between reliable values and market price. Just as many of the giants of previous takeover booms were the targets of the next one, so too the fall in the oil price in 1984 made that industry, the world's strongest just a few years before, the number one target now. And since oil, with the exception of Shell and BP, is essentially an American industry, the action was all on Wall Street. The much hackneyed phrase of the time was that it was 'cheaper to dig for oil on Wall Street than in Texas'. Unbelievable as it would have seemed at the height of the oil boom, by the end of 1984 almost every oil company in America, regardless of size, was watching out for one man: a raw Texan from Amarillo called T. Boone Pickens Jr. He was to have a profound influence on the whole direction of takeovers – and of the oil industry.

Bill Douce was tired but happy. He and his buddies Fred and John were having their first drink of the evening after the kind of bird-shooting day that took Douce back to his Kansas boyhood. There was the feel of taut leg muscles, the warmth of the fire and the whisky, the pleasant pain in the right shoulder from the recoil of the rifle. He liked to say there was sex and there was whisky, but then there was bird hunting. Other bird hunters knew what he meant.

Bill Douce was no longer a Kansas farm boy but the chairman of Phillips Petroleum. Fred was Fred Hartley, the head of Unocal; and John was Texaco boss John K. McKinley. On this day early in December 1984, the heads of the second, third and tenth largest oil companies in America were in a Spanish duke's estate north of Granada. Just three good friends, off on a bird shoot with good ground, good whisky and talk that wouldn't leak out to some nosy Wall Street analyst or some bright spark in the US Justice Department.

The telephone interrupted their laughter. It was for McKinley; his Houston office was calling. The three oilmen were mildly surprised. They had been teasing each other all weekend about whose company was going to be the next major takeover target in the wave of frenzied merger battles that had rocked the oil industry all year. It had to be either Hartley or Douce, they agreed. But it was McKinley being called to the phone.

He was back in the room a moment later, grinning. McKinley's office in Houston had called with news off the Dow Jones news ticker. He cocked a finger at Douce and squeezed off an imaginary bullet.

'It's you, old buddy,' he said. 'It's Pickens.'

Far off in the other room the sound of the telephone could be heard again. This time it was Douce's secretary in Bartlesville, Oklahoma with the news that T. Boone Pickens and his Mesa Petroleum investment partners had filed a New York Stock Exchange notice of a $50 tender offer for control of Phillips. There was other annoying news. None of the top officers of the company were in Bartlesville at that moment. Some had slipped away for a bit of skiing in Colorado, but most were in New York City attending an awards banquet for a board member. Never mind, Douce told her. Hold everybody in New York and get me out of here first thing tomorrow. Then he went back to the fireplace.

The three were no longer in a teasing mood. The takeover wars would engulf the other two in any event and they knew it; it was take over or be taken over these days. For Douce, it was a battle for which he'd been preparing for two years now, ever since rumours began that Mobil Oil was planning a takeover run at Phillips. He was in a grim, fighting mood now.

'That venal son of a bitch,' Douce said. 'He may get us, but he'll know he was in a fight.' The others nodded.

The Boone Pickens stories started to flow – in particular they liked the one about how after finally being elected to the board of the American Petroleum Institute, the trade association and social focus for the major oil companies, Pickens was to be dropped off the board at the end of this year. After all, Mesa Petroleum might be a $400m-a-year oil and gas producer, but, hell, what was that against the billions that the big boys pumped?

'There we were in the hotel lobby, a bunch of us, and Boone walked right up to us and started talking about something without so much as a hello,' McKinley marvelled.

'He made some crack about me having a piano in my airplane in front of some of my people,' Hartley fumed. 'First of all, it's not even a piano. It's one of those electric keyboards – and my staff gave it to me while I was recuperating from my heart attack.' The others nodded.

Douce lowered his voice even though there was no-one else in the room. 'Boone's been sniffing around Boots Adams' widow.'

Now that really was low. It also might have been slightly questionable under the rules of the US Securities and Exchange Commission, but that wasn't the point. It was a matter of taste, of style, as far as the three men were concerned. There were some things you just did not do.

From Pickens' standpoint, however, a gentle exploratory base touching with Dorothy Glynn Adams and her children was only prudent strategy. No insider information, mind you. Just some attitude testing; what would the Adams family reaction be if Boone Pickens were to take over Phillips Oil, as it is still called in Bartlesville?

Frank Phillips and his brothers had struck it rich in the Indian

Territory oil fields around Bartlesville in 1905 and had moved beyond wildcat rich to manufacturing rich during World War I when oil went from 40 cents a barrel to $1. They went beyond that when the Texas Panhandle boom of 1925 trebled the company's size and made Phillips the nation's largest producer of natural gas.

The Phillips brothers – Frank, L. E., Ed, Fred and Waite – were genuine American industrial founders, lucky, tough and as eccentric as any Ford or Firestone. But they were more – Uncle Frank especially. The Phillipses looked beyond the huge riches that could be earned from the finding and getting of oil and gas to finding ways to increase America's appetite for their products.

Through most of the 1930s, Phillips aviation fuels were publicised widely by such heroes as pilot Wiley Post and such celebrities as Will Rogers. Phillips service stations, with their pledge of clean restrooms, dotted the motoring landscape. Research breakthroughs such as the first 100-octane aviation fuel and various chemicals kept the company growing at an explosive pace, even during the Depression.

There is a photograph of the five brothers, seated precariously on picnic chairs at some family-company outdoor gathering in 1930. All are wearing the high-cut suits of the times. Frank, L. E., and Ed are wearing their trousers tucked into ornate calf-high cowboy boots and they are sporting wide-brim, high-crown Stetsons. It looks like a joke picture, these owlish Phillips brothers in their rimless glasses and dour faces; perhaps they are a group of school superintendents at a masquerade. But a second look shows what tough characters these brothers were. The snapshot catches them in a split second of motionless time; they have paused to sit back in their chairs to accommodate the photographer and they watch him at his work. A moment later they will be out of those chairs, talking about the thing that consumed them. To joke about the 'oil game', as was the fashion at the time of those in the steel 'game' or the tool-and-dye 'rackets', would draw icy stares from the Phillips brothers. They were not playing at a game.

Kenneth Stanley 'Boots' Adams made it into that circle of brothers by working harder and knowing more about the inner workings of Phillips Petroleum than anybody else outside the family itself; soon he was inside the family circle working 18 hours a day, seven days a week at the side of the driven 'Uncle Frank'.

'Boots' Adams was a go-getter, a classic Corn Belt drummer at heart, who was happiest when he was on the road for Phillips buying drilling rights and recruiting new service station operators for the ever-expanding retail network. When Frank Phillips finally retired in 1949, Adams became his successor as president and took Phillips into the next frontier as an international competitor for oil reserves and marketing outlets.

The Adams' presence in Bartlesville went beyond the street and office building they had named for him after his death. Dorothy Glynn Adams and their adult children were a constant reminder of the good old days when the grimiest roughneck expected to be called by his first name either by Uncle Frank or Boots.

It was not that Douce and his already-announced successor Glenn Cox and C. J. Silas had done anything in particular to anger the Adams family. It was more a case that they enjoyed being courted and paid attention to, and Boone Pickens had worked for Phillips as a geologist when he was just starting out. Certainly Uncle Frank and Boots would have admired a get-ahead kind of guy like Boone.

Douce knew this and knew that the small newspaper run by the Adams family in Bartlesville would be weighing in with pro-Pickens editorials soon enough.

That was all right with Douce, who had very little in common with the old guard families who still insisted on their perquisites but who were not actively involved in the company operations. Indeed Douce saw himself as a bridge between the old, paternalistic, seat-of-the-pants management style of Uncle Frank and Boots Adams and this new breed of business school manager – 'numbers crunchers', he called them – who didn't know a tool pusher from a drill bit.

Douce may not have been as familiar with the latest business theories as Glenn Cox and C. J. Silas, the men who would succeed him at the top; it didn't really matter since he was to retire in early 1985 anyway. But he had known that Phillips was a likely takeover target and, now that the raid was coming, he knew what he had to do. He would show these business schools boys how to mount a defence that would go into the business textbooks.

The casebooks of the world's business schools already have lengthy chapters on takeovers. They should be rewritten, if for no other reason than the great raid on Phillips, its sequel, the great raid on Unocal, and the tidal side effects that continue even today. More so than any other of the latest series of battles for corporate control, the Phillips raid was the first of a series of bitter challenges to the way everyone thinks about the big, multinational corporations. For at least four years now the international corporate scene has resembled nothing so much as one of those horrible nineteenth-century Russian lithographs of the troika sled dashing across the frozen wastes just ahead of the pack of ravenous wolves, the mother poised to chuck the bundled babe over the side to gain a few precious seconds.

In the battle for control of Phillips, it finally came to pass that all the aberrations of tactics and doubts about the final results would come together; the takeover battlefield would never be the same. New tactics, new troops and new objectives replaced the old game for management control.

A year later, one result is that we must call into question even the most basic assumptions about what we know and have been taught about the ways of business in this final 15 years of the century. We must also reexamine the responsibilities we impose on those who manage our major corporations, on those who want to manage them, and on those workers and individual investors who until lately have been passive bystanders.

Several such commonplaces were shattered at once on 5 December, 1984, the day a group of investors headed by T. Boone Pickens Jr the flamboyant corporate raider, made public its tender offer for control of Phillips Petroleum Co.

Pickens, like most of the practitioners of the takeover gambit, loudly proclaims that he only seeks target companies that are so listlessly managed that the price of the target shares often are less than half the 'real value' of the underlying assets and profit potential. One of the more graphic images that he sketches for questioners is that of 'management which spends more time on the golf course and no time in the boardroom'.

As the tenth largest petroleum producer in the world, Phillips hardly fitted that image as 1984 came to an end. For the second straight year, the company had increased both its earnings and its return on revenues. Earnings for 1984 were $810m, a 12 per cent rise over 1983.

More to the point, Phillips management had not been sitting idly on its oil reserves, counting on the rise in OPEC prices to lift their boat as well. Its substantial investments in the Ekofisk fields in the North Sea had been matched by ambitious exploration and development projects in southern California and it moved as quickly as the changing demand market to convert a 500-mile oil pipeline into natural gas conduits between Texas and Oklahoma.

As a result, the stock market rewarded Phillips with a share price rise during the year from $33.50 to $44.50, despite the fact that Phillips had spent $1.6bn of its capital to buy Aminoil Corp, the oil and gas subsidiary of R. J. Reynolds. The year before Phillips perhaps had sealed its fate as an eventual Pickens target by outbidding his Amarillo-based Mesa Partners investment group for control of a smaller oil producer, General American Oil Corp. These two takeovers are instructive not only for what they tell us about the oil game, but also for what it shows about the rules of the takeover game. From time immemorial, companies have pursued others whose assets could be acquired more cheaply than those same raw materials and resources could be developed and discovered elsewhere.

By buying Aminoil, Phillips acquired 1.1m acres of rich oil and gas reserves, most of it in Oklahoma and nearby Arkansas. Thus the Aminoil buy was part of an industry trend of consolidation brought on by the fall in world demand and prices plus the skyrocketing costs of finding new reserves of commercially developed hydrocarbons. But the pressures of the takeover game also dictated the Aminoil buy because it forced Phillips to siphon off some of its surplus cash and thus made for a less attractive target for someone else to seek. Moreover Phillips management had signalled to the world that it would be an aggressive defender of its own integrity and that it had devised a game plan of its own.

Indeed it had. The plan was dubbed Operation Porcupine and its details and alternative strategies had been worked out in precise detail as a strategy exercise by the public affairs department in 1983 when it appeared that Mobil might be planning a raid on Phillips.

Douce and other Phillips top brass had decided early on that if a potential buyer were to show up with an undeniably top dollar bid – say of $60 a share or better – they would not follow the 'scorched earth' tactics of some managements, but would sell out. A buyer who paid top price would be more likely to keep the company intact and try to recover his investment through enhanced profitability. If someone could make more money with Phillips' assets, so be it.

But the Phillips team was under no illusions about the real goal of the new breed of corporate raider who had come on the scene in the last five years. This new variation on the takeover theme sought not undervalued commodity assets such as oil and gas reserves. Cash – surplus cash or cash from liquidation – was the true objective. Take the money and run is what the name of the game had become. Indeed the most popular version of this current takeover tactic does not envision a hostile bidder actually taking control of the target company.

As practised by Pickens and others such as New Yorkers Ivan Boesky, Carl Icahn and Saul Steinberg, it is infinitely preferable to have the target company management buy back one's shares at a premium as a price for being left in control of their company. It is this threat of seizing control coupled with the willingness to be paid off that has led the tactic to be tarred with the epithet 'greenmail'. The green stands for money, the mail is as in 'blackmail'.

In fact, the way a 'greenmail' strategy is usually fashioned, the unwanted suitor does not even have to seek majority control of the firm to be considered a threat to a management's control. To defeat such an attack, one needed a far more sophisticated defence than one could cook up oneself, and Douce and Cox knew it. Operation Porcupine showed, if anything, that Phillips' management would have to place its defence in the hands of professional strategists.

Just as the creation of the nineteenth-century German Imperial General Staff ended the European tradition of armies led by the noble-born amateur, so the takeover wars of the twentieth century were about to shift out of the hands of the company managers and into the hands of the hired takeover specialists – lawyers, public relations firms, and especially investment bankers – who could mount a successful corporate merger attack for one client and then mount an equally effective defence for another client.

The significance of the Phillips raid and the subsequent skirmish over Unocal is that the same general staff-for-hire was marshalled to develop strategies for both battles. Specialists had been used by raiders and defenders in other struggles, but this would be the first head-on clash of the first teams, the superstars of specialists, for the control of first-tier *Fortune* top 500 corporations. New tactics and new weapons would be displayed in a bewildering array.

The opening skirmishes of the battle had begun nearly two years earlier when Phillips had made a friendly $1.14bn bid for General American Oil Co., a Texas producer whose reserves would boost Phillips' domestic oil output. Douce was playing the white knight in this bid, since General American management badly wanted to fend off a lower bid by Boone Pickens' Mesa Petroleum Co.

Pickens had to be placated to be sure, for he had bought his 15 per cent interest in General American at $35 a share and he wanted some of the $50 a share that Phillips was paying the company's two big stockholders – the Meadows family and Southern Methodist University, which held 45 per cent of the stock in various trusts. Part of the settlement involved a 'standstill agreement', a fairly common bit of self-protection on Phillips' part. In effect, Pickens would promise that if he got the money he wanted, he would 'stand still' – that is, he would refrain from any more raids against General American.

But what difference would that make, if General American were to be owned by Phillips? Most standstill agreements merely seek to buy the friendly suitor enough of a peaceful interlude until the shareholders, in this case General American's, had a chance to ratify the merger. At that point Douce missed an opportunity to tie Pickens' hands forever and bar him from raiding Phillips as well.

'It is true that in one of the early draft agreements it was specified that Boone not only agreed not to pursue General American, he also was barred from making a takeover bid for us. We did ask it. But when you get into those contract negotiations, you can get distracted by other issues that appear more important at the time. We wanted General American at the price we wanted to pay and in getting it, that specific standstill clause got dropped out,' Douce would recall ruefully after it was all over. There also was a very firm impression in the mind of Douce and the other Phillips executives that it didn't matter anyhow, that a standstill agreement against General American perforce had to bar Pickens from making a run at Phillips.

At any rate, by the spring of 1984, Douce was convinced that while Boone Pickens may not make a run at Phillips, somebody was bound to.

Mobil was the most frequently mentioned suitor, so Douce deduced that the best legacy he could leave Cox and Silas was to shore up the defences according to the best tactics of the day. At the annual shareholders meeting, Phillips' dutiful shareholders approved a set of new rules that would daunt all but the most ardent suitor. Either a takeover bid had to be approved by the Phillips board of directors or the suitor had to win the support of 75 per cent of the outstanding common stock.

It was a good move. Until then, the way takeover and greenmail raiders had operated involved a considerable amount of bluffing and stampeding. A raider could buy 15 to 20 per cent of a target company's shares at market. Then he could make a tender offer for cash at a premium price for just enough shares to acquire a 51 per cent interest and offer a substantially lesser price to the remainder.

Often that was all it took. One of the facts of corporate life in the 1980s was the heavy percentage of share ownership that had become concentrated among institutional investors. These mutual funds, insurance companies and pension plans owned one share out of every three traded on the New York Stock Exchange in 1984. More impressively, they generated eight out of every ten trades, the vast bulk of them in huge, 100,000 or greater share blocs.

As we will see later, the pressure on the American institutional portfolio manager is a double-barrelled one that compels him to take an extremely short-term view. Tremendous profits can be gained by trading on an eighth of a point. Tremendous losses likewise threaten. If a raider is offering a premium for a limited amount of a company's shares, the portfolio manager who holds some of those shares would be foolish indeed to pass up what might be a once-in-a-lifetime – within his timeframe – chance, as well as to risk the almost certain downdraft that will hit the company's share price if the raid is a success.

The Phillips move made certain that, at the very least, a raider had to attract a substantial number of individual shareholders as well to successfully dip into the company treasury. It also gave the management a strong card to play at the very outset, for it tended to counter the 'Saturday night special' – that raid, frequently timed for the weekend, that sought to stampede the institutions as quickly as possible into selling out before the target board could even meet. Now a prudent raider would be tempted at least to sound out a target management; if not, the board still had bought time with its veto to marshal a defence.

On 11 October the *Wall Street Journal* noted 'Pickens On the Prowl'. It was one of those what's-going-on pieces the *Journal* does so well. Why, the *Journal* asked, 'had Mesa's Chairman T. Boone Pickens, Jr., in recent weeks been lining up the investment banking team of Drexel Burnham and the takeover legal specialists Skadden, Arps, Slate Meagher and Flom? Why had he hired Kekst & Co., a public relations firm that specialises in putting a good gloss on hostile takeover battles?'

The conclusion was hardly surprising; Pickens was either getting ready for another proxy fight for another big oil company – such as his epic 1983 battle for Gulf Oil Co. – and Mobil is the rumoured target, or he is planning a hit and run raid on a company such as Phillips or Unocal.

Almost a year before, Pickens had reaped a $400m profit in a David versus Goliath bid for Gulf Oil that stampeded Gulf's management into the arms of Chevron Oil Co. Half the $13.3bn Chevron paid for Gulf went to the shareholders, who made Pickens something of a folk hero among individual shareholder rights groups. Newspaper cartoonists rejoiced at the chance to caricature the rutted Pickens face and cowboy gear. There were plenty of other amusing clichés – including the Mesa minnow trying to swallow the Gulf whale.

If the big oil fraternity disdained Pickens before as a brash bumpkin, in their eyes the Gulf Oil suicide made him something of a traitor to the industry, especially when he began to call the oil industry 'a sunset industry', one that was already in liquidation.

Well, they never could stand the truth. [Pickens explained.] Look, I know my industry. I started off as a trained geologist and I have been all over this country looking for oil. But I also know that between 1980 and 1983, the United States only replaced half of the domestic oil it consumed and that it has gotten worse since then. I also know that the average cost of finding new reserves is $10 per barrel and, as a rule of thumb, those finding costs should not exceed one-third of the price you receive in order to provide a reasonable return over the life of the prospect.

Now the big producers were able to paper over this, thanks to the OPEC price rises and they got all awash with cash in the 1970s and while they tried to find new oil in some cases, they also put a lot of those paper profits into department store chains and copper mines and experiments in shale oil.

As the head of Mesa, I had been committed to the oil industry's future just like the rest of them. But it dawned on me that it was getting harder and harder and more expensive to find new reserves. I resisted that truth for a while, just like they have. And I spent a lot of Mesa money in the Gulf of Mexico before I finally just called it off.

You just can't escape the truth forever [Pickens concluded]. I just had to face it that the big producers were in liquidation by living off old reserves. And they weren't giving the shareholders the proceeds of that liquidation. If I could get the money for the shareholders and profit myself, well then, that was where we had to go.

On 20 October Pickens formed a limited partnership to buy oil shares on speculation with Texas investors Cyril Wagner and Jack Brown. The next day the Mesa partners started to buy shares on the market of both Phillips and Unocal. In the next month the partners would secretly amass 8.8m Phillips shares – 5.7 per cent and just over the percentage limit at which the Securities and Exchange Commission requires a statement of public disclosure.

Even in the best of times, secrets don't remain secrets for long on Wall Street. Bill Douce soon learned who was buying his shares and quickly guessed what was up. On 29 November Phillips sued the Mesa partners charging that Pickens had violated the 1983 standstill agreement by trying a run at Phillips. Douce had no illusions that the charge would stick, but he wanted to smoke Pickens out of the woods, choose where to fight or cash in. The next day at the Amarillo headquarters of Mesa, Pickens and his partners decided to shut down the share buying campaign against Unocal and concentrated on Phillips.

Thinking that at the least the standstill suit would slow Pickens down a bit, Douce went off after pheasant in Spain with Hartley and McKinley. What he didn't know was that Pickens was gathering support for his raid from such Wall Street arbitrageurs as Ivan Boesky and Carl Icahn. The arbs, as they are called, can read a stock ticker better than most and they had reached the same conclusion that Douce had. Pickens raid, even if it failed or ended in a dismemberment à la Gulf, probably meant a rise in Phillips' share price and some quick profits. Indeed, profits could be had already, since Phillips' stock had risen from its summertime low water mark of $33.375 a share to $44.50

in November, strictly on anticipation. By contrast, even though Pickens had been buying Unocal shares at the same time, the price had fluttered between $40.125 and $43.25 – as if the arbs had had some advance knowledge that Pickens was really going after Phillips after all.

Just who knew what about Pickens' plans for Phillips probably never will be known, despite some half-hearted attempts by a Congressional committee a year later to find out.

Yet Wall Street knew the raid was coming. A wire service story on the morning of 4 December that Pickens and his Mesa partners were meeting in Amarillo sent Phillips shares up another $3.75 to $48 in heavy trading. That afternoon at four o'clock, after the stock exchange had closed, Mesa filed the required notice that the partners held 5.8 per cent of Phillips stock and were seeking another 14.9 per cent at a $60-per-share price. If successful, the notice said, the partners would try to gain control of Phillips.

So Pickens was not trying to take full control of Phillips with this 4 December bid; he just wanted 15m shares or 9.7 per cent of the company's outstanding common. Coupled with the shares he already owned, Pickens was effectively seeking a 20.6 per cent interest in Phillips, enough to put himself and at least one of his Mesa Petroleum investment partners on the board. Since the Douce management team had only five of the sixteen Phillips board seats, the Pickens threat was a very real one.

Since Pickens' bid was not for total control, Phillips' management understandably decided to defend against the tender offer. But in deciding to fight, the management then did something that even its own senior members find hard to explain now that it's over.

The bristling counterattack options of Operation Porcupine were forgotten. Instead of mounting an aggressive counterbid or spending still more capital on a takeover attempt of its own, management shelved its prepared plan of action and sought outside help in mounting its defence.

In hiring First Boston Corp, adviser investment Morgan Stanley, and Wall Street corporation lawyer Martin Lipton as its advisers and strategists, Phillips' management certainly was following a growing trend in recent greenmail cases. After all, Pickens' partners had armed themselves with the expertise of the Drexel Burnham firm of money raisers. In fact, Douce had originally wanted Joe Flom to head up their defence team, but Flom had opted out (despite Phillips' $50,000 retainer) because he already had worked for Pickens and had been hired again to head the attack team against Phillips.

Upon the advice of these new advisers, Phillips went into the submarine warfare equivalent of the crash dive; management departments back in Bartlesville were sealed off from one another. About a dozen top management moved camp to a suite at the Helmsley Palace Hotel in Manhattan to be near their new counsellors and the public relations firm, Adams Rinehart Inc., that had been hired. One of the first steps counselled by the public relations firm was to cut off the flow of public statements and to restrict the flow of internal corporate communications to prevent leaks to the press.

One questions the revisionists of corporate textbooks will have to address is whether the kind of financial strategist/hired gun employed by both suitor and takeover target aren't more akin to doctors who welcome the next patient so they can try out some newly devised wonder cure, whether the diagnosis warrants it or not.

Certainly Morgan Stanley, First Boston, and attorney Lipton were acting in Phillips' best interest as they perceived it. But just as surely, it must be taken into account that their professional reputations rest on their ability to concoct novel defences and ingenious schemes beyond the ability of mere mortal corporation management. After all, that is why one goes to specialists in any discipline; they can see the forest for the trees – and the underbrush as well.

The team went immediately into its standard drill that included retaining the private detective agency headed by former New York federal district attorney Jules Kroll. Kroll and his operatives are the top of the line in corporate investigators. They can track down a senior manager who may be defecting to another firm with sensitive data, they can break a sophisticated trademark piracy case, or they can do a discreet background check on a potential chief executive.

It was this latter chore that Martin Lipton had in mind for Kroll's agents. Boone Pickens seemed too controversial a character not to have some dark part of his past hidden away somewhere. But this time, Kroll's agency blundered. A New York detective pounding the streets of Amarillo trying to find dirt about Boone Pickens was about as undercover as a cowboy hat and boots on Wall Street. Pickens was properly outraged when he found out about it, especially when he found out the detective was concentrating on the breakup of his first marriage and subsequent second marriage. In retaliation, another set of detectives was set to photograph the comings and goings of the Phillips officers at the Helmsley Hotel, in hopes of catching call girls being brought in. Douce found out about that and was, in turn, outraged himself. Personal feelings were bruised beyond healing and the bitterness would get worse as the battle raged on. When Douce and Pickens finally did meet to sign the final settlement papers in April 1985, even though their wives were in the room, Douce confessed later to a wild urge to punch the much younger Pickens in the jaw. So much for the coldly rational decision making process.

The Phillips defence team had other tricks on tap as well. The counter-tactics were to make history of sorts. Of the various standard anti-takeover defences that have come to dominate today's battlefield, the one called 'shark repellent' envisions a target company making itself as financially unattractive as need be to dissuade a suitor's bid. Phillips' bids for General American and Aminoil were variations on the repellent theme. But an extreme version has acquired a name of its own – the 'poison pill' defence.

Like the fashion designers of Paris, Lipton and Morgan Stanley were the premier designers of shark repellent and poison pills.

By Wall Street's definition, a poison pill is a rival offer to shareholders that gives those shareholders the right to buy new shares at a special price, or to get other benefits, whenever a hostile bid is offered by an unwanted suitor. Usually a poison pill is triggered by some automatic mechanism, say when the unwanted suitor is able to acquire 10 per cent or more of the outstanding shares in the open market, and then makes a public offering for the remainder of what he wants.

Thus the pill offers shareholders a benefit for remaining loyal to the company management and also makes further tenders prohibitively expensive for the suitor. A politic defender does not publicly acknowledge using the 'poison pill' defence; rather, he refers to a 'fair value' plan or a 'redemption rights offering', arguing with some reason that if anyone is going to pull capital out of the firm's treasury, it ought to be the longer-term shareholders.

One of the advantages of turning to specialists is their ability to respond speedily to takeover raids. Within ten days of the Pickens announcement, Phillips counterattacked on multiple fronts. First they filed court suits to try to block Pickens from proceeding with his own tender offer. A friendly judge in Oklahoma issued a temporary injunction against Pickens proceeding with his tender offer until there were hearings on the 1983 standstill agreement. Pickens turned to the Delaware Chancery Court – which was to loom larger as the body of takeover and merger-defence law developed – and got an injunction against Phillips' lawyers getting any more injunctions. Lipton then went into the federal courts in Delaware to overturn the Chancery Court injunction.

By 17 December, Morgan Stanley had lined up $5bn in defence financing for Douce and Cox, which was just as well since on 20 December, the Delaware Chancery Court ruled that Phillips could not hide behind the standstill agreement. A day later, Pickens and Douce were in negotiations through their advisers over a recapitalisation plan that involved a counter bid for its own shares. As devised by Lipton and Morgan Stanley, Phillips offered its shareholders a 'recapitalisation' plan in which the poison pill was not used to menace the current unwanted suitor, but to ward off other raiders such as Icahn and Boesky who had big stakes in Phillips and who might try raids of their own, even as Pickens was being bought off. This had happened a year before in the siege laid to Walt Disney Productions first by Saul Steinberg, who collected an $85m greenmail payoff, and then by Milwaukee arb Irwin Jacobs, who carved out another $43m.

The basic offer asked Phillips shareholders to swap 58.8m shares – 38 per cent of the 154m shares outstanding – for 'a package of debt securities' that allegedly had a total value of $60 a share. Then the company would create a special employees stock ownership plan (called an ESOP). That stock plan would buy roughly 32m newly created shares to be held in trust for the firm's 7000 workers.

Assuming the plan was approved by the shareholders, Phillips proposed that in the year to come, it would spend at least $1bn to buy up to 20m ordinary common shares on the open market at prices not to exceed $50 a share.

The result was that Phillips would have to sell off $2bn of its assets to cover the cost of the plan. But the company would have bought back 46m of its own shares, while its employees would hold another 32m.

The key to the Phillips plan – and its Achilles heel as well – was the special treatment afforded the Pickens group of investors over the rank and file shareholders – and other raiders who had speculated heavily in Phillips stock.

The whole deal came down to a classic greenmail payoff of the Mesa partners who sold their stock at a guaranteed $53 a share price, garnering at least $383m or a $88m clear profit over the purchase price plus another $25m for the expenses the partners were put to chasing around from one courtroom to another fighting the Lipton firm lawyers.

Phillips' advisers were due another $35m in fees. Additional millions were paid out in expenses to the public relations firms, and so on.

Why then did this first Phillips payoff plan for Pickens fail when even Pickens ostensibly was satisfied with his payoff?

One easy explanation is that between mid-December and the end of February, when Phillips shareholders were called upon to ratify the deal, so many extraordinary reactions occurred that the defence team was unable to move fast enough to head off disaster.

One immediate outside factor was the community of Bartlesville,

Oklahoma, itself. The rebellion staged by the people of Bartlesville was not a case of the people of a small, one-industry town becoming alarmed at the prospect of lost jobs. The prospect of a Pickens takeover seemed to threaten the very lives of people who felt they had invested in Phillips' future, even though they owned no shares nor perhaps ever even worked for the company.

One of the common wisdoms about American multinationals that surely must be reexamined is the accepted reputation that big companies have for being impersonal entities whose hometown responsibilities and preoccupations end only at the factory gate or at the bottom line of the annual report.

A quick examination even of such a huge and diverse corporate headquarters village as New York City shows that this is not so. The spread of Wall Street's data processing operations across the river to Newark and Hoboken has prompted as much controversy as Citicorp's decision to shift some of its functions to North Dakota.

The simple fact is that people – whether they live in Hershey or Boeing's Seattle or the now one-brewery town of Milwaukee – look to their principal employers as more than a source of jobs. The leaders of these companies invariably are the leaders of the community who determine the quality of the lives that the majority will live. We are talking about more than just payrolls and who buys the season tickets to the local symphony orchestra. It is the influences that spring from the corporate presence that often shape a community and help individuals decide whether to live there.

Just as obvious, the wider the variety in the industrial base, the more diffuse the influence. But even Pittsburgh was jolted when Gulf Oil was taken over by Chevron three years ago. And the people of Marathon, Ohio, literally took to the streets to protest the loss of what they saw as their economic independence. In that, their demonstration was the forerunner of what was to happen in Bartlesville. But at the time, the rebellious protest was dismissed as a one-of-a-kind civic blip.

Bartlesville is stuck in the wind-seared corner of northeast Oklahoma between Kansas and Arkansas. Its vulnerability to the changing fortunes of Phillips was writ far larger than 7000 jobs (about 40 per cent of the workforce). It is no exaggeration that the people of the village of Bartlesville see themselves as a mirror of the failing times that have engulfed the entire Oil Patch region of Oklahoma and Texas.

Pretentious? Certainly not. The history of Bartlesville is a history of the American petroleum industry. After all, Uncle Frank Phillips was not the only one to bring in his first gusher here and found a family fortune. The town was home to a young boy named J. Paul Getty, who began accumulating his fortune by selling subscriptions to the

Saturday Evening Post on Bartlesville's main streets. The fortunes of other families who specialised in oil tools, pipelines and other services made Bartlesville one of those plump Akrons, Clevelands and Elkharts that stitch America together.

Long afterwards, when Getty had become a recluse on his English estate and the Getty interests were spread from Tulsa to Beverly Hills, Bartlesville benefitted from the largesse of a hometown boy made good. As for the empire created by the Phillips family, Bartlesville residents properly thought themselves as entitled heirs. There were not only hospitals and an auditorium and football parks donated by the company and family; the company's own corporate headquarters served as the village social hall for workers and unaffiliated residents alike.

But more than that, Bartlesville (and nearby Tulsa) had been big-print names on any map of the world's industrial might. Like Akron with its tyres, Detroit with its cars, Ft Wayne and Hammond, Indiana, Birmingham, Alabama and Durham, North Carolina, Oklahoma could boast its villages where world-class wealth could be had and enjoyed.

First came the oil boom of the turn of the century and twenty years later, as transcontinental air travel developed (and Phillips pioneering interest in aviation fuels grew), the area became a vital, vibrant grid-point for air travellers that thrived well into the 1950s.

Celebrities flocked to the area. Tom Mix, Hollywood's first cowboy superstar, was a frequent visitor to the Phillips homestead. Humorist Will Rogers grew up in the nearby Osage Nation Indian Territory and owned a ranch there. Explorer-pilot Wiley Post flew a series of Phillips '66'-sponsored planes in his record breaking attempts, including the ill-fated Alaskan flight that killed him and Will Rogers.

To live in Bartlesville in 1984 was to have had the best of all possible worlds and still to have it pretty good. One had the rural attractions of Oklahoma just a few miles from the architectural wonders of Frank Lloyd Wright, who designed the community's civic centre and museum. One lived in a bucolic suburbia where folk spoke knowledgeably of events in the major capitals of the world. The register of the Phillips Hotel noted visiting officials from Hong Kong, London, Paris and the Middle East. But senior executives could still walk to work down tree-shaded streets. People joked about having to drive the fifty miles to Tulsa to have a good time, but few people made that trek with any regularity.

Withal there was unease. In 1984 Getty was long gone as a corporate identity, let alone as a regional presence. So was Tulsa's Cities Service Oil Co. The absorption of those two petro-giants had cost Tulsa more than $3m a year in subsidies to its local education and arts programmes, not to mention the lost jobs and empty office space. Perhaps worse was the hard-to-define loss of self-worth that even non-oil people felt at their passing.

Boone Pickens should have known all of this. He had begun his career as a Phillips engineer in the 1950s. He knew many of the men whose lives he was threatening but who never thought for a moment that Pickens could be considered a threat.

After the first series of impromtu local protest meetings was held and the media began to cover the uproar, Pickens announced with ill-timed grace that if he were to take control of Phillips, he would be happy to move to Bartlesville and become part of the community. While the community newspaper owned by some Boots Adams offspring made initial welcoming noises about how Pickens would sure pep the old burg up, the almost universal public backlash and anger soon caused them to become ardent foes of the takeover. To Pickens' open chagrin, he was told that no-one in the area would sell him a house and that he would be safer never to set foot in the area again.

That heated and most personal rejection hurt Pickens. He was even more nonplussed when the television news carried pictures of citizens sporting tee shirts with the international stop symbol imprinted over a caricature of him. Copying the logo of the hit movie *Ghostbusters*, the shirt's legend proclaimed, 'Boone-busters'.

Here again is something the casebooks overlook. After years of being treated with deference by his associates and as a colourful celebrity by the financial press, Pickens was confronted by the spectacle of a large group of people who actively disliked him. By rights this should have been a mild annoyance to the kind of hard-minded capitalist we have been led to believe most corporate executives are. But Pickens was not alone (as we will see later) in chafing at the growing notion that he was somehow an unsavoury character. While he was no politician crying for public adoration, the outright hostility of the Bartlesville community unsettled him and gave him second thoughts about his takeover objectives.

At first Pickens' acceptance of the Phillips recapitalisation plan fuelled the image of Bartlesville as the little village that stood off the tyrant's raid. Coming as it did a day or two before the Christmas holiday, the press made the most of headlines about how 'the Grinch that stole Christmas' had to give it back this year. A palpable feeling of relief swept through the town and spread to the eighteenth floor of the Phillips corporate headquarters on Frank Phillips Avenue. It was only after the holidays that it began to filter through that not everyone was as happy with the Phillips payoff to the Mesa partners as Pickens and

Phillips and the corporation's advisers.

The least happy were several other corporate raiders who had invested heavily in Phillips shares before the price ran up to its $55.75 high and then who watched it drop $10 on 15 December when the management offer was accepted by Pickens. Ultimately the Phillips share price would hit a low of $42.75 in early January, when arbitrageurs liquidate untenable positions.

The total loss to the arbitrageurs was estimated by Wall Street insiders at $200m; Ivan Boesky suffered at least half that loss. Boesky had hung onto his Phillips stock by selling off sizable stakes in other companies. He ultimately would buy up the shares held by sometime-rival Irwin Jacobs of Minneapolis.

Uncharacteristically, Boesky went public with complaints about the Pickens payoff. It was greenmail, Boesky said, something he had never countenanced, and it was unfair to all shareholders. As a shareholder he intended to become the rallying point for all the other little individuals who were being screwed by the deal and would vote to reject the management plan at the special meeting on 28 February.

Boesky suddenly found an unlikely ally in another corporate raider, Carl Icahn, who had lost heavily in Phillips shares and wanted a better deal as well. With Boesky's (roughly 5 per cent) and Icahn's (at least 2 per cent at the time) shareholdings, the nucleus of a formidable opposition group suddenly began to form. Their cause was helped by the annoyance individual shareholders were feeling when their attempts to get information from the company were met by the wall of silence Phillips' strategy advisers had imposed.

If for nothing else, the Phillips case will live in the business casebooks because it helped coalesce a movement that until then really had existed in the telephone conversations between Jess Unruh and Harrison J. Goldin. Unruh, the shambling bear-god of California Democratic politics and 'Jay' Goldin, the natty comptroller of the City of New York. What a combination! David and Goliath, Inc.

The two men were something more than politicians who knew a good issue when it was dumped in their laps. Both men were trustees of multi-billion dollar pension funds for the workers of their respective state and city governments. The California State Employees Pension Fund, which includes the state's school teachers as well as government workers, has a common stock portfolio worth $4bn. Goldin's fund, which covers New York's subway, some police and emergency workers, as well as local government employees, manages $2bn worth of stocks.

'We got tired of being the big losers in these greenmail raids. In many cases the pension funds held far larger blocs of stock than the raiders and yet both the management and the raiders treated us as if we did not exist. Our pension fund alone holds millions of dollars worth of Phillips stock that was jumping around in $10 a day increments and no-one would even acknowledge that we had a right to information, to find out what the hell was going on,' Unruh said later.*

Actually Unruh and Goldin had gotten together before the Phillips raid took place. In August the Council of Institutional Investors had been formed with a membership that included enough state and local government employee pension funds to account for a $20bn holding in New York Stock Exchange listings.

But it took the Phillips raid to get the state pension funds to deal themselves into the game. Unruh and Goldin's group had to move cirmcumspectly. Federal law forbids such groups from voting or threatening to vote their shares in concert. So when Unruh and Goldin called a meeting of the CII, its stated purpose was to gather information. Goldin volunteered a high-ceilinged conference room in his municipal building headquarters across from City Hall. A press room was set up and the invitations went out. The date was set for 19 February, 1985. The Pickens–Phillips battle was now headed into its fourth month without resolution.

By then both Boesky and Icahn had made counter offers for Phillips control that they said they intended to take to the company's annual meeting. Douce and Joe Fogg, Morgan Stanley's merger maven, also were summoned. So was Boone Pickens. Among the pension funds represented were the States of Massachusetts and Connecticut, Michigan and Illinois, the cities of Boston, Detroit, Chicago and a score more; managed by individuals with legally-defined but personally-felt fiduciary responsibilities to get the best deal possible for their pensioners.

Douce and Fogg first presented the bare bones outline of the recapitalisation plan. What about Wall Street estimates that the rank and file shareholder was not going to get $53 a share, as Pickens would, but a package of debt and securities worth maybe $42 a share?

'I won't comment on speculation. We promise that all shareholders will get equal value,' Douce said. Take it or leave it. Oh, really?

While Pickens was before the institutional group, Douce moved into the press room and presented much the same public response. 'It is the best deal we could cut and we think our shareholders will trust our judgement enough to back us.' He left and Pickens took his place

*Interview with the authors

in the press room seat, giving a ringing defence of free market capitalism and his right – nay, his duty – to 'maximise the values of company shares for all shareholders'.

Were Unruh and his group getting shares worth $42 or $53 as a result of the diluted assets going into Pickens' pocket?

'Look, boys,' Pickens drawled. 'They say $53, I believe them. I'm getting $53, why shouldn't the other shareholders do as well?'

The succeeding interviews and press conferences wore the morning on with Boesky and then Icahn pitching first to the pension funds and then to the press that they and all the other mom-and-pop shareholders were being squeezed by the Pickens-Phillips deal. The press corps, rebuffed by Douce and annoyed by Pickens, began to get testy.

'Mr Boesky, what do you say to people who call you a pirate?' a television newsman called out from the back of the room. Boesky, in his late forties, has the oval, extended face of an early Egyptian pharaoh. He also has an unfortunate tic. When he gets nervous he exhibits a reflexive, Jimmy Cagney 'allll-right, you guys' grin.

Grin, went Boesky. He leaned into the battery of microphones trying to be charming. 'Do I look like a pirate?'

Grin. As a matter of fact, he looked like a shark at that moment.

'Yes,' somebody said, and the press room gave a guffaw.

Boesky sought to recover the lost ground. He went into a soft pitch about how he was glad to live in a country where it still was legal to try to win an honest profit by maximising the values of undervalued companies and putting those assets to work creating new jobs, before he was cut off by the same newsman in the back of the room.

'But Mr Boesky,' the voice boomed. 'Some people say the way you seek profits makes you little more than a thief.'

The grins were coming one every three seconds now. Boesky was shooting his white cuffs out of his London-tailored suit as a gesture of self control.

'You know, I am not just a risk arbitrage investor,' he said softly. 'I am on the faculty of Columbia University as a lecturer in finance at their business administration school. I also lecture at New York University. Now do you think that those two fine institutions would have a thief on their faculties?'

'I dunno, they also teach criminal law there, too, don't they,' the television man riposted. Again, laughter. It was a good New York wisecrack; Boesky had it coming.

'Yes,' Boesky said, then paused. 'They also teach journalism there, too.'

Good. It was a nice comeback. The laughter gave him a chance to catch his breath and get out of the room. There he ran into two unexpected cast members in the drama – Lucy and Vivian.

Their names were not really Lucy and Vivian. They had named themselves that after Lucille Ball and her madcap television sidekick, actress Vivian Vance. Lucy and Viv were two Bartlesville housewives who had flown to New York with two local businessmen to hand out hundreds of rock-hard, heart-shaped cookies that had been baked in a hundred Bartlesville ovens and decorated with icing that bore the Phillips '66' logo and such messages as 'Love our Cookies, Save our Town.'

Lucy and Viv gave Ivan Boesky a particularly large cookie with an especially photographic Phillips logo and his eyes lit up. Photo opportunity. He popped back into the press room and held up the cookie.

'Eat the cookie,' somebody shouted. The television cameras whirred, the flashguns whined.

'No,' cried Boesky. 'And I don't want to devour Bartlesville, either.' Needless to say the six o'clock news and the next day's newspapers dwelled not on Boesky the pirate, but on Boesky and his cookie. Score one for Ivan, Lucy and Vivian.

But going down in the elevator, Boesky was furious.

'A pirate,' he repeated. 'A thief. Don't these people understand anything?'

Meanwhile Carl Icahn was getting an even worse drubbing.

'Look, I'm no Robin Hood,' he said at one point and was amazed when the room again dissolved in derisive laughter. Icahn's problem is that he comes across like a right-wing Ralph Nader, rumpled, humourless, zealous – true believer. But in what?

The bottom line of the confrontation, and the one that followed ten days later in Washington before a Congressional committee, was that no-one thought Boesky, Icahn et al were such great guys. But neither did anyone pat William Douce on the back for the smart way he handled Boone Pickens. The bottom line turned out to be a month of bad vibrations beamed out to the various blocs of shareholders, the real mom and pop. But weren't mom and pop just as dependent on their pensions as they were on their private shareholdings? Weren't Jess Unruh and Jay Goldin working for mom and pop too when they demanded that capital assets be sold off in order to boost the share price? If the shareholder is the true and absolute owner of the company whose shares he holds, then who speaks for him when his own interests conflict?

One of the immediate observations was that the institutional shareholder representatives had immediately made common cause with the corporate raiders. Despite what Unruh and Goldin said, they made it plain that they would throw their weight with the raider who could maximise the return on the shares held in their portfolios.

But then, soon afterwards, the common cause between raider and representative became even further blurred. First, a born-again Boone Pickens formed his own United Shareholders of America to campaign for greater leverage on the corporate cash box. Later a New York City investigation would be launched into a series of telephone calls which Comptroller Goldin had made to a number of important Manhattan investors on behalf of his very good friend – Ivan Boesky.

In the end, Phillips management failed to garner the necessary majority share votes at the 28 February meeting, largely because of the defection of the major institutional holders of stock who thought they were getting a raw deal.

One side note is that by this point Phillips' internal public affairs department had broken with its New York advisers and was secretly travelling around the country to meet on an off-the-record basis with financial editors of major city newspapers and business magazines to explain both the rejected deal and the revised plan that was unveiled by management on 7 March. This off-the-record public affairs push also should go into future textbooks on takeovers, because although no newspaper or magazine ever wrote about the campaign, it did produce a remarkable turnaround in the publicity Phillips was getting in the final days before its shareholders were to vote the deal up or down on 16 March.

In this new deal, the Mesa partners would sell back to Phillips its 8.89m shares for $53 a share. So Pickens gets his $89m profit as it stood in the new plan.

Phillips also was to offer to exchange a package of three issues of debt securities nominally worth $62 a share for another 72m shares of its own stock. When 'blended' with the remaining common shares, these debt securities should have a value of $57 a share.

Assuming Carl Icahn were to sell the 7.5m Phillips shares that he had acquired at roughly $46.80 a share, he would walk away with at least a $46.5m profit, if one were to value Phillips stock at the $53 Pickens is getting as much as $75m if one believes the Phillips valuation.

In buying back its stock and paying off its tormentors, Phillips management (Douce retired at the end of the annual meeting) intended to spend $4.5bn that it would have had to raise by trebling its debt to $7bn and selling off $2bn in to-be-announced assets. The

Ekofisk field is the most frequently mentioned of the firm's distress sale assets.

For this Douce, Cox and Silas were to get a legally binding promise from Pickens, Icahn and Drexel Burnham (the financier of these various attacks), that they will not participate in a raid on Phillips for eight years.

Pickens by this time had made a fatal error. Thinking the Phillips campaign all but won, he and the Mesa partners had begun buying shares of Unocal and by 14 February owned a 7.9 per cent stake that was described as 'for investment purposes only'.

Fred Hartley, Unocal's crusty chairman, knew better. On 28 February Unocal's board endorsed his plan to hire Goldman Sachs and Dillon Read as investment bankers, the Hill & Knowlton public relations firm, and the D.F. King firm that recruits and solicits proxies from individual shareholders as the defence team. The Unocal board also began to spread shark repellent with a new bylaw that required anyone who wanted to nominate a director to the board or to bring up any new business to give at least 30 days' notice.

At the same time, Hartley realised how well prepared Boone Pickens was when he launched such a campaign. Hartley discovered to his horror that Mesa Petroleum had become a favoured customer of Security Pacific Bank of California, the lead bank for Unocal for more than forty years. Indeed, with one hand Security Pacific was lending Pickens money to buy Unocal stock, while providing Hartley with strategic advice. Hartley promptly sued; the courts have not yet moved on that particular case.

Even with that betrayal out in the open Hartley could not shake off the feeling that someone was eavesdropping on his innermost thoughts. He had his office 'swept' for bugs; nothing turned up. Some of his aides wondered whether the boss wasn't going a bit paranoiac. It would be more than two years later that he learned the truth: Robert Freeman, the Goldman Sachs investment banker assigned to plot the defence for Unocal, was accused by Marty Siegel of leaking information to him so that he, in turn, could divert two of his trading colleagues at Kidder Peabody in trades that would make all of them a bundle in advance of the market. Freeman and the two Kidder Peabody traders have since contested the accusations.

Pickens too had lost the advantage of surprise. Moreover it was clear to the most casual newspaper reader that he intended to take his greenmail profits from the Phillips raid and use them to prise even greater sums out of Unocal. At least that is how Fred Hartley and the Unocal strategists put it; they also put it about that unlike Phillips, there would be no compromise with Pickens. He could have a battle to the death if he wanted it.

At that point, Pickens showed no sign of giving up. The Phillips shareholders endorsed the new recapitalisation plan on 18 February. Within a week Pickens and his partners had boosted their stake in Unocal to 13.6 per cent with a $322m share purchase and he announced that he intended to seek control of the company and oust Hartley. In the weeks that followed, Pickens and Hartley raised each others' bids. Pickens announced a $54-a-share cash bid for shares up to 51 per cent and junk bonds for the rest. Hartley countered by offering $72 a share for the remaining 49 per cent – a variation on the poison pill that sought to encourage the institutions to hang on.

The courts of California and Delaware also became a side arena as each side sought to nullify the other's tender offers. Hartley finally took the poison-pill defence to an extraordinary extension. On 16 April, he replaced his original share repurchase scheme with a $72 a share tender offer for 29 per cent of Unocal's shares, but excluded the Mesa partners specifically from the tender offer. On its face, this was a flagrant violation of the New York Stock Exchange's one-share, one-vote rules that forbid discrimination against shareholders of the same kind of common stock in a company. In effect, Hartley was dictating a second class of corporate citizenship that would be unthinkable in any other form of business dealing.

With only days remaining until Unocal's annual meeting, Pickens rushed to the Delaware courts. They stunned him by ruling that the 'business judgment rule' (a legal standard that effectively bars a shareholder's ability to question or second-guess the acts of boards of directors unless there is compelling evidence of fraud or negligence) allows boards of directors to discriminate against minority shareholders if they think it is in the best interest of the majority of the shareholders.

On 20 May, Pickens surrendered and withdrew his bid in exchange for Hartley's agreement to buy one-third of the Mesa partners' 23.7m shares at the $72 price. There also was a standstill agreement that Pickens stay away from Unocal for twenty-five years. In order to win the approval of other shareholders, Hartley had to extend his offer to 38 per cent of the total, for a total outlay of $2b. On 21 May, Unocal's shares dropped $10.125 to $35.875 and have not varied much above that since then.

So who won?

According to *Business Week*, 'It seems that all the players in [the Phillips raid] get half a loaf.' Pickens did not get control of Phillips, but he did clear an $89m profit. Rival Carl Icahn clouded his reputation by threatening to raise $4.5b in 'junk bonds' for his attack. But he, too, was paid off by Phillips and cleared a $75m profit – plus a $25m payment to cover his legal and other costs. The investment advisers on both sides ended with their reputations for probity tarnished. Indeed all the banks and law firms who play in the greenmail game are facing growing outrage from other sectors of Wall Street at the potential conflicts of interest and corruption involved in firms that have clients throughout the corporate community using privileged information to help one side take over another.

The big losers, of course, were the target companies Phillips and Unocal and their workers and the communities they serve. An estimated 8000 jobs have been cut by the two companies one year later. Massive properties, many of them vital oil and gas fields, have had to be sold off in the middle of a world oil price slump, to service the billions in debt that both companies had to take on just to stay free.

As we shall see in other chapters, the losses are incalculable in terms of scientific and industrial breakthroughs that now must be delayed or bypassed entirely. The target companies also are reduced now in their ability to serve their home communities, both as a source of jobs and as a supporter of the quality of life Americans have come to demand.

The winners got money that they say was being squandered by lazy corporate management. It was a lesson that had to be learned the hard way, they say. Shareholders, passive and disorganised, can now demand and get the maximum yield for the risks they take with their investments, either by joining a shareholders rights group, à la Goldin and Unruh's, or they can join forces with a real risk taker like a Pickens or an Icahn.

From the interesting vantage point of hindsight, Phillips' Bill Douce draws another lesson. 'I had been raised to be a prudent businessman, to keep a manageable balance in your capital strength and not to have too high a ratio of debt to your equity shares. For all the good it did, I could have run our debt up by $2bn or more early on and given all of it away to the shareholders right then. They might have been better off; Phillips wouldn't have been better off, but nobody else seems to care.'

CHAPTER FOUR

The Claimants

Mark Twain called them 'the claimants'. Bitter and bereft in some part of their souls, there was, Twain argued, something in the American ethos that produced a person who pushed past the point of greed, past the love of wealth and power and on down a terrifyingly lonely road where ambition is a goad not a goal.

Certainly, as we have already seen, the personality trait which exaggerates a sense of entitlement, which distorts personal and business judgements, is not an exclusively American phenomenon. At least, not any more. Yet the fact remains that in the early 1980s, the United States became a magnet for similarly driven men. There was a confluence of law, finance, business climate and especially of personality that transformed previous cycles of merger and acquisition into a protracted siege of American capitalism and all that it had stood for since the Great Depression. American takeovers had become the game of choice for American 'claimants' and others who came from overseas. To assist them arbitrage specialists such as Ivan Boesky and Carl Icahn had been on the scene for some time and, after the Phillips and Unocal battles, had become national celebrities of sorts.

'I can introduce you to a girl you've never seen before and after hearing you two talk for just a half an hour I can make a bet whether you are going to get her into bed or not,' Boesky says in explaining just what the secret is of his success. 'I can calculate the odds on whether a thing is going to happen or not and I can do it better than nearly anybody else in the world.*

*Interview with the authors.

But by that standard alone, Boesky should be as happy on a race track as in a corporate board room; that he wants more, that he wants to be inside the inner circles of American high finance is also part of what makes Boesky run; just as Icahn frequently portrays himself as an outsider, a lone ranger whose lightning intellect helps him confound and snatch wealth from an American business establishment which he professes to disdain as 'a bunch of fraternity boys'.

So it is that Boone Pickens tried to crack the Oil Patch's good-old-boys club and Carl Icahn would rail against the insiders from his pretend position on the outside. And Ivan Boesky regularly pauses to shake hands with acquaintances in the members lounge of the Harvard University Club in Manhattan where he goes to take his noontime exercise.

Robert Edward Turner III is another classic 'claimant' personality. *Fortune Magazine* in an unabashedly admiring profile described Turner in these words, 'Cocky, shrewd, and so wildly unorthodox that even some admirers [*Fortune?*] regard him as slightly crazy.'*

Crazy? No, Ted Turner is not crazy. None of the men he would soon test himself against in that summer of 1985 were crazy. At its simplest, this book is the story of men who had become wildly successful in the world business arena through a strong sense of intuition, hyperenergy and a single-minded commitment to success. What happened next, and the theme of takeover battles that followed in the mid-1980s, was how some of these men pushed their ambitions beyond the reach of their normal limits of business judgement, how others kept a check on their passions and what happened to us all as a result of their actions.

It would be particularly easy to turn a Ted Turner into some sort of cartoon monster. Turner himself is not above a flamboyance that lapses into self-parody; he spends millions on a racing yacht and then wears a locomotive engineer's cap when he is at the helm; he cavorts in costume at the games of the Atlanta professional basketball and baseball teams he owns. Padding shoeless through the night-darkened offices of his Turner Broadcasting Co. headquarters in Atlanta, the 48-year-old often discomfits aides with his grasp of his world-flung enterprises. Like many of the men he was about to compete against, Turner could be brash and charming sometimes and childishly cruel at other times. He won world applause for his fearless performance as a yachtsman when he won the Americas Cup in 1977.

Fortune, 7 July, 1986.

Turner's bravery was put to an even greater test two years later in the 1979 Fastnet race across the Irish Sea to Britain. Turner, at the helm of his boat *Tenacious* pushed through 40-foot waves and a 65-mile-an-hour wind that had sent nearly all of the 306 boats entered scuttling back to ports with cracked masts and blown-away sales. It was one of the great tragedies of English racing; only 87 boats finished, and 19 sailors were killed in various wrecks and sinkings during the gales.

Turner had scarcely tied up his boat and accepted the winners' trophy before his weakness for the shocking tease got the better of him. To the sombre race officials (and with the press in earshot) he quipped, 'You ought to be thankful there are storms like that or you'd all be speaking Spanish.' It was supposed to be a joke about the Spanish Armada; the race committee merely lapsed into stricken silence.

The dark history of Ted Turner is common enough knowledge. Unlike many of his rivals in the takeover wars, Turner was born wealthy, the son of a Savannah, Georgia, billboard advertising tycoon whose own ambitions and alcohol problems led him to an early suicide.

Until his father's death, Ted Turner had been pretty much typecast as the well-to-do Southern party boy who treated his brief foray at Brown University as a prolonged sexual escapade. But the tragedy and the financial crisis that quickly engulfed him produced a new Ted Turner. Even though his father's will left the billboard company to Ted, the elder Turner agreed to sell it before his death without telling anyone. As soon as Ted realised he was about to lose his inheritance, he threatened the buyers that he would shift the site leases with the landowners where his billboards were placed to another company unless they gave up the deal. They did and Turner was off and running.

Within 7 years, Turner bought an Atlanta UHF television station that proved to be the hub of his WTBS global television empire. The property was a bargain since UHF stations, with their weaker signals than VHF frequency broadcasters, normally sell at a discount. But Turner beamed the station's signal to the rest of the nation via communications satellite and created a cable-pay-television network which began to attract paying subscribers nationally. By 1977, Turner also was broadcasting the games of his Atlanta Braves baseball team and Atlanta Hawks basketball team to sports-starved Americans via the network. In 1980 his 24-hours-a-day Cable News Network went on the air and within three years its programmes were being beamed as far away as Europe, Japan, Canada and Australia; within the United States his network reaches more than half of the nation's cable television viewers.

*

101

CBS, the old Columbia Broadcasting System, had been a ripe takeover target for years. The network was the number one television broadcasting corporation in the United States. Its programmes reached 75m adult viewers every day, it had the number one evening news programme – an important headstart on the lucrative prime time evening programming sweepstakes. CBS also had dominated those most-expensive evening viewing hours for the past five years and the last 25 of the past 30 years.

But CBS was more than just a broadcasting giant. That was part of the trouble. There was a division that made children's toys and which in the period 1983–5 was costing the corporation $125m in losses. The CBS records division had made money early in the 1980s with superstars such as Michael Jackson and Bruce Springsteen but the company's expensive talent properties were less popular now.

The real disaster in the making that faced CBS chairman Thomas Wyman was of his own making. Since taking over from founder-chairman William S. Paley in 1980, Wyman – a methodical corporate grey-suit of the kind Carl Icahn despises – had made only two dramatically important policy moves since taking command. Late in 1984 Wyman agreed to buy 12 magazine properties from publisher Ziff-Davis at a $362.5m purchase price that CBS accountants later determined was about $100m too high. Early in 1985 the litigation over the purchase made the gaffe public knowledge; the scandal spread when CBS executives so infuriated David Davis, the popular editor of *Car and Driver*, that Davis persuaded Rupert Murdoch to underwrite the publishing of a new car fan magazine, *Automobile Magazine*.*

Indeed, since 1980 CBS had only enjoyed one truly successful new venture and that was put together by the old founder-owner William S. Paley in 1982 when the company and Marvin Davis' 20th Century Fox formed CBS/Fox Video to market prerecorded video cassettes to the booming home video market. It would be a significant deal in many ways. It demonstrated what everyone knew already, that Paley was still running CBS, not Wyman. It also put Davis firmly in the Paley-CBS corporate orbit a few years later.

Although CBS remained in the black it was facing increasingly tough competition for broadcasting advertising revenue from the other networks and a malaise within its own broadcasting structure. This could be fatal, and Wyman and other observers knew it. CBS got 8 per cent of its $500m plus in operating profits from broadcasting. Yet its programmes were losing the race to attract the up-scale viewers that

New York Magazine, 4 November, 1985.

advertisers prize to rival NBC, a subsidiary of the powerful RCA Corp.

Wyman's response in the opening months of 1985 was drastically to slash the operating budgets of CBS's news division and many of its popular entertainment programmes. Warranted or not the cost cutting, salary disputes and open squabbling merely added fuel to an already hot-burning political controversy over whether the network's news broadcast unfairly slanted their presentation of events to meet some liberal bias. By attacking the funding for such controversial programmes as *Sixty Minutes* and the *CBS Evening News*, Wyman was adding to the public impression that something was out of balance within the broadcasting giant's programmes. The network also had been caught up in a bitter and hideously draining libel trial involving General William Westmoreland, who had sued for $120m.

The image of CBS, both as a corporation which had lost forward momentum and as a powerful news media force whose impartiality was being publicly questioned, was very much the problem. When combined with its vast resources, its huge volume of cash flow, this dangerous lack of direction and muddled image made the company a prime target as the takeover and merger battles over oil ran out of potential targets.

The first shot fired at CBS came from the network's conservative critics who had decided in late 1984 to do more than protest news broadcasting policies.

On 10 Janauary, 1985, the Raleigh (NC) *News & Observer* reported that Senator Jesse Helms was drafting a letter which would call on political conservatives to buy stock in CBS so as to win a proxy fight at the April annual shareholders' meeting and force a change in the network's news and entertainment programming attitudes.

The five-page letter, the newspaper reported, promised the share buyers they would become 'Dan Rather's boss'. The proxy drive was being mounted by Helms, and there was rich irony in his complaints that Rather and other CBS 'liberal' news reporters and commentators slanted their presentations to the public by skilfully sly changes in tone of voice and facial expression as well as in the more blatant selection of news stories and content.

The irony was that 20 years earlier, Helms himself had become something of a Southern celebrity for his own television news broadcasting style which made no secret of his opposition to the Civil Rights movement and the demonstrations led by North Carolina black leaders to gain equal access to jobs, public facilities and to education. Jesse Helms had proved a master of the raised eyebrow and the vengefully turned phrase now he was after CBS.

Nor was Helms merely a regional politician on the make. As North Carolina's senior US Senator since 1972, Helms had been one of the leaders in developing mass fund-raising technology on behalf of conservative political candidates who met his ultra-right standards. His National Congressional Club, based in Raleigh, NC, raised scores of millions each year and parcelled the money out to help build a farm system of young conservative political candidates at the local and state level and to nurture them into candidates of national potential.

In so doing Helms became a national figure of compelling power among the American right. When Ronald Reagan was trying to cement his conservative credentials for his 1976 run for the Republican nomination against incumbent President Gerald Ford it was Jesse Helms who introduced him at the announcement press conference.

It is interesting to note that Helms chose the proxy fight as his method of attacking CBS. There was no thought at the time of launching a takeover bid. Helms strategy was to get conservatives to buy as many of the 29.7m shares of CBS stock as they could. Since every shareholder had one vote inside the company's annual meeting the idea was to control the company's policies by forcing specific votes on the management that would set a new news (and personnel) policy on the CBS management.

To do that, the letter that Senator Helms' Congressional Club mailed out asked the one million conservatives listed on the group's various mailing lists to buy 'just 20 shares of CBS stock' apiece. That way, the letter said, 'we would have enough votes at the stockholders' meetings to end CBS's bias forever.'*

This was no mean undertaking. At the current New York Stock Exchange listing price ($72.50) for CBS, Helms was asking his fellow conservatives to shell out $1bn even if all they won was a simple 51 per cent majority. Nor was this a simple matter of upping the price offered to big institutional traders for CBS shares were held among 24,000 stockholders, many of them small and most of them fiercely loyal to the house that Paley had built.

Helms' ploy was a no-lose proposition as far as he was concerned. Even if he did not come close to controlling a large proxy block of CBS stock the publicity would be well worth the effort. He counted on the national news media's horror at the idea of a political-cum-economic attack on one of their power centres and the resulting publicity and controversy would be worth gold to future fund-raising efforts.

*Associated Press, 10 January, 1985.

Ted Turner was equally fascinated by the Helms gambit. Turner had been a long and vocal critic of the programming habits of the major broadcasting networks. His CNN network was making money but not as fast as he wanted; between his broadcast and sports properties, Turner was still a shaky proposition.

Moreover, Turner was up to his bushy eyebrows in collateralised bank debt already. He had raised $191m to repay old bank debts and expand TBS. He then paid off $133.7m of the old bank debt but was left with only $57.3m in cash and had to go back to the banks for another $190m credit line.

This left Turner in possession of a fund for expansion that totalled $247.3m - an amount that was laughably short of what a major acquisition would cost - and Turner needed to take over something really big, some operation, preferably broadcasting, which would generate enough cash flow to feed his other hungry enterprises. Worse, the expansion fund was tied up by the banks six ways from Sunday. Under the terms of the bank credits he could spend only $15m a year for ventures outside his already existing properties. At risk was Turner's personal control of TBS; he had pledged his personal holdings of 16.6m shares and another 600,000 warrants.

The only way was to leverage his way out into something far bigger and more liquid. But how? And what to takeover even if he could raise the money?

The two obvious broadcasting properties were CBS and the American Broadcasting Corp. While ABC was smaller than second ranking NBC, it was a separate corporate entity while NBC was secured by the vast RCA Corp. corporate bulwark. But while ABC was more digestible and its shares were discounted because of its poor audience showings, it also did not have the alluring non-broadcast divisions which could be sold off at once for instant cash. Only CBS had those extra subsidiaries.

The Helms proxy fight intrigued Turner. He had been a loud critic of network entertainment and news programming. He had decried, even testified before Congress, calling prime time sit-com shows 'stupid and anti-family' and raking over the inaccuracies of network news. Turner also was something of an admirer of Senator Helms, at least he enjoyed the outrage that Helms' barbed rhetoric provoked among the blacks and liberals of Atlanta's ruling elite. Lately, however, Turner was seeing himself more as a world figure. His international broadcasting net afforded him a global celebrity that required a more mature, more internationalist pose. Still, to get one's hands on CBS using someone else's money, that would show Wall Street something.

But the meeting that took place with Helms Congressional Club aides were dissatisfying to both sides. Turner's idea was that if the Helms group could wrest control of CBS away from its present management it would entrust the prize to the professional skills of TBS management and to the ideological instincts of Ted Turner. To his amazement, the other side proposed that he be something of a professional caretaker of CBS, strictly following a political agenda dictated from Raleigh.

Worse, it also was evident in late February that the Helms group was not getting the response they had hoped for from American conservatives. There was large-scale buying of CBS stock going on but it was mainly arbitrageurs such as Ivan Boesky and Carl Icahn who were betting on Wyman and the rest of CBS management to win through.

It was a good bet. Wyman was assembling a first-rate defence team. Morrow & Company would be the proxy solicitation firm; that is they would develop the lists of names and addresses of as many of the individual CBS shareholders as they could and identify the major blocks of institutional holdings. Contrary to popular belief, most major companies do not know who their shareholders are since it is a constantly shifting population and many individual names are lumped into the far larger house-trading lists held in strictest secret by the major brokerage houses.

But since the struggle would be more than just a simple bid-price auction, the proxy fight would be crucial and Morrow's role would be vitally important. Once the lists were assembled a casting call would go out through Manhattan's theatre haunts and scores of actors and actresses would be hired to telephone each individual shareholder and argue a precisely designed script to the shareholder as to why he or she should remain loyal to the current management.

The general business press had to be massaged as well, so Burston-Marsteller was hired to do the public relations work on the defence. Two law firms were hired: Cravath, Swaine and Moore to fight the courtroom legal battles with the Helms group and a supporting set of litigants called Fairness in Media which was demanding from CBS the very precious shareholders list that Morrow & Co. was assembling.

The internal tactics of the defence were to be handled by Joseph Flom of Skadden, Arps, Slate Meagher & Flom. The firm, and Flom personally, was the favourite of Morgan Stanley & Co., the investment adviser Wyman turned to for broader strategy.

Scarcely had the CBS team been formed than they were in court battling the demands of the Raleigh group for shareholder identification. Between 14 and 21 February the two combatant groups sued and countersued each other over the shareholder lists.

By 28 February, however, the battle was on another point altogether. Attorneys for TBS approached the Federal Communications Commission in Washington to sound out the regulatory agency as to its reaction if Turner were to make a run for CBS. Rather than wait to see what the outcome would be, CBS lawyers quickly included Turner in the list of witnesses who were to have their depositions taken in the network's effort to prove that a political conspiracy was underway to seize control. The suit alleged that Fairness in Media was violating federal securities laws and rules that restrict some tax-exempt groups from political activism.

By this time Ivan Boesky was taking a major position in CBS, not so much in support of CBS management anymore, but as a potential target for his own brand of greenmail. By 17 March, Boesky acknowledged to the SEC that he had 7 per cent of CBS. By 24 March the Boesky holding was up to 8 per cent. This was the same day CBS turned over its shareholder list to the Helms forces; but even though the conservatives would remain on the scene, the battle front had shifted away from them at this point. It was no longer a proxy fight. The battle now was for control.

On 31 March, Boesky announced he had an 8.7 per cent stake in CBS and wanted to meet with management. Flom signalled to Wyman to say no, Morgan Stanley was on the verge of setting up a $1.5bn line of credit to fight Boesky or anyone else. Turner by this time was canvassing many of the same bankers to see if they would back his own attack on the network.

Meanwhile rival network ABC was suddenly in the headlines. Capital Cities Broadcasting, a much smaller publishing and broadcasting conglomerate, bought control of ABC for $118 a share, or roughly $3.5bn. It was the first time any of the three major networks had changed hands and was the biggest takeover outside the battles for control within the oil industry.

The Capital Cities/ABC deal galvanised Turner to action. Capital Cities was raising nearly $2bn of the purchase price through bank financing and the new owners were paying a hefty premium for control considering that the stock for ABC was trading at $64.50 the day before the deal was announced.

Yet the takeover was a good deal for whoever emerged the winner. As with any company, broadcasting network share prices are compared with what the firm would produce if its separate entities were broken up and sold on the marketplace for cash; another way of looking at the price is to weigh it against the cash flow the firm generates per share.

Wall Street quickly turned to John Bauer, an analyst for the small firm of Duff & Phelps, who was recognised as the leading authority on bust-up analysis for the big networks. Bauer estimated that the 'takeout value' of ABC was somewhere between $140 a share and $155, which meant that it was trading at a 20 per.cent to 25 per cent discount to the market price just before the deal. Since Wall Street shares were trading at an average discount of 16 per cent it was a pretty good buy.

But CBS was a better buy still by Bauer's lights, even with the current share prices pushed up to $78.25 in the early weeks of March by all the other share interest. Bauer estimated the 'takeout value' of CBS as between $175 and $190 per share and a cash flow of a whopping $721m washing through the network's 29.8m shares.

What that calculation meant to Bauer was that if Turner could raise roughly $100 a share, or about $3bn, from *somewhere* he could make a credible bid for CBS that would be both attractively above the current price yet well below the idealised and unrealistic upper levels of what the network would yield if it was broken up. Even if he paid top interest rates, then at 12.5 per cent, such a financing would cost Turner a million dollars a day and that could easily be handled by the wash of CBS's revenues through the Turner Broadcasting books.*

Turner embarked on a campaign to raise the money from the banks or from anybody with an interest in seeing CBS go under the auctioneer's hammer. He even secured tentative credit lines from MCI, the telephone competitor of AT&T, and from William Simon, the ex-US Treasury Secretary and financier for rightist causes. But they were barely $100m in seed money, really not enough to get started. Try as he might, Turner was being impelled in one direction. Junk bonds were the answer. High interest yielding bonds secured against the assets and cash flow of the target company. A simple rush to buy up CBS shares in order to stake out a big minority holding would not do it; not even if Turner could borrow some more money to buy on margin because then he would only be a shareholder and not have ownership of all that lovely cash flow. No, it must be complete control or nothing at all. Turner called his lead banker First Boston Co. One of the ironies of the CBS saga is that First Boston would be used a few months later by another unsuccessful bidder for the network – Marvin Davis, late of Denver and of Twentieth Century Fox.

At the moment, Davis was in the midst of his own transactions, selling off half of Twentieth Century Fox to Rupert Murdoch for

Barrons, 4 March, 1985.

$162m. Murdoch also loaned Davis $88m which enabled him to pay off the final bank loans on the studio. Davis also dumped the last of his oil and gas properties for $180m just as oil prices started to slide.

By the end of March 1985, the list of players in the CBS drama were expanded to include a rumour that CBS founder Bill Paley, who held 5.6 per cent of the shares himself, was sounding out financiers for a leveraged buyout of his old company in order to keep it from falling into evil hands. The market fever burned hot when Goldman Sachs was spotted buying 100,000 shares for its own account. The price of CBS stock hit a high of $110 as rumours about Paley, Boesky and Turner dominated the business press headlines.

Indeed, at one point Boesky was set to push his holdings above the 10 per cent mark when his ubiquitous intelligence service informed him that Paley was not a serious contender after the old man's banks had given back a cool response to his feelers. Boesky held the line and word filtered out to allied arbs elsewhere on the street. CBS shares dropped to $105 in a twinkling.*

Boesky decided to fold soon afterwards. With Paley out, the prospect of a real run-up in CBS shares seemed dim. The Helms-FIM campaign was going nowhere and he could not believe that Turner's financing efforts could be taken seriously. With CBS dug into its bunker and bolstered by a $1.5bn line of credit he had just about decided (later he would say he had already begun to sell) to sell off his CBS gamble and take a nice profit when CBS sued him in federal court alleging a series of securities laws violations, including illegal margin trading and trying unlawfully to force CBS to buy back his shares at above market prices.

Boesky was easy to spook at this point. The public shellacking he had taken in the Phillips-Unocal raids had stung. He also had learned the hard way that sometimes his vaunted intelligence network and odds-calculating skills were human after all. In 1982 Boesky had been caught going and coming in the takeover battle over Cities Service; he bought 400,000 Cities Service shares at roughly $40 a share when it looked as if Gulf Oil would come in with a $63 a share bid and then was forced to dump them all at $30 when the Gulf pulled out. A day or two later Occidental Petroleum Corp. stepped in and bought Cities Service at $55 a share. In the Phillips raid he had watched his holdings of the target company drop $10m in value in a single day's trading.

There was a time to stay in and a time to go and this was one of those times to get going, Boesky reasoned. His 2.6m shares of CBS had cost him $247m, or $95 each on average and he could unload at $105 for a

*Wall Street Journal, 22 March, 1985.

tidy $26m profit. And time was rapidly moving in CBS's favour. The 17 April shareholders meeting now in all probability would result in a resounding vote of confidence for Wyman and the management and they would be even less willing to buy up some of their shares with their $1.5bn warchest (and inflate the value of Boesky's holdings) after that. Besides the lawsuit had provoked the popular press into that old story about how the other arbitrageurs called him 'Piggy' for his greed. He hated it. So he moved quickly and unloaded half his holdings to fellow speculator Irwin Jacobs of Minneapolis.

This time Boesky's luck held. Had he sold into the market that first ten days of April he would have had to sell CBS into a market that dropped quickly to $100 a share and ultimately to near the $95 price at which he had bought into the game. On 12 April, CBS stock suddenly rebounded back over the $100 mark and the next day rose $3.25 to $103.75 on rumours that E. F. Hutton and Shearson Lehman Brothers had put together a financing package that would enable Ted Turner to offer $175 a share for CBS. Turner by now had mounted his own takeover team of outside specialists including Doremus and Co, for public relations.

When the market reopened on Monday, 15 April, CBS shares were up to $109 and the *New York Times* was openly speculating that the share price would rise further since Turner's reported offering price would be $175 a share. There was a note of caution, however. The same sources which informed the *Times* also warned 'that the market might value his securities, presumably including so-called junk bonds, at only $130 to $150 a share.' That day, CBS shares jumped another six dollars to $115.75 in active trading on the New York Stock Exchange. Ivan Boesky's remaining 1.3m shares now offered another $26m profit.*

On 17 April, the CBS shareholders meeting convened at 2 pm in the studio auditorium of WBBM-TV, the network's Chicago affiliate. The choice was deliberate, only 200 shareholders could fit into the room, limiting the amount of harassment Wyman would be subjected to by the various protest groups in addition to the Helmsites. It was a bitterly tough meeting with the professional corporate gadflies carping about low dividends and poor earnings performance in the toys division while the right wingers even raised such arcane complaints as the alleged liberal bias in news anchor dean Walter Cronkite's reporting of the 1968 Tet offensive during the Vietnam War.

The next day was not much better for the CBS team. Turner finally dropped the other shoe. He filed notice with the Federal

New York Times, 16 April, 1985.

Communications Commission in Washington that he would seek agency permission to make a takeover bid for CBS. The company's shares slipped to $110 after some Wall Street stock traders cashed their clients out for a quick profit, betting that Turner's financing would be less than credible.

In what the *Wall Street Journal* called 'an extraordinary repudiation of Ted Turner's offer', CBS shares dropped almost immediately to $106.50 when the terms of Turner's bid was made public. It was for $175 a share, to be sure, but only on the face value of the Turner securities being offered.

Edward Atorino, Smith Barney's broadcasting analyst, summed up the mood of the rest of the brokerage community after a briefing held by Turner in New York. 'It's nothing but paper, nothing but paper. There's not a dime of cash in it. It's a serious offer... but the probability is zero that Turner will end up owning CBS.'

Indeed, what Daniel Good, head of E. F. Hutton's mergers and acquisitions department had done was take junk bonds to the outer limit. In other takeover attempts in the past the shareholders of the target firm had at least been offered half the face value of the offering in cash and the rest in high-risk, high-yield 'junk' debt securities. In Turner's bid for CBS the shareholder was asked to turn over shares that were still worth more than $100 on the open market in return for a variety of debt securities – a 7-year senior note valued at $46, another 15-year debenture also valued at $46, there was $20 worth of non-interest bearing notes, and another $30 subordinated debt as well as some shares of stock in the combined Turner Broadcasting/CBS which were valued at $33.

Wyman quickly dubbed Turner 'the paper tiger' and the Wall Street snickering extended to E. F. Hutton. Dan Good, it was said, was a good man who had had a rocky past as head of A. G. Becker Paribas Inc., before its French owners had sold the house out from under him to Merrill Lynch. Now he had taken over Hutton's tiny six-person M&A department and was determined to take it into the big leagues. There were doubters that Hutton had the capacity to pull off a big-league deal. So far that year Good's team had earned a hefty $7m fee for helping Rockwell International Corp. pull off a takeover. But First Boston, Morgan Stanley and other junk bond impresarios were already in the $100m league.

What Good and Hutton had to offer was a network of 6000 brokerage salesmen who could individually seek out customers who held CBS stock and convince them that the Turner junk bonds had the promise of $175 per share and more. For that, and the fees that subsequently could come from dismantling CBS to redeem those bonds, Good and Hutton could rake in fees of $50m or more.

At the end of course, it would come to nothing like that. Turner would make a million or so on the run-up in the CBS shares he ultimately acquired, but he would have to pay the lawyers, the public relations men and others $23m in fees, about $10m of which went to Good and Hutton. It was not a triumph.

What happened was that Wall Street did its sums and concluded that it was largely irrelevant whether the securities Turner was offering were worth $174 or $175. There was no way he could win control of CBS at any price and make it all work. First of all Wyman and CBS had amended the shareholder rules so that any takeover offer had to have 67 per cent of the shareholders votes. Moreover to finance the deal as it stood, Turner would immediately have to sell off $2.7bn of the broadcasting giant's assets and here, of course, is where the merger theories of 'break-up value' and 'take out value' fall apart.

The fact of the matter is that while CBS as a corporate being might have been worth $5bn or so as an entity a sudden rush to break it up and sell off even a large portion of that entity would immediately lessen the value of the parts being put up for sale. Moreover, once the company was essentially cut in half, where would the cash flow come from that Turner needed to build TBS? Equally important, no-one believed Hutton could sell the junk bonds to enough institutional investors to raise the purchase price in the first place.*

Yet Turner tried. Within a few days of the tender offer Hutton M&A specialists were busy calling prospective buyers of the pieces of CBS, in effect trying to presell the network's subsidiaries, the toys, the television stations; in all Turner said he would sell $1.3b of CBS assets in 1986 and another $500m a year later.

CBS counterattacked on all fronts, alternatively pretending that Turner did not exist, then going into court to accuse him of cooking his own TBS books to help finance the takeover raid. Suits were filed. The FCC was criticised, with some reason, for literally washing its hands of so clumsily put together a takeover bid for a major broadcasting network. On 3 May, CBS entered into a 'standstill' agreement in which the network dropped its suits against the arbitrageur in return for his agreement to keep his CBS holdings at no more than 4.3 per cent and to stay out of any other takeover bids for the next two years. On the same day, the network spent $100m to buy five radio stations from Taft Broadcasting. It was business as usual, Wyman was signalling.

In the end, CBS beat Turner with his own junk bond weapon.

*Wall Street Journal, 19 April, 1985.

Using the time-honoured poison pill defence, the network made itself less attractive to takeover suitors by loading itself with debt; $1bn, in this case.

The CBS plan, launched in July, was to buy back 21 per cent of its stock with the $1 billion. To pay for the stock repurchase, CBS issued $123m in preferred stock, made a $137m short-term borrowing from its bank credit line and issued $700m in 'senior notes'. Thus anyone trying to take CBS over would not only have to pay the full price but assume the extra indebtedness as well. Those who wanted to sell would get a package worth $15 a share, or $32 over the current market price for CBS; not bad for Ivan Boesky nor for anyone else since unlike Turner's $175 offer, CBS would still exist intact.

After a few weeks of trying to stir up investor interest in a sweetened offer, Turner decided, on 28 July, to take what profit he could and sold his CBS shares. A year later he would pay $1.6bn for the failing MGM-United Artist movie studios, paying the wiley Las Vegan Kirk Kerkorian several hundred million dollars more than what the vast film library and production facilities were worth in some analysts' eyes and leaving TBS saddled with horrendous debt. Yet Turner finally found the cash producer he wanted to fatten up TBS. Film revenues plus the advertising income from showing such film and television sit-com classics on his cable network have pushed sales towards the $500m mark.

Turner's defeat by CBS did not bring rest to the network nor honour to Thomas Wyman. Others had been eyeing the vulnerabilities the network had displayed during the battle with Turner, Boesky and the Helmsites, who in the end never accumulated more than a few thousand shares for the April confrontation.

Laurence A. Tisch, chairman of Loews Corp., was one of the circling sharks. So was Marvin Davis, the Denver oil billionaire, out in his Beverley Hills mansion. Tisch, prodded by his son, Dan, who was head of Salomon Brothers arbitrage department, had begun buying CBS at $118 on the morning of 3 July, the day Wyman announced the stock buyback plan to thwart Turner. The idea was that Tisch could sell back half his investment at the $150 Wyman price and thus lower the cost of the overall investment to roughly $105 a share. There was no way he could lose. But by the end of July, Tisch owned 7 per cent of CBS, a greater holding than Bill Paley himself and by August the holdings would exceed 15 per cent.

In September, Marvin Davis would make his move against CBS. What would happen from this point on is currently under investigation by the SEC and other securities regulators who are worried about controlling the spread of insider information which can be used for unfair and illegal trading advantages.

Federal rules that prohibit insider trading are explicit enough as to what corporate 'insiders' may do or not do with information not shared by the general public. But Davis was not an insider; indeed, he was an outsider planning his own investment strategy. Nevertheless, the story that follows demonstrates too clearly how difficult it is to keep takeover and merger information from spreading and it raises serious questions about the ability of financiers, their investment bankers and other participants to avoid conflicts of interest.

Davis first became interested in CBS in September 1985 when he contacted First Boston Corp., one of his long-running bankers and advisers and asked them to do a work-up on the broadcasting company as a possible target. Davis felt comfortable with First Boston because a number of its senior deal makers had been Harvard Business School classmates of his son, John Davis, now 31 and a key aide to his father. The First Boston reports were good and a draft of a takeover strategy was given the code name 'Project Charlie' and presumably kept within the close circle of First Boston analysts who were directly advising Davis.

Towards the end of 1985, the circle of awareness about 'Project Charlie' widened. Davis asked Bruce Wasterstein, the deal maker for First Boston's merger and acquisitions department, and three of his aides to meet for lunch at Davis' Beverley Hills mansion. Also present was John Davis and the brothers Tony and Richard Fisher, whose family firm had been sometimes partners of various Davis investment schemes.

Davis had just bought out Marc Rich (soon to be the fugitive financier) and was in complete control of Fox. The question at the luncheon table was whether the Davis and Fisher groups were interested in a joint takeover bid for CBS. The Fishers decided they were not interested, but now they carried away the knowledge that Davis would soon put CBS into play.

In that fall of 1985 First Boston would get the green light on 'Project Charlie' from Davis even as Tisch was strengthening his influence inside the boardroom of CBS. Both men were becoming increasingly fascinated by the network, its cash flow, its prestige, its power.

Also fascinated were surveillance officials at the Chicago Board of Trade where the super-hot market for investments in stock options trading was at its hottest in the options on CBS shares. Options are not the shares themselves, but contracts to buy an announced quantity of shares in a given company at a fixed date in the future at a given price above or below the current market price. If it sounds like a horse race, it is. But it also has become a valuable hedging tool for those investors who buy huge blocs of shares on margin.

What the surveillance officials spotted was unusual activity in CBS options from a New York brokerage firm partly owned by the Belzberg brothers of Vancouver, sometime partners of Boone Pickens, and takeover artists in their own right. In this case they had formed a partnership with none other than the Fishers to invest in CBS; they had done Davis the courtesy of asking if he wanted in.

The Chicago Board of Trade and the SEC were to launch an insider-trading probe into activity in CBS options in the spring of 1986 even as Davis and his First Boston team put together a $150 a share offer for CBS which Davis put personally to Wyman on 26 February. Prudential was backing him, Davis told Wyman, but the deal had to be friendly to all sides. Wyman, being a prudent man, checked with Prudential executives and found that Davis did not have a firm financing commitment. Meanwhile the arbitrageurs had begun pushing up CBS stock by $15 a day until it hit $142.25 on 28 February.

On 3 March, according to most accounts, Wyman politely declined Davis' offer but told Laurence Tisch about it. What the SEC and other regulators were belatedly trying to find out was who else was privy to the information and the subsequent Davis raise to $160 a share and the rejection that followed. By the end of March, CBS shares were up to $146 a share on heavy trading volume almost every day as the arbs backed their bets.

In the first week of April, Tisch made his move, buying 1 million more CBS shares, this time from the Fisher brothers at $143.50 a share. This put Davis out of the game for good and that sent CBS shares plunging $12 by the end of the week.

Later that summer, Paley and Tisch would make common cause and in September oust Wyman with the founder resuming the role of chairman and Tisch becoming chief executive. None of the SEC investigations ever did determine the extent of insider dealings in the CBS battles; the truth of that may never be known.

CHAPTER FIVE

Hanson is as Hanson Does

The Rolls-Royce glided past Horse Guard's Parade, along the back of Downing Street and turned left past the Foreign Office and the Treasury into Parliament Square. Sitting in the back, the six foot four figure of Lord Hanson was at ease, smoking a cigar left over from his lunch at his favourite restaurant, the Mirabelle, in Mayfair. Although in the middle of his biggest in a long line of takeover battles, Hanson was now on his way to a relatively new task to which he had greatly taken: defending the government in the House of Lords. The government whip had asked for extra support on the benches, and the loyal Hanson was about to provide it. 'Hanson has three loves,' a friend had remarked: 'Mrs Thatcher, free enterprise and the United States – in no particular order.'

Under the Thatcher regime, Lord (James) Hanson is in his element, feeling free to make the type of takeovers and achieve the scale of rationalisation of whole industries he had only dreamed about in the 1970s. By the early 1980s he had emerged as the greatest practitioner of the art of bidding for companies ever seen in Britain – and Sir Gordon White, who handled the American side of his business, had few equals in the United States either. 'Hanson has a good track record on Wall Street,' said Ivan Boesky respectfully in September 1985, after he had bought 12 per cent of SCM, the New York-based chemicals to typewriters conglomerate for which Hanson had just bid $900m. 'The market regards him favourably.'

At that time, praise from Boesky still meant something. There were not many men who *could* impress Boesky, but Hanson and White, although neither had ever met the man, did. They impressed a good many others, too. For over 20 years they had defied the laws of averages and of the stock markets which said that conglomerators would fall flat on their faces – or at the very least would, after the initial glamour had worn off, be rewarded with a market raspberry, more technically known as a 'conglomerate discount'. Essentially that means its shares should be selling at well below asset value. Hanson's sold at a premium.

No study of takeovers is complete without a close look at James Hanson and his mode of operation. At this time – 1985/6 – he was the most successful operator on the bid scene in Britain; and White was among the top half dozen in the United States. In the 1960s when Hanson first emerged he was wrongly categorised as a Jim Slater lieutenant, one of a not-very-special breed who revolved around the star of the moment. By the 1970s he was the great survivor, one of the few who had not perished in the chill of the great bear market and secondary banking crisis which had killed off so many of the hothouse plants of that time. But it was the early-1980s before Hanson was taken seriously. Only then had he become, in the eyes of British industry and the City of London, something more than an opportunist conglomerator with a keen eye for undervalued assets and an even better eye for converting it into profits.

The fate of other would-be Hansons, particularly in the United States where conglomerates had their hey-day in the 1960s, should have deterred most companies from pursuing that route. Professor Michael Porter of the Harvard Business School points out why Hanson is such an exception:

> Study after study in the United States has shown that unrelated diversification is extremely risky and that conglomerate corporate strategies have largely failed. My recent study (1987) of the diversification track record of 33 major American companies from 1950 to 1980 found that a startling 74 per cent of acquisitions in unrelated new fields were divested.*

There are no equivalent figures for Britain, but the same pattern is broadly true. It takes no great genius to point out the failures of conglomeration and diversification in Britain, ranging from Distillers' disastrous move into pharmaceuticals and chemicals, to Imperial Tobacco's many false starts at getting away from its own declining industry. In the whole of British industry and commerce in the mid-

Competitive Advantage to Corporate Strategy, Harvard Business Review, May–June 1987.

1980s, there was only one other figure who could stand beside Hanson: Sir Owen Green, who had built up BTR from a collection of uninspired engineering and rubber companies, won one of the more dramatic early battles of the new takeover wave when he took over Thomas Tilling (another conglomerate) and finally Dunlop, the latter an example of a company which should have been taken over a decade before.

Hanson however was very different from Green, both in his style of operation and in his personality. Green was, in many ways, closer to Arnold Weinstock at Weinstock's peak, much more interested in running the companies he acquired than in the acquisition process, controlling costs and return on capital to the third decimal point. Hanson, although interested in his return on capital and the profitability of the companies he retained, was more at home in the bid arena, directing the latest bid from his pool-side in California, where he kept in touch with the Fax machine, which continually spewed out new documents from London or New York (documents which Hanson, always worried about leaks, instantly fed into a shredder as soon as he had read them). Alternatively, he worked from his London office near Harrods in Knightsbridge.

Green had few imitators in British industry, in the sense that one seldom heard a young entrepreneur say: 'I want to be the next Owen Green.' Hanson had many, perhaps partly because he was a more glamorous figure, but also because – whatever the pitfalls – conglomerate takeovers still offered a quick and attractive route to the top. In his piece for *The World in 1987* (Economist Publications November 1986), Professor Porter pondered: 'Why are British conglomerates so in fashion in the London stock market today?' To find the answer, Porter took a look at Hanson and immediately found a clue: 'compounded annual turnover growth of 31 per cent in the last five years, average annual earnings per share increases of 36 per cent in the same period, and Hanson's emergence as the fifth largest British company in terms of stock market capitalisation.' Hanson Trust was one of the most successful investments a shareholder could have made in post-War Britain: an investment of £100 in 1964 was worth £70,000 22 years later, although the shareholder would have to have invested a further £8900 over the years in rights issues.

Hanson himself, although certainly thoughtful and perceptive, would not pretend to be the philosopher king of the takeover world. What he has done has been to a large extent instinctive, without the benefit of an elaborate plan of campaign. Like most of the raiders, he has basic tenets; and unlike most of them, he has stuck to them. Professor Porter reckoned that Hanson's success was due to a strict and skilful adherence to what he calls 'the restructuring concept of diversification'. The three elements of this model, he explains, are (1) acquisition of firms with potential for restructuring; (2) active management, post acquisition, to transform the new units, and (3) disposal of the restructured assets once the job is complete and the results are clear. 'Hanson's approach, if one looks at it carefully, goes a long way to meeting these tenets.'

Academic analysis does not help a great deal in deciding what, if any, types of takeovers are good in the long-term; nor what takeovers should be discouraged. Companies, which have spent millions on market analyses and programmes identifying what industries they should buy into, have met with no more success than the instinctive, opportunistic bidder. In more recent years Hanson had become more analytical, with access to the increasingly sophisticated tools which were available for studying companies and industries. But he seldom used them. When his partner Sir Gordon White, cross-examined in an American court about how he had valued SCM, replied 'gut feeling', he was not being evasive. On the contrary, he was answering as truthfully as he knew how. Professor Porter and the other academics, who seek patterns and rationales in the takeover world, do not factor 'gut feeling' into their analyses. There is no place for it on the computer or the statistical analysis. Yet many of those involved in bids knew exactly what White was trying to say. One raider, asked how he decided on his targets, sided with the Gordon White view. 'Sure, I have studies and papers and valuations. But they're just rationalisations for decisions you've already taken. You do what your gut tells you and find the reasons for it afterwards.'

Hanson and White had been serious players on the American bid scene since they first bid $180m for McDonough Corporation in February 1981. In 20 years of serious takeover activity in Britain and 12 in the United States, they had gained more experience of the takeover scene than almost anyone in the business. When White talked about his 'gut' what he really meant was his experience, his knowledge – and a belief in his own instinctive feel for a situation. He and Hanson, after all, had been right more often than they were wrong. They had taken a small Yorkshire-based transport company into the biggest league in Britain; the SCM takeover pushed the Hanson interests in the US into the 120 biggest American companies in its own right – and, by the time it was completed, Hanson was involved in something far bigger and much more adventurous. He was bidding over £2bn for Imperial Group, for many years the biggest tobacco company in the world (originally it even controlled BAT industries, which had passed it in terms of size some years previously).

By 1986 there seemed to be very few bid situations in which Hanson did not have some involvement – or more often a share, somewhere along the line. He had discovered, a full decade before many of the players on today's scene, that, by regarding takeovers as his main activity and running the companies taken over as something separate, he had a considerable advantage over more traditionally minded managers. He set up two acquisition teams – one in New York under Gordon White, the other in London under himself and his close lieutenant Martin Taylor – each of them constantly calculating and re-calculating the values of potential targets. Yet, when it came to it, either Hanson or White could decide to make a bid, or increase their offer, on their own feel for it.

Through 1984 and 1985 probably no company of any size in the United States or Britain escaped the Hanson scrutiny. In the London stockmarket there was a new rumour almost every week, often caused by some investment buying from a fund which Hanson kept just to play the market. In one month alone in the autumn of 1984 the financial press named Hanson as the potential bidder for Pilkington Brothers (glass), Hepworth Ceramic (pipes and sanitary ware), Distillers (whisky), Marley (roofing tiles) and Thorn EMI (TV, electronics and entertainment). Then there were Charter Consolidated (mining), Babcock International (engineering), Tate & Lyle (sugar), and a dozen more. Hanson did indeed have a stake in several of them – Distillers, Babcock and Tate, to name three.

Even while they hummed with rumours, the stock markets on Wall Street and in London had little real concept of the scale of Hanson's plans and ambitions. During 1985 he had his team prepare a report on some of the most prestigious British companies, regardless of size and reputation. The bid he eventually made was not only twice as big as anything he had yet attempted, either in the US or Britain – it was also a watershed in the whole takeover movement. On the day he made it *The Times* forecast that it would 'mark a major turning point – for Hanson, for the market and for Mrs Thatcher'. The target was Imperial Group. And on its own it did not fulfil *The Times* forecast. But by an extraordinary coincidence it was to run alongside, day by day for the next four months, the bid which did eventually kill the takeover boom and lead to some wholly unforeseen repercussions: the battle for Distillers.

For all their success, it had taken the City and the international financial scene many years to accept that Hanson and Gordon White were serious about what they did. Until well into their 50s, both men still had reputations as playboys, Hanson's a long-outdated hangover from the days when he was regularly seen squiring the pretty young film stars of the day, and from his much publicised year-long engagement to Audrey Hepburn in the 1950s. Sir Gordon White (he was knighted for his services to British industries overseas) was linked in the gossip columns of the time with a variety of stars too, Grace Kelly and Ava Gardner among them.

As the *Financial Times* wrote in December 1983:

Few playboys of the '50s jet-set have made it to the House of Lords. Fewer whizz-kids of the '60s City have become captains of British industry. James, now Lord, Hanson, has pulled off both feats – and become in the process one of the least known public figures controlling a major international company in Britain today.

Virtually all the practitioners in the 1960s and early 1970s had attracted considerable stigma to themselves. Hanson had been as active as anyone in the Slater 'whizzkid' era of 1968–73, when in five years more fortunes were made and lost than in any other period in British commercial history. When Jim Slater and his protégés, notably John Bentley, were pilloried by both the Left and the City as 'asset strippers' and pushers of useless bits of high-priced paper, Hanson had managed to avoid the worst of the antipathy of both sides and, more importantly, to avoid financial ruin.

Hanson was a product of the North Yorkshire gentry, not by any means part of the established British aristocracy, but acceptable enough in post-War Britain. His father, when James was born, was Master of Foxhounds for the local hunt and ran a prosperous family transport company originally started in the mid-nineteenth century by a grandmother who ran packhorses and who, according to Hanson, started the family tradition of 'line management', or what he himself later called 'free form' management. The young James had some early training as an accountant but the war interrupted that. Life seems to have begun for Hanson at the age of 26 when the post-War Labour government nationalised the company, paying the Hanson family some £3m in compensation.

That gave him both the capital and the incentive to start out on his own. But not in Britain, then a dark and gloomy place for potential entrepreneurs. Hanson and his brother Bill went to Canada where they started in the business they already knew something about: haulage. It was then that Hanson acquired his love for North America; he and his brother each spent five months of the year there, and Hanson has more or less maintained that practice ever since. By no means all that five months was spent running the haulage business in

Canada: Hanson had by now discovered the delights of Hollywood and, with his money, charm and looks, seems to have been a welcome addition to the scene. He brought some of his girlfriends back to the family home in Huddersfield: friends remember Jean Simmons, then only 19, as a regular visitor, and there was the much more serious romance with Audrey Hepburn.

One relationship however outlasted the more fleeting ones with the starlets: his friendship with Gordon White, who came from the same area of Yorkshire and had been a friend since childhood. The two men are remarkably alike: almost the same age (White is a year younger), and the same height, accent and even tastes. In the late 1950s the two men went into partnership, importing US greeting cards. The business did well enough but they sold out at a profit and moved on to other things. In 1964 they bought into a little public company called Wiles group, and Hanson Trust was born. Hanson by now had married Geraldine Kaelin, a New York divorcée, and had sold the Canadian business. His playboy days were behind him, but he had already set the pattern for what was to come: he now had four homes, two in the United States, two in Britain, and divided his life between the two countries.

His partnership with White has emerged as one of the most important in post-War British commercial history, to be compared with, say, the partnership between Arthur Anderson and Brodie McGhie Wilcox which was the foundation of the P&O shipping group in the 1820s, or of William Jardine and James Matheson who founded the great Hong Kong trading empire, Jardine Matheson. The two are 'more like twins than brothers' according to Hanson and both of them speak of their almost telepathic relationship – 'we sometimes turn up wearing the same ties'.

Before 1964, business for both men had been more of a past-time than a profession, and neither was suited for the monotony and hard work involved with running any normal business. The discovery of the takeover, short-cutting as it did years of painstaking build-up and at the same time providing instant excitement and all the thrill of the hunt in finding and then catching the victim, thrilled them both. Wiles Group had a brief history under that name: both White and Hanson agreed to rename it Hanson White in 1969 but legal problems got in the way. They settled for Hanson Trust which is what is has been ever since.

By then Hanson and White had thoroughly revamped the company. They had sold the Wiles fertiliser business, bought a company called Scottish Land which moved muck, and developed the practice they have taken to a fine art since: they retained the bits of the companies which seemed to have a future, and ruthlessly sold or closed those which were no-hopers. Increasingly they were setting the pattern for all that would follow. Hanson and White had taken up headquarters in an elegant mews in Chelsea, commuting between their growing number of businesses in a red and white helicopter, in those days a spectacular way for a company boss to behave.

By 1969 Hanson had met, come under the influence of, and become an associate of Jim Slater. The two men were naturally drawn to each other, with Slater, socially shy and gauche at the time, the dominant one in business philosophy. Hanson never became a Slater satellite, but he entered the periphery of the orbit. In 1968, in a whirl of other deals, Slater announced a complicated £5.5m share exchange deal, in return for which Slater received a 15 per cent stake in Hanson's company, plus £2.5m in cash. 'This exchange,' Slater later wrote laconically in his book *Return to Go*, 'consolidated the already strong business links between James Hanson and myself.' They were consolidated in the sense, however, that Hanson was the junior of the two – although he was several years older and had much wider international experience than the still insular Slater – and was seen by the City, if not necessarily by himself, as one of the Slater stable of bright up-and-coming men. Slater after that continually offered him shareholdings in various companies he had targeted, and Hanson gradually perfected the art of the successful takeover, learning tactics from the master. Later in his book, discussing the nature of the problems and benefits the wide circle of satellites and spin-offs presented to him, Slater wrote: 'There were some cases in which the relationship became difficult and others in which, over a period, it became completely impossible.' With Hanson, he went on, there was never a problem; he had 'always been in command, and did not feel the need to prove anything to anybody'. With him, added Slater: 'I had a simple and effective business relationship' in which Hanson could be better described as an 'associate' rather than a 'satellite'.

By 1972, partly prompted by Slater, Hanson and White had turned their group into a low-key, well-run industrial conglomerate, having acquired a brickmaker (Butterley), a construction equipment business, property and an agricultural services business. Slater by then was increasingly building paper empires.

Hanson, however, refused to join the great paper chase, preferring to keep most of the companies he had acquired, once he had done his initial re-shaping. He enjoyed being a brickmaker, for instance, and found he could build himself a profitable niche in the building materials market. Slater urged him to sell and move on; he refused, again setting an important precedent. Only a handful of the active bidders of the day would survive the 1970s.

The prospects in mid-1970s Britain were too dismal for Gordon White. He left for a land where capitalism still thrived: the United States. 'I was finished with England,' said White in an interview with the *Observer* in May 1984.

I felt it was the end. I was leveraged up to the eyebrows and technically insolvent. If my agreed loan of £150,000 had been an overdraft, they could have called it in, and I would have gone down.

I did not leave England as a tax exile. I left broke, and came here [New York] to start on my own. James said: 'Why not do it for Hanson Trust?' and I said OK – but not without equity, so we agreed 10 per cent. I left England as deputy chairman of Hanson Trust and I came out here like an errand boy. They [the investment banks on Wall Street] said: 'Who are you? What do you want? And goodbye.' I sat around in waiting rooms, and I lived in a hotel for a year.

That hotel was the Pierre in New York, a comfortable hotel by any standards, but at one point the management decided they had had enough of this restless Englishman after they logged a hundred calls to White in a single day.

It did not take White long to hit his stride in the US. 'James and I had been partners for a long time and we both felt that while a Labour government ruled in the UK, America was the place to make money.' He set off to do just that. He founded a new American company, Hanson Industries, on just $3000 of capital. White later paid a nominal $500,000 for his 10 per cent stake in the American end of Hanson, and was bought out by the parent company for many times that sum in 1979.

White took to the US the same basic takeover philosophy which he and Hanson had developed together in Britain, and which academics like Professor Porter of Harvard would later attempt to formulate. 'Philosophy' is probably too high a word for it. What they essentially had was a few rough principles which they had discovered worked for them. For instance, they had long ago decided that they did not want glamorous, high-tech companies – quite the opposite. They made money in simple, straightforward, even dull businesses which were largely ignored by the more fashionable corporations. There was another principle too, which Professor Porter missed – they would never overpay. 'I've always thought about the downside risk on a takeover, rather than the upside potential,' said Hanson later. 'We don't gamble.'*

In a separate interview White echoed his words almost exactly. 'I never ask myself how much can we make out of this? I ask: what can we lose?'†

It was this principle which lost them their first major acquisition: the chance to buy 51 per cent of Avis, the car hire business, for what White remembers as a mere $17m cash payment. He said he told Hanson, '"it could put us straight into the big league, but if it goes wrong it would bust us." We didn't have to talk about it for very long.' There was also an abortive bid to take over the United Artists Theatre Circuit – both Hanson and White have retained an enthusiasm for the world of showbusiness.

Three months after he arrived, White made his first real acquisition in the United States: he bought Seacoast, a fish processor (he sold it again ten years later, for $30m, roughly what he had paid for it, although Hanson had of course enjoyed the cash flow). He was away. Through the '70s there was a steady flow of acquisitions, most of them distinguished only for their ordinariness. In April 1984 the *Wall Street Journal* had some fun at White's expense:

> After a thorough review of its business, one of Hanson Trust PLC's US subsidiaries last year decided to throw caution to the wind and introduce an array of new products.
>
> In short order, Ames Co of Parkersburg, W. Va, brought out a line of wheelbarrows, a selection of fertilizer spreaders and a variety of picks and mattocks to complement its other lawn-and-garden tools.

Hot-dogs, shoes, yarn and garden tools were not exactly on the frontiers of technology. But after Hanson acquired them they made money. And they were providing the base for the much bigger things that White had in mind. By the time the American takeover boom got fully under way, Hanson and White were as well placed as anyone to take advantage of it. They had a track record and the resources to fight it out.

The two men had another tenet, too, as rough and ready as the others. They had long ago agreed that the company should be balanced 50/50 between Britain and the United States. They never intended to stick to it slavishly, and it would certainly not prevent them making

Financial Times, December 1983.
† *Observer*, May 1984.

another bid in one country or the other even if the balance was wrong at the time. But if it could be managed, that was the way they preferred it. As the size of White's American assets grew, James Hanson decided it was time to step back into the bid arena in Britain in a major way again.

He had not been entirely idle through the 1970s, but they were not good times for the bidder. With the emergence of the Thatcher government in May 1979, however, that changed. Market economics and free enterprise ruled the land; competition was to be king. Hanson who had personally become surprisingly close to Harold Wilson when he was prime minister – it was Wilson who knighted him in the same honours controversial honours list that included Sir James Goldsmith – entered a significant new phase.

It was late 1981 however before he made his first major move: a £100m bid for the Ever Ready battery company, which had renamed itself, in a moment of aberration, Berec. It was a bruising, hostile bid, with Hanson showing just how rough he could play if he had to. That again was valuable experience – when it came to his really big battles a few years later, Hanson and his team were fully battle-hardened, proof against the many personal remarks that would be made about them.

He won Berec, then began to sort it out in what was already long-established as the Hanson pattern from which he seldom varied, either in the US or Britain, and which would come under Professor Porter's second heading of 'active management, post acquisition, to transform the new units'. Most of the headquarters staff went, as did the subsidiaries in Nigeria and Hong Kong. Then came Hanson's master stroke, one that perhaps established the creed and completed Professor Porter's third stage: he sold Berec's loss-making European operations to one of its major rivals, Duracell Europe, which is owned by the US group Dart & Kraft Inc. That in effect left him the profit-making parts of the company in Britain and South Africa for the modest investment of £60m. He changed the name back to Ever Ready, which is how the majority of the British public knew it anyway. To emphasise his insistence on low technology, he also sold a research centre where a group of scientists were working on solar-energy projects. And he introduced a long-life alkaline-manganese battery that had been developed by the old management but never introduced. 'Berec (management) was very slow,' Sir Gordon White explained to the *Wall Street Journal* (April 1984). 'They couldn't make a decision to go to the bathroom.'

Here the academics and Hanson were in agreement. Professor Porter correctly identified the philosophy at work: 'The typical Hanson target company is not just any company in the industry. It is a market leader that is asset rich but has a recent record of poor management. The common thread in all of Hanson's acquisitions are situations in which there is under-utilisation of assets – both economic and human.' Ever Ready was merely a rehearsal for the next big bid, however: for the retailer United Drapery Stores. This was Hanson at his opportunistic best, his only display of the 'white knight' technique.

In January 1983 Gerald Ronson, owner of Britain's second biggest (after Littlewoods) private company, Heron International, had put together a consortium of City institutions under a new company called Bassishaw Holdings and somewhat ponderously bid £200m for UDS, owners of the Richard Shops and John Collier chains. The battle that followed raged for four months. One month into it, with Ronson seemingly unstoppable despite the opposition of the UDS board, Hanson entered. It was no ordinary entrance. The UDS board was actually in session, all ready to change its mind and finally accept an increased offer it had wrung from Ronson. 'We were actually talking about it [the increased Ronson offer],' said the UDS chairman, Sir Robert Clark, later, 'when who should ring but Sir James Hanson.'* The board instantly changed its mind again. It was delighted to accept the new offer, not just because it was £30m higher, but because it preferred the personality. 'We like Hanson. I don't think there will be any problem about his shares holding their price. He's got a terrific profit record,' said Sir Robert.

The sceptic might have wondered what Hanson wanted with a major retailer like UDS, but the timing of the entrance was so perfect that Ronson never regained the initiative, and the rationale soon appeared. Hanson had to raise his bid and in the end paid £265m for a group which only six months before had been capitalised at less than £100m. Yet within a year he had sold a series of subsidiaries, mostly to management, and raised £190m. Again, as with Berec, he had received a large part of his investment back – and still held assets worth much more than he had paid for them. Professor Porter when he came to examine it gave his approval. 'Hanson also aggressively disposes of strategically ill-fitting businesses for cash, reducing the effective acquisition cost. On average, nearly a third of the cost of a Hanson acquisition is recouped through disposal in the first six months of acquisition.'

There was one sidelight to this bid which was of some import in the City where these things were as significant as the bids themselves: for his UDS bid, Hanson used the merchant bank Schroder Wagg, one of the most established, but at that time going through a rough patch

*Daily Mail, 18 February, 1983.

particularly on the takeover front. Schroder had acted for the conglomerate Thomas Tilling which made a rival bid for Berec – and of course lost to Hanson, which used – as it usually did – Rothschild as its merchant bank. But when he came to bid for UDS, Hanson found that Rothschild was already tied up – acting for Gerald Ronson. He went to Schroder, which won for him. But Tilling, furious that Schroder was acting for an old enemy, moved banks, too – and went to Warburgs, adding to the already considerable prestige of that bank, and doing considerable harm to Schroder. Then in the biggest battle yet seen, Tilling was taken over by another conglomerate, BTR – whose merchant bank was Morgan Grenfell, and the accolade of the most successful merchant bank passed from Warburgs to Morgan.

When Hanson won Berec, Schroder celebrated with champagne. It was premature – for his next bid, Hanson went back to Rothschild, to whom he remained loyal. It was an action with profound importance for Michael Richardson, the head of corporate finance (which means mergers and acquisitions) at Rothschild. With UDS, Richardson had now lost a major bid, and his reputation would be severely damaged if he lost two in a row. Hanson, on the other hand, had won with Schroder; he was taking a risk in changing from a winning team to a losing one. If the next bid was lost, his reputation, too, would suffer – although not half as much as Richardson's and Rothschilds'. The stakes were now becoming very high indeed.

His next bid was London Brick, again a dull old company, making dull old things – it was the biggest maker of bricks in the country, not exactly a high techonology or even a growth business. Afterwards one London stockbroker was quoted as saying, 'Some people like fast cars and women. Lord Hanson seems to like bricks.'* Hanson's playboy image had at last been forgotten. He himself expressed a genuine and long-held affection for the brick industry, which he had been in for 20 years. But there was no hint that his liking for one business as opposed to another ever influenced his takeover decisions. Hanson was far too clinical for that, and he had also learned a great deal from some of Slater's wiser judgements. He reckoned he could make money out of the London Brick takeover, which was the only reason he made his bid for it. At the end of his £250m bid, Hanson said: 'It doesn't matter what you are making. We cannot boast a single glamour business. What matters is how you go about what you are making. Shareholders realise that these days. Our strength . . . is that we are good managers with bold objectives.' †

---

*The Times, 6 March, 1984.
† The Times, March 1984.

Just as Hanson had learnt the art of the predator, others had learnt the art of self-defence. Even in Britain (which was pale by comparison with the US) defences were now fierce, personal, and often very effective. Hanson's bid for London Brick, which should have been a walk-over, was a real cliff-hanger.

Two years before Hanson made his bid the shares languished at 30p; Hanson ended up paying 165p, and even then only squeezed home by a tiny margin, despite his most aggressive tactics yet. He was left with the lingering impression that he had been forced to overpay, trapped by his own reputation and his need to win a bid once he had set it in motion. Machismo had entered the London bid scene, and winning seemed to matter almost as much as the price paid.

The London Brick bid brought out some fascinating new tactics. Hanson had now been taking over companies for 20 years; the management of London Brick knew about bricks and not a great deal else. They threw themselves on the mercy of their merchant bankers – who rose brilliantly to the occasion. Hanson himself stayed aloof from the public running of the bid, as he invariably did; the London Brick chairman, Jeremy Rowe, was by contrast on full public display, briefing the press and the City institutions continually. Hanson and Rothschild were in a position of having to win to retain their reputations; the advisers to London Brick, Lazard Brothers of London, had nothing to lose, but a great deal to gain.

The young Marcus Agius, one of the new generation of mergers and acquisitions specialists, made his reputation – and that of Lazards – on defending London Brick in a situation where no outsider seemed to give them a chance. Agius read engineering at Cambridge, went to Harvard Business School, and married a Rothschild – not a bad background for a career in the City. His opponent, Michael Richardson, had been a senior partner at Cazenove, easily the most establishment of all the stockbroking firms in the City of London, then moved to Rothschild to take over the job vacated by Jacob Rothschild after internecine warfare in the Rothschild family caused Jacob to move out and start his own financial group. Richardson's reputation was based on his skill for judging market forces, a skill that he was required to use to the full to win London Brick (he was later the man responsible for setting the price of British Gas).

Hanson, legendary for never over-paying, raised his bid not once but twice. Yet even then, there was no certainty at all that the institutional shareholders in London Brick, the same institutions which had accepted his offers in the past, would come through for him. The institutional shareholders were trying to lay down some principles, ones which they believed would help them in future bid situations. For one thing there was the 'premium for control' – buying a stake in a company was worth one price, but buying control was worth something more, and the institutions were insistent that Hanson would pay it. 'If you weaken and accept this bid, the premiums offered on future bids will slide,' one fund manager was quoted as saying.*

Then there was the principle of supporting a management which, although it had not produced miracles in the past, might at last be doing well – as the management of London Brick showed signs of doing. 'You do not part company with a management which has done its work well, if rather late,' said the Norwich Union, one of the bigger insurance groups, and a major shareholder in London Brick. Agius at Lazards had persuaded the City that London Brick was at last waking up and that Hanson was being opportunist again, getting in at a time when the results of the improvements had not yet shown through. Others felt that the Hanson bid by itself was enough to revitalise any management. Hanson's reputation was beginning to work against him. If he was willing to pay £240m for the company, then his past record showed he believed it was worth considerably more than that. 'You can be sure if Hanson is seen to be getting London Brick cheaply, someone else will be interested,' said one institution in the final days of the bid.† His own past success was beginning to prove a problem for Hanson, forcing him to pay higher prices than he ever intended; he was unable now to convince the City that he was paying a fair price.

There remained one final tactic and, with time running out, Hanson gave Richardson the go-ahead for a most dramatic market swoop. The plan was put forward by Richardson, who was as aware as Hanson of how badly it could misfire. What he proposed was to send the brokers into the market to mop up every share they could, taking the shareholding up to 30 per cent. Above that 30 per cent level, every shareholder would have to be offered similar cash terms to the highest price Hanson's brokers had paid in the market – and he wanted them to take his share offer rather than the cash. Hanson had started the bid with just under 10 per cent of London Brick. Now he knew that every share might count in the end. But it would mean that Hanson was going to have to commit himself to spending £80m to buy a minority stake – which he could be left with if the bid failed. Furthermore, the fact that Hanson was in the market buying so many shares would effectively underpin the London Brick price, and persuade the majority of shareholders to hold on until the last moment. It was not a

*Financial Times, 27 February, 1984.
† Financial Times, 27 February, 1984.

pleasant prospect. Hanson agreed – but, before the raid, he himself took the decision to raise the bid for the third time, offering 165p in cash or 175p in paper. It meant he was now offering £77m more than he originally intended.

Within four days of the higher offer, Richard Westmacott and Peter Meinertzhagen of Hoare Govett, Hanson's brokers, had used their team to pick up 18m London Brick shares. They bought another 167,000 on the morning the bid closed, such was the need for every share. Even so, just 20 minutes before the bid actually closed, Richardson, tense and desperately anxious, had to confess they were still 1.5m shares short of victory. At Lazards they were ready to get the champagne out. But it was premature.

The final 15 minutes changed everything: the professionals accepted Hanson's share offer. In that final quarter of an hour, Hanson's acceptances swelled from 49.8 per cent to 54 per cent.

In the words of *The Times* the next day 'the whole episode has left the City faintly puzzled. London Brick is undoubtedly a desirable property, but the price Hanson paid was hardly cheap.' The quality of the defence, which had exploited Hanson's own reputation, had cost him dearly. As the *Financial Times* wrote afterwards: 'London Brick used every financial trick it could think of.' One London stockbroker remarked: 'It revalued its assets. It doubled its dividend, made a high though realistic profits forecast. I can't think of anything it should have done that it didn't.'

London Brick was later seen as one of Hanson's less clever bids, particularly when a year later Hanson found himself making massive redundancies, closing down some of its major brickworks. There were at the time simply too many bricks around for a British construction industry which still remained depressed even as the economy expanded again. Hanson, however, insisted that it was an excellent buy and that, once he had it sorted out, it was a valuable profit contributor, particularly when the housebuilding industry improved through 1986.

In any case Hanson was big enough and rich enough to carry it. There were enough overheads and assets to be squeezed out to make the acquisition wash its face. And it fitted the philosophy. 'Hanson has built its strategy on acquisitions such as London Brick and Ever Ready batteries,' wrote Professor Porter, 'which the City rather disdainfully calls "low tech". Although mature and low growth, however, the typical Hanson target benefits from an attractive industry structure. Customer and supplier power is low and rivalry between competitors is controlled. Given the maturity of the target industries, there is usually little threat of new entry and also few substitute products.

Since it is the structure of an industry, not growth or "sexiness" that determines industry profitability and cash flow, Hanson has been rewarded handsomely.'

In a year Hanson had been involved in two tough, bruising takeover battles in Britain, worth between them £500m – not large by comparison with what has happened since, but very big indeed by the standards of the day. Hanson, who had always enjoyed a lower profile than some of the rasher figures on the scene, was now becoming a national figure. Mrs Thatcher awarded him with a peerage but at the same time warned him not to indulge in asset stripping of the kind which had done capitalism, the City and the Conservative government so much damage back in the early 1970s.

Most bidders might now have paused for reflection but, even as he took control of London Brick, Hanson was already looking forward, outlining the course of his next bid. White in the US had got behind – it was his turn to make a takeover. White's less aggressive tactics were meeting with less success than the blitzkrieg that Hanson had employed. One problem, of course, was that the US banks until the early 1980s simply did not finance hostile tender offers, and Hanson was not in a position to offer shares in the United States. It was not until junk bonds and new forms of financing came along that White was able to get going in earnest, a point not always appreciated of Hanson's US build-up. As the Lex column in the *Financial Times* remarked barbedly in April 1984

The harpoon tactics so successfully employed by Hanson Trust for acquisitions in the UK have been eschewed by Hanson Industries, the US arm of the group, in favour of some old-fashioned fishing expeditions. These have provided scant reward over three patient years.

White had not managed to make a single significant acquisition in three years (although trading profits increased every year). He had looked at the consumer products group Scott & Fretzer, only for Ivan Boesky to step in with a $420m leveraged buy-out. He had looked at Tiger Airlines and then at the toy company Milton Bradley, where he even bought a 5 per cent stake (and then sold it at a profit). At one stage he even reckoned he had tied up the acquisition of the motel chain Howard Johnson, only for Imperial Group of Britain to come along and outbid him with $670m (White's offer, which he thought was agreed, was $240m less – and Imperial was forced to sell HoJo off in 1985 for half what it paid for it). There had been plenty of others, but none White could quite pull off – until he opened his paper one morning at the end of February 1984 and read the story that a group of senior managers at US Industries, based in Stamford, Connecticut, were preparing to offer $20 a share for a leveraged buy-out. A number of shareholders, however, opposed the deal, and had filed suits claiming that the buy-out was unfairly priced. White knew US Industries, in many ways a mini-Hanson Trust, having studied it carefully for two years. US Industries was at the time going through a major reorganisation, after a period of rapid expansion in the mid-1960s, followed by a period of declining earnings. In 1981 it had produced a detailed 'strategic redeployment programme' pinpointing 14 operating units that should be sold. By the time of the management buy-out, it had sold 13, including its financial services subsidiary, and was concentrating on low-technology unglamorous products – building materials, industrial equipment for the auto industry, furniture, clothing. It was right up Hanson's street. There was another key factor: US Industries' debt represented only 20 per cent of its total capital. Commented the *Financial Times* in London: 'Hanson rarely if ever buys if its target cannot produce positive cash flow for its new parent.'

White made a bid of $22 a share, or $449m, for a company which would double Hanson's US revenues. It came as a rude shock to USI which had no love for the English in the first place: three years before they had been forced to surrender to 'greenmail' after Clabir Corporation, a group headed by Ralph Ehrmann, once chairman of the defunct British toy group Airfix, and supported by the English Association and its clients, had bought 7.7 per cent, sold it to the Beltzberg family in Canada, and USI had to buy it back. And the USI management did not welcome its management buy-out being wrecked.

Once again White was being opportunistic and once again it paid off, this time without a serious fight. Hanson's machines could react instantly and professionally, without needing batteries of lawyers and bankers to brief themselves or even to read themselves in. There was no question of them having to spend weeks organising the resources to make what was at that stage their biggest bid yet – they now had more than £400m, or $600m, in their balance sheet, should they need to use it. When Kelso and Co, the New York investment bank acting for the management, lifted the original $20 a share offer to $24, White responded the next day by adding another dollar to his original offer, making it $23 a share. Kelso had no real chance of responding. The management buy-out, everyone realised, would take months to organise. A month later the management caved in, and White was back on level terms with James Hanson, now with an American organisation which could boast total sales of more than $2.3bn. By itself that bid put the American end of Hanson into the 150 biggest corporations in the United States. Yet even as he put the finishing touches to the takeover, White was already looking to bigger things. He was rapidly getting into the really big league.

US Industries had been Hanson's and White's biggest, and probably their easiest, takeover yet. There would not be many more like it. Their next bid was actually one of their rare failures, although theoretically the target was a sitting duck. Hanson bought a stake in July 1983 in Powell Duffryn, a shipping, engineering and heating oil conglomerate, and, as he did with many companies, ran feasibility study after feasibility study on it. Again the timing was immaculate – Britain was half-way through a year-long miners' strike, which had depressed Powell's business, the benefits of a major rationalisation and capital programme had yet to come through to profits – and it was also Christmas time. A year earlier Hanson had spoiled the festivities at London Brick by launching his bid just as the company's Christmas party got under way. Now he did the same for Powell Duffryn, although with slightly more courtesy he announced his £150m bid in the morning, rather than his usual practice of leaving it until late afternoon when the market was closed and rival management could reasonably be expected to be fighting their way home through the rush-hour traffic. His bid-machine this time looked, as the *Sunday Times* commented, 'almost as if it were on auto-pilot'. He may have been over-confident. More likely, however, Hanson was setting out to show the City it could not always force him up, as it had done in the case of London Brick. This time again the City expected him to raise. Coolly he refused to better his terms. A majority of shareholders voted against the bid, and Powell Duffryn lived to fight another day.

As the *Economist* said at the time: 'Lord Hanson raised doubts in the City. Was he losing his touch? Has he found a juicier takeover target?' In fact it was neither. Hanson's director Martin Taylor explained that the group was merely sticking to its original view: Powell Duffryn was worth no more than it had originally offered. Hanson had abandoned that principle in the case of London Brick and was regretting it.

Hanson now began preparing himself for what many believed might be the final splurge of what had already been the greatest takeover period in the history of capitalism. There would be time for one, maybe two, more big bids in the United States before the boom had run its course. In Britain, Hanson's company, still only 21 years old, was the 15th biggest, and he wanted to get it into the top five at least before the party came to an end.

*

In the summer of 1985 Lord Hanson had a call from Geoffrey Kent, chairman of Imperial Group, one of Britain's largest and sleepiest companies. Could they meet? Hanson was immediately intrigued. He had known Kent for years, and the two of them were non-executive directors of Lloyds Bank, one of the few outside directorships that Hanson had taken. For several years he had had Imps high in his target sights. It met all his criteria: low technology (cigarettes, beer and food), underutilised assets, poor reputation in the City after years of poor performance. In the past it had posed problems for him, however: first it was too big, being two to three times his size; secondly, it had a major difficulty in the United States with its Howard Johnson motel group subsidiary.

Now however the size differential had narrowed sharply. And Imps was negotiating to sell HoJo, albeit at a substantial loss. In anticipation of his meeting with Kent, Hanson asked Martin Taylor and the acquisitions team to get out their figures on Imps again. Kent, he surmised, had at least recognised the fact that he was highly vulnerable, and that, given the type of geared takeovers that were now happening all the time in the US, it was only a matter of time before someone had a go at him. The most likely aggressor would be Hanson. Was Kent about to propose a preemptive deal?

Hanson was to be disappointed. Kent did not want to talk mergers or takeovers at all. He was, he told Hanson, thinking about strengthening his board, and he hoped Hanson would make a major addition to it. Would he be interested in joining Imperial as a non-executive director? Hiding his disappointment, Hanson courteously refused. He spent nearly half the year in the US, he said. The Lloyds board meetings fitted neatly with those of Hanson when he had to be in London. The Imps meetings did not. But from that moment on, although Kent still did not suspect it, Imperial's days of independence were running out.

CHAPTER SIX

The Pill that Poisons

Hanson's story so far is merely the prelude to the epoch-making events on both sides of the Atlantic.

So far, we have concentrated on telling the story of how the current merger frenzy has come about, of how more often than not it leaves the shareholders of both suitor and target firm with little advantage; and we have tried to make the point that the frenzy itself has had a disturbing impact on the business judgement of the financiers and chief executives who get caught up in these contests. This is not so much an indictment of the individuals as a recognition that, in the heady atmosphere of wasteful raids, the rules change in mid-play. It is hard to keep perspective when a lifetime of experience turns into the Mad Hatter's Tea Party.

In this chapter we will look at another part of the takeover dilemma: in the United States in particular, but to an increasing degree in Britain, the rule makers are at a loss about how to design a set of legal relationships for corporations that preserve the free functioning of the marketplace while at the same time providing a fair but not suffocating level of protection for the various interests involved – those of individual shareholders, institutional investors, the corporations themselves and, not least, the general public.

The US Congress lacks the research or intellectual base to understand fully what is going on in the running battles of the last five years; the lawmakers themselves are preoccupied with the more pressing conflicts of politics and their staffs are generally too thinly spread to devote much thought to legislative remedies, except for the most pressing emergencies. The perfunctory hearings held in 1985 by the House Subcommittee on Telecommunications and Finance (what kind of jurisdiction is that?) were nothing more than an opportunity for the Congressmen to trade quips with celebrities such as T. Boone Pickens, Carl Icahn and Sir James Goldsmith.

Nor has the Reagan Administration helped with its 'what merger crisis?' attitude. Even among regulatory agencies such as the SEC and FTC which maintain a fairly non-ideological attitude there has been little incentive to go beyond the rather strict jurisdictional turfs to look at the takeover frenzy in its totality. Local remedies turn out to be no better. Whenever state legislatures got involved in trying to correct takeover abuses – as New York did in the Turner raid on CBS – the lawmakers discovered the crisis was over and the situation changed before they could act effectively. As a result, Governor Mario Cuomo vetoed the new rules which were both moot and ill-considered.

Small wonder, then, that early in 1984 a frightened herd of corporate chief executives began energetically to seek out ways to protect their control over their domains. Even when there was little immediate prospect that their company would be a takeover target, bosses were circling their wagons and looking anxiously into the dark landscape for moving shadows. The world was turning upside down. One could not be too prudent.

Indeed, prudence was what was at issue. There is no national corporation law in the United States that spells out specifically the rights and duties of management. Instead, most major corporations have used the artifice of incorporating themselves in the state of Delaware because its liberal rules and technicalities are the most convenient and least onerous of the 50 states. At the same time, corporations are bound by the ever-growing body of state law court decisions; those of the federal courts are often guided by precedent-setting decisions that are tried first in the Delaware Chancery Court and which then work their way up through that state's appeals system before going on for review by federal judges and appeals panels.

Needless to say much of what constitutes corporate law in America is not law at all. Rather, it is what is understood to be the law of the moment. In part this is because of the ad hoc way in which case laws are decided. One by one, each case presents a different set of facts, each seeks some common guide for resolution, while still addressing the specific needs of plaintiffs and defendants.

Through this constantly evolving fabric of precedents, certain set standards of corporate conduct have emerged. Chief among them is the standard of prudence. A legal fiction has emerged, that of The Prudent Man. This make-believe business persona never enters into a contract that is not written or which lacks due consideration. He takes risks normal to the marketplace but only after making the enquiries and doing the diligent questioning needed to frame a rational *prudent* decision.

This mythical presumption leads to another. While case law has endorsed the idea, as Phillips Petroleum's Bill Douce has expressed it, that 'corporate management are just the keepers of the store – the real owners are the shareholders', this idea itself is relatively new. Back in the days of the South Sea Bubble management and investors were one. The whole idea of incorporation was to set up a mythical dummy which would shield the risk takers from having creditors try to collect bankruptcy debts from personal assets. Look to the corporation, the sorrowful debtors could say.

Small wonder that the nineteenth-century corporation did not have a good name. Smaller businessmen and the ordinary citizen suspected the corporation as a form of legal chicanery; all the more so towards the end of the century when monopoly was the name of that first great wave of mergers and takeovers.

The vision of management as the custodian for thousands of individual owners was a Depression era concept as economists of fifty years ago sought to create a new set of relationships that would haul the world out of an economic stagnation that was, at its most simple, an expression of universal mutual distrust.

Except that leading theorists of that day, such as Adolph Berle and Howard Means, never actually meant to imply that the shareholder-owner actually could claim his $52.50 share price worth of the *assets* of the corporation.

No, the management was the custodian all right. And management owed a duty to those shareholders not just to squander those assets away. It was a fiduciary duty that was owed, one of prudence. The corporate chief executive was expected to behave as a prudent man. So was the board of directors, especially those directors who were 'outside directors'; board members who did not hold management positions inside the company.

As for the shareholder, he had certain rights too in the theoretical kingdom. If dissatisfied, he could organise enough of his fellow shareholders and, with their proxies in his pocket, vote the current management out of office, or force on it a new corporate attitude or policy. Indeed, as this theory evolved into the 1970s the concept of 'shareholder democracy' took on an activist hue and the American corporation found itself called upon to right social ills, to be a good environmental neighbour and indeed to become a political spear-carrier for the United States in its dealings overseas, whether it meant refusing to bribe a tribal chief or in opposing political oppression.

The disaffected shareholder had another right, according to this modern corporate theory. He could sell out and buy shares in another company. It was the liquidity of the common ordinary share that was the shareholder's greatest prize, the theorists held. No prudent man could envision that shareholders would gather outside the company gates one day and actually take away corporate assets equal to their market share price. That share price was for the resale of the share, not for the liquidation of the company. Wall Street is two marketplaces, after all. There is the primary market where businesses go to raise capital through the sale of shares, notes and other instruments. And there is the secondary market for those shares and, nowadays, for options on those shares and for contracts to buy mythical groupings of shares tied to the Dow Jones and other stock indicators – themselves composites of shares.

But it was never imagined that a shareholder could wheel up a wheelbarrow, or otherwise command the dismantling of even part of the assets of the firm simply because he wanted a higher price for his shares. If one thought about it, the idea was a non sequitur; the price of a share had to do with the share and its saleability in the secondary market, not with the underlying assets, 'the break-up' or 'take-down' value of the corporation's properties.

Perhaps it was because those early theorists could not envision such a turn of events, that they never addressed such a possibility. And, since the question as such has never been taken squarely before any court, that helps us to understand why the courts have been loath to address the issue.

Instead American courts have tried to ensure that economically viable takeovers which appear fair to the target shareholders are conducted as openly as possible in the marketplace to whatever conclusion the market dictates.

Court challenges to the management responses to the American takeover frenzy of the 1980s lagged behind the public's perception of the danger. And even in 1983–4 most lawsuits were specific challenges to specific violations of the federal securities laws. One reason for the inviolability of management law was another legal fiction – the Business Judgement Rule. This rule has been a longstanding bulwark set up for management against insurgent shareholders. The rule short-circuits shareholder attempts to seek redress in the courts when their proxy battles fail to carry. The rule simply states that courts will not second guess the decisions of management or boards of directors unless there is clear evidence, provided by the plaintiffs, of the grossest self-dealing, conflicts of interest, or outright fraud.

And in the case of management responses to hostile takeover attempts, early court rulings were quick to say that the chief executives and their boards could take extraordinary steps to protect their control over corporate assets since there was a presumption that those managements were acting in the best interests of the majority of shareholders.

Fred Hartley of Unocal did not need to be told twice about these early rulings. He took what was a still developing trend and pushed it to the limit of the day, literally setting up a defence strategy that pitted the interests of one group of shareholders against another. What Hartley did with his two tier share repurchase offer was say that management could single out a bloc of ostensibly anonymous shares held by hostile forces and discriminate against them and their holders and the Business Judgement Rule would protect him in court.

An interesting footnote is to speculate what would have happened if the merger battles we will examine later in this chapter had been fought out on Hartley's line. For 60 years the New York Stock Exchange has stood alone in its demand that for corporations listed on its trading posts, each share of stock shall carry an equal voting right to all other common shares of that company. Other stock exchanges, even the over-the-counter market, have allowed various classes of common voting stock with some having more voting power than others. Indeed the notion that corporations can set such standards is now even honoured at the New York Stock Exchange where two dozen member firms want the SEC to permit variations on the one-share-one-vote theme as a flexible anti-takeover weapon that, at least insofar as Boone Pickens was concerned, was unassailable.

Yet others were watching and looking for newer weapons and tactics. By 1985 it could be noted that the public outcry over bust-up takeovers was being reflected in the courts. Martin Lipton, a senior partner of the New York firm of Wachtell, Lipton, Rosen & Katz is one of those scholarly, gentle members of the bar who give the legal profession the veneer of academic sanctity that it cherishes so much.

Lipton had concluded back in the late 1970s that an increasing number of takeover bids were aimed less at improving the manufacturing competitiveness or productivity profits of target firms and increasingly aimed at closing the perceived gap between what a company's shares might fetch on the stock market and what the company's assets might fetch if put on some hypothetical auction block.

'In the last three years, we have had a dramatic shift to an objective of achieving financial profit by busting up the acquired company. We've had a shift in the factors that affect the relationship of share price to takeover price,' Lipton says.*

'Greenmail,' he went on, has become part of our everyday vocabulary and takeover abuses have become a pressing national problem. During the past three years there has been sharp growth in highly-leveraged takeovers by entrepreneurs who are not interested in operating the target companies, but seek the opportunity for profit through greenmail, bust-up liquidation of the target or forcing a white knight transaction that usually also results in bust-up liquidation of the target. These takeovers are not for the purpose of diversification, expansion or growth, but are financial transactions for the profit of the takeover entrepreneurs. They do not add to the national wealth. They merely rearrange ownership interests by substituting lenders for shareholders and shift risk from equity owners to creditors. They place our banking system and credit markets in jeopardy and restrict the ability of the affected businesses to grow and provide increased productivity and employment.

Not that Lipton opposes all takeovers or mergers.

The Reagan Council of Economic Advisers and the Office of Management and Budget, as well as a large number of private economists, argue that hostile takeovers move assets of the targets into the hands of more efficient management and therefore are economically desirable. This is correct with respect to soundly financed acquisitions by operating companies that are seeking to diversify or expand. Mergers by successful operating companies have been an integral part of our economic development. They should not be restricted. They improve the economy. But this is not true with respect to bust-up liquidation takeovers by takeover entrepreneurs. They do not move assets into more efficient management. They move assets into hands that profit by reducing expenditures for research and development and capital improvements. After a highly-leveraged takeover, a very high percentage of the revenues produced by the acquired assets are diverted to paying the debt incurred to acquire the assets.†

*Interview with authors.
†Interview with authors and testimony before US Senate Subcommittee on Securities, 3 April, 1985.

Lipton's argument rings true enough from some of what we have seen. But it does not answer the tough underlying question. How does the casual lay observer – judge, stock analyst or investor – tell the difference between a takeover bid that is 'economically desirable' and a 'bust-up liquidation'? The problem is compounded for the besieged (or apprehensive) corporate manager who is haunted by a 'takeover entrepreneur' who has been happy in the past to take the 'greenmail' or to strip valuable assets away from conquests but who protests mightily that *this time* his motives reflect a wholesome desire to operate the target company more efficiently. What if he's telling the truth?

Theory and philosophy are further complicated by reality. Take Jules Kroll of New York who formed his own private detective agency staffed largely by other ex-federal prosecutors and FBI agents. The agency's original focus was tracking down corporate miscreants – the patent stealer, the embezzler – but during the early 1980s the Kroll firm became the pre-eminent 'due diligence' investigators for the merger and takeover combatants. If you wanted to determine the accuracy of an annual report, get a vivid character reading of a firm's top executives or just find out whether an unwanted suitor really had his finances lined up properly, Jules Kroll was the man you turned to, that is, if the other side had not already lined him up on their side.

Kroll observes,

You have to beware of the temptation to portray these guys as chess players who operate in some rarified atmosphere. I suspect that we have worked with most of the major players in the takeover era at one time or another. First off, most are men of their word. And most do have a philosophy that does guide their decisions. Certainly Marty Lipton does.

But Marty Lipton does not operate in a vacuum. Neither does Joe Flom; none of them do. In Lipton's case, their firm is very small by Wall Street standards, only eighty-five partners or so. What that means is that everybody is extremely busy all the time and everybody is usually involved in whatever is going on. So Marty does not just sit there like some guru and hand out new ideas. It's the other way around. He has guys like Ed Herlihy just as Joe Flom has his Finn Fogg, who are always thinking, always coming up with new ideas, new tactics, new ways to finance this or that. And when a specific set of facts lends itself to trying one idea or another, then they run it by Marty and he tests it against his own intuition, his own analysis, his own philosophy, if you will, before they go ahead. That's how it works, very fluid, very busy, very creative and, of course, very risky. If it weren't risky there would not be any need for our services, would there?

Kroll is right. In a sense, the merger wars of the 1980s are not ideological contests at all; rather there is an underlying willingness by both sides to let the market sort out such final questions as to moral right and wrong. Of course this makes a hash of the myth of Marty Lipton and his struggles with his leading adversary in so many of the major takeover battles of the decade, Joseph Flom of the firm of Skadden, Arps, Slate, Meagher & Flom. Lipton and Flom are personal friends, the myth has it, and this has led the business press to repeat the fiction that they lunch together every Wednesday the way two old warring generals might get together to push the salt shakers and wine glass about the table as they relive their greatest battles.

Aside from the fact that the clubby weekly lunches are a fiction, such a press conceit diminishes the deep feelings both men have for their points of view. Neither is a cynical hack for hire. Just as Lipton genuinely opposes the economically destructive bust-up brand of takeovers, Flom genuinely puts his faith in the marketplace as final arbiter. Who knows better how to deal with a Boone Pickens? And of course, by the time Unocal was wiping up the last of the bits of business left over from the Pickens raid, Flom and Lipton were not seeing each other socially that often anyway. Flom by then had become the gun you hire when you want to stage a takeover raid; just as one hired Lipton to set up the defences if you were the target.

In fact, Flom and Lipton were on opposite sides of two battles already brewing over a little invention of Lipton's that was the potential Doomsday Weapon of the takeover battlefield – a manoeuvre called the Share Purchase Rights Plan, known forever more as the Poison Pill Defence.

In the summer of 1984, Lipton had convinced two corporate clients to adopt share repurchase plans that effectively poisoned any investment a raider might make in a target company if he triggered the plan. According to the outline of the strategy, any time a raider aquired a certain percentage of a target's assets (say 50 per cent), or merged with another company, then a 'flip-over' provision would be triggered that would allow the remaining shareholders to buy newly issued shares in the target (or the newly merged firm) for half price. So whether a raider bought stock on the open market or stampeded his target into the arms of a white knight, his investment would be instantly diluted by hundreds of millions of dollars. The target management, however, was still free to seek favourable deals by merely buying back the repurchase rights and cancelling them by purchasing them from shareholders at 50 cents each. This latter safety catch also allowed shareholders themselves to respond to tender offers from white knights which might be deemed more favourable.

In the case of Crown Zellerbach, the forest products giant, a fail-safe provision was added since management was convinced that Sir James Goldsmith had already begun to buy up their shares. Once any holder had acquired more than 20 per cent of Crown Zellerbach shares, the 'flip-over' provision was activated and could not be repurchased by the board for at least ten years.

An earlier version had been sold to an Illinois-based financial services conglomerate, Household International, but had run into immediate objections from some shareholders who feared that the poison pill would drive away all potential suitors and merely preserve management's control at a penalty to the share price. John Moran, one of the shareholders, had hired Flom, who in turn had deputised no less than Irving Shapiro, the recently retired chairman of DuPont and now legal associate, to conduct a test of the poison pill defence in the Delaware Courts. One point of attack was that no-one was actually pursuing Household.

The same could not be said of Crown Zellerbach. If anyone had a reputation for being a predatory asset stripper it was Sir James Goldsmith, another survivor from the Slater era who had in the late 1970s sought his fortune in the United States. Goldsmith is in many ways the most interesting of all the raiders, a man who abided by few conventions or mores, and who had spread controversy across three countries. As Geoffrey Wansell, who has written two biographies of Goldsmith, said of him:

> There is none of the restraint of a financier about him. He lives out the fantasies of others with a flamboyance that is unmistakable. His takeovers have been some of the largest and most controversial in the history of the United States economy. His political opinions have attracted the strongest criticism in France and Great Britain. His unorthodox private life has been the subject of persistent speculation throughout the world. It is a lack of inhibition that still attracts the strongest reactions. To his enemies he is always a monster, to his friends an angel.

Goldsmith's career had been chequered, verging from the edge of bankruptcy to millionaire several times. But by 1978 he had built up one of the largest grocery businesses in the world, with the highly successful Grand Union stores in the United States and his Cavenham foods business in Britain which included Liptons and Presto stores. But he had also become depressed by Britain, then still under a Labour government. He had fought a long and savage libel case against *Private Eye*, which called him Goldenballs and sneered at his political views. He had created one of Britain's most successful companies, but in the atmosphere of the time that was more a cause for sneers than accolades. Goldsmith himself became increasingly bitter and critical. In 1979 he spoke at the annual convention of the Institute of Directors at the Albert Hall and uncomfortably reminded his audience of a few home truths: Britain's share of world trade had declined from 25 per cent to 8 per cent since the war; the average standard of living, which 25 years before was among the highest in the world, was now around the same level as Spain or Greece; steel production per man was a quarter that of the US steel industry; and so on. 'Economically, in one generation we have been transformed from a rich country into a poor country.' He was listened to in stony silence.

He remained domiciled in France where he had grown up, but when that country elected a socialist president in François Mitterand, Goldsmith cut many of his ties there too. Except for a few small interests – the Laurent restaurant and the magazine *L'Express* in Paris, a stake in Aspinall's casino in London, plus families by different women in both capitals – Goldsmith was finished with Britain and France. 'It seemed to me that both nations were set on paths which, unless radically changed, would lead to decline, poverty and unhappiness,' he wrote later in his book *Pour La Revolution Permanente*. 'And perhaps to subjugation.'

Goldsmith's first major bid in the United States, for the forestry group Diamond Corporation, illustrates clearly the gambler's instinct at work, and the type of chances the raiders are prepared to take. After several years of stalking and being rebuffed, he eventually made a cash bid of over $660m. 'I was going to be borrowing $660m at 16 or 17 per cent,' he said later.* 'The interest payments alone were $120 to $130m a year, and Diamond was losing money. It wasn't just double or quits, it was worse. It could well have been costing me more than $180m in a year to hold on to the whole company when it was losing money.' He was banking everything on Wall Street turning up. 'If my view was wrong, even by a year, I was blown away, bye-bye.' Not without difficulty, Drexel Burnham found $440m of the money he needed, and he sold his British food interests to James Gulliver for the rest.

By the end of 1982 the Diamond board had caved in and Goldsmith began one of the biggest and most successful liquidations of the whole

Tycoon, by Geoffrey Wansell.

takeover boom. Within seven months of the takeover he sold six Diamond divisions for $334m; in the next three months another three went for $253m. Goldsmith repaid all his $436m of bank loans plus Diamond's existing debts of $162m. He was left with 1.6m acres of timberland in Northern California and New England. Goldsmith's profit on the deal was at least $500m. By the summer of 1983 his declared shareholdings in his companies were valued at $940m – a four-fold increase in a year. From now on Goldsmith was taken very seriously indeed on Wall Street. He ploughed some of his profits back into St Regis Corp and the Continental Group, in each case surrendering his shareholding for a handsome profit. The *New York Times* began a main editorial by saying, 'T. Boone Pickens... Carl Icahn... Saul Steinberg... Irwin Jacobs... Sir James Goldsmith. Their names are spoken with a shudder in boardrooms from Pittsburgh to Bartlesville. They are the new buccaneers of capitalism, making millions by taking over, or just threatening to take over, America's largest corporations.'

Yet the concept of Goldsmith as a dangerous destroyer of companies does not stand up well to close examination. He had owned the Grand Union grocery chain in the US for more than a decade before his emigration from France and Britain, and he has promoted and redesigned the network into the number three, ranking behind Safeway and Kroger nationwide. In St Regis, as would be the case of Crown Zellerbach, Goldsmith's strategy had been concentrated on forest products, an investment he believes has tremendous long-term prospects. One does not invest in trees for the short haul; but whatever Goldsmith's motives, Crown Zellerbach were not having any of it.

The run on Crown Zellerbach started in December 1984, when Goldsmith began buying shares quietly on the open market. In April, Sir James got Drexel Burnham to arrange a junk bond financing so he could offer $42.50 a share for the remaining Crown shares. Just as quickly, the takeover bid came unstuck when a counterproposal from Mead Corp vanished as mysteriously as it had been proposed.

So back went Goldsmith to the open market, but this time he was not the only buyer of Crown stock – Dennis B. Levine, who was one of the senior managers in Drexel's merger department, would later stand accused of plunging heavily into Crown stock based on the inside information he was gleaning from meetings with Goldsmith. This would not come out of course until a year after the deal was over and Levine was embroiled in the headline-grabbing scandal with Ivan Boesky.

On 14 May, 1985, Goldsmith's holdings of Crown Zellerbach crossed the 20 per cent mark and the poison pill provision was

Ernest Saunders, chairman and chief executive of Guinness. This picture was taken in his office in the middle of the bid for Arthur Bell when his reputation stood high.

Tiny Rowland, Lonrho's chief executive, fought for eight years to win House of Fraser.

Professor Roland Smith fought Rowland off – and agreed to a bid from the Fayed Brothers.

Mohamed Al Fayed, eldest of the three Egyptian brothers who now own Fraser.

Sir Hugh Fraser, the tragic figure caught in the centre of the bloodiest takeover battle of all.

T. Boone Pickens, the man who changed
the world of Big Oil.

William Douce, chairman of Phillips
Petroleum. Life was never the same
after Pickens.

Carl Icahn, winner of TWA, and master
of the use of "junk bonds".

Ivan Boesky, king of the Wall Street
"arbs", enjoying the Phillips battle.

Ted Turner put CBS "into play" – but in the end his fees totalled more than his profits.

Rupert Murdoch's takeover bids have made him the biggest media tycoon in history.

Sir James Goldsmith's takeover of Diamond Corporation was one of the most profitable in the history of takeovers.

The Hanson Trust twins: Lord Hanson (left) and Sir Gordon White. Among the most professional – and most successful –practitioners of the hostile bid.

Sir Hector Laing, the gentle and evangelical head of United Biscuits, who found himself up against Hanson.

The City's takeover kings: Christopher Reeves (left), chief executive of Morgan Grenfell: and Roger Seelig, sought out by Ernest Saunders to win Distillers for him.

The watchdogs: Sir Godfray Le Quesne (left), chairman of the Monopolies Commission; and Sir Gordon Borrie (right), director-general of the Office of Fair Trading, who decided which bids to refer to the commission.

James Gulliver, the boy from Campbeltown, who came close to becoming the world's biggest distiller.

Lord Weinstock dropped his support for Gulliver.

The winning team: toasting Guinness's victory over Distillers (from left) Thomas Ward, the Washington lawyer; Ernest Saunders; Vic Steel, the Guinness executive put in to run Distillers; and the French consultant, Olivier Roux, who acted as Guinness's finance director.

Sir Thomas Risk. Saunders changed his mind and refused to have him as chairman.

Gerald Ronson, a leading bidder himself, supported the Guinness bid.

The insiders: Dennis Levine (left), the first "big fish" caught by the SEC. He led the investigators to others. Marty Siegal (right).

triggered. By 4 July another compromise that looked set with Crown management collapsed and Goldsmith pushed ahead and acquired 50 per cent of the shares. On 22 July, Goldsmith flew to San Francisco to become chairman of Crown Zellerbach. Goldsmith's task now was to dismantle the poison pill trip wires, prise loose the forest products division and sell the rest off to recover the best profit possible.

The poison pill defence at this point looked tough to beat. The Delaware Supreme Court would soon uphold the Household poison pill provision which had the disadvantages of not having an active pursuer and being challenged by current shareholders as well. The day after Goldsmith arrived in San Francisco, Martin Lipton's invention was explained by Revlon's general council in a meeting of the board of directors in New York City.

Revlon had reason to be worried. A month before, Ronald Perelman, chairman of the aggressive Pantry Pride, had told Michel de Bergerac, chairman of Revlon, the cosmetics manufacturer, that he was interested in a friendly takeover priced in the $40 to $50 range. Bergerac dismissed the offer but took the intention seriously enough. On 14 August, Pantry Pride's board authorised Perelman to offer $42 to $43 a share for Revlon if it was a friendly takeover, otherwise he could go as high as $45.

The Marty Lipton prescription that Revlon purchased to ward off Pantry Pride gave existing shareholders a dividend in the form of rights to exchange each common share held for $65 worth of notes. This dividend was to be triggered whenever anyone acquired at least 20 per cent of Revlon's shares, unless the acquirer promptly bought up the 8 per cent balance for at least $65. Before being triggered the management could redeem the rights for 10 cents.

Even though the Delaware court system had supported the poison pill genre of defences, that support had been qualified. Basically what the judges had said was that the Business Judgement Rule which protects managements and directors blocked the courts from second guessing tactics such as rights issues. But in the Household case particularly the various courts which heard the case in Delaware agreed that while the share rights plan was permissible, it also imposed a higher duty on the board to make sure that subsequent takeover offers, which increased the price offered, would be dealt with in good faith and with the shareholders' interests in mind.

Moreover, Marty Lipton realised that at some time, in some state court *somewhere* his invention would run into a judge who would rule against it; what that would do is tip the weighing scales of court precedent back to zero and increase the risk that all of his plans would end up being challenged in the federal courts. Not that Lipton minded fighting in federal courts; it was losing that he minded very much.

More to the point, Lipton's arch rival Joseph Flom of Skadden Arps was developing a counter-argument of his own which was being tested out in those same state courts. Specifically, in a case involving Dart Group Corp's efforts to take over Safeway Stores of Oakland, California, Flom argued that Safeway's shareholder rights plan violated the law by issuing 'fictitious warrants or options with no economic value'. The argument was that a defender management's issuance of rights to buy a large volume of existing shares for a small price was beyond the power of the board of directors and that it violated tender offer laws for the state (Maryland, in this case) and the Commerce Clause of the US Constitution.

Flom's position might have been stronger if Skadden Arps had not been advising dozens of clients into share rights plans remarkably akin to the one deemed unconstitutional in the Dart-Safeway conflict. But the point was taken; share rights plans were all right for the moment. But some variation, some more potent elaboration of the theme, would have to be found by Lipton for his growing list of corporate patients.

He could not know it at the time but the battle for Revlon would give him his first test case and a more significant example was getting underway at that very moment.

Another polished Engishman decided to yield to a hunch as he reviewed a list of possible American takeover targets. In early July Sir Gordon White began to buy a small amount of shares in SCM Corp, at one time the old Smith-Corona typewriter concern, but then a conglomerate which owned Durkee's Famous Foods, paint and pigments divisions and other profitable properties. He sent a copy of the annual report to Lord Hanson in London and set his two assistants, Chris Guntner and Eric Hanson (no relation to Lord Hanson) to work on a report on SCM's prospects and how they might fit in with Hanson's.

At the end of July 1985 the shares of SCM stood at $45 on Wall Street and White had concluded he might be able to take the company over if he offered $60. The next step was to appoint a merchant bank to help raise the money. He had no regular bank at this time although Hanson had used N.M. Rothschild in London for 20 years. White had met and liked Robert Pirie who had turned the New York branch, Rothschild and Company, into a major takeover player.

Pirie, at 51, was something of a Wall Street character in his own right. Indeed, Wall Street was of two minds about Bob Pirie.

... the scion of Chicago's Carso Pirie Scott department-store furniture has no trouble standing out in a crowd – *any* crowd. He's the kind of guy who put in a bid for an island off the coast of Britain with 'cousin Adlai' Stevenson III, the former US senator and son of the late Democratic Party standard bearer, while still at Harvard College and the kind who, while at Harvard Law School, bought a vast estate outside Boston. He's the kind of guy who collects rare books and who moors his 50-foot sloop at Northeast Harbor in Maine in the warmer months and at Virgin Gorda when it's colder. He is, in the words of his admirers, 'a gentleman', a bona fide 'class act', a man Skadden Arps's Joseph Flom lauds for his 'catholicity' of interests.*

What caused less flattering descriptions of Pirie by competitors was a tough-minded attitude and fearlessness which White found attractive; he played the investment game with no thought of ever losing. Pirie shoved Rothschild into the big leagues of investment advising by offering clients a personal style of concentrated service while cutting prices for those services well below what the heavier-weight firms charged – fees cut as low as one per cent of the value of the transaction.

Pirie was busy charting the strategy for Sir James Goldsmith as he slogged through the negotiations that would, at the end of 1985, result in taking over Crown Zellerbach. What Pirie had done was find a way of defusing the poison pill tripwire which Crown management had set up against Goldsmith; he simply triggered the explosion so the damage was done to Crown itself and not to his client.

'As long as we didn't do a merger, we didn't trigger the pill and that made the pill a tremendous weapon on our side in a transaction, and against the management. That was something they never dreamed of. Crown management never sat down and figured out what way we were going until it was too late,' Pirie recalled later.†

In effect, if Goldsmith was not actually after a merger, it followed that if he triggered the share rights distribution by buying a majority of Crown shares, then it made it impossible for Crown management to recruit a white knight rival.

'I talked to one of their bankers later and he told me that when Sir James got over 19 per cent they were convinced we would quit. They never imagined that we didn't give a goddamn about the pill and that when we triggered it, it made it impossible for them to find anybody else to merge with,' Pirie said.

Institutional Investor, March 1986.
† Interview with authors.

Still, the tricky part lay ahead for the Pirie-Goldsmith-Fogg team; the trick was to dismantle the poison pill mechanism so it would not explode a second time, this time against the new controlling interest of Sir James Goldsmith who wanted to sell Crown's paper division to James River Paper. That would send Crown's rights holders into high gear to buy Crown shares at 50 cents on the dollar.

'The plan was to be seen, in the legal sense, to be exchanging property, not to merge Crown properties with James River. We had to come up with something that would be agreeable both to the courts and to Crown's other shareholders,' Pirie said.

The battle for Crown thus shifted out of the investment banker's hands and back into those of Joseph Fogg who took until the end of 1985 to hammer out a complex swap of timber lands, cash and legal agreements that gave Goldsmith control of Crown so that he could sell off the pieces he wanted to James River while paying the pillholders an estimated $20m *not* to exercise their rights.

This left Pirie free to take on Hanson's battle for SCM Corp. and by 2 August White was in London, fresh from a Mediterranean holiday, ready to do combat. On 21 August White and Hanson flew back to New York in Concorde. Between mid-July and that Monday, 19 August, White's staff had been quietly accumulating small blocks of SCM shares until they now held a small 2.9 per cent interest in the company. It was also obvious to White and Hanson that others, including management, were buying into SCM as well. Whether prodded by inside information or keen guessing, the trading in SCM pushed the price of the shares up steadily from $46.75 when White first authorised the buys to nearly $56 a share in mid-August.

So it was now or never as far as Hanson was concerned. White now had two studies available to him, one from his own staff, one prepared by Pirie at Rothschild. But for one of the most successful bids ever made – and Hanson's biggest to date – it was all remarkably casual. The SCM accounts were still on Hanson's desk, barely read. Rothschild had produced its report on 7 August, and that too had barely been glanced at – White admitted in his court deposition later that he had barely skimmed it. Even the discussion between the two men was, according to both their testimonies, remarkably cursory. 'Going out in the car to the airport to catch the plane, Gordon said to me "I am due to have a meeting tomorrow with Robert Pirie of Rothschild whom I have engaged to advise us on this,"' said Hanson. There was no talk about values, what price to go at, or the tactics to be used. When he was questioned later on how he *did* value it, White simply said, 'I've got a few simple formulae on which I work.'*

*Interview with the authors.

On SCM I could see from the accounts that they had a corporate overhead costing $35m a year. I walked down Park Avenue and I looked at their offices, and saw that it was a nice 160,000 square feet of office. That could go. Then I saw that in the last year they had made a profit of $115m. I was going to borrow all the money, and we went up to $930m. Now we were paying 10 per cent, so I estimated that 10 per cent of $930m is only $93m. And if you add on $35m of overhead savings, plus the sale of their office, I reckoned profits in the short term were running at $160m. That means I could in theory have gone all the way up to $1.6bn if I had needed to – although I wouldn't have done.

At that stage I had no intention of selling anything off. But then ICI and Reckitt & Colman, two British companies, approached me during the bid, asking to sell them the paints and food divisions. I said, well, we'll see after the bid. But we could see there was potential there.

The price White at the time intended offering was well below this level: he decided to go at $60 a share, valuing SCM at just over $800m. That in fact was what the Rothschild report valued the company at. White's 'gut feeling' was in the event a far better guide to the true value.

That afternoon in Hanson's Park Avenue office White borrowed a sheet of Hanson's London notepaper, and addressed a note to SCM chairman Paul H. Erlicker informing him that Hanson intended to make a tender offer for control and that he wanted to discuss a friendly takeover.

An attempt to telephone Erlicker was unsuccessful because the SCM boss had no intention of talking to any possible unwanted suitor. There was a very good reason: the SCM management was already involved in discussing a possible leveraged buyout that would put him in the driver's seat for good. The Hanson bid could not have come at a more inconvenient time; the SCM management had to act quickly or stand to lose a fortune and their jobs as well.

SCM management were not the only persons moving quickly. On the very day that Hanson and White were flying to New York, the shares of SCM had suddenly soared by $8 to close at $63. The next day they jumped another $1.25 after Erlicker told the *New York Times* he wanted to 'see this management in an independent mode'. The market was also prompted that a fight was brewing by analysts' predictions that SCM was really worth 12 to 13 times earnings (not the ten times of Hanson's offer) and that meant a probable final price closer to $73 to

$79 a share. Among the undervalued properties noted in various newspaper articles was SCM's 'flourishing titanium dioxide business ... SCM's most attractive asset. Titanium dioxide is a white pigment used in paint and other products,' as the *New York Times* noted on 23 August, 1985.

Still, Hanson and White stuck to their schedule of making their tender offer begin on Monday, 25 August even though the intervening two days gave both arbitrageurs and SCM management an effective free period to make their own plans.

On Thursday, Erlicker and SCM's advisers from Goldman Sachs met with Martin Lipton and determined to push through the leveraged buy-out which had been on the minds of senior SCM management since July. It was then that the company had authorised 'golden parachute' triple pay cheques for 23 of its top executives in the event that any outsider bought 20 per cent of its shares and then forced any of them out within two years.

Also as part of the deal SCM agreed to pay Goldman Sachs a fee-and-bonus deal for finding a buyer for a leveraged buy-out that would still leave the management with at least a 15 per cent interest in the surviving company. The deal specified that in the event an outsider acquired 25 per cent of SCM's shares, the company would pay Goldman Sachs a 4 per cent bonus on the portion of any share sale over $60 a share. SCM also would pay $625,000 every three months for the next year to the investment brokers while they sought such a friendly buyer.*

Goldman Sachs' Willard Overlock was enthusiastic about the group's chances to defeat Hanson. Kohlberg, Kravis, Roberts and Co., the merger partners, were interested. So, too, were a group of senior executives at Merrill Lynch's venture capital division. The idea was to draft at least the preliminary outline of such a plan and have a working agreement from the prospective buyer already in place when Erlicker summoned the entire SCM board of directors for a meeting at the company's 299 Park Avenue offices. At that point, the directors had not even been informed that the company was under siege unless they had read the news in the morning papers. They would not be consulted until Sunday, 25 August, the day before Hanson's tender became effective.

In the meantime, Marty Lipton had other irons thrust into his fire. On Friday, 23 August, Pantry Pride began its tender offer for Revlon at $47.50 a share. On Monday, as prearranged, the Revlon board would reject the bid and put its own leveraged buyout scheme into

Wall Street Journal, 27 August 1985.

motion. There was little to worry the small (only 88 lawyers) Wachtell Lipton firm; their principle deals were well under control. Even SCM could be won.

At 11 am, that Sunday, SCM's 12-man board met their defence team; Overlock, Charles Davis, Christopher Flowers and Barry Zubrow from Goldman Sachs plus Lipton and his top aides Ed Herlihy, Eric Roth and Steven Rosenbloom. Also on hand was Benjamin Stapleton II of Sullivan and Cromwell, the law firm retained by Goldman actually to go into court, if need be, and fight the litigation battles.

The minutes of this meeting, and the lengthy depositions that were taken later on from those who were present, make astonishing reading for anyone who has accepted the notion that directors, especially outside (non-management) directors, are an effective check and balance on behalf of the shareholders' interests.

After Overlock delivered Goldman Sachs' opinion that the Hanson bid was too low, Lipton took over and put the case for a leveraged buy-out either with Kohlberg, Kravis and Roberts or the Merrill Lynch partners. As the record showed, the directors in the main sat mutely through the exercise. No-one asked what chances there were that Hanson could be pushed into a higher offer and, if so, whether such a higher bid might be acceptable. No-one asked whether the LBO being put together would be in the best interests of SCM or the shareholders.

On Friday, 30 August, the SCM board met again, to view the latest Lipton creation. The new SCM Corp. would include Erlicker and the other managers, plus the Merrill Lynch investment partnership. The deal would be a $70 a share cash offer for 85 per cent of SCM's existing shares and the remainder to be paid off with junk bonds valued at the same $70 price. The SCM management would own no less than 15 per cent of the company. Prudential-Bache would help with the financing.

The deal was a sweetheart for the Merrill Lynch partners. For openers there would be a 'hello fee' for agreeing to the deal that was worth $1.5m. Then there was the 'good-bye fee' of an additional $9m which would be paid in the event that an outside party acquired more than one-third of SCM's shares at a price of $62 or more. In effect, SCM's directors were being asked to pony up the equivalent of $1 per outstanding share of their own shares to attract someone who wasn't even offering to buy the whole company. It was an expensive way to rent $450m (for that was the extent of the Merrill Lynch partner's funds) but the SCM management and their legal advisers were in a hurry. As an afterthought, Lipton also told the board that Merrill Lynch wanted 'reimbursement of expenses and indemnification against all losses in connection with its acquisition proposal'.

That final disclosure finally did provoke some of the outside board members but that line of questioning was quickly subdued by Goldman Sachs' Overlock who noted that the size of the deal merited such protection. After all, the SCM board was raising $854m with approximately $129m of that amount still having to be raised in the junk bond market. Now was no time for dissension. Indeed, if the board would act today, the whole deal could be commenced on 9 September, just ten days away.

After all the parties returned from the Labour Day weekend on Tuesday, 3 September, the bidding contest began in earnest. The SCM board approved the definitive agreement with the management – Merrill Lynch group that morning offering $70 cash for 85 per cent of SCM's shares and junk bonds for the rest. White immediately retaliated by publicly announcing that Hanson had upped its all cash offer to $72 in cash. But, suspecting that the Merrill Lynch partners might be demanding, White added the condition that SCM must not grant any 'lock-up' options to another bidder which would enable them to carry off one or more of the company's prize assets as booty.

Pirie also tried conciliation. He called Marty Lipton and suggested a meeting which would work towards some sort of compromise. 'I said I think it would make sense for our clients to get together. Maybe there is something we can discuss, maybe there is something that can be worked out here.'

He was not prepared for the explosion from the other end of the telephone. The normally controlled, gentle Lipton shouted that Hanson and White were 'bad people' and that he would never allow the SCM management to speak to them. Pirie asked what was bothering him so much about the Hanson Trust duo. Lipton charged that they had never paid a legal fee due to Wachtell Lipton in their bid for US Industries.

Pirie, who has a disdain for such cheap tactics, confessed surprise and shock and offered to straighten the matter out. After checking it out thoroughly, he found that Hanson's had indeed paid Wachtell Lipton's legal bill and he called Lipton to assure him of that fact and to renew the request for a meeting with SCM's management, if not the board itself. But the lawyer was adamant. There would be no discussion of any deal whereby Hanson would end up with any part of SCM.

What Pirie did not know at the time was that the SCM-Merrill Lynch partnership was already on the move to a more elaborate and more profitable merger relationship. For public consumption the announcement was made that Merrill Lynch had dropped out of the bidding. The $9m 'goodbye fee' was not triggered but, at the partners' request, SCM management transferred the corporate funds into an escrow account payable to the partners, while the talks continued.

One of the early points of agreement was that if a new agreement were to be reached, the Merrill Lynch partners would get a $6m signing bonus (the Hanson lawyers would later insist on referring to this in court documents as the 'hello again fee'). Other fees were insisted upon. The Merrill Lynch partners were designated the investment bankers for the deal (fee, $8m) and they were given a 'dealer-manager' fee worth $2.75m. Thus even as the deal came out of the starting blocks, the Merrill Lynch partners were ahead of the game by a cool $27.5m.

The deal itself would better Hanson's bid by $2 more a share to $74. But, of that total SCM shareholders were to get $59.20 in cash and the rest in junk bonds. But the best was yet to come.

SCM management still wanted to end up in control of a company that was virtually takeover proof. They needed the money offered by the Merrill Lynch partnership. Lipton's latest invention, 'the crown jewel lock-up', fulfilled all those needs.

The 'lock-up' was a device that had the effect of letting the Merrill Lynch partners carry away the most attractive bits of SCM in the event that the unwanted suitors, Hanson, began to close in on control of the overall company. By promising to sell off the crown jewels and locking them up for the favoured suitors, SCM executives secured themselves some cash to continue their own war for control, while making the company less attractive to Hanson.

And what a bargain the deal was. The option gave the Merrill Lynch partners the option to buy the two most profitable divisions for obviously cut-rate prices. Specifically, the option gave the partners the right to buy SCM's pigments business for $350m and the Durkee Famous Foods firm for another $80m. In other words the partners had an option to buy, for $430m, SCM properties which other analysts (and not just those hired by Hansons' lawyers) firmly held were worth $125m to $195m more than that (and in the event to be worth even more). All that plus the various hello and goodbye fees. All that to coax a group of supposed strangers into making a takeover offer that provided SCM's putative 'owners', the shareholders, with $14.80 a share *less* cash than Hansons' improved bid.*

*Hanson Trust plc v. ML SCM Acquisition Inc., 774 F 2d 47 (2d Cir. 1985). Also note Revlon Inc. v. MacAndrews & Forbes Inc. Fed Sec L. Rep (CCH) para 92,357 (Del 1 Nov. 1985) and Moran v. Household International Inc., Fed Sec L. Rep. (CCH) para. 92,371 (Del Nov. 19, 1985).

Now it was Sir Gordon White's turn to take a gamble. On 11 September, the day after the new SCM deal was unveiled, White announced that Hanson had dropped its $72 a share cash bid. Even as that information was being sent about town on the financial news wire, White and Pirie were busy buying SCM shares from arbitrageurs at prices shaded to within 50 cents of its $74 a share old bid. The market tickers began to pick up the trades and before the closing bell roughly 3.1m SCM shares had been taken out of the market and into the Hanson holdings. The *New York Times* (12 September, 1985) reported that 'Ivan F. Boesky, the Wall Street arbitrageur, who reported as late as a week ago that he owned about 1.1m SCM shares, is thought to have sold them yesterday to Hanson. The sale price was said to be $73.50 a share. Neither Mr Boesky, who was said to be in an airplane, nor Robert Pirie, president of Rothschild Inc., adviser to Hanson, returned phone calls for comment.'

The White-Pirie gamble was a daring one. In order for the SCM investors to trigger all the parts of the merger agreement, the shareholders had to turn over to the Merrill Lynch and SCM executives 67 per cent of the oustanding shares or at least 8.25 million. Every shape held by Hanson was one less for the opposition. By spending $23m in a few hours, Hanson had bought up nearly 25 per cent of the outstanding shares, bringing its total holdings to nearly 30 per cent. White and Pirie were very close to triggering the 'lock-up' option.

Indeed, they actually may have triggered the device. It all depends on whether one counts the percentage of shares in the hands of Hanson against the number of present common shares or the number of possible common shares once all the convertible and preferred stock was factored in.

The SCM-Merrill partners immediately cried foul on two counts. One was the lightning raid on their shares by White and Pirie just hours after they had publicly dropped their bid. Surely that violated federal securities laws. And they protested against Hanson plans to contest the 'lock-up' option which had been allegedly set in motion already.

The next step was into the courtroom. SCM immediately charged Hanson with violating the Williams Act, the federal law which requires that takeover bids observe a 20-day auction period. By secretly buying up SCM shares, the Sullivan and Cromwell lawyers charged, Hanson was breaking the law. They applied to the US District Court for the Southern District for an order requiring Hanson to divest itself of its purchases and for an injunction barring them from buying more shares. Hanson's lawyers applied for a stay order until the case could be heard before a judge. There also were counter-charges about whether the 66 per cent trigger had been tripped by the Hanson purchases.

Sometimes the gods step into the affairs of men and amuse themselves by throwing a wild card into the game. In this case the wild card proved to be the Honourable Shirley Wohl Kram, a former New York domestic relations court judge who had been elevated by the Carter Administration to the federal bench. Judge Kram complained that she did not understand what was going on during some of the more complicated stages of the proceedings.

But as is a time honoured remedy of the bench, Judge Kram made up for her own uncertain grasp by opening the record to almost every submission by both sides – including some of the most genuinely funny deposition records around – and then bucking the whole matter up to the District Court of Appeals to settle.

To add a surreal note, the SCM–Merrill Lynch group was represented by two attorneys with the same name: Bernard Nussbaum, one a courtly partner in the Chicago firm of Sonnenshein, Carlin Ranth and Rosenthal of Chicago; the other, from Wachtell Lipton, introduced himself to Judge Kram as 'Mad Dog' Nussbaum.

'So, you're a *lord*,' snarled Mad Dog Nussbaum during one examination of James Hanson. 'Well, just what does a *lord* do? How much money do you get paid for being a *lord*?'

Before Hanson could fully explain, Nussbaum was off on another tangent, accusing the bewildered and increasingly disconcerted Hanson of having been charged with criminal fraud in a business dealing in the United States in the 1970s. Sir Gordon White endured similar chaffing. He was a playboy, wasn't he? And asset stripper of no real reputation, wasn't that true?

Even Pirie came in for a grilling from Nussbaum who dominated the questioning and introduced every bit of extraneous character assassination that the bemused Judge Kram would allow. Hadn't Pirie hired a French chef, no less than Claude Mare from New York's famous Luctece, to be the in-house chef at the Rothschild executive dining room? Indeed, hadn't Pirie been so wildly extravagant after taking over the banking house that he was desperate for the fees the Hanson takeover of SCM would generate? Isn't that really why he had counselled Sir Gordon to violate the securities laws with his post-withdrawal raid on SCM shares? The Judge Kram took it all into the record.

'It was awful,' Hanson would later recall. 'I will never knowingly allow myself to be trapped in such a situation again.' (White on the other hand visibly relished his verbal bouts with 'Mad Dog'.)

At the same time, the SEC launched its own investigation into the 11 September market raid and among the persons questioned were Ivan Boesky, as well as arbs at Jefferies & Co., Jamie Securities Co. and Oppenheimer & Co., as well as Sir Gordon and Robert Pirie. Moreover the agency examined telephone and stock trading logs from the six companies, all looking for evidence of collusion and insider trading.

One of the interesting questions asked by the SEC was whether Pirie talked White into his raid because Sir James Goldsmith had done a similar flanking movement against Crown Zellerbach. There also was the issue of whether White should have tried to buy a share of SCM's shares knowing that it would have triggered the 'lock-up' option and given the management-Merrill Lynch partners the right to carry away Durkees Famous and the pigments divisions at cut-rate prices. In the end, the agency gave up and let the battle proceed.

Yet, as unpleasant as it all was, Pirie did not lose sight of the goal – to block the bust-up of SCM and to win control of *all* the company at a reasonable price – if not in Judge Kram's court, then on appeal where the parties would end up in any event. And that, by the way, is the risk one takes when one runs the kind of adverse, investigative deposition taking operation that Wachtell Lipton's Nussbaum conducted; there is a risk of learning things you don't really want to know.

At one stage in his questioning, Pirie was being pressed on whether he or Gordon White had been willing to sell their shares in SCM and take a profit for walking away. No, Pirie answered. Why not? Had he actually ever talked to anyone on the SCM team about it? Yes. Who? Mike Overlock of Goldman Sachs. Aha, and what did you say to Mike Overlock of Goldman Sachs and what did he say to you. Right there, Nussbaum violated one of the canons of the art of legal questioning; never ask a question unless you already know the answer.

To Nussbaum's chagrin, Pirie recounted in some detail a series of telephone conversations with Overlock during which the investment banker confessed that Goldman Sachs had sat by while the SCM board was told the two crown jewel divisions were worth much less than they actually were. Worse, Overlock revealed that he had done the actual estimating and that there were documents floating about (and easily subject to subpoena) which showed how much Durkees and the pigments divisions were worth and what a bargain the Merrill Lynch partners were getting. That valuation and those documents would be important ammunition later on when the case would certainly go to an appeals court. Pirie was feeling rather optimistic given the circumstances.

Pirie recalls,

'A very interesting thing was going on at that time. The poison pill defence had been upheld in two trial court level cases – one was a minor case in Nevada and the other was the Household decision in the Delaware Chancery Court with Judge Joseph Walsh presiding. In the midst of our arguments before Judge Kram, the same Judge Walsh ruled in the Revlon case and while he upheld the pill there he said something that slipped by nearly everyone; he said he was having serious doubts about the propriety of poison pills in deals where one of the parties is making an all cash offer to any and all shareholders. That was a significant change of heart, all the more so when Judge Walsh was suddenly elevated to the Delaware appeals court where he would be reviewing both the Household and the Revlon cases.

'I never really worried about the outcome of our challenges to the lock-up because, and this is really just a private theory of mine, I didn't think that the jud̄ es, whoever they are, would rule against us. My theory is that you can explain the legal results in most of the tender offer litigation of recent years by whether they were all cash or not. In an all cash bid for any and all shareholders the shareholders aren't going to get screwed. In a bid that's tacked on the back end with a lot of junk bonds, the judges don't know what the shareholders are going to get in the end.

Now that is not how the law is supposed to work but it is the way the law *does* work. There is an emotional logic to it all. The business judgement rule is fine as far as the judges are concerned until they confront a situation where they don't know whether the shareholders are getting screwed or where they suspect the shareholders *are* going to get screwed. So it really is emotional logic at work; the judges will find a way.'

Pirie was right enough. Judge Walsh and the entire Delaware Supreme Court was unhappy with its early acceptance of poison pills and they began, on review, to draw distinctions that weakened the early findings.

What Lipton had convinced the Revlon board to do, in the face of Perelman's threat of a $45 hostile bid, was to adopt a rights plan which gave holders the right to exchange each of their common shares for $65 worth of notes. The rights were to be triggered into effect whenever anyone acquired at least 20 per cent of Revlon common, unless the suitor promptly acquired all the shares for at least $65. Before being triggered, the rights could be recalled by the board for 10 cents.

Originally, Judge Walsh had said that the Revlon board had acted within the Business Judgement Rule. They had made a determination

159

that $45 a share was grossly inadequate and they had investment banking advice that Pantry Pride would be likely to have to finance its offer by 'junk bonds' (remember Pirie's theory about the fate of all cash offers) and that, as a result, there probably would be a subsequent sell off of Revlon assets to pay off Perelman's debts.

But at the time Judge Walsh had left himself an out. While the board had acted within the play, there was no doubt that its defensive tactics effectively 'substituted its judgement for the marketplace (therefore) the directors assumed a greater degree of responsibility in responding thereafter to acquisition attempts and were not absolved from having to demonstrate the rationality of their subsequent decisions'.

But the initial defence was not the only contested item before the courts in Delaware. A bidding war spilled over into October during which time Pantry Pride raised its bid price to $50 a share, then to $53 and Revlon's board went a step further to dig itself in. Revlon offered and ended up buying a surprising 30 per cent of its own shares for a $57.50 package of notes and preferred stock. The notes contained covenants, which could be waived only by Revlon's independent directors which had the effect of severely limiting Revlon's ability to sell off other assets, to incur new debt or to declare dividends. It was the ultimate barbed wire entanglement poison pill defence.

Hardly had Revlon's shareholders absorbed this news, than there was another development. In October, Bergerac convened the Revlon board to approve a surprise $56 a share tender offer from a white knight, the Forstman Little investors group. Within a day or two an irate Revlon shareholder had taken the deal into courts, charging the board with misleading the other shareholders by not disclosing Bergerac's desire to take the company private.

After meeting with its bankers, Perelman came back into the game with $56.25 but was stalled when Forstman Little offered $57.25 *all cash*. Revlon's board was under some pressure from its shareholders by now. Between 3 October and 12 October the price of its new notes had dropped from $100 to $87 and the shareholders were screaming. In the negotiations with Forstman Little, Bergerac's board tried to peg the deal down by agreeing to a Lipton 'crown jewel lock-up' option whereby Revlon's two most attractive divisions, its skincare products and health care laboratories, could be sold off to Forstman Little at a knock-down price of $525m (which Revlon's own investment banker estimated was $75m too little) in the event that anyone else acquired more than 40 per cent of Revlon's shares. Just so there would be no mistaking the Lipton trade mark Revlon also agreed to escrow a $25m 'goodbye fee' and sign a 'no shop' covenant that it would not seek an alternative bidder other than the Forstman Little partners.

In the meantime Pirie and company were making headway on the legal front. They had been successful in severing the matter of whether the 11 September raid was legal and taking Judge Kram's predictable adverse ruling directly to the US Court of Appeals.

On 2 October, the Appeals Court ruled that Hanson had not violated federal securities laws. 'Mad Dog' Nussbaum and his trial team had not been prepared for the court's willingness to create 'a gaping hole in the Williams Act', as he called it. If one accepts Pirie's theory, the decision makes sense; the judges simply found facts to support an all-cash bid. Specifically, the appeals decision rested on the conclusion by all three judges that by confining their purchases to four highly sophisticated professional investors, the Hanson purchases did not jeopardise the Williams Act protective restraints on behalf of the general, more vulnerable, mass of public shareholders. A bit hard to swallow perhaps, but effective enough. On 11 October the court allowed Hanson to continue buying shares of SCM.

On 15 October, White and Pirie headed for a final showdown with the SCM–Merrill Lynch partners. They sued the group in Judge Kram's court alleging unlawful conspiracy for the control of SCM and demanded an injunction against the Merrill Lynch group to prevent their exercising of the option to take off SCM's 'crown jewels' – the pigments and foods divisions. All the cases were consolidated and Merrill Lynch volunteered to stand still until a final ruling was achieved.

It increasingly appeared as if Judge Kram would get an additional and new precedent to complicate her final decisions. On 18 October Perelman lined up new financing and announced a $58 a share all-cash-any-and-all tender offer for Revlon and demanded the Delaware court enjoin Revlon from issuing any more of its 'junk rights'. On 22 October, Household International agreed to sell its household merchandise division to a Donaldson Lufkin and Jenrette group for a leveraged buy-out worth $700m. On 23 October Pantry Pride won its preliminary injunction against Revlon. As an echo from a now distant battle, the next day's newspapers also record that Phillips Petroleum will sell or has contracted to sell assets totalling more than $1b and that it intends to shed $2b more in assets by mid-1986 in order to reduce its debt burden from the Boesky-Icahn-Pickens takeover raids.

In granting the injunction, Judge Walsh invalidated the lock-up option granted to Forstman Little and, in reaching its decision, actually cited the Federal appeals court's preliminary decisions in the Hanson–SCM Case. Surely Judge Kram would pay attention to the way the wind was blowing. Perhaps not.

In any event, Judge Walsh began by observing that '[Revlon's] board's self interest in resolving the noteholders' problems led to concessions which effectively excluded Pantry Pride to the detriment of Revlon's shareholders'. He then banned the 'goodbye fee' and the 'no-shop' concession.

Walsh's line of argument would later be refined by the Delaware Supreme Court when it sorted out the various final appeals. Revlon's management and board had the right to become an auctioneer, in effect, by not just rolling over and accepting the first cash offer that comes along. But, the courts ruled, once a board sets itself up as an auctioneer, it has a duty to secure the highest reasonable price for the company's component parts.

The Delaware courts also hung some restraints on the Business Judgement Rule which had protected boards and managements from second guessing by shareholders for so long.

'While the business judgement rule may be applicable to the actions of corporate directors responding to takeover threats, the principles upon which it is founded – care, loyalty and independence – must first be satisfied.'

But the rule also had held that in such questions, there was to be a *presumption*, an assumption, that the directors were acting in good faith. It was up to the rival bidders to prove that the directors were acting in bad faith, without 'care, loyalty and independence'. What about that?

Delaware's courts chopped the rule back a bit more. The three judge panel would harken back to its early ruling which allowed Unocal's Fred Hartley to declare that *some* shareholders could be discriminated against in a takeover battle if the board's objective was to save the company as an integral whole. The judges reminded themselves that they had said at that time [Unocal Corp. v. Mesa Petroleum Co., 493 A. 2d. 946 (Del. Sup. 1985)] that when directors react to hostile bids there is 'the omnipresent spectre that a board may be acting primarily in its own interests, rather than those of the corporation and its shareholders'.

And then the Delaware judges added for Revlon's benefit, 'this potential for conflict places upon the directors the burden of proving that they had reasonable grounds for believing there was a danger to corporate policy and effectiveness, a burden satisfied by a showing of good faith and reasonable investigation... In addition, the directors must analyse the nature of the takeover and its effect on the corporation in order to ensure balance – that the responsive action taken is reasonable in relation to the threat posed.'

In effect, Revlon was all right when it issued the first poison pill defence because it resulted in Pantry Pride jacking its tender offer price. But later, Revlon's board had switched from being 'defenders of the corporate bastion to auctioneers charged with getting the best price for the shareholders at a sale of the company'. When it fought to preserve its sweetheart deal with Forstman Little and shut out any compromise with Pantry Pride, the Revlon board violated the duties of care, loyalty and independence.

By 1 November it was all over for Revlon and Pantry Pride, which gave a $58 a share all cash offer that pulled in 88 per cent of Revlon's shares within one 24 hour period. For $1.9bn, Revlon now belonged to Ronald O. Perelman. By January he would have turned down a chance to recoup $900m of that money by hiving off Revlon's beauty business.

On 26 November, Judge Kram handed down a decision that was based, in part, on her reading that the Delaware Supreme Court had said there was nothing inherently wrong with crown jewel lock-ups as a takeover defence. Since, under New York state law, the Business Judgement Rule put the burden on the plaintiffs to show that SCM's board had violated the duty of loyalty, Judge Kram concluded she only had one other test to administer, the duty of due care on the part of the board to make an informed decision. The fact that the board heard expert advice from investment bankers of the stripe of Goldman Sachs and attorneys of the stature of Martin Lipton satisfied her that the board had taken due care in informing itself. Case dismissed.

Not quite, of course. The US Court of Appeals for the Second Circuit was quick to enjoin SCM from handing over its two crown jewels to the Merrill Lynch partners. And it would take until 7 January to reach its decision but as so often happens with the legal system of examining the decisions of other courts, the judges pulled their growing doubts about Marty Lipton's creation a further notch tighter.

The appeals judges agreed that a corporate board that sets itself the task of defending against a takeover bid moves beyond the normal protective barriers of the Business Judgement Rule. The rule is not a blank cheque and the court has the right to pursue plaintiff complaints about both the basis and the results of a board's defensive actions.

Not surprisingly, the New York judges read the Revlon case reasonings into their own deliberations. A crown jewel lock-up is not illegal *per se*, but it may be improper in a certain case. In the SCM case, the appeals court found that the SCM board had acted in unseemly haste and had not looked into the details of the Hanson bid as they might have. Instead, they had relied on their advisers, accepting without question assertions that they should have examined; the valuation of the two assets to be sold off to the Merrill Lynch partners was just one item.

Indeed, and here the court went a step further, the SCM board had a heightened duty to examine and question the assertions and proposals of their management and the team of lawyers and bankers for the very reason that they knew the management had a self-interest in the outcome. Delegating those judgements that had to be made to outside lawyers and to investment bankers did not absolve the board members of their own duty, especially since the lawyers and investment bankers were being paid by management in the final analysis.

The SCM directors, in a three-hour, late-night meeting, apparently contented themselves with their financial advisor's conclusory opinion that the option prices were 'within the range of fair value', although had the directors inquired they would have learned that Goldman Sachs had not calculated a range of fairness.

There was not even a written opinion from Goldman Sachs as to the value of the two optioned businesses... Moreover, the board never asked what the top value was or why the two businesses that generated half of SCM's income were being sold for one third of the total purchase price of the company under the second LBO merger agreement, or what the company would look like if the options were exercised... There was little or no discussion of how likely it was that the option 'trigger' would be pulled, or who would make that decision... Merrill, the board, or management.*

White and Pirie knew victory when they heard it. Within minutes of the appeals court decision being handed down, and well ahead of an SCM announcement that it would ask for a rehearing, Hanson announced it would resume its $75 a share cash offer to any outstanding SCM shares. Within hours the group had 4.2m SCM shares or 66 per cent of the outstanding stock. It was a victory with a $926.5m price tag.

Except for the Merrill Lynch partners, who took away not even the first 'hello fee' in the end, the SCM battle had a happy ending. Unlike the Revlon case where Michel Bergerac was out of his executive offices within a few days, Gordon White recognised that SCM possessed a good, tough management in Erlicker and his team. There were no sackings or corporate reshufflings of consequence and SCM is now the jewel in Hanson's American crown.

It is easy to count the winners and losers in this story.

*Hanson Trust PLC v. SCM Corp., 774 F. 2d 47 (2d Cir. 1985).

Marty Lipton was a big loser, having developed a defence tactic that exploded in his clients' faces. In fact, 1985 was not a good year for Lipton at all. Even as he was plotting strategies for Crown Zellerbach, SCM and Revlon, Lipton was on the defensive himself in the biggest legal battle over a corporate takeover attempt in legal history; one of the lawyers involved called the $10.5bn damage suit won by Pennzoil over Texaco Inc. the 'most important case in the history of America'.* Pennzoil sued and won because of Texaco's interference in a deal to take over Getty Oil. Lipton was one of Texaco's star defence counsellors and testified to a number of intricate legalisms. The Texas jury later would single out Lipton as an incredible witness.

Sir James Goldsmith and the Lord Hanson–Sir Gordon White duo not only emerged as winners but further confused the merger debate by proving that corporate raiders are not always more dangerous to shareholders than the entrenched managements. Goldsmith would get another chance to prove that point in sharper relief in the autumn of 1986 when his takeover run for Goodyear Tire Corp proved the inability of Congress to grasp what is going on as well as highlighting the shareholder-be-damned attitude of some corporate executives.

Charitably, one might also declare the American court system winners of a sort, for managing, just, to keep up with a rapidly changing set of legal concepts and yet to sort things out with fair equity. In the end, one must admit, the courts did protect the broader interests of the shareholders and the *corporate entity itself*. The decision making was not a pretty sight and no definitive set of rules for or against the 'poison pill' genre of defences, let alone the obviously questionable 'crown jewel lock-up', has been set down as yet.

However, the disturbing thought remains that one comes out of these stories as one went in. There is an element of irrationality, of emotions out of control, or self-interest driven beyond prudence, beyond greed, even. In all of these cases there were instances where one party or the other was literally willing to burn down the structure that was to be protected rather than see it fall into enemy hands.

There was also a troubling unwillingness to let the marketplace actually judge the outcome fairly. And the footprints of Ivan Boesky and Dennis Levine taint many of the final results as well. Conclusions seem harder to come by the closer one looks at the issues.

*The American Lawyer, January–February 1986.

CHAPTER SEVEN

Morgan: The Deal-Maker

By the mid-1980s a new element had entered the London bid scene which contained within it, although few were prescient enough to see it, a sinister force which would eventually encourage, if not directly cause, some of its worst excesses. Bid battles were no longer just between a strong individual, such as Lord Hanson, and a worthy but dull chairman fighting on the other side. Nor were they one company battling against another.

Bid teams had become bigger and more complex, bid fees had escalated, and new 'success bonuses' had been added on. Now it was often merchant bank versus merchant bank in a more nakedly aggressive way than anyone in the City could remember. There had, of course, always been rivalry between the so-called 'first layer' of merchant banks (which essentially meant Warburgs, Rothschild, Morgan Grenfell, Schroder Wagg and Kleinwort Benson) and the position, not measured on any charts or league tables but nonetheless known to all, of the City's number one merchant bank was eagerly coveted. But the competition had never been as intense as it was now. A decade ago, the heads of merchant banks used to point out scathingly to journalists that they were wrong to pay so much attention to the one bit of their business they came most often into contact with, which was corporate finance, or mergers and acquisitions as the Americans insisted on calling it. It was, the senior bankers would reiterate, only one part of the bank, and not that important either. Even in the 1970s, this was never entirely true, but it was a message most bankers wanted to get across – they were already keenly aware that takeover bids were glamorous, and straightforward banking business was not. For the press to make stars out of bid specialists caused jealousies and friction inside. But by the 1980s, that facade had long been dropped. Corporate finance was huge business, and with it came other banking business, too: if you could win a big company as a client in a takeover battle, there was no end to the other services and products you could flog to him. Corporate finance had become the best way to win new business – and was highly profitable in its own right. Financial journalists were now invited into the banks to be told how well they were doing in the mergers business.

And there was all to play for. No one bank ruled the roost. A new bank could come along, establish itself with new ideas and aggressive thinking, and win for itself the top spot from banks that had been around for centuries. In the early 1970s, Schroder Wagg was generally seen as the bank most companies wanted on their side; but that gave way to Warburgs, a relative newcomer, which enjoyed perhaps a ten-year run at the top. Warburgs' legendary founder, Siegmund Warburg, set the style for the bank in the 1950s and 1960s: punch with style. And it worked remarkably well. Through the 1970s Warburgs was the bank to have on the bidders' side, even more than on the defence. By the early 1980s, however, another bank was fast challenging Warburgs: Morgan Grenfell, much older but considerably smaller and less successful, was growing rapidly.

The crown tacitly passed from Warburgs to Morgan when BTR won its battle for Thomas Tilling in 1983. Morgan acted for BTR and Warburgs for Tilling. After that the flow of business to Morgan was overwhelming. The shipping and property conglomerate P&O, now under new management and totally revitalised, moved its business from Schroder to Morgan. Corporate finance profits, which in the 1970s had run at around £3m a year, were suddenly ten times that and still rising. Scarcely a bid went by without a Morgan involvement, and the members of the corporate finance team became some of the most sought after and best known in the City. Most banks had one takeover star; Morgan's trick had been to pull together a team of them. The head of the team was a former director-general of the Takeover Panel, and one of the City's greatest experts on the technicalities of a takeover bid: Graham Walsh. A mild accountant, renowned in the bank for his health worries and his fussiness, Walsh presided with a loose rein over the real stars.

George Magan came from an old Irish family, and privately complained he had never been accorded the recognition he deserved from his snobbish colleagues. Magan wore his hair slicked back, earning himself the nickname 'Teddy', and his suits, even with the gold watch-chain, were seen as just too smart for the austere and old-fashioned partners' room of Morgan which was more like a country house than a modern bank. It was Magan who had piloted Sir Owen Green to victory in the Tilling bid, and it was Magan whose tactical and strategic skills had done as much as anyone to push Morgan to the top. 1985 was Magan's big year, when he did six of the top ten bids in Britain.

Even Magan, however, was overshadowed by Roger Seelig, the most inveterate deal-maker in the whole City. In 1985 Seelig had just turned 40 (he and Magan are the same age), and had already put together some of the most spectacular mergers of the whole wave; he had landed Currys for Dixons, a classic of its kind because of the way Dixons' share price soared both during the bid and afterwards as the realisation sank in of how good a deal it was for the electrical retailer. His close friendship with Terence Conran had helped propel the Habitat group into the big-time, first with the merger with Mothercare, then with British Home Stores. He could be seen late at night in the Annabel's night-club in Berkeley Square, chatting to potential clients or putting into place another bit of his latest deal; or at the theatre, mobile telephone beside him for emergency calls. Seelig would fly in from New York and talk about his meeting there with 'Gordon' (White) or 'Jimmy' (Goldsmith); there were few of the major players either in London or New York to whom he did not have a direct line. There were constant rumours that he was about to leave Morgan and head up a new team somewhere else at an astronomical salary – he earned £200,000 a year at Morgan – but he stayed. He was a millionaire from his shareholding in Terence Conran's companies, and in another Morgan client, the Underwoods chemists chain. But he was also intensely loyal to Morgan, even if there was often friction with Walsh and some of the others. Seelig was much more of a free spirit than the others, working his own hours (which included most weekends) and tending his own clients and contacts. He could often disappear, out of contact except for emergencies, and return triumphant with the next deal planned.

However well known the stars were, much of the credit for Morgan's premier position went to its chief executive, the tall, patrician Christopher Reeves, who presided over the partners' room at 23 Great Winchester Street, the bank's headquarters. Although the bank had been founded in 1838 by George Peabody from New England – the 'Morgan' in the name came from J. Pierpont Morgan who annexed it to his own empire after becoming a partner there when he worked in London as a young man – Morgan Grenfell had over its

150-year history been through a series of crises. Its most recent was a major move into financing films in the late-1960s, which resulted in the inevitable disaster; the Bank of England had intervened to put in one of its own men. Morgan's reputation at the time was in stark contrast to its 1980s fame. Christopher Fildes, a veteran financial journalist, later recalled:* 'My City Editor twenty years ago kept a headline in standing type: First Win for Morgan Grenfell. The time would come, he said, when he might have to use it.' Much of the credit for the change in status was given to Reeves who had joined as one of the new team in 1968 after being recruited from Hill Samuel where he was assistant personnel manager.

Reeves gloried in the esteem now accorded his bank. He bubbled with some ideas of his own: a takeover of a public company which would give Morgan its own quote (a bid for Exco, the money-broker, was later vetoed by the Bank of England), or a full public quotation (the direction he eventually went in mid-1986). Reeves had successfully combined all the aura of Morgan's position as one of the pillars of the City establishment with the modern, aggressive style of Magan and Seelig – and for a five year period no-one could touch it. In 1985 Morgan acted as financial adviser in 32 takeovers worth between them over £3bn, keeping it in number one spot ahead of Warburgs, Kleinwort and Schroders. In 1986, the height of the boom, it would handle bids worth £14bn, more than the total of all bids made in Britain in any previous year. True, some doubts about the style, management and takeover tactics at Morgan had begun to appear as early as 1985, but on the whole they were dismissed as petty jealousy on the part of rivals. One critic was quoted as saying: 'They are trotting into action with all the arrogance of a crack Polish regiment in 1939.'† No-one at Morgan paid much attention to the carping. Life was too busy. The bank was making money as never before, and salaries with bonuses on top were high and getting higher.

Others, however, had begun to note some disturbing elements of Morgan bids. It was one thing to be aggressive, in the way Magan and Seelig were, but too often Morgan seemed to be continually going to the very limits the takeover rules allowed. Seelig's response to that, when it was put to him by an Institutional Investor writer in December 1985, was that his rivals 'may just be reading the rules. We *changed* most of the rules.' Magan had enraged the board of BAT

Daily Telegraph, June 1986.
† *Business Magazine*, September 1986.

Industries during its battle for the insurance company Eagle Star, the largest bid made in 1983, when he announced that his client, Allianz, was interested in making a higher offer. After weeks when no offer emerged, Magan was called before the Takeover Panel, given a ticking off, and Allianz called off its bidding altogether. But the tactic was unique in British takeover history and its effect had made it almost impossible for BAT to buy Eagle Star stock in the market. Magan passed it all off as the difficulties of explaining things to a foreign client, but such was the reaction that no-one has even tried anything similar since. The Panel changed the rules to make sure they didn't. Today there is a strict takeover timetable that companies have to adhere to.

Morgan lead the way in other bid tactics, too. It had discovered that simply advising and helping with a bid was not enough; financial muscle helped, too. It soon gained the reputation for aggressively using its balance sheet to support its clients, a perfectly legal thing to do, but a relatively new tactic in the takeover game which Morgan had adapted from the American banks. It developed new systems of underwriting generous cash alternatives to share offers, and also used its own cash to buy shares in the target companies in the market. The more traditional bankers were increasingly antagonistic. 'Their attitude is, "Let's not worry about self-regulation, and let's not worry about any other merchant bank," one rival was quoted as saying.* For all that, no-one suggested they were breaking the rules. It was more a case of stretching them to the limit, or as Magan put it 'using every inch of the playing surface'. At times the Morgan team were on the very edge of the touchline.

'Did Morgan Grenfell get a little *too* aggressive in the bitter battle of the retailers between Dixons and Currys?' asked the *Institutional Investor* in December 1985. 'Its clients Dixons had less than 50 per cent in the closing days of the bid when a blitz of buying in both stocks lifted Dixons's price (which would allow it to buy *more* of Currys).' A review by the Takeover Panel assigned no blame, but the Panel ruled that in order to prevent the appearance of tampering with the price, henceforth neither side could purchase a target's stock within 24 hours of the purchase of the acquirer's stock. Seelig, who handled the deal, says the interest in Dixons's stock actually came from the institutions, not for the bank. "If you believe it's a coincidence," snapped a competitor, "that's up to you. They've got a fairly well tuned system."'

Remember that this article in the *Institutional Investor* was written at the end of 1985, more than a year before Seelig and Morgan got

Institutional Investor, December 1985.

involved in the bid that would do so much damage to both of them, the Guinness bid for Distillers. By that stage the suspicion that Morgan was able to support its clients' share price, which would later be at the centre of the Guinness affair, was already widely established. Other banks did the same of course, but not with the same aggression and success as Morgans, which led the pace. In the climate of the time, the rise in the Dixons share price went largely unnoticed, and what criticism there was soon died away as the price continued to rise after the bid was finished, when all support operations would have been unwound. In any case the Takeover Panel had held an enquiry, and decided there was no case against Morgans or Dixons. The bid stood, and provided Dixons with the platform to bid (unsuccessfully) for Woolworth later. From now on support operations for the share price of the bidding company became more and more of a feature in takeover battles.

Financial muscle had become every bit as important as financial advice. And no bank used its well-exercised muscles more effectively than Morgans.

On the evening of Monday, 2 December, 1986, Christopher Reeves took his wife and a party of friends to the theatre. He was visibly pleased with himself. His corporate finance team, working through the weekend, had that morning put the final touches to one of the biggest mergers they had yet been involved in: for the princely sum of £1.22bn, Imperial Group, one of Britain's biggest companies which had since the 1960s moved outside its traditional Players and Wills cigarettes business into brewing (by taking over Courage), and food (Ross and Youngs frozen food), would take over United Biscuits, another major food company. More to the point, almost alone among the recent run of takeovers, there was nothing hostile about it. The day had been a historic one which Reeves, with his unrivalled position as the lead merchant banker in London, could appreciate: it had seen bids made worth a record £3bn, three times the total for the whole of 1981.

Reeves was not immediately involved in the other big bid of the day: James Gulliver, after being prevented by the City Takeover Panel from making a bid for the last four months, had finally unveiled a £1.8bn offer for the Distillers drinks company, which, like Imps, was one of Britain's last remaining sleeping giants. But within a few weeks, that bid, too, would come to be every bit as important to his merchant bank as United Biscuits was.

That night at the theatre Reeves talked enthusiastically about his own deal. As it turned out, one of the principal guests of the evening,

David Davies, then the chief executive of the Hong Kong Land company, was late and the party missed the first act of Congreve's *Love for Love*. So Reeves had an unexpected hour to relax in the foyer and discuss the bid scene in the middle of the busiest period in the history of his bank.

Imps, which once controlled the much bigger British-American Tobacco, had long lost its way, and diversification after diversification to get away from its dependence on the tobacco industry had given it major problems, the final one being the acquisition – oddly enough in competition with Sir Gordon White of Hanson – of the Howard Johnson motel chain in the United States.

United Biscuits, on the other hand, had undergone a new lease of life under its almost evangelist chairman Sir Hector Laing. In contrast to Imps, United Biscuits was an outstanding example of how takeovers can be made to work. Pre-tax profits of Laing's group had grown 20 times since 1965, three times the rate of inflation. Over the same period, as he liked to remind people, £100 invested in his shares would have grown to £2400, an annual average rate of return of 17 per cent as he had added a series of new products and activities to his traditional McVities's biscuits: Meredith & Drew and KP nuts in the mid-1960s, Keebler, the cookie company, in the US in 1974, the Wimpy and Pizzaland fast food chains and the chocolate firm, Terry's of York.

Laing's style was highly individual, and more reflective than many of the big players on the takeover scene. Unlike Hanson, he was very much a 'hands-on' manager, insisting on visiting one of his plants almost every day, continually preoccupying himself with the welfare and health of his staff; he was a paternalistic, almost nineteenth-century, capitalist, who had translated his old-fashioned wisdoms into the modern world with considerable success. 'I was born into wealth,' he once wrote. 'But I was also born into a practising Christian family so my attitude to personal wealth had always been that it is a privilege and therefore carries a responsibility.' Like Hanson, he was a friend of Mrs Thatcher, and often described as her favourite "Anglo-Scot industrialist'. Laing could even take responsibility for giving Britain the services of Ian MacGregor, the Scottish-American veteran who first ran British Steel and then the National Coal Board. MacGregor, in his book *The Enemies Within*, described how at a dinner party one night in New York, as he was discussing the problems of the US steel industry, Laing suddenly exclaimed: 'My God! You may be just the person we need. I was talking to the prime minister just the other day and heard her concern as to how she could find someone to get British Steel into better shape. Maybe you're just the man she's looking for.'

In the harsh world of the hostile takeover, Laing seemed to have placed himself at a disadvantage. But in the weeks that followed, he would show, as he had done in business, that his strong humanist streak and his Christian commitment were no deterrent to his combative skills. But he would also show he was no match for the reigning champion of the British bid arena: Lord Hanson.

Laing's style of management and record had certainly influenced Christopher Reeves and other City men, who perceived him as the salvation for Imps. Morgan Grenfell's team had structured the Imps deal in such a way that effectively it was a reverse takeover: although technically Imps was the acquisitor and United Biscuits the target company, it was agreed by both sides that Laing would run the enlarged group, with the Imps chairman Geoffrey Kent agreeing to take a back seat.

In the National Theatre foyer that evening Reeves was jubilant as he described the details to his guests. 'What about a counter-bid?' he was asked.* There had been a lot of rumours about Imps. Now that it was in play, might not some of the rumoured bidders enter the scene? Reeves was disdainful. 'It would take a mighty brave bidder to come in and disturb an agreed deal like this.' Only Hanson, he agreed, had the resources and the nerve to do it. But he had his hands full with his $1bn bid for SCM in the US, now bogged down in the courts. Even Hanson, Reeves suggested, was unlikely to disturb a party as large and as well tied up as this one.

It was a major misjudgement, not the first that had been made of Hanson. As Reeves and his guests were filing in to watch the second act of the play, Hanson at that very moment was toying with the idea of breaking up Reeves' carefully arranged deal. He did not want United Biscuits: that was too well managed and fully valued for him. But he had long been thinking about Imperial Group, although as he said later 'there were more attractive situations around at the time.'† He had also given considerable thought to making a bid for Distillers, and had even bought a stake, usually his first step before launching his offer. He and Gordon White had discussed it together as they were travelling to New York. 'But we made the decision not to go for it, because we couldn't get it. Not because of the Monopolies Commission, we didn't think that was a problem. But because it was a big Scottish institution and we just felt we wouldn't be acceptable. We didn't want to take on the Scottish lobby, and that's another reason for not doing it. Added to that, it was a high risk one, because with whisky you have to wait seven years before you can even call it whisky. There

*The question was asked by Ivan Fallon, the author.
† Interview with the author.

were a lot of problems.' These remarks were made to the authors during the bid, and long before what became known as the Guinness affair blew up. But, in retrospect, there is little doubt that Hanson made the right choice. He switched all his energies back to Imps, knowing that, if he was ever going to get it, it had to be now. Once Laing's reverse takeover went through, the joint group would be beyond his reach.

It was a pure coincidence that Distillers and Imps were put into play on the same day. Either of them in its own right would have been the biggest bid ever made in Britain. For the next four months they would dominate the City scene, overwhelm the Monopolies Commission, bring a new level of bitterness to the hostile bid scene, and cost many millions of pounds in fees and underwriting costs. No-one dreamt for a second that events had been set in motion which would cost Reeves, Seelig and Walsh their jobs, would dramatically topple Morgan from its top position, and would lead to the biggest scandal in the City for fifty years. The Reeves party happily went on for a late dinner at Harry's bar, with their host still basking in the excitement of his day.

While Sir Hector Laing moved into his merger with smiles and goodwill on all sides, James Gulliver was hitting stiff opposition from the start. The 55-year-old Scot had always known he would, but his City advisers insisted that the door to Distillers was open and all it needed was a firm push.

Distillers was one of the most traditional and conservative companies in Britain. It was also among the most badly managed. The average age of its board was 60 and for years its once dominant position in the Scotch whisky industry had been eroding. Gulliver had spent painstaking months compiling the most detailed analysis ever done by a bidder on a target company in Britain. It showed a depressing picture: in the early 1960s, Distillers had 75 per cent of the British market for Scotch. By 1984 it was down to 15 per cent. Worldwide, its share of the market had fallen from 48 per cent in 1973 to 35 per cent. Its Johnnie Walker Red was still the market leader, with 10 per cent of the world market, but others were closing up: J & B Rare, part of Grand Metropolitan, and Bells, now owned by Guinness, were second and third. Scotch whisky still accounted for 80 per cent of Distillers' profits, and its attempts to diversify had often backfired. At one stage it had decided to become a pharmaceutical company as well, and then ran into the most celebrated of all scandals, when its thalidomide drug began causing children to be born without arms or legs. Distillers had tried to hush up the thalidomide dangers, and fought for four years to prevent the *Sunday Times* from printing a series of articles on the full effects of the drug and the fight by the parents of the children for compensation. The reaction of the directors was to get out of the drugs business altogether, leaving Distillers in 1985 dependent on a declining world Scotch whisky market. From then on, the Distillers management shunned publicity, something which Gulliver, Hanson and the others had all learned was an invaluable weapon when it came to takeover battles.

Gulliver had one advantage over Hanson: he was Scottish, and if the Scottish lobby, ferociously defensive of the few remaining independent Scottish concerns, had frightened off Hanson, it held fewer dangers for him. He would point out later that, despite their professed Scottishness, only three of the Distillers directors actually lived in Scotland, the others finding the climate of the home counties around London more congenial. Furthermore, London contained not just one Distillers headquarters but four. He had gone to elaborate pains to become accepted by the Scottish establishment. A year before he announced his bid, he had begun to work his way through a list. 'According to a leading member of the Scottish council for Development and Industry, a Scottish pressure group, Mr Gulliver ... requested a list of the "great and the good" in Scotland. Soon afterwards Mr Gulliver became a member of the Scottish Economic Council, the "think tank" which meets regularly with Mr George Younger, Secretary of State for Scotland.'* While the Distillers board seemed to regard itself as a permanent part of the Scottish landscape, Gulliver was assiduously establishing his own credentials with a view to taking it over.

In Edinburgh at the same time Ernest Saunders, the chief executive officer of Guinness, was making a similar systematic assessment of the Scottish establishment, spending more and more time convincing the big investment houses, the banks and the Scottish politicians that Guinness was acceptable north of the border. 'Now they call us McGuinness,' he joked at one stage. Later this would become a sour joke and the name Saunders would not be mentioned in polite Scottish society. But for a brief time, long enough to win two takeovers, Saunders was perfectly acceptable.

But in the highly class-conscious world of Scottish business, Gulliver was still not entirely acceptable. The son of a grocer, he came from the small distillery town of Campbeltown, in Argyllshire. He had studied engineering at Glasgow University, and won a Fulbright scholarship to the Georgia Institute of Technology, spending, he says,

Financial Times, 19 December, 1985.

'some weeks' at the Harvard Business School studying marketing. Later he had become the protégé of the Canadian food retailer Garfield Weston, who owned the Fine Fare supermarket chain and Fortnum & Mason in Britain. Weston had given Gulliver a taste for the better things in life. He loves the South of France, spending up to three months a year there, holding his management and board meeting there through the summer, working long hours on the detail of his business and planning his takeovers. Once, looking out over the Mediterranean, Gulliver described how Weston had given him an award as his best manager of the year: a holiday with his first wife (he has had three) and children in his superb house at Eden Roc, one of the most glorious places on the French coast. Gulliver had been bowled over by it and bought himself a house in the hills behind Cannes.

Although Weston made Gulliver managing director of Fine Fare at 33, Gulliver was in his late 40s before he ventured off on his own. From losses of £300,000 in 1965, he had transformed the fortunes of the supermarket group to the point where in 1972 it made profits of £5.4m. Gulliver's reputation as one of the ablest of British managers had been established. When Weston refused to float Fine Fare, Gulliver left, borrowed £1m, from a City merchant bank, and bought into a company called Oriel Foods. Two years later he sold it to RCA and became a millionaire. Shortly after that he teamed up again with his old friends Alistair Grant and David Webster to form one of the most able management teams in Britain today. They did a series of deals: they bought the Manchester meat wholesaler Louis C. Edwards, which also gave Gulliver a stake in the Manchester United Football Club, one of his other great interests. Then he bought back Oriel from RCA for £19.9m cash, and in June 1982 did his biggest and most important deal: he bought out Sir James Goldsmith's British food retailing interests, which included Presto supermarkets and Lipton and Templeton shops for £104m in cash, although Gulliver's company at the time only had a market value of £45m. 'I wanted to build a big food multiple,' he explained later* 'but with the concentration of market shares in the hands of a handful of major food retailers in Britain, I realised we would have to be bold enough to grow through acquisition, and quickly, if we were to reach a critical mass – the point where we were obtaining the economies of scale to enable us to grow organically. This meant having the support of the bankers and financial institutions of the City of London.'

Gulliver's interest in Distillers dated back to 1984 when he actually tried to put together a bid. He argued to his bankers that the company

*_Tycoons_ by William Kay.

was 'woefully undervalued', but could not get the backing he wanted. The climate was not yet right for the leveraged bid, the aggressive Davids against the sleepy Goliaths, that were already happening in the United States and that the more farsighted players in London could see would arrive in the City too, given time. John Connell had just taken over as chairman and chief executive of Distillers and there was a general feeling in the City that he should be given some time. Gulliver's market value at the time was £400m, and Distillers was valued at £750m. Gulliver would have to offer at least £1bn – and the biggest bid ever made at the time was BTR for Thomas Tilling which was £600m. 'We talked to an eminent bank and an eminent broker about it,' says Gulliver. 'They were very taken by our presentation and our plan – but they felt the institutions would decide to give the new boy a chance.'

In the spring of 1985 Gulliver decided to have another go. By then, however, word began to get around that Distillers was undervalued, and one of the people to notice was Lord Weinstock, managing director of GEC.

Weinstock at the time was coming under increasing criticism for the size of GEC's cash pile, then roughly £1.5bn, while British manufacturing industry was suffering from lack of investment. Weinstock appeared in a new guise: he suddenly decided GEC could take stakes in some of the more badly run groups, with the object of galvanising them to greater effort. High on his list was Distillers. He began buying the shares, and by the summer of 1985 had 3.4 per cent. He invited John Connell to lunch at his office, and was unimpressed. One GEC director afterwards remembered Connell's 'wonderful brown shoes', polished to a high sheen – but little else. Later Weinstock's closest associate, Sir Kenneth Bond, went round to see Connell, but there was little meeting of minds. Weinstock by July was in a mood to support action on the Distillers front.

GEC's money and Gulliver's management skills were an ideal combination to tackle Distillers – a thought that occurred that summer to Sir Ian MacGregor, who had just finished a year-long strike with the miners, and was now working out his notice period at the National Coal Board. MacGregor was a Gulliver fan; his Scottish hideaway at Ardrishaig was only 40 miles from Gulliver's home in Campbeltown, and the two often saw each other at weekends.

MacGregor still retained a connection with the New York house Lazard Freres, and had a relationship with its London counterpart, Lazard Brothers, headed by Sir John Nott, the former cabinet minister. That summer MacGregor heard the rumours in the banking parlours that Gulliver was considering mounting a bid for Distillers, a task which seemed to him impossible without some help. MacGregor decided to provide that help.

Early in July, he telephoned Gulliver. He had a proposal which might interest him. They met a few days later in MacGregor's London flat in Eaton Square; with MacGregor was a senior director of Lazards, Peter Grant, a friend of Weinstock, and a man who commands considerable power and influence in the City. Their proposal was music to Gulliver's ears. They had been looking at Distillers, said MacGregor, and had spoken with Arnold Weinstock who wanted to use his holding as a catalyst for putting the company right.

Gulliver and Weinstock had never met, and knew each other by reputation only. MacGregor had been making the right noises behind the scenes, and believed that Weinstock would like Gulliver to make a move. 'He believes you are the right person to do it,' he told Gulliver. They were, he went on, speaking with Weinstock's knowledge and approval. Weinstock would not get directly involved. But what he might be prepared to do was underwrite a core part of Gulliver's financial package – say £350m. His name could also be used, indicating he was behind the deal, thus making it easy for Gulliver to raise the rest. MacGregor and Grant also believed Weinstock would support a Gulliver offer with his shareholding. And Lazard reckoned it could deliver another block of shares: the South African industrialist, Dr Anton Rupert, who controlled Rothmans and Dunhills, owned another three per cent of the equity. The two blocks together came to nearly eight per cent, which, MacGregor indicated, Lazard hoped would support a Gulliver bid. In return however Lazard would want to be 'lead' banker on the bid.

Weinstock remembers being favourably inclined towards the concept outlined by MacGregor. 'It was quite a romantic idea. MacGregor said "You've got these shares, Gulliver is a good young chap – why not do something together?" And there was MacGregor in the background.' Both Macgregor and Weinstock seemed taken with the idea of "this young Scot" from humble background taking on the stuffy Distillers. In fact Gulliver was 55, only six years younger than Weinstock.

Gulliver was on holiday in the middle of July, so it was 25 July before he met the GEC chief at his unprepossessing offices just off Park Lane (Weinstock did not believe in spending money on frivolities such as comfortable offices). Gulliver reckoned the meeting had gone well and that both men were impressed with the other. Weinstock, however, had doubts. 'I thought I detected a hint of ego, and I don't like ego.' He wondered privately whether Gulliver was quite as good as MacGregor had built him up to be. 'I was slightly nervous. I didn't know if he was the man to take on a situation as big as that.'

But he agreed that in principle he would support the scheme. That was enough to send the spirits of the Argyll camp soaring. Gulliver's right hand men, Grant and Webster, were less enthusiastic about Weinstock than their boss was, but the bankers disagreed. 'Our advisers thought Arnold Weinstock could be of crucial significance,' said Gulliver afterwards.

The financial package was fashioned on the basis that GEC would underwrite a major chunk of the core underwriting, perhaps as much as £350m; other core underwriters would take another £550m. 'It meant we would have £350m in the bag before we started,' says a Gulliver colleague. The rest would be easy. But it was all predicated on Weinstock definitely supporting it; and as time went on, and in the heightened atmosphere that prevailed through August, no-one paused to consider what might happen if Weinstock did not come aboard. His presence was taken for granted. Many people, both in government and the City, have learned never to take Weinstock for granted. Probably no-one in British industry today is as hard-headed and analytical as Weinstock. As far as he was concerned, he would decide on the merits of the proposals put to him. And he had not yet seen the written proposal.

Gulliver knew he was venturing into uncharted waters. There had not yet been a leveraged hostile bid for a big company in Britain – John Elliott was lining one up for Allied-Lyons at the same time but had not yet launched it. But Gulliver was vaguely conscious of the change of climate which was just reaching the British bid scene. 'We didn't fully realise the mood for a mega-bid was there,' said Gulliver later.* 'The United States had seen a number of major leveraged bids and it was seen that beneficial corporate change could be achieved by aggressively run smaller companies bidding for larger businesses.' The excess liquidity in the system, which had fuelled the American bid boom, had also built up in Britain and was now waiting for the raiders to come along and use it.

But all of this was only glimpsed dimly through the busy days of that August. Gulliver, for all his success, lacked the self-confidence to believe the City institutions would support *him* against the might of the Scottish establishment, which he knew he would be taking on by bidding for Distillers. He was greatly comforted by his belief that

*Interview with Ivan Fallon.

179

Weinstock would be behind him. 'Weinstock was to be the sort of father figure, not actually doing anything but putting his seal of approval on James,' said one of the Gulliver side afterwards. There is some disagreement between the bankers, and Gulliver and his directors, even now, over the importance of Weinstock. At Lazards, there is a view that Gulliver could not have raised the finances for his deal that summer, and Samuel Montagu tends to agree, although less vehemently. Gulliver himself insists he could have done. 'When they heard that Weinstock was probably going to be involved, they felt it was the credibility we needed,' he said. 'Until that moment, they had been telling us we couldn't do it. But we were already well down the road, we were going ahead even before Weinstock ever showed up.'

With Weinstock apparently aboard, the pace through August speeded up. Few of the team took a holiday that August; Gulliver reckoned the Distillers board would be caught off their guard, and the bankers agreed. 'Let's shoot them up the backside while they're out on the grouse moor,' remarked Peter Grant; it became one of the catch phrases of the campaign.

The written proposal to Weinstock, drafted by Lazard, was finally ready on 21 August, and arrived at GEC's offices just before the Bank Holiday weekend. It proposed that GEC take up £350m of the core underwriting, and also contained a recommendation that Gulliver and his senior directors would be issued new warrants on what were described as 'favourable terms'. The Argyll bankers seem to have believed that Weinstock's approval for the terms was already assured and that the papers would come winging back with a signature and the agreement to go ahead. It did not work that way.

In the tight programme Gulliver was working to, even minor hold-ups were serious worries, and were often misinterpreted. Weinstock did not even see the proposals until after the Bank Holiday weekend, by which time all sorts of rumours were circulating through the Argyll camp.

'Unfortunately, when it came to the launch, no-one could get hold of him, and he never returned James' calls. We just couldn't get a decision out of him,' says an Argyll director. Weinstock's 'elusiveness' became part of folk-lore. Yet his diary records the fact that he was out of the country for six working days that August, and was, he insists 'never out of contact'.

Gulliver was not dealing direct with Weinstock – in fact they only had that one meeting during the bid. Contact with GEC was largely through Malcolm Bates, GEC's deputy managing director, and through Philip Ralph, another GEC finance man. At that level, the view was that Weinstock would almost certainly support the scheme.

But everyone was aware it needed Weinstock's personal confirmation. Just after the proposals were delivered, Gulliver rang Bates. They needed a quick decision. The press releases had been drafted with Weinstock's name prominently on them. 'Look Malcolm,' said Gulliver. 'We're right up against it now. We just have to get a decision. If we don't get one by tomorrow, we may have to pull the bid.' Gulliver related his version of the Bates reply back to his team with wry amusement – and some dismay. 'I'll tell you how you'll know whether you will get a decision tomorrow,' Bates is said to have replied. 'When you wake up in the morning, look out of the window. If it's raining, he should be here, and you should hear. If it's fine, he'll be in Deauville.'*

Weinstock did not see the Lazards proposal until after the weekend. He did not like it. 'It took me ten minutes to turn it down.'

Some of his colleagues argued that GEC should go ahead, but Weinstock was adamant. GEC, he pointed out, could end up with £350m locked into a Gulliver-run company, with no way of getting out. That, of course, was on the worst possible scenario – an underwriter is providing a guarantee, and is only left with the stocks if no-one else wants them. 'The terms were unacceptable,' he said bluntly. He did not rule GEC out of the deal altogether: if Lazard wanted to reconstitute the terms, then he would agree to participate. But not on the basis proposed.

It was a major setback for the Gulliver camp. In the final days of August, there was a desperate attempt to reconstitute the bid. There was a frantic few days while Gulliver and his team tramped the City, trying to piece together a new package. But it was the height of the holiday season, and few of the senior fund managers were in their City offices. The chances of launching in the first working days of September looked increasingly remote.

'If Gulliver wanted to launch a thing like this in August, he had only himself to blame,' said a GEC director afterwards. Weinstock was also apparently unimpressed with the way the banks were operating, unable to agree on some of the details. And he did not like the fact that the Distillers share price was rising, indicating there was a leak.

But there could have been another reason which influenced him: Weinstock was working on a bid of his own. He had decided to bid for Plessey, one of his few serious rivals in a number of areas in the electrical business, although now less than a sixth GEC's size. Weinstock prepared his Plessey bid in great secrecy.

By the end of August the inevitable happened: the story leaked.

---

*Bates denies that he said these words.

The *Sunday Telegraph* carried the first real hint of it. Then on 1 September, the *Sunday Times* commented: 'Jimmy Gulliver... is costing himself a fortune by delaying a bid for Distillers. If he is serious he must now move fast.' In the past 10 days, commented the paper, the price had risen 70p 'costing him an extra £300m just to fire a realistic first shot'. The previous Friday alone it had risen 47p.

But still Gulliver waited for Weinstock. Grant and Webster urged him to launch as planned in the first week of September but, without Weinstock, Gulliver refused to accept he had the necessary credibility, and insisted he must have more time to win the support of the institutions. As September opened and the City returned to work after the holidays, Gulliver still dithered. Weinstock indicated he might still support a bid, if the terms he was offered were very different; he would not support anything which he felt was 'over-egged' with warrants for the Argyll directors. 'We would not have minded something reasonably modest,' said Weinstock later.

The reaction over the next few days proved beyond doubt that the City believed Gulliver more than capable of swallowing Distillers, despite the disparity on the market values: Distillers now at £1.3bn, Argyll at £616m. The bid had now acquired a momentum which could not easily be stopped. The Distillers price took off as the arbitrageurs and speculators piled in. Gulliver however still hesitated, deciding he must have a few days to assess the scale of support. 'James made the mistake of spending too much time with the brokers, and not enough with the institutions,' said a colleague later. It was the institutional shareholders who would decide the bid one way or the other. They were at the point where they would have supported almost anyone against Distillers. They regarded Gulliver very highly, partly because of his record, but also because of the time and effort to which Grant and Webster had gone in explaining what the Argyll team was about.

The speculation following the weekend was frenetic. *The Times* headline reported it as *'fever pitch'*. Gulliver was expected to announce any moment a bid of 375p a share, worth £1.36bn. When he didn't, the shares fell back. It was the type of situation the Takeover Panel could not ignore. It called in Gulliver's advisers, Lazards, and insisted on an immediate statement clarifying Gulliver's intentions. Gulliver was given a choice of what he could say, with the implications of each laid out carefully. He could deny he had any intention of bidding, in which case he could be forbidden to do so, unless there was a material change of circumstances, for a year at least. Or he could announce immediately he was considering a bid. Or he could go for something in between. Gulliver chose the 'in between'. That day he put out the following statement:

Argyll, which has as its long-term strategy the development of a major food business, has for some time regarded Distillers and a number of other companies as possible opportunities for growth by acquisition or association. The reports, however, of an imminent bid are inaccurate and the company does not intend to make an offer for Distillers at the present time.

It was Gulliver's biggest mistake.

The Panel had carefully explained to him that the words 'at the present time' would be interpreted to mean something more than a week – in fact it would mean three to four months. Gulliver's advisers suggested the Panel did not seriously mean three months, because if the Distillers share price continued to rise, and the speculation refused to die down, then they would be in a new situation and the Panel would have to treat it as such. On the other hand, the statement might just cause the speculation to cool, and allow Gulliver to get his act together.

The crucial element, however, seems to have been Gulliver's own self-doubts. Despite his success, Gulliver underestimated his own standing in the City. Short and stocky, with an almost cherubic face and a mass of wavy, grey-flecked hair, he was in appearance the opposite of the tall, elegant Hanson. Hanson had the ability to make an instant decision and launch a bid, with his team already in top gear, within a matter of hours. Gulliver was far more cautious, weighing up every possible aspect, researching his target as no-one else had ever done, running through pro-form balance sheets at a whole range of prices, paying more attention to the downside than the upside. In this case it was his undoing.

'James was like a kid fighting in the playground,' said one person involved in the bid. 'He had half made up his mind to fight, but was still hesitating. He could not quite bring himself to put his head down and go in, fists flailing.'

By the end of the week all Gulliver's doubts had been removed. The City had rallied overwhelmingly to him, grateful that someone at last was seriously going to tackle Distillers, even more grateful that it was someone they admired as much as Gulliver.

Weinstock by that time, however, was largely out of the picture. Only lukewarm at any stage, he was now positively cool. 'When he made that [Panel] statement, we stopped taking him seriously,' he said later. 'We were mystified by this statement, and our confidence in the judgement of those concerned in Argyll was weakened.' By now, however, that no longer mattered. Even without him there was no problem finding institutions willing to underwrite the bid. Gulliver was ready to go. His advisers trooped back to the Panel.

Tim Barker, director general of the Takeover Panel, now delivered a rude shock. He attached great importance, he told the Gulliver camp, to 'the public being able to rely on statements of intention'. It was completely unacceptable for a statement of the kind Gulliver had issued a week before to be followed now by an announcement of an offer. Gulliver's advisers, Lazards and Samuel Montagu, had been clearly informed of how the statement would be interpreted.

At Guinness, Ernest Saunders was just putting the finishing touches to a bid for Arthur Bell. It had been a major and exhausting battle, and in mid-September, as Gulliver was arguing with the Panel over whether the words 'the present time' could be interpreted as three to four months (as the Panel insisted) or two to three months (as Gulliver claimed), Saunders was sending in his management team to begin the task of incorporating the group's biggest ever acquisition into Guinness. Saunders might have cast an envious eye in the direction of Distillers, but it did not seriously occur to him at that stage that he would be in a position to get it. Bells had been tough enough, and it was less than a quarter the size.

Distillers belatedly moved to prepare its defences. For years it had relied on the merchant bank Robert Fleming, which has strong Scottish connections, but was now firmly advised that it needed a real heavyweight in the corporate finance field (Fleming is one of the biggest fund managers among the banks, with over £17bn under management, but it is relatively small in the corporate finance area). Now Distillers brought in Kleinwort Benson, one of four or five first division City merchant banks. It also announced a major management reorganisation and some better than expected profit figures. Kleinwort appointed a new director to the board: Sir Nigel Broackes, himself one of the ablest and most experienced bid experts.

Meanwhile, as Gulliver continued to get his financing and his team ready for the delayed start, the Distillers share price kept on rising. By early October it was well past Gulliver's original target price of 375p and was 420p, 120p above its level before the 'rumours began. Adamantly the Panel refused to accept the Gulliver argument that there had been a 'significant change of circumstances' since the statement. 'Last night Peter Lee, a Panel executive, confirmed that an increase in the Distillers share price would not rate as a "significant change",' wrote *The Times* on 9 October. Time was working against Gulliver in a number of ways: Distillers was becoming more expensive by the day as the stock market rose and speculation continued; the defence was now getting into its stride and Distillers executives were touring the institutional shareholders, armed with flip charts and slide shows, telling them of the change of the direction the company was now experiencing. And although he was not aware of it at the time, something else was happening behind the scenes: Ernest Saunders was steadily getting himself into a position where he might be a contender for Distillers, after all.

Gulliver first heard the rumours of Saunders' interests in October. Olivier Roux, the 36-year-old French management consultant whom his employers, Bain & Co, had hired to Guinness, lunched at the City offices of Hoare Govett, brokers to Distillers. At the end of the lunch, Roux casually mentioned that Saunders had asked him to say that if there was anything Guinness could do in the coming battle against Argyll, he was very willing to get involved. Gulliver, when he heard, was immediately on the alert. He rang Saunders. Was it true? Saunders denied it. 'I can assure you, James, that the wear and tear of the Bells bid was so great that we could not consider another bid.' Gulliver believed him. He felt he was on friendly terms with Saunders, whose management abilities greatly impressed him. Gulliver was a keen football fan, a major shareholder and director of Manchester United. Saunders too was a football fan, devoting his energies to Queens Park Rangers, where he too was a director. Gulliver had entertained Saunders on a couple of occasions in the directors' box at Old Trafford; they had met once at a dinner party; they had bumped into each other on half a dozen other occasions. Gulliver felt he had done Saunders a favour during the Bells bid, when the Bells chairman Raymond Miquel went to see him and suggested he might enter as a 'white knight'. Gulliver had said no, and had dropped Saunders a letter telling him he would not get involved. It had been useful information for the Guinness chairman at that stage of the bid.

Despite all the delays, disappointments and rumours, when Gulliver finally launched his bid on 2 December, three months after his fateful statement, he was still the favourite to win. He offered 513p a share, valuing Distillers at £1.9bn, the biggest bid yet made in Britain, just topping the £1.8bn that John Elliott of Elders-IXL had offered for Allied-Lyons. Argyll's own market value by contrast was £700m. Even Gulliver's £1.9bn however was already being dismissed as a 'sighting shot' and 'unwelcome and inadequate' by the Distillers board, which was typically scornful of this upstart daring to bid for the pride of Scotland. 'Mr Gulliver deals in potatoes and cans of beans,' said one director. 'We are not selling brown water in bottles. We are selling Scotch.'

Gulliver had now moved out of the period which had become

known as the 'phoney bid' into full-scale bid warfare. He was now a different man from the hesitant, self-conscious figure of three months before. He might have been offering some £500-600m more than he originally considered a good 'sighting shot', but all his research still showed that Distillers was worth it. Furthermore, in their early days, the clear view both in the City and in Edinburgh was that Gulliver would win. He had avoided some of the indignation of the Scottish lobby with his careful wooing of the past few years, and also with another move: he offered to shift the headquarters of Distillers from its elegant office in St James Square to Edinburgh where all Scots felt it rightly belonged.

His financing package also minimised the pain of the higher price he was now forced to pay. A similar bid in the United States would have relied heavily upon junk bonds. For Gulliver and Argyll, the financial team of Samuel Montagu, Charterhouse Japhet and Lazards had arranged loan finance of £600m, and another £1.2bn of Argyll's shares underwritten (or guaranteed) by a group of institutions. It had been so designed that, if the bid failed, Gulliver would pay less than £10m in costs for the financial facilities; if it succeeded, he would pay a different rate: some £74m.

There were other differences, too, in the way such a bid would have been arranged in the US: instead of the normal cash tender offer for over 50 per cent of the shares, the now standard American practice, with a mixture of junk bonds and cash for the rest, Gulliver was essentially offering shares in his own company for shares of Distillers. If all Distillers shareholders accepted, it would mean they would be in the ascendant in the enlarged company. But by accepting Gulliver's offer to exchange their Distillers shares for his Argyll ones, they were voting for his style of management. The indications in the early days already suggested that Distillers shareholders would indeed support Gulliver.

In that first week in December 1985, both Sir Hector Laing and James Gulliver could be forgiven for believing they were only a matter of weeks away from their ambitions of running major international concerns, fully capable of competing with most of the world. Laing did not know that Hanson was about to shatter his carefully worked-out plan; and Gulliver did not know that Distillers, in its desperation to avoid his clutches, was casting around for a 'white knight' who would ride onto the stage.

Hanson at the time was still at a critical stage in his bid for SCM, where it had become not so much a battle of Sir Gordon White versus the SCM board, as White versus Merrill Lynch. The value of that bid was fast approaching $1bn. Could Hanson/White really take on another bid three times the size of that? There was already another proposition in front of Hanson: he had been approached by a group of individuals which included Nicholas Berry, son of the *Daily Telegraph*'s 74-year-old proprietor Lord Hartwell, and asked to help save the struggling newspaper which in the absence of a rival bid was headed for control by the Canadian businessman, Conrad Black. As late as the afternoon of Thursday, 3 December, three days after the two big bids had opened, Hanson went to a meeting at N.M. Rothschild, merchant banker to both Hanson and the *Telegraph*, to talk about the fate of the newspaper. Hanson, however, decided he was not interested in bailing it out – there were too many problems in that industry. Now he was interested in a much bigger proposition.

The previous day Hanson held his quarterly board meeting. Sir Gordon White had flown in for it and had become involved in the *Telegraph* discussions. One item on the agenda was, as it always was, a discussion of takeover plans. The range of companies Hanson might be interested in buying was discussed. Distillers, now in play with the Gulliver bid, was ruled firmly out. But Hanson indicated he would like to make another bid, which was desirable for a number of reasons. Hanson Trust was, after its rights issues, now overcapitalised, an unusual but easily resolved problem for a company. Imperial Group had been on the list for over a year but, with the proposed deal with Sir Hector Laing, it was now in play. If Hanson was ever going to go for it, the time was now. If the current deal went through, it would have got away. The board agreed.

Distillers for Hanson was out; Imps was in.

On Thursday afternoon, when the *Daily Telegraph* discussions ended, Hanson instructed Rothschild to put a package together. By seven that evening it was ready. And there were no leaks. The next morning the normally perceptive Lex column in the *Financial Times* gave its view:

> Pity poor Lord Hanson. He has spent much of the past few months sitting in the ante-rooms of successive New York courts waiting for judgments which have tended to make the takeover of SCM a rather remote proposition... The SCM involvement has more or less precluded Hanson Trust from tackling a UK takeover at a time when its war chest had never been fuller and the list of British targets is being whittled down by defensive mergers and hostile bids elsewhere. It must be very frustrating.

Not a bit of it. Hanson was in fact feeling on top of the world. That day, just four days after Christopher Reeves and his Morgan contacts had announced their carefully crafted Imperial-United Biscuits merger, Hanson made his move: he offered £1.9bn for Imps.

Imps, like Distillers, was one of the last great asset situations available at the time. It was also, again like Distillers, the market leader in a declining business, cigarettes. It had seen its share of the marker drop from a seemingly permanent two-thirds through most of the 1960s and 1970s, to 40 per cent by the mid-1960s. It had tried for 30 years to reduce its dependence on tobacco, and had made a series of diversification takeovers, many of them poor. Its worst was the takeover for $360m of Howard Johnson (HoJo), in 1980 which it had just sold to Marriott, the US hotel chain; that move had savagely damaged its City reputation, and still stands as one of the worst takeovers in British history. It had also led to a boardroom coup in 1981 when the then chairman, and the man responsible for the HoJo acquisition, Malcolm Anson, was dismissed as chairman after only a year in the job. He had been replaced by Geoffrey Kent, who ironically had known Hanson for 20 years. Kent introduced a new reign of tight centralised 'hands on' management. He also sold off some of the odd acquisitions already made (a poultry, meat and animal feeds operation was sold in 1982 for a net loss of £54m), many of them to a little known company called Hillsdown Holdings, which turned them into a major success and provided the base for that company to achieve spectacular earnings growth. Under Kent, profits had more than doubled in five years, but even so its John Player and W.D. & H.O. Wills tobacco subsidiaries accounted for half of profits, its brewing (Courage and John Smith), food (Ross and Golden Wonder, HP sauce) and others accounting for the rest.

For all Kent's better management, however, by the time of the Hanson bid, Imps was still only making profits of £220m on sales of £4.66bn. Hanson by contrast made £250m on sales of £2.7bn. Furthermore, Hanson, even before SCM, was by far the bigger company, with a market capitalisation of £2.5bn.

Hanson from the start controlled the pace of the bid, settling in for what he knew would last four to five months, and would be determined – unless the Office of Fair Trading decided otherwise – in the final weeks. There is no doubt that his years of experience in the bid arena gave him a considerable, and perhaps even a decisive, advantage in the biggest takeover yet. By contrast Gulliver, battling for Distillers, was running in bursts, putting in great bouts of energy, then in the middle of the bid disappearing from the scene altogether. Hanson never seemed to doubt he would win, whereas Gulliver had had major doubts from the start. Given the scale of the stakes, confidence was vital, and Hanson had it in abundance.

In February Hanson got a tremendous break when first of all the government, now deeply embroiled in the Westland Helicopters drama, referred Imperial's bid for United to the Monopolies Commission – and then announced it would not refer Hanson's bid for Imps. Imps' deal with United Biscuits lapsed and Hanson seemed to have the bidding all his own way. The confidence of Reeves and his Morgan Grenfell team was shown to be doubly misplaced. A deal which had seemed to be cut and dried had now run into two seemingly insuperable problems: first a counter bid had appeared from the man everyone feared in the takeover arena (because he seldom lost) and secondly that bidder had a clear run thanks to the Monopolies Commission reference. Paul Channon had now taken over as Secretary of State for Trade and Industry from Leon Brittan, who had become the second cabinet casualty of the Westland affair. It was obviously a contentious decision, but Channon was able to argue it on pure competition grounds: Imperial and United Biscuits between them had 41 per cent of the £360m a year snacks market, and that, the OFT had recommended, should be examined by the Monopolies Commission. Channon agreed. On the other hand there was almost no overlap between Hanson and Imperial, which raised still another question. Did conglomerate mergers, whatever their size, have nothing to fear from government intervention just so long as there was no duplication of assets? That of course was the logical extension of the Norman Tebbit doctrine, as laid down in July 1984. But the political pressure to interpret that doctrine loosely and subjectively was already beginning to build up on Channon.

There was another question being asked about the government actions over the bid. Was Hanson being shown special favouritism? For Hanson, for reasons never fully explained, had entered the Westland fray. He could claim some helicopter interests: he operated a tiny fleet of them. But Westland was a deeply troubled helicopter manufacturer, with no commercial interest to Hanson. Yet at the height of the Westland embarrassment for Mrs Thatcher, Hanson bought 14.9 per cent and wrote to the chairman, Sir John Cuckney, to pledge his support for Cuckney's proposed link-up with the American group Sikorski. It was widely interpreted at the time as a gesture of support for Mrs Thatcher, who favoured the Sikorski option, as opposed to her former Defence Secretary Michael Heseltine who had resigned over it. As *The Times* commented: 'As a gallant gesture by an ardent Thatcher fan, Lord Hanson's move has a certain style. As an attempt to win friends and influence people in the United States, it has some merit. As a straightforward commercial decision, it defies analysis.' The Westland purchase was now being presented by critics of Mrs Thatcher – and of Hanson – as a gesture of another kind. Hanson was accused by MPs, notably the Liberal Leader David Steel, of buying the shares to influence the outcome of the Monopolies reference. 'Anyone disposed to cause mischief might be tempted to suggest that the Hanson bid was given the all clear as a "thank you" for Lord Hanson's role in the Westland affair,' said Steel.

In the raging argument, several points were overlooked. First, Hanson's interest in Westland went back much further than the immediate fracas. Early in 1985, Hanson and White had decided to take over Westland; but first they needed to ensure there were some orders to see it through into the 1990s. According to White* they made an appointment to see Michael Heseltine, then Secretary of State for Defence. Would he oppose a bid for Westland? Heseltine indicated he had no objection. What about orders from the Armed Forces, the only serious customer for the Westland range of helicopters? Heseltine, according to White, was brutally frank: there was no prospect of him bringing forward any orders just to save the British helicopter business. Without those orders, Westland was clearly headed for serious financial crisis. Hanson and White pulled out. But they kept a watching eye on the company.

Secondly, White says he was very anxious about anti-American feeling in Britain creating a backlash in the United States. If Britain were seen to be refusing to allow an American bid for Westland, might not the Americans start to get nasty with British companies?

Thirdly, the critics chose to ignore the fact that the recommendation to refer the rival United Biscuits bid had been made by the independent OFT and its director general Sir Gordon Borrie, not renowned for delivering the decisions the government wanted.

It was now that Sir Hector Laing suddenly showed a different side of his character – and Morgans showed why it had such a reputation as a winner.

Hanson had outgunned the Imperial board, shooting down Kent's defences with consummate ease. Laing had been forced to take a back seat during the bid so far: he was, after all, technically the target company of Imperial. The Imperial bid for United had died with the Monopolies Commission references. But there was a way round that.

At 9.30 on the morning of Monday, 17 February, 1986, Hanson stepped up the pace, now determined to go for a quick clean kill before

*Interview with the authors.

Kent and his team could gather themselves from the blows he had already hit them with. He increased his offer to £2.3bn, reckoning that, with the opposition already demolished, that would win it for him.

At the same moment however, Laing was making an announcement of his own: if Imperial couldn't bid for him, he would bid for Imperial, despite the disparity in size.

He topped Hanson's offer with a £2.5bn bid, yet another new record, and at the same time revealed he had found a way round the Monopolies Commission reference. The OFT was worried about the monopoly position in the snacks field. That was no problem. He would sell off Golden Wonder, part of Imps, and leave the competition position in the snacks market unchanged. It was a breathtaking move, for once rocking even the calm Lord Hanson.

Nothing like it had ever happened before in the history of takeover bids in Britain. Normally a Monopolies Commission reference either meant the bid died there and then, or there was six months of argument and discussion in front of the Commissioners. True, the new bid, recommended by the Imps board, meant that instead of ending up with 41 per cent of the enlarged company, United Biscuits shareholders would now get around 28 per cent, but Laing argued that was a small price to pay for the benefits that would undoubtedly follow. It was, he insisted, well worth it in order to get a group which could take on the American giants in the rapidly growing food markets of the Third World. Golden Wonder could be sold for £100m or so. It was a small part of a combine which would command a market value of over £3.5bn if it went through.

Once again Christopher Reeves and his men at Morgan Grenfell were in the ascendant. Again they thought they had won: 'Hanson has to live by making good financial deals,' said a Morgan Grenfell man that day. 'He never thought he would have to go to this level. He can't just match us, he has to go beyond by some margin; and if he does that it's our judgement he won't have a good financial deal.' Later, even allowing for the rhetoric that is part of the merchant bankers weaponry, that judgement did not look too good.

The battle for Imps had now become a straightforward fight between Hanson and United Biscuits. Now was the time when market muscle would decide things. The City institutions had made money from Hanson succeeding before. They reckoned they would again. At this crucial moment, his share price rose, tilting the balance back to him. As the Hanson share price moved up, the value of the bids was roughly the same: £2.5bn each. Hanson's was a hostile bid, vigorously resisted by the Imperial board. United Biscuits was making an agreed bid, which gave Laing an advantage, but not a crucial one. The government, in the shape of the OFT and the Monopolies Commission, played no further part. The bid would now be fought in the market, and would be decided by shareholders. Both sides set off to get the magical 50.01 per cent they needed for victory.

The bid now moved into the endgame. Hanson had steered well clear of the controversies that were raging on the Distillers bid, and had also remained aloof from the counter-attacks from Imperial. Now he quickened the tempo at just the right time, displaying a calm certainty that would not fail to impress the big shareholders. He bought shares heavily on the market, while the rise in his own share price allowed his offer first to catch up with United's and then to pass it. He was inching ahead just when it mattered. Laing was still running hard, but his early bursts had left him with little new to say at the end when it mattered. It was as if Hanson had slipstreamed in Laing's wake until the final lap, and now pulled out to overtake in the back straight according to a plan he had worked to from the start. There was no sign of greater effort, as there was in the United camp which was visibly running as hard as it could. Laing had fought a valiant battle, but his race was run. When the counting was done, Hanson had won easily. His crown as the king of the takeover world was safe.

Morgan had suffered one crushing defeat, and desperately needed victory in another battle to redeem it.

Its chances of achieving it were evenly poised. In the Distillers bid, James Gulliver had sailed past the one obstacle that initially worried him: the possibility of a Monopolies reference. But an even bigger obstacle had suddenly appeared. Gulliver now had company: Distillers had found its 'white knight'.

Ernest Saunders of Guinness had entered the fray. And the merchant bank behind him was Morgan Grenfell.

• CHAPTER EIGHT •

Guinness Isn't Good For You

Even before Ernest Walter Saunders and Guinness moved into what developed into the biggest scandal the City had known in generations, concern about the level of takeover activity was already growing. The farsighted in the City were forecasting that 'short-termism', complete lack of interest in the longer-term implications of industrial concentration, plus the worrying level of abuses, would inevitably lead to the same type of reaction the Square Mile had witnessed at the end of the Slater era – and this time it could be much worse. That concern however had not yet touched official level. The Thatcher government had its hands full with the Westland affair, and the man whose job it was to watch over competition policy, Leon Brittan, was fighting for his political life. When he was forced to resign, the new man, Paul Channon, started uncertainly, and from the beginning found himself at a terrible disadvantage: he was a member of the Guinness family, and therefore had to disqualify himself from any involvement in that battle. In any case, it would probably have made no difference: competition policy was not high on the government priority list, even in Norman Tebbit's or Leon Brittan's time. The essential philosophy was that the markets, with the help of the City Takeover Panel, should decide.

And in the City, the mood now fully endorsed the mega-bid. There were at least half a dozen names who could have raised almost any amount for a leveraged bid: Gulliver, of course, had already done it; Sir Jeffrey Sterling of P&O; Sir Nigel Broackes; Sir Ralph Halpern of

Debenhams; Sir Philip Harris of Harris Queensway; Sir Terence Conran; Alec Monk of Dee Corporation, the food group; and a few others. Hanson and Sir Owen Green came into a different category; they could have had as much as they liked. The City was awash with money – Japanese, German, American and domestic money, seeking a quick return before chasing the next hot market. The merchant banks were working around the clock, dreaming up new deals to put to their clients, suggesting mergers, purchases, sales, leveraged buy-outs, anything to increase their business. Roger Seelig and George Magan of Morgan's seemed to be everywhere, with Christopher Reeves and Graham Walsh moving smoothly behind them, setting the fees, putting the seal on deals, soothing clients. It was a time when no company, even ICI and BP, the giants of Britain, seemed safe. There were merchant bankers running the rule over every single company in Britain, and working out strategies for taking them over. American banks, desperately trying to break in and make a mark, figured out new ways of taking over some of the great companies of the day: Sears Holdings, owners of Selfridges and most of Britain's shoe shops; Pearson Group, owners of the *Financial Times*, Lazards, Château Latour and Madame Tussauds; Woolworth and many, many others. Potential raiders were bombarded by every post with ingenious schemes for making a dramatic takeover. Where the merchant banks were not able to dream up a takeover, they sold their services as defenders, persuading their clients to get the walls in place before the invaders appeared over the horizon.

Even though the freneticism was largely confined to the City and the offices of the raiders and target companies, all the signs that it would get out of hand were there. Insider trading was rife, and everyone knew it and turned a blind eye. Many of the bids made no sense, but were being shuffled through anyway. The tactics of both bidder and defender had developed far faster than the rule-makers could cope with. It was only a matter of time before it all went too far – and the whole takeover scene blew apart.

That is exactly what happened. The bank at the centre of it all was Morgan Grenfell. And the company that set it all in train was Guinness.

It is easily forgotten today, but in January 1986 few executives enjoyed a higher reputation than Ernest Saunders. As a marketer, a manager and a raider, he ranked among the highest in Britain. 'Saunders could have walked on water,' says James Gulliver. 'He was regarded, like his advertising, as near-genius. And he *had* done an amazing job. You have to give him that.'

Just turned 50, Saunders was a tall, handsome man, with the nose of a Roman senator. His grey hair was thinning, he had to be careful about his blood pressure, and there was a suggestion of a middle-aged paunch. But he had the commanding bearing and presence expected of the head of one of the country's great corporations. In his large office, furnished more in the fashion of a living room than a work-space, he was invariably shirt-sleeved, delicately twirling a pair of glasses that he seldom wore. Although he was frequently pictured holding a pint of Guinness or toasting victory with a glass of Bell's whisky, he barely touched either, carefully watching his weight, and one felt, unwilling to be out of control of himself, even slightly.

He spoke slowly and deliberately, with just the faintest hint of a lisp, more marked when he was tired. During the Bell's bid, he had discovered the habit of breakfast meetings, and during his takeover bids started with meetings before eight each morning. By late evening, he could appear drained and grey, but was still invariably courteous and charming.

Long-term relationships seemed to mean less to Saunders than to most senior businessmen. Journalists who had known him for years but dared to oppose him in his bid battles suddenly found themselves regarded as enemies. He several times complained to proprietors, and he also spread around legal threats, even to leading City editors who regarded themselves as his friends. The City, used to ambitious and driven men, detected an extra dimension to Saunders: a man determined to climb by quantum leaps into the premier division, and prepared to pay a high cost to get there. Someone gave him a nickname 'Deadly Earnest' and it fitted so perfectly that he was seldom called anything else. People would say 'What's Deadly Earnest up to this week?' and everyone knew who they meant.

Yet there was another side to him, too. His family mattered to him a great deal, and few people realised that, in the immediate aftermath of the Distillers bid, his wife Carole was seriously ill and underwent a major operation. He found himself spending more time at her bedside than running his company, but she mattered more to him at that point even than his ambition. He was deeply involved with his children, particularly his son James, who had followed in his father's footsteps by going to Cambridge. Later, in the one-dimensional way we like to depict our villains, he would be shown as the inhuman, manic ogre, but through the Distillers bid and through the Thomas Risk affair that was to follow it, he was perfectly balanced and as subject to human emotions as anyone. He genuinely could not understand why he was accused of doing wrong. The word 'ruthless' when applied to him 'make the hairs stand up on my head', he said once. His executive directors were intensely loyal to him, and the Guinness family had come to believe the sun shone out of him.

From the beginning, well before the Bell's bid even, he took a great interest in the preparation of this book, and frequently offered suggestions. He indicated he was putting aside private papers and memos which could be reviewed once the bid was over and they were no longer confidential. He even offered to make available documents relating to the Distillers bid for the preparation of a major *Sunday Times* colour magazine article on the anatomy of a bid. 'It's important that all the issues, all the tactics, the strategy, why we did certain things when we did, are understood,' he said on several occasions. It was his own idea, and in retrospect it is fascinating to consider what papers he might have made available. Perhaps the papers he would have shown would have been selectively edited, but he never appeared secretive. In the event, we never saw any papers he might have set aside for us – Ivan Boesky's confessions intervened. But Saunders, two days after Department of Trade inspectors marched into the Guinness offices on 1 December, 1986, carefully went through an early draft of this and other chapters in the book. At that stage we only dimly suspected the type of revelations that lay ahead. Saunders himself stated he had absolutely no idea why the inspectors were there. Was there no clue, not even the slightest? 'None.' Was there anything which might come out which might alter the manuscript he had just read? 'Nothing – you've got it all.' Of course we had *not* got it all, far from it. We make no claim to have got it all, even now. Saunders himself later insisted that many of the revelations relating to events in the Distillers battle were as new to him as they were to the rest of us. But there is little doubt he could have shed more light on events at that point.

What follows is written without the benefit of the report from the inspectors, and will no doubt be further overtaken by events even while this book is being printed. It is based on interviews with Saunders, with Lord Iveagh, with Gulliver, with Seelig and with many others, both during the bid and later.

Even in its early days the Distillers bid battle was something out of the ordinary, not only because of its size, but for the fascinating clash of Gulliver versus Saunders, for the tactics used, and because it coincided, almost day by day and event by event, with the battle for the Imperial Group. Yet it was months later before even those most closely involved with the Distillers bid realised its full significance. In the end, it made even the battle for Harrods almost look pale.

Saunders was born Ernst Walter Schleyer in Vienna, on 21 October, 1935, the eldest son of Emanuel Schleyer, an eminent Austrian gynaecologist. His father appears to have been from a Jewish family, although Saunders always said he genuinely wasn't sure what his religion was. His mother was a Protestant, and had the baby Ernst christened at the British embassy church in Vienna – presumably a precaution against the rising tide of anti-semitism in Austria at the time. Saunders never remembered his father even talking about religion. But Emanuel's fears of Hitler were sufficient cause for him to take his wife and two sons out of the country. In 1937 they arrived in Britain, unable even to speak the language. The first years were far from easy. Schleyer was in his 40s and his medical qualifications were not accepted in Britain. He retook his medical exams in Glasgow and Edinburgh, then moved to a lowly post at the Hospital for Women in Soho Square. But he soon prospered. By the mid-1950s, when the family name was changed to Schleyer-Saunders, he was able to move to his own practice in Wimpole Street where he stayed for many years.

By the time Ernest arrived at Cambridge in 1954 to study law, he was plain Ernest Saunders. He never practised his law, but went instead straight into industry, working first for 3M, then in 1960 moving into the marketing department of J. Walter Thompson, the leading advertising agency in London of the day (although of course American-owned). JWT, he would later claim, was his university, and it is from that point that his love of marketing began. In 1962 he met Carole Stephings, an attractive student radiographer, and they soon married. In 1966 he moved on again, this time to Beechams, one of JWT's major clients, and a group which was especially marketing-oriented, with its Lucozade, Macleans and other products. Saunders clearly had a flair for it. Sir Ronald Halstead, later Beecham's chairman, reckoned that Saunders could have succeeded him at the top of the company if he had stayed long enough. But his restless ambition drove him on, first to Great Universal Stores, where he ran the international mail order side and hated it, and then overseas to a Swiss company called Eutectic. That lasted a couple of years. By the age of 40 he was ensconced at Nestlé, the Swiss food group, then run by a man who was to have a significant bearing on his days at Guinness, Dr Arthur Fuehrer. When Nestlé became deeply involved in a scandal over the sale of powdered milk to the Third World – mixed with contaminated water, it resulted in thousands of infant deaths – Saunders was the man selected by Fuehrer to handle the publicity in the United States. He did so with some skill, although with methods which would later be questioned by investigative journalists following his departure from Guinness. It was during this time that he met and came to know well another central character in the Guinness affair; the Washington lawyer Tom Ward, who advised Nestlé on how to handle the milk scandal.

In the summer of 1981, Ernest Saunders was sitting alone in his elegant lakeside office in Vevey, Switzerland. He was about to take a fateful decision. At the age of 47, he was a member of the top international management committee of Nestlé. Accounts differ as to whether he was headed still higher, or whether the baby food scandal had left its mark on him; at any rate he was a highly marketable manager, and still registered, as he had been for years, with a number of international headhunters. He had never occupied a really senior post in Britain, and essentially his culture was that of the international nomadic executive, in Geneva one day, Washington the next, London or Paris the day after. He was multilingual, energetic, personable – and a skilled marketer of proven experience. But for all his experience, he lacked one attribute which may help explain what happened later. He was at this stage almost a total stranger to the City. He had no financial training, and others would later be surprised by his inability to grasp intricate financial points. He had never been involved, even peripherally, in a takeover bid. He had inherited none of the tradition, none of the relationships, which provided a degree of restraint on other bidders, such as Gulliver. Instead he had found that the way to cope with a major problem was through clever and inventive lawyers, such as Tom Ward, or by employing high-powered consultants (at Guinness later he would have up to 15 consultants provided by the Boston-based Bain & Co.).

Now, in that summer of 1981, he was in a mood to move on. He and his wife Carole enjoyed the Alps, not to mention the Swiss francs, on which he paid little or no tax. By European standards their life style was high. They had a house in southern France which they had bought some years before, and were within a couple of hours drive of the best skiing in Europe. But the view of their friends is that Carole missed England, and for Ernest there was a lot of action going on back in Britain.

It was that summer that Lord Iveagh personally offered him the job of running Guinness. Benjamin Guinness, who had succeeded to the title of the Earl of Iveagh, found himself out of his depth at managing the family business. Founded in 1759 by an Irish brewer who signed a 9000 year lease on the St James Gate brewery in Dublin, the firm of

Arthur Guinness had not changed all that much. It was still essentially a family business, run by Arthur's direct descendants, who by the 1980s had long been established in the British aristocracy under such titles as the earls of Iveagh and the barons of Moyne. More importantly, it still had the potential only of a one-product business, despite a wild and unplanned takeover spree to diversify. The Guinness acquisition programme worked on the principle that if you scattered enough seed around the place, something surely was bound to take root. In 1981 the brewing side still accounted for 92 per cent of trading profits – and its sales were slipping in the home markets of Ireland and Britain, not dramatically, but every year for nine consecutive years they had been lower. Guinness' share of the total British beer market had halved in ten years and profits had fallen three years running. The City had long been worried about the lack of management and direction. In 1981 the family had become worried, too. A large number of comfortable existences depended on the success of the family business. The chairman, Iveagh, was a mild-mannered, bright and perceptive man who felt keenly the damage done to the company by the ill-considered diversifications of the 1960s and 1970s, a criticism as much aimed at himself as anyone else. Guinness, he would say later* was going through 'a hiccup' in the 1980s, moving into film finance and other areas which could have bankrupted it. It needed a professional outside manager to get it out of its decline and pointed in the right direction again. Hence the call to Saunders. Would he come to the rescue?

For several weeks, Saunders thought about it, then finally accepted the challenge and a salary of £110,000 a year. Before moving to London, where Guinness had long had its head office, however, he took the Guinness accounts and a set of brokers' circulars to his house in France for a two-week break. The picture that emerged was worse than he thought. Guinness had acquired an extraordinary dog's breakfast of companies: a confectionery business, Callard & Bowser, canal boats in France, an orchid grower, a company that made injection plastic fenders for cars and many, many others; between them they turned in a thumping loss.

While he was on holiday in France, the implications of Guinness's poor financial state were beginning to get through to the London stock market, too. Iveagh made a statement with the latest set of figures, indicating that the dividend might be in danger. A great shudder went through the entire Guinness family.

In Saunders' first week in office, the Guinness share price stood at a

*Interview with the author.

low point of 49p, capitalising the company at just £90m. That made Saunders a minnow compared to the players of the day to whose ranks he aspired. Hanson Trust, before its big burst of takeovers, was already three times the size of Guinness. BTR, the great success story of the 1980s, was capitalised at over £800m. No-one, including Saunders himself, could seriously believe that four years later he would be able to mount a takeover bid worth £2.7bn for one of the most established and venerable of British institutions – and to pull it off. Or that, from that £90m base, Guinness would rise to £3.5bn, which put him still behind the high-flying Hanson (by then £5bn) and the shyer, more retiring but extraordinarily effective Sir Owen Green of BTR, whose own series of takeovers, including the Thomas Tilling conglomerate and the ailing Dunlop, had given him a capitalisation of £5.5bn; but placed him where he wanted to be: among the world's biggest players in the drinks world.

How Saunders transformed Guinness is one of the most dramatic examples of professional management seen in Britain in recent years. After his downfall, it became fashionable to detract from his achievements, but those involved with him at the time, although pointing critically to a number of decisions, still insist that as a manager Saunders had few equals in British industry.

Saunders cleaned out the mess left by the previous management without too much trouble, albeit with some pain: in his first two years at Guinness he sold or closed no less than 140 companies, writing off £49m in the 1982 accounts. He got out of a potentially lethal (for the company) commitment for a major financing of a string of Hollywood movies. He changed the thinking – and the advertising – from the traditional manufacturing-oriented philosophy which had reigned for so long, into a modern, marketing-conscious line of thought. He came up with a complete new advertising policy. Young people were not drinking Guinness, so he abandoned its lengthy relationship with his old firm J. Walter Thompson and its series of stylish and memorable ads, and went to a new agency, the younger, and brasher Allen Brady & Marsh. 'Research showed,' said Saunders, 'that the advertising was so powerful that one almost felt that there was a second product: there was Guinness beer and Guinness advertising.' Allen Brady came up with a new campaign designed to attract what their research showed were the real drinkers in Britain: the 18–35-year-old working class, who regarded Guinness as both expensive and toffee-nosed. The new campaign, which cost £10m, was the now legendary 'Guinless' campaign, when the drinker was told he could not do without it. It did not increase Guinness sales – but for the first time in a decade they were no longer falling. Saunders claimed the tide had been turned.

All of these and much more were relatively straightforward management decisions. They put Guinness on the road to recovery and the financial statistics soon told the tale: over the next three years profits after tax increased 240 per cent, return on capital employed increased from 16 per cent to 22.1 per cent, and the share price increased eight-fold.

The Guinness family 'regard me as an adopted Guinness,' remarked Saunders.* But Saunders still felt that in their eyes he was still a hired hand, a servant paid to do the work while they lived off his efforts. One little incident in particular stuck in his mind. Soon after he joined, he was invited to a Guinness family wedding. As the chief executive of a world-renowned group, Saunders felt himself to be a person of some importance, but he found himself at a table some way removed from the top; with him were a group of other family retainers, the agent who ran the estates, the tax adviser and so on. 'I suddenly realised how the family saw me,' he remarked afterwards.

This may have been a factor in pushing him onwards to achieve even more. But he still had the problem of relying on one product and, no matter how clever the advertising, demand for that product was in decline in the home market, although still expanding overseas. New and more fashionable drinks were taking over. He had to get his growth from elsewhere. And that meant through takeovers. 'You can't just have a business which makes more profit by cost-cutting,' said Saunders.* 'You've got to find businesses with real growth potential.'

Saunders was by no means alone or unusual in facing this dilemma. Almost every company does so at some stage in its career. All the tobacco companies have sought to use their cash flow to build up other interests; brewers have gone into hotels, and food chains; food groups have gone into brewing; shipping companies have bought property companies; and property companies have moved into financial services. Everybody had gone into everybody else's industry, hoping it would somehow be greener on the other side of the corporate hill. The history of takeovers is littered with diversifications by one-product companies which have gone awry. Guinness's own previous record was often cited as a case of how not to do it.

What singles Saunders out is the speed with which he moved. In 20 months he spent £500m on acquisitions, starting with the Martins newsagent chain in June 1984. He bought the famous British health resort Champneys for £3m. He added other newsagents businesses and the British franchise of the Seven-Eleven Convenience Stores,

*Management Today, May 1985.
† Euromoney, April 1986.

open when the local shoppers want them to be. They solved another problem for him too: 'We needed the acquisitions to give us British earnings,' he said afterwards.* The tax system in Britain, through Advanced Corporation Tax, penalises companies with high overseas earnings and low UK earnings. Guinness had a classic ACT problem, which the acqusitions resolved.

All of this, however, was fringe stuff. The more Saunders researched the beverage business, the more he realised that this was where he had to expand. He had to have strong international brands if Guinness was ever to get into the big league. He steadily became aware of the concentration taking place in the drinks industry worldwide. 'Everywhere one went, one was conscious of the same names popping up all over the place. In bars, hotels, duty frees, on aeroplanes, the same groups were pulling together the brand names.' Saunders could see what the Saatchi brothers had already seen in the advertising world, and what was becoming apparent in other industries too: that by the 1990s, his industry would have gone international, and would end up dominated by half a dozen big international groupings. The Japanese group Suntory was rapidly advancing; Anheuser-Busch, producers of Budweiser, were taking a dominant position; Seagrams and Hiram-Walker from Canada were big players on the international stage. From Australia John Elliott had emerged to make a £2bn bid for the British group Allied-Lyons and his Elders-IXL was bidding fair to become one of the giants, too. Guinness would be swallowed into one of the big groups if he didn't do something about it.

In the summer of 1985 he did. His target was a Scotch whisky company, which had won itself the reputation as an aggressive and successful marketer, and which had been making major inroads into the dominant market share held by the giant of the industry, Distillers. It was Arthur Bell. 'The takeover of Arthur Bell & Sons by Guinness was hailed by the City as one of the best-planned deals of 1985', remarked *Euromoney* later. But it was by no means all smooth going. There were various lobbies to be overcome, not least the Scottish lobby which had won out in a number of previous bids: Hong Kong and Shanghai Banking Corporation had tried to take over the Royal Bank of Scotland, and run into a minefield of opposition which had resulted in a Monopolies Commission reference and a firm 'no'. Similarly Hiram Walker had been repulsed in its attempts to extend its interests into the Scotch whisky industry. It was called the 'Tartan fence' and was designed to protect Scottish companies from 'foreigners'. Guinness, although very much a British and Irish

---

*Interview with the authors.

establishment company, was a foreign company in Scotland. Saunders in laying the groundwork for his bid spent days touring the Edinburgh financial establishment, one of the most conservative – and chauvinistic – in the world. He carefully explained what Guinness was about, extolled the new marketing skills, and the potential for his own group. 'Market research shows that Guinness is the second best known brand in the US,' he explained, 'topped only by Coca-Cola. But we hardly sell any stout over there. Instead it is known for the book of records. We can build on that, through our drinks distribution agency in the US, selling Guinness as a luxury import.' He wanted, he hinted, to add on some of Scotland's better brand names.

When he finally made his bid for Bells, the work he had put in served him in good stead. Bell's tough, no-nonsense chairman, Raymond Miquel, was in New York and didn't bother to return. He learned about the bid in his hotel bedroom, not because Saunders deliberately wanted to catch him at a disadvantage, but because news of the bid had begun to leak, the Bell share price was moving up, and Guinness had to hurry out its announcement. But once having lost the initiative, Miquel never recovered it. Everything that could go wrong in a defence did so. As the *Financial Times* later commented:

> The initial bid had caught the company on the hop and the chairman in America; the appointment of the mighty House of Warburg to partner the less mighty House of Ansbacher was made after an inexcusable delay and in a fashion which left it unclear which bank was doing what. The public relations advisers changed (twice) and the defence itself was almost devoid of substance: the profit forecast was weak, the dividend increase implausible and the asset revaluation absent. Shareholders were left with arguments which were advanced – on both sides – with the tit-for-tat puerility of the lower fourth form.

Saunders exploited the enemy's confusion with considerable skill. He raised his bid from the initial £327m to £340m, just enough to split the board. Saunders had been talking seriously for weeks to one director, Peter Tyrie, who ran the Gleneagles subsidiary. Unknown to the Bells board, Saunders had agreed to pick up Tyrie's costs of consulting lawyers and of preparing a circular to be posted to shareholders when the time was ripe. That time came when the bid was raised. Tyrie issued a statement saying he disagreed with the rest of the board, still opposed to Guinness. Large shareholdings, including many of the big Scottish institutions, began changing sides. Bell's own neighbouring institution in Perth, the General Accident company, opted for Guinness. In desperation, Miquel tried another and even more damaging ploy: the 'white knight' defence. The board, he said, was 'seeking an alternative offer'. That could not have suited Saunders better. Miquel, he charged, had 'put the company up for auction'. But who would buy it? Miquel, in his desperate search for any other partner than Guinness, had briefly held talks with the South African Dr Anton Rupert, head of the Rembrandt Group which with the US Philip Morris group controlled the Rothmans International tobacco combine. In the final weekend before the bid closed, the South African connection leaked in the financial press, which made a great deal of what had only been a brief chat. Rothmans issued a denial a few days later, but the damage had been done. The 'white knight' defence had boomeranged badly. The battle was all over. Guinness registered over 65 per cent acceptances when the counting was done. As the *Financial Times* remarked, Guinness's announcement that it had won 'was among the least surprising statements of the takeover battle'. The ten-week contest, it added, had 'contained more bizarre incidents and false turns than any in recent memory'.

Afterwards, weighing up the reasons for Guinness's easy win in the face of Bell's ten-year profit record of unbroken growth, commentators picked out not just Saunders' own public relation skills – the press was unanimously on his side – but also the advisers he had assembled. Morgan Grenfell was his merchant bank, and had displayed the skills which had now put it at the top of the corporate tree (although he had not had the services of either of the big stars – Morgans had fielded Tony Richmond Watson, who had performed more than adequately, but would not be used again by Saunders). The stockbroking had been split between Wood Mackenzie, the king of the Scottish brokers, and Cazenove, the king in London. On the PR front, Brian Basham, who now had such a reputation that every major bidder (or target company) wanted him on their side, had skilfully masterminded one of the most effective campaigns yet seen, involving another of his own clients, Saatchi & Saatchi, to help with the script-writing. Sir Gordon Reece, image maker to Margaret Thatcher, had been used as a consultant. There were the best solicitors, the best accountants, the best of all types of advice. That was the Saunders style.

Against this formidable array, the disorganised campaign on the other side was always on the defensive, and never seriously slowed the Guinness momentum. Saunders had discovered the importance of public relations and of advertising (full page ads, with the big headline: 'How to make your Bell's investment worth 90 per cent more. Accept the Guinness offer'). These were to play an even bigger role in what lay ahead.

During the struggle for Bells, one event had occurred which was to have major implications for the next stage. As part of his wooing of the Scots, Saunders had not stopped at the big institutional investors in Edinburgh, or the various politicians and officials in the Scottish Office who could influence events. His path at one stage took him to the office of John Connell, chairman of Distillers. Saunders saw it simply as a courtesy call, a visit to the giant of the industry just to show his face and let him know what his thoughts on the business were. Connell, however, saw it in a different light – according to one source afterwards, he thought Saunders was going to announce a bid for him there and then. That had become his reputation, and was an indication of how vulnerable Distillers had come to feel.

Saunders had not seriously thought of bidding for Distillers at that time. But, as he researched Bell, so he discovered more and more about the Scotch whisky industry. He began to cast longing glances at the giant of the business, measuring his own market value against that of Distillers, and anxiously watching the progress of Gulliver's attempts.

The first time Saunders publicly showed his hand was in October, 1985. Gulliver was still in baulk, with another two months to go before he could bid again. Distillers was using the time to prepare its defences. It was Olivier Roux, the young French management consultant who had increasingly become his right hand man, who gave the first hint.

Roux, a slim, charming and popular man with a boyish grin and a Maurice Chevalier accent, was never actually a Guinness employee. He worked for the management consultancy business Bain & Co., which Saunders used extensively and had come to rely on heavily to supply him with managers and advice. Born in Marseilles in 1950, Roux had a business degree from Paris, and then worked for Esselte, the Swedish office equipment group. In 1980 Bill Bain, who ran the secretive and selective Bain consultancy business, had hired him and a year later, shortly after Saunders arrived at Guinness, he was seconded to the brewer. The two men clicked instantly, and in 1984 Saunders promoted him to the Guinness board, as director of financial strategy and development. He was responsible for all the financial departments of the corporate office, one of the key jobs in the whole group. Saunders tried several times to hire him away from Bain, but gave up when he discovered what Roux was paid by the consultancy: Roux confided to him that the figure was even higher than Saunders' salary at the time, and a figure which, if published, would have put Roux among the two or three most highly paid men in Britain. If the

Guinness board had any objection to an outsider, paid by his consultancy rather than directly by Guinness, occupying such an important position, there was never any outward sign of it. But again, Roux's background may have had a bearing. Roux was French, married to a German and employed by an American business – in effect, like Saunders, a homeless, international executive of which the 1970s and 1980s have bred thousands. He had never worked in the City, and had little feeling or particular respect for the way things were done there. As far as he was concerned, Guinness could have been shipped offshore to Japan or Zurich. Nor had he any real experience as a finance director, which is what he now in effect was.

All that late autumn, Saunders was getting himself into position to make a run for Distillers. He had decided it was the right thing for Guinness, but was it right for him? Later it would be claimed that Saunders was single-minded, but that was never so. He was actually ambivalent. 'The professional in me was saying I should do it, the personal was saying I shouldn't.' He was worried about the health of his wife, now facing a major operation. He was also preoccupied with running a much enlarged company, and streamlining a management structure which had not yet digested Bells. And the Bells bid had taken a greater toll of his energies than he expected. Nonetheless it was a chance in a lifetime. His own momentum, and his own strategic reasoning of where he wanted to position Guinness, pushed him inevitably towards a bid. But it was going to take careful and skilful handling, and he had accepted that he had no chance with a hostile bid. He had to be invited in by the Distillers board. He began to work on some of the big Scottish institutions, hoping to get a lobby going which would push Distillers towards him. Later he claimed he only entered the bidding at the request of the Scottish institutions. 'That was never true,' says Gulliver. 'We looked and we could never find any Scottish institutions who had made any request to him.'

At the end of November Saunders went to Morgan Grenfell. For two hours he chatted to Roger Seelig about the prospects of making a major bid in the retail sector. The subject of Distillers was not even raised. Saunders had never met Seelig before and this was a test. Seelig passed. The next day Seelig was called in to see Christopher Reeves. Guinness, Reeves told him, wanted to enter the bidding for Distillers. And Saunders wanted Seelig to run the bid for him. It would be the biggest bid ever handled by the bank. Seelig could see lots of problems, particularly with Gulliver so well out in front in his preparations. 'But how could I refuse?' he said later.

After Christmas Saunders and Seelig hit their full stride and, as 1986 opened, they had their teams up and running. Early in January

Saunders brought Tom Ward over from America, and put him up at his house in Penn, Buckinghamshire, with a team of lawyers. The stalking of Distillers was done in the utmost secrecy; not even Gulliver, plugged in as he was to the slightest nuance, suspected it until it was too late. By mid-January, Saunders was in position and ready to go.

Saunders initially did not intend making a full-scale offer for Distillers. He had a different idea. The two merchant bankers working for his scheme, Seelig, acting for Guinness, and Bay Green of Kleinwort Benson, acting for Distillers, had just finished work on an imaginative scheme whereby the two stores groups, British Home Stores and Mothercare-Habitat had been put together under the umbrella of a new holding company called Storehouse. It was a pure coincidence that they now found themselves acting for another two clients wanting to do the same thing. It did not involve a takeover, with all the cost in fees and underwriting. 'I thought that made a lot of sense,' said Saunders. 'And I decided that was what I wanted to do.'* There would of course be no doubt who would run the new holding company: Saunders and his team.

The bankers went away to study it and came back the next day. 'It won't fly,' said Seelig.

In the Habitat case, there were only two companies involved, and both of them had agreed to merge. In this case there was a hostile offer from Gulliver on the table. 'You can't counter that offer with a concept,' the bankers said. There would have to be a matching offer by one company for the other. That posed the question: who should bid for whom? The Argyll bid had driven the value of Distillers to nearly £2bn, while Guinness was only half the size. Guinness's City credibility, the bankers advised, was considerably higher than that of Distillers, whose reputation, never high, had now been shredded by Gulliver. 'So it was agreed that we would have to do it, we would have to mount the bid,' said Saunders.

Fresh from picking up the cost of the Bells bid, he was wary of the expense. Suppose he bid for Distillers and lost? He realised it could cost his group over £50m, compared to pre-tax profits of £80m. It was too big a risk. It was Distillers who wanted him in as the white knight. He would make Distillers pay. Later the Distillers board would be accused of offering to pay his costs as the price of getting him in. That was never even a proposal. 'One aspect one ought to clear out of the

*Interview with the authors.

way,' says Saunders, 'is that there was never any suggestion that Distillers said to me: "Come and help us out of this situation and we will pay your costs." It was never that – it was the other way around.' Saunders negotiated hard for the toughest terms he could squeeze out. 'I basically took the view that I didn't see why my shareholders should pick up the tab for a takeover when we were going to do it the other way, through a holding company. And I just told the lawyers to come up with an agreement which did not involve us in picking up all the costs. And that is how that particular agreement came into being.' Would he still have gone ahead if he had to pick up his own costs? 'Probably. But the costs of a bid are certainly a factor in deciding whether to do it or not.'*

That agreement would later be interpreted by Gulliver as a form of 'poison pill', an extra cost that he would have to pick up if he succeeded in taking over Distillers. Gulliver now faced his own costs, which would be £60–£70m (about half that if he lost), Distillers' costs, which would be about half that, and Guinness's costs. The whole lot would be about £160–£170m, which would make it a hugely expensive acquisition, and leave even less room for manoeuvre if he did eventually get control.

Gulliver, of course, did not know about this arrangement until some days after Saunders launched his bid. And there was something else he did not know until later still: Saunders initially demanded an even higher price. Probably influenced by Tom Ward who played a major role in designing the bid package, Saunders went for a variation of the 'crown jewel lock-up' which Hanson was faced with in his bid for SCM. Even with the Distillers support, Saunders could not be sure of winning. 'I was very conscious of my shareholders,' he said later. To protect his interests in the event of failing, he demanded a chunk of Distillers' business, which would be transferred to him at an agreed (low) price, whether he won or lost. He chose the Distillers brandy brands, Denis Mounié and Hine. After lengthy discussion, however, it was dropped. The Distillers management, desperate though they were to evade the clutches of the upstart Gulliver, baulked at that. They did not think much of the cost proposals either – even within hours of the bid being announced, there was still furious argument going on. Saunders, however, held on. 'I'm very cost-conscious,' said Saunders afterwards. 'And before I spend even a million pounds, I think very hard. Before I spread myself a little, I think very carefully. But then you make a commercial decision. In this case there was also the unknown. We had had a good indication from the Office of Fair

*Interview with the authors.

Trading that there would be no problem, but you never knew. The idea of some cost sharing seemed reasonable.'

By the second week of January there was broad agreement on the terms – Guinness would top Gulliver's latest £1.89bn offer by another £350m. But as they moved into the final few days, there were still a few issues to be cleared up – and a huge amount of detail. There were teams of people working all over the City: at Kleinworts, where the bulk of the work was being done, at Morgan Grenfell, at Freshfields, solicitors to Guinness, at Cazenove and Wood Mackenzie, Guinness's two brokers, at Hoare Govett, brokers to Distillers, and of course at the offices of the two groups. For the Bells bid, Saunders had created a special little 'war cabinet'; he tried with Distillers, but soon discovered he could not get the team together easily. Everyone was too busy, in too many different directions.

Although there were a few runners in the market, security this time was much better than it had been for Guinness' bid for Bells which had leaked badly. If Gulliver did hear anything, he dismissed it as unfounded rumour.

The news eventually broke on the morning of Saturday, 18 January. It came in the form of an article in *The Times*, delicately written, but clearly informed. The executive editor of the business section, Kenneth Fleet, picked up the mood of defeatism that was increasingly gripping the Distillers camp.

There has been a distinct and radical change of mood in the Distillers boardroom. The beleaguered directors, handicapped by their appalling past record, have accepted that a merger would be good for the company, its employees and shareholders, but not a 'merger' with James Gulliver's Argyll Group, which has already made a hostile bid worth £1.89bn. Although the company adheres to 'no comment' with an implied negative, Guinness is expected to emerge officially next week as Distillers' preferred suitor.

Early that morning Brian Basham, the PR man acting for Gulliver but still (for a few hours more) also retained by Saunders, rang Gulliver. 'Have you seen *The Times*?' Gulliver had not. 'Well, read Ken Fleet. It looks informed to me.' Fleet, Basham went on, knew members of the Distillers board who could have leaked it to him. He also knew Saunders, and there could be an element here of trying to bounce the Distillers board into a decision over the weekend. 'I think you should ring Ernest straightaway and ask him.'

Basham of course knew Saunders well; they had become friends as well as professional allies; Basham had attended most of the morning meetings on the Bells bid, and knew his style of operation as well as anyone. He also knew Kenneth Fleet, a veteran financial journalist of considerable reputation. To him it was immediately obvious. To Gulliver, however, it was just another newspaper rumour which he did not need to take too seriously.

'I didn't believe the story,' he said later. But at Basham's insistence he agreed to telephone Saunders. He rang the office at Portman Square first, and then Saunders' home in Penn. To his surprise, it wasn't Saunders who came to the phone, but the American lawyer Tom Ward. Gulliver had vaguely heard his name, but had never met him. He was aware, however, that he was close to Saunders and, like others, he wondered what a Washington-based lawyer, who was not even a specialist in mergers and acquisitions, was doing on the board of Guinness, and working so closely with the chief executive officer.

'Hello, it's Tom Ward here,' he began. 'I'm a close associate of Ernest's. Can I help?'

Gulliver wanted to talk to the boss.

'Ernest's driving around the country just now, and I don't think we can reach him.'

Gulliver plunged in. *The Times* that morning, he said, indicated Guinness was about to make a 'white knight' bid approach to Distillers. 'Is there any truth in that whatsoever?'

Ward, according to Gulliver, was adamant. 'There's no truth in this whatsoever. I'm here with a bunch of guys from the United States and we're discussing the acquisition of a drinks distribution business in the US. That's why we're all here.'

But, added Ward, he had been meaning to ring Gulliver about something else. 'Ernest and I would like a chat. Could we meet early next week?'

They settled on Monday at 3.30, just two days away. By that stage, as Ward clearly knew, the bid would be announced.

('I'm still waiting on that meeting!' said Gulliver ruefully after the battle was over.)

But as the morning wore on, Gulliver became increasingly concerned. The bankers and brokers agreed with Basham, and were making their own enquiries. There had been hints that Morgan was about to launch another mega-bid, as big as the one they were involved in already with United Biscuits/Imperial Group. Basham learned that the Sunday papers were being briefed and that all three quality Sundays would carry stories the next day, indicating that Guinness would be making a bid first thing on Monday morning.

Gulliver tried ringing Saunders again. The Portman Square office told him that Saunders was still out in his car. He kept ringing. 'I must have tried eight times. I got Tom Ward again who repeated what he had said already.'

It was Saturday afternoon when Saunders finally came through. He was ringing from his car phone, he explained, and was some way away from London. Gulliver says he asked him for 'an absolute assurance that there is nothing in this suggestion that you will enter the bidding for Distillers'.

Saunders, according to Gulliver, gave it to him. 'It must be your man Brian Basham putting around this story,' he said. 'We're not interested.' As Gulliver continued to press him, the phone went dead. Gullvier, now increasingly convinced there was something up, says he managed to get hold of Saunders' carefully guarded car telephone number (he would not say who gave it to him) and rang back. All he got was the signal 'The Vodaphone subscriber you are calling is not available. Please try later.' His doubts deepened. 'He's taken it off the hook,' he told his team.

Gulliver the next day elaborated on this conversation to the *Daily Telegraph*. According to this version, Saunders was in his car, and he was phoning, he told Gulliver, to indicate that he was upset by the way the press that day had handled the story. 'I said are you interested in making a bid for Distillers,' Gulliver was quoted as saying.* 'And he said "I can tell you I'm not interested." I went on to say are you interested in the possibility of a merger? And he said that Distillers had formed a view that Argyll were winning and they were looking for a white knight.'

This version was contained in an earlier draft of this chapter which we showed to Saunders. He reacted strongly to it, insisting he had not mislead Gulliver. 'Gulliver called my home and Carole called me in the car. I then called him on the car phone. What I told him was that I was not interested in making a *contested* bid for Distillers – but everyone knows they're interested in a white knight.'

Gulliver, according to Saunders, then said, '"But would you be interested if they approached you as a white knight?" And I replied, "I'll have to think about that."' Saunders says he remembers making a distinction 'between making a contested bid and being a white knight. Then the phone went dead, and I wasn't able to call back.'

This incident, possibly more than any other in the whole bid, sticks in Gulliver's mind. He has repeated it to us three or four times, either in casual conversation or in formal interview, since then. It still puzzles him. 'He could quite easily just not have been available that

Daily Telegraph, 20 January, 1986.

day,' he says. 'He didn't have to talk to me at all. But he saw the balance of advantage in misleading someone he could have continued to be friends with, even if we were going to be on opposite sides.'

Saunders however disputes Gulliver's memory of the conversation. And there was little that Saunders could hope to gain – the Sunday newspapers (available by eight on Saturday night) left no room for doubt. In the City the Kleinwort camp was easing its careful security, knowing the cat was out of the bag, and that the bid would either be announced first thing on Monday morning (before the markets opened) or would get through the awkward Distillers board meeting scheduled for Sunday afternoon. There was no longer any doubt.

The *Financial Times* understood the situation clearly the next day: 'A stream of calculated leaks to newspapers over the weekend setting out the terms of a merger with Guinness . . . had caught the [Distillers] board wrong-footed. At least one senior Distillers director felt that he was being "bounced" into a merger whose merits had yet to be fully agreed.'

There was no question of insider dealing because Guinness proposed to make the announcement when the market opened on Monday morning. But it was pressure tactics.

Everyone was aware that the Distillers board would object to the cost arrangements, and that Kleinwort, which supported the Guinness proposal, would have a hard job talking them through. There was still some argument over who should be chairman of the joint group, but Saunders was not worried by that; it was, he claimed afterwards, just another detail which he left to the bankers to resolve.

It had been agreed, indeed it was a central part of the merger philosophy, that the Guinness management under Saunders would be in full charge of sorting out Distillers. That was stressed several times in the draft press release. In this context, the role of a non-executive chairman would not be too vital, except perhaps as a figurehead – at least that is how Saunders, used to Lord Iveagh, saw it. On Sunday morning, when Bay Green and Roger Seelig met to go through the unresolved items left on their list, neither was perturbed by it. Nor was Saunders, preoccupied as he was. No-one that day seems to have properly thought through the implications of the board structure they were now designing; it was an oversight which would come back to haunt Saunders long before the DTI enquiries began, and involve him in a controversy which raged all through the summer of 1986 and which at one stage was being depicted by the financial press and many leading City figures as the biggest challenge yet to the self-regulatory system.

Saunders had worked very happily with Lord Iveagh, who supported him when he needed it, but seldom stood in the way of a decision, however painful. Iveagh, as titular head of the Guinness family, was keen on remaining chairman of the enlarged company, but the bankers argued against it. They presented a variety of reasons: for a start, the enlarged company, including Distillers, would have such a Scottish bias that a Scottish chairman would be a good idea, and would help appease the Scottish financial lobby which otherwise might swing towards the Scottish-born James Gulliver. Secondly, once the bid had gone through, any pretence that Guinness was still a family company would disappear, and Iveagh was really only chairman because he was a Guinness. There was a third reason: John Connell, the Distillers chairman, also wanted the job. And both Green and Seelig were fully aware that this would not find favour with the institutional shareholders after the systematic way in which the Gulliver campaign had already dented the Connell reputation. But if Connell, who was chairman of the bigger of the two companies, was not to be considered, it would not look right to appoint the Guinness chairman either.

That Sunday morning the two bankers had one name on their list as acceptable compromise chairman for the enlarged group: Sir Thomas Risk, a Scottish banker, governor of the Bank of Scotland which had recently become Distillers' principal banker. Risk was a man of considerable standing in the Scottish financial establishment, and also had many contacts and powerful friends in the City of London. At 62, he was approaching the time when he would have to step down from the Bank of Scotland, which is Scotland's second biggest commercial bank after the Royal Bank of Scotland (the title 'governor' is grander than it sounds: it simply means chairman, and in no way is the governor of the Bank of Scotland the equivalent of the governor of the Bank of England, who is appointed by the prime minister and is Britain's central banker).

That weekend the virtues of Risk as chairman were extolled by another Scottish director of Distillers, Charles Fraser, an Edinburgh lawyer, who was also the head of Morgan Grenfell in Scotland. Fraser carried considerable weight with both camps, and when the Risk proposal was finally put to Saunders, he nodded approval. He knew him slightly: Risk had been banker to Bells and, in the tight circles of the Scottish financial world in which Saunders had been moving with growing assurance, their paths had crossed a number of times. One of the bankers that Sunday morning told him that Risk saw himself as a

'Scottish Lord Iveagh', and that suited Saunders perfectly. He wanted total management control, the same system in effect that he had enjoyed in his four years with Guinness. If Risk offered that, then that was fine with him.

And so the decision was confirmed. Risk was offered the job and accepted it. His name went onto the draft press release.

Everyone was focusing on the issue of the fees, and how to persuade the Distillers board to accept the proposed arrangement, and then how to present it to the financial world. It had never been done before, and the bankers in particular foresaw storms ahead. By the early afternoon of Sunday, 19 January, the broad details of the bid had been sorted out. Now all that remained was for the Distillers board to agree it. That was not going to be easy.

At 4.30 on Sunday afternoon the Distillers directors met for one of the most important board meetings they would ever hold. The venue was 6 St James Square, an office unprepossessing on the outside, but inside one of the most elegant buildings in London. The boardroom, with its painted ceiling and carved panelling, was a particularly classic room. What followed was, in the words of one Distillers director, Sir Nigel Broackes, 'one of the most tiring events of 1986'. It ended at 2.30 the following morning after long and often angry discussion.

The merchant bankers Lord Rockley and Bay Green, both of Kleinwort, set the tone at the start. In their professional opinion, said Rockley, head of corporate finance at Kleinwort, Distillers had little or no chance of remaining independent. Gulliver was winning the takeover battle, and there was no ammunition left to throw at him. The principle of independence therefore had to be abandoned. What they recommended that day was a bid from a friendly quarter: Guinness was prepared to offer £2.5bn, £350m more than Argyll. Without that bid, Gulliver would probably win on the existing terms of 485p a share.

Ernest Saunders, he said, had an excellent track record, and he would be the chief executive of the whole outfit. But to tempt him, he wanted Distillers to pay his costs: that was a condition of the bid. It was that issue which dominated the discussions for the rest of the meeting.

Nine of the 12 Distillers directors were being told that the terms of the merger meant they would not get a place on the new board. It was from them, in particular, that the opposition to the tough terms being laid down by Saunders came through. The defence so far, they pointed out, had been based on the oft-repeated assertion that Distillers did not need Gulliver's management skills – it had enough of its own. Just a week before, Distillers had claimed it had 'got it right' – the right management structure, the right marketing organisation, the right production base. Now the board was being asked to admit publicly that this was untrue, and that the existing Distillers executive directors were not good enough to be considered for the senior roles in the enlarged company. Later Gulliver could claim, with some justi-fication, that this move alone meant the Distillers defence 'is history'.

Against the opposition was Sir Nigel Broackes, the chairman of Trafalgar House (a group which had once been well ahead of Hanson in the takeover race). Broackes had been drafted onto the Distillers board by Lord Rockley of Kleinwort, and had agreed to do it, he said later,* 'because I owed Kleinwort a favour after their help with the Channel crossing', a venture which Broackes had been instrumental in reviving but which he had lost to the Channel Tunnel Group. 'I hadn't been asked whether my name should be on the list for the new holdings board,' said Broackes. Nonetheless it was. And he was keen on the bid. 'I had thought, a year before that meeting, that the fit between Distillers and Guinness would be excellent,' he said. He greatly admired what Saunders had achieved at Guinness. At the same time he could see the great potential at Distillers, *if* there was a change of management. A merger of the two groups, with neither side having to pay a takeover premium and no argument over the fees, seemed to him the ideal. With Gulliver at the door, that of course was not possible. But Broackes was still keen on Guinness, and argued that evening that the issue of fees was a small thing. For £30m or so, Distillers was about to persuade Guinness to increase the bid by an extra £350m. From the shareholders point of view that seemed to be good business.

In the midst of the bigger matters of the day, the decision on who would become the non-executive chairman barely surfaced. The bankers had thrashed out the details in advance of the meeting. Now all the Distillers board could do was ratify them – or vote against them. At the meeting, aware for the first time of how low their standing among their own shareholders was, the Distillers board accepted defeat. A group of them were appalled that the once great Distillers should so abjectly surrender to a company which they had despised for years and which even now was less than half their size. In looking for a white knight, they had been thinking about someone more amicable, and they began to feel that they had chosen the wrong man in Saunders.

*Interview with the author.

215

A reporter from the London *Standard* was asked to be in Morgan Grenfell at 8.30 on Monday morning to pick up an important press announcement and receive a briefing. He waited for an hour while John Connell, the Distillers chairman, refused to agree the statement. Everyone was keenly aware that an agreed statement had to be put out by the time the market opened, and early comment in the *Standard* could also set the tone for the rest of the day, and therefore for the rest of the daily press to pick up on. Finally, Connell agreed, and the statement went out. Connell from that moment played little part in the bid.

The banking mechanism now slid smoothly into action. Morgan Grenfell and the brokers Cazenove and Wood Mackenzie took just two-and-a-half hours to persuade the City's banks and institutions to underwrite £1.6bn of Guinness shares. The battle was on.

Distillers, like Imperial, now had two bids, one 'hostile', one 'friendly'. And Christopher Reeves at Morgan Grenfell was in place to crown his bank's position as the unrivalled king of corporate finance: he was acting for Guinness bidding for Distillers, and for United Biscuits bidding for Imperial. Of the four main players on the stage (Hanson, Laing, Gulliver and Saunders) there would be two winners who would get immense prizes; and two losers who would pick up huge fees and even bigger loss of prestige. The stakes in the British takeover arena had never been higher.

Guinness had made one curious miscalculation, however. That Monday Saunders talked confidently of getting the bid through the government regulatory machine without problems. Yes, he owned Bell, which had 20 per cent of the British Scotch whisky market. Distillers (Dewar's, Johnnie Walker, White Horse and other brands) had around 18 per cent. Control of more than 25 per cent of a market was usually cause for a reference to the Monopolies Commission. Saunders, however, reckoned he had an invincible argument to counter that point: 90 per cent of Distillers production went *abroad*. He was creating one of the world's great drinks groups, and it had to be looked at in a broader context than just the home market. He was convinced there could be no monopoly problem on just 10 per cent of the group's production.

Informal approaches had already been made to the OFT in the way that had long become traditional. Roger Seelig of Morgan's was skilled at reading the OFT nuances. But that day the wires seem to have become crossed. 'We clearly would not have embarked on this course without taking full benefit of the informal guidance procedure at the

OFT,' said Seelig on the Monday.* The OFT responded frostily. 'There is no, repeat no, question of any bidder having been told at any time that any bid other than that by Argyll for Distillers would not be referred to the Monopolies and Merger Commission for fuller investigation.'

Gulliver saw his opening. Over the next few weeks he concentrated on building up the public pressure to get the Guinness bid referred. When it became clear that one obstacle was the fact that his offer was lower than that of Guinness, and that a Guinness reference might therefore be seen to be depriving Distillers shareholders of a higher bid, Gulliver raised his offer, taking it to £2.3bn (before he began, the value of Distillers was just over £1.1bn). Gulliver sent his brokers into the market to buy more shares. 'We were going to have to increase the offer at some stage,' said Gulliver. 'So we thought we would confer an element of surprise by doing it now.' Without the intervention of Guinness he would not have had to raise his bid at all. And now his own colleagues were getting anxious at the high price. David Webster, the cool financial brain of the Gulliver team, began to argue that Distillers at this price was fully valued, and that Argyll should not offer more. By now, however, Gulliver was so far down the road that there was no turning back without considerable lost of face. He needed to win.

'There was a massive PR and press campaign which only had one object,' said Saunders later. 'And that was to get us referred.' Guinness was doing some campaigning itself: it was at this stage spending heavily on advertising, extolling its own virtues, and knocking Argyll and Gulliver. Saunders was also presenting his carefully reasoned and worked-out case to the Office of Fair Trading, using many of the statistics accumulated when he bought Bells. At one stage there was a suggestion he should offer to sell Bells on the grounds that Distillers was a prize many times bigger.

In mid-February Sir Gordon Borrie at the OFT was ready with his ruling on the Guinness bid. On the evening of Thursday, 13 February, Ernest Saunders got a call around nine o'clock. It was from an OFT official. 'He told me there would be bad news,' Saunders recalled. 'I was furious. All the discussions we'd had directly and indirectly had been very positive, and I really was very upset. I thought I'd had no indication there was a problem, and I was very concerned about this aspect of even-handedness which would have resulted in a situation where the shareholders in Distillers would have been deprived of a choice. Nobody was going to wait six months while we cooled our heels

*Financial Times, 22 January, 1987.

in the Monopolies Commission. Argyll would have won.'

Saunders went around to the Department of Trade and Industry. 'I demanded to see people and I got to see an official and he was very polite and he said to me, "We can't really talk to you – you are now in the hands of the chairman of the Monopolies Commission." It was like being told that one was on probation and should go round to see the probation officer. Anyway I went. I went round to the Monopolies Commission in Carey Street, I'd never been there before, and I found Sir Godfray Le Quesne a most distinguished and charming man who I felt was a sort of judge. That was the Friday night. He explained the situation to me, that I was now in the Monopolies and Mergers Commission, and I was now to think about the options, would I sit through the thing for six months, which would involve a lot of management time, or drop the bid.'

Either option, Saunders knew, meant that Gulliver would win. He went home to think about it over the weekend.

'I thought for one day. Then I started making a few phone calls.' He started with some legal friends, notably he said, Tom Ward. All Sunday he consulted a stream of lawyers. 'One lawyer I spoke with recommended me to another lawyer and I ended up with John Swift QC, who came down that Sunday from All Souls' College, Oxford.' Swift arrived at the Guinness offices, and talked through the position with Saunders. 'We arrived at the conclusion that there was another alternative, which was withdrawing bid one, and coming up with a different bid, which was something I'd never heard about, so I spent the whole of that night – and I had a few late nights during this thing – talking with John Swift here, and Tom who was in Washington, and because of our time differences we were able to talk most of the night. And so in the morning Swift and I went around to see Sir Godfray Le Quesne again.'

The two mega-bids, for Distillers and for Imperial Group, had, up to this point followed remarkably similar lines. They started on the same day; in each case another bidder had entered the arena; they were for very similar amounts; Morgan Grenfell was involved in both; and in each case the defending boards had recommended one of the two bidders.

But there was another similarity which was even more important, and which now surfaced. When Sir Hector Laing found that Imperial's agreed bid for his own United Biscuits was referred to the Monopolies Commission, he dropped out of that bid and launched a bid the other way round: he made an offer for Imps. That morning in

February, as Saunders arrived at Sir Godfray Le Quesne's office, the competition machinery of the government was wrestling with the question of Laing's new bid. If Imperial bidding for United Biscuits was reckoned a serious enough matter to be referred to the Monopolies Commission, should not the same bid the other way round be referred too? (Even though Laing had suggested that the Golden Wonder potato crisp subsidiary should be sold off.)

Now Saunders presented his own little package to get round Guinness's problem: he proposed to withdraw his first bid, and make a second one, which would involve stripping out some of the Distillers brands and selling them to another party, thus reducing the monopolies element. It was an ingenious and novel scheme, and according to Saunders owed much to Tom Ward.

Many British managers would have accepted the rulings they had been given, and the bid would have died there. Saunders, however, chose the legal route, as he had done before, to dig himself out of a hole. But he needed Sir Godfray Le Quesne's approval to withdraw the first bid, and his judgement that the second bid was indeed a new one. It was now legalistic, unplumbed territory, not reached in any previous takeover. As the *Financial Times* commented on 21 February, 1986:

> The repackaged takeover bid for Distillers made yesterday by Guinness, and the similar one unveiled on Monday by United Biscuits for Imperial group, could prove landmarks in the way British companies approach potentially anti-competitive mergers. They also appear to introduce to Britain a faint echo of the US system of negotiation between companies and the regulatory authorities in cases of mergers with anti-trust implications.

There is no doubt that this particular point in the two bid battles marked a significant shift in the course of competition policy in Britain. As Saunders said later:

> I effectively changed pace completely and went into a legal kind of frame of mind. And you know I hadn't really thought about the law since leaving Cambridge. Now it needed a lot of intellectual work to understand what one had to do to proceed in the way that we were talking about. These QCs are all very clever and I hadn't fully understood what they were about. But what type of bid should we come up with which would give us a chance of not being referred a second time around was a different matter. The obvious thing was to sell Bells. But I refused to do that, because we'd bought Bells for a particular reason. We felt very strongly about the brand and its

potential, particularly in the States. And I had already developed a strong relationship with the management of Bells who, having fought and lost a battle, have been tremendous and we've worked very well together. I wasn't going to sell off my people. So I saw we absolutely won't do that, so what is the alternative?

There *was* an alternative. It was to construct a package of some of the Distillers/Bells brands which could be sold to a third party. Thus the share of the *British* market which Saunders would control would be reduced to around 25 per cent. Four of the five brands they came up with were Distillers: Real Mackenzie with 0.8 per cent market share, John Barr (0.16 per cent), Buchanan Blend (0.2 per cent), Claymore (5.91 per cent) and Haig Gold Label (2.77 per cent). The impact of their sale on the group as a whole would be miniscule because, as Saunders stressed at the time, 90 per cent of the combined group's Scotch whisky production was destined for overseas markets and 95 per cent of Distillers' profits were earned overseas. Initially the brands would be sold to Morgan Grenfell so as to get them out of the stable; they would be resold later.

Now the package had to be presented to the competition authorities – and it had to be done fast and in great detail. 'We had to put to the Monopolies Commission a reasonably detailed proposal there and then,' said Saunders:

That was a period of late nights, setting out from scratch to say that these are the brands and this is how we would do it. We had to put it down in a sort of form that had to be agreed by the chairman of the Monopolies Commission, cleared with the office of Fair Trading, which had to recommend to the Secretary of State, that the first bid had lapsed, which would enable a second bid to take place. And then the Secretary of State would have to say, 'Yes, the first bid has lapsed,' which would enable the Stock Exchange to allow us to proceed with the second bid.

It was unprecedently complex and delicate. And it all had to be done in three or four days, with Gulliver and his team doing their best to run a spoiling operation.

Sir Godfray Le Quesne made the first crucial decision in the many decisions taken: he agreed, against Gulliver's protests, that the first bid had technically lapsed, thus lifting the situation out of the Monopolies Commission. The other decisions flowed from that and soon Saunders was back on top, launching his second bid. Now he had to begin the process of getting it through the OFT as if it were an entirely new situation. 'We then had to knock on their door all over again,' said Saunders:

Because although the OFT had knowledge of what was going on – in fact because we had a meeting with the OFT during the discussions with the Monopolies Commission – in law they do not recognise those previous discussions and they start again. You knock on the door and say 'here I am' and in you go. And they go through the thing all over again.

Gulliver hit back by demanding a judicial review of the decision of Sir Godfray Le Quesne, supported by the government, to 'lay aside' the Monopolies reference to the first bid. First of all, argued Argyll, the bid had not been properly abandoned since Guinness had every intention of continuing with it, albeit in a slightly revised form. And secondly, its lawyers insisted, Sir Godfray did not have the legal right to make the judgement he did. And so the battle continued to takes its much more legalistic course. 'When Argyll decided to go for judicial review, we then had a second legal process to get involved in,' said Saunders. 'We got rid of one and now we had to think about preparing the case for the High Court and later the Court of Appeal.'

The High Court ruling went against Gulliver, with costs given to Guinness.

Now it moved to the Court of Appeal, which rejected the first part of the Gulliver claim – that the bid was not properly abandoned. The Court said it wasn't sure about the position of Sir Godfray Le Quesne, but overall it rejected the appeal and refused leave to appeal to the House of Lords. Gulliver had been beaten in the courts not once but twice. And this may have been far more important even than appeared at the time. According to Saunders:

I believe this was a decisive step in the end in having us approved the second time round by the OFT. The public read in the newspapers that the courts had cleared the Guinness bid twice and against that background it might be difficult to throw the bid out. Obviously we had removed the competitive element, but I'm sure that it had an extra sort of authenticity.

So in fact we were clear. But it had been a whole legal phase: the Monopolies and Mergers thing; getting the second bid going; then the judicial review; then the court of appeal. And then there was a final thing: the ads, which were disgracefully bad. There was one absolutely foul ad, which put our products into a dustbin, with a bottle of Bells on top. It was revolting. I don't mind being insulted myself but I won't have my products damaged. So I decided enough was enough and I issued some writs against Gulliver and Saatchi & Saatchi and others involved in them. And that was the end of the legal phase, and after that for the first time we were able to concentrate on the market and think about the insitutions and the shareholders.

It may have been the end of that phase for Guinness, but for other bids it was just beginning. Merchant banks, which had once never even thought about a court room, were now consulting barristers as a regular routine. There were legal challenges to the City Takeover Panel, which had originally refused to join the new statutory self-regulating board set up to see the City into the Big Bang, the time in October 1986 when deregulation at last came to the financial services industry. The brewer Matthew Brown sought a judicial review of the Monoplies Commission judgement on its bid from Scottish & Newcastle; Rank Organisation, attempting to take over Granada, threatened to haul the Independent Broadcasting Authority into the High Court when the IBA refused automatically to transfer Granada's TV franchise with a change of ownership in the parent company. Until that time judicial reviews were almost unprecendented in takeover battles. Now there had been three in the space of a few weeks.

Hanson Trust soon joined Guinness in suing the other side over the newspaper ads, and Weinstock, whose bid for Plessey had at last emerged (and was referred to the Monoplies Commission – and turned down), threatened similar action. Argyll sought to have Guinness's argreement with Distillers over its costs overturned in the courts. And everybody seemed to be complaining to every regulatory body imaginable, about everything imaginable: the Bank of England, the Stock Exchange, and the Department of Trade and Industry, which was still reeling from the Westland scandal.

The takeover scene had worked itself into an extraordinary frenzy, never seen before and unlikely to be seen again for many years. The merchant bankers were working around the clock, as were those involved in the bids. Fees were huge, and advertising expenditure even greater: in the month of January 1986 Guinness and Distillers between them spent £1.9m, and Argyll spent £820,000, arguing their cases through the newspapers. The Thatcher government observed it all with some misgivings, but it was more alarmed at the time by other excesses in the City: Lloyd's scandals were still surfacing, there was the affair of the crash of Johnson Matthey Bankers, bailed out by the Bank of England, which had become the subject of loud and ill-informed attacks from a group of left-wing Labour MPs, and of course there was Westland. But its own monopolies machinery seemed to be breaking down under the tactics used by the big groups and their merchant bank advisers. In all areas, there was growing alarm that the takeover boom had got out of hand, and somehow it had to be slowed.

But, in the meantime, all four mega-bidders (United Biscuits and Hanson bidding for Imperial, Argyll and Guinness bidding for Distillers) were clear runners for the first time, all ostensibly free to persuade the shareholders of the two target companies that theirs was the best offer, on price and on future management, which are the two principle considerations of institutional shareholders in making up their minds in a bid. But, to get there, new ground had been opened up, which raised profound implications for the way future bids would be handled. In each case, the bidding companies had proposed selling off those parts of the merged businesses which had provoked the Monopolies references. United Biscuits and Guinness, both Morgan clients, had apparently opened up new avenues through the thicket of Monopolies Commission enquiries: from then on, some observers noted, other companies, impatient with the the time enquiries took, could follow the same route. Competition policy seemed to be headed into still deeper waters.

The mega-battles at last moved into the marketplace which, as we shall see, was not precisely a marketplace of unfettered and free competition. Morgan (acting for United Biscuits and Guinness) switched to a new tactic: aggressive purchases in the market. It spent £360m buying shares in Imperial and another £70m buying shares in Distillers, not directly on behalf of its clients but on its own account. The buying created yet another furore when Morgan admitted it had an indemnity from both companies against any losses on the purchases. It was a clever way round the Stock Exchange regulations which insist that, before a company makes an investment amounting to more than 25 per cent of its capital and reserves, it must first seek the approval of its shareholders. The purchases in Imperial easily exceeded a quarter of United's net worth, which came to only £410m, as Hanson quickly pointed out. Argyll joined in to show that Guinness's net worth was £264m, so the £70m purchases also exceeded 25 per cent of that. There were other indemnities being given by Morgan at the same time in support of the Guinness bid, but they would not become known until later.

Morgans, to the dismay and fury of the opposing merchant banks, got away with it at the time – or more or less did. The Stock Exchange refused to censure it, although it did politely ask it not to act in the same way again. The Bank of England, however, was less polite. Late on a Friday evening at the end of February, it issued a sternly worded statement indicating that whatever everyone else was doing about the excesses which had crept into the takeover scene, the Bank of England at least was standing no nonsense. It announced that from then on it was severely restricting the extent to which banks could use their own capital to further the takeover ambitions of their clients. It would not regard as 'prudent' share purchases exceeding 25 per cent of a bank's capital base, which in the case of Morgan's would have been £55m at the time, compared to the £430m already committed.

It named no names, but there was no doubt in anyone's mind whom it was aiming at: Morgan Grenfell, which had now agreed to buy Golden Wonder crisps in order to get United's bid through the Monopolies Commission, to buy five whisky brands from Distillers in order to do the same for its other client Guinness, and had spent over £430m buying shares in their target companies. As Neil Collins, the *Sunday Times* City editor at the time, commented:

> Friday's public rebuke from the Bank is as hard a rap on the knuckles of a leading merchant bank as I can remember, and is a direct response to the swashbuckling tactics Morgan is developing to avoid losing takeover tussles.

No-one had any idea of just how light that rap on the knuckles was in relation to what was really going on.

It was at this stage that the Guinness share price, which had been lagging during the bid, suddenly began to defy the laws of gravity and rise. Argyll watched in disbelief as the value of the Guinness offer began to catch up with its higher offer – and then pass it. It had long suspected that Morgan was organising one of its famous support operations for the Guinness share price, talking to friends, getting institutions and others to buy some more Guinness shares on the grounds that they were bound to rise once Saunders got his hands on the potential of Distillers. It had now become a feature of all major bids, particularly when Morgan was involved. A support operation is not illegal – but it is a grey area of the City takeover code. The Argyll camp complained, but not with any great enthusiasm, knowing that its banks were doing something similar. There seemed to be something different about this one, and Gulliver was deeply suspicious. But there was no proof, and the Panel threw the complaint out.

Both mega-bid battles, for Imperial and for Distillers, were now in the endgame. Hanson's share price rose sharply at this stage too, indicating that the Hanson camp was not to be left behind when it came to the well-timed support operation (there was never any suggestion that there was anything illegal or improper about it). Laing had fought bravely but Hanson won easily in the last lap.

The other great battle, for Distillers, was a closer run thing. Gulliver was a fighter to the last. He had spectacularly overcome most of the disadvantages of the early stages to stay neck and neck with Saunders. His bid was opposed, which was a disadvantage, but on the other hand he was the man who had made all the running, and Guinness and Morgan had made little impression on the loyalty of the big institutions.

'We believed we were going to win, and we would have done, if they had not cheated,' says Gulliver. 'We were advised that we were going to win. We got the support of all the major Sundays, including the *Sunday Times*. Our cash alternative was 630p – Guinness's was 600p. But their paper offer in the end was worth more than ours and that's what settled it. If their shares had not been gunned up in the way they were, we would have won.'

Guinness in those final weeks had come to the same conclusion. It was in that period that dubious tactics got out of hand. They would give Guinness victory. But they also caused Saunders to lose his job, would result in the resignation of a dozen others, in the end of some of the most promising careers in merchant banking, and in a scandal such as the City has not known for 50 years.

CHAPTER NINE

Rigging the Market

Traditionally when one company makes an offer for another, using as
its currency its own shares – which is usually the case in Britain, but
almost unheard of in the United States where it is cash and bonds – its
share price falls. There is a logical reason for it: its share capital is about
to be enlarged considerably, and there may even be a surplus of its
shares on the market. An increase in the supply of any commodity
classically leads to a lower price – unless demand keeps pace. The trick
in the takeover world in the 1980s was to create that extra demand.
And the means of doing it became more and more dubious as time
went on, and bids got bigger.

With the Guinness bid for Distillers, it finally went over the top.

Until the early 1980s, the advice of most independent analysts was
to sell a stock when it became involved as the bidder rather than the
raider. Indeed practically all of the academic studies of takeover
activity on both sides of the Atlantic make the point again and again:
there is advantage to the shareholder in the target company. There is,
on average, disadvantage to the shareholder in the raider.

From 1982 on, however, the opposite began to happen – the share
price of the raiding company often rose spectacularly during a bid.
There were several reasons why it was so. First, the academic studies
were hopelessly behind the times – companies such as Hanson and
BTR had proved that they could gain considerable advantage from
takeovers, and their share prices actually rose *because* of the takeover
bid. During a battle, therefore, the price should – and often did – begin

to rise in anticipation of victory. By applying their own management techniques, their own accounting skills (which were often largely cosmetic, but still impressed the market), and their own market charisma, raiders successfully argued, they would make the acquisition worth more than they had paid for it. This message was not new in the 1980s, but was actually hammered home in two successful Morgan Grenfell takeovers: BTR's acquisition of Thomas Tilling and Dixons' takeover of the Currys electrical chain. The respective bidders, Sir Owen Green and Stanley Kalms, persuaded the big institutional investors that these were cases where two and two would not just make five but six or seven. As it began to look as if BTR would win, its shares took off, putting victory beyond doubt in the end. And Dixons' share price doubled during the bid, leaving the defence with no chance. Furthermore, in each case the share price went on rising afterwards as analysts produced new optimistic calculations of the full scale of benefits that would flow from the merger. Even Dixons' rivals pointed to the extra profits that Kalms could produce from Currys' run-down and old-fashioned structure.

In both cases, the share price probably had a little help from Morgan Grenfell's friends; but no-one shouted too loudly. The reaction of the competitor merchant banks, after squealing un-availingly to the Takeover Panel, was to set about doing the same themselves. From then on, merchant bankers would cite Dixons or BTR as an incentive to their clients and institutions to purchase shares in the raiders *now*. The raiders themselves became slicker and slicker, touring the City, as both Green and Kalms had done to great effect, with flip charts and slide shows, explaining to the big shareholders just what the enlarged companies could achieve. They were no longer saying: 'Accept our offer for your shares in the target company;' they were saying: 'Accept our offer – but also help us, and help yourself, by buying some of our shares.' The regular raiders had their own group of friends or 'fan clubs' who had stuck with them for years and who, they knew, would help them at the time of a bid. They had long seen the advantage of countering the natural propensity for a share price to fall during a battle.

Of course, defensive tactics had developed in parallel. If a share price could be supported, it could also be undermined, particularly coming up to a crucial underwriting time. Defending merchant bankers developed the habit of persuading *their* friends to dump the raider's shares just when it hurt the most. In turn that had to be countered with a support operation, persuading friendly buyers to appear just at the right moment. As the bids got bigger, so the market tactics became more sophisticated and professional (or unprofessional, depending on your point of view). It was all legal, even if it was not necessarily always above board. The practitioners of the art of support operations seldom talked about it; they would often cite others as doing it, but never *them* – perish the thought. Even then they were – and still are – coy about it; after the Guinness affair it is almost a taboo subject. Few will admit to even having been within a million miles of a support operation.

Support operations worked on the basis of a widespread system of unwritten and sometimes even unspoken deals. If you were part of the club, and asked for help, you paid up – and expected to receive the same favour yourself when it was your turn. But as the bids became bigger, and the stakes became outrageously large, members of the club began asking for something more: indemnities against loss, or worse still, 'success fees'. In the nastiest and hardest fought battles, the club was no longer big enough – the raiders had to go outside. And the payments became greater. It was only a matter of time before a ruthless raider, his back to the wall, would step over the ill-defined boundaries where the rules ended – and get caught.

That raider was Guinness.

Ernest Saunders was aware that it was not enough to have persuaded the Distillers board to invite him to bid, although it was certainly a vital step. He still feared, with some reason, the opposition.

From the beginning there was a phobia on the Guinness side about the vulnerability of the share price. Again and again this is cited as the reason for the initiation of the support operation. There was a fear that Gulliver and his supporters were going to mount, or indeed had already mounted, a major bear market operation to force the Guinness share price down, persuading all their friends to dump Guinness shares at the worst possible moment. There may be an element of truth in this – 'we were not exactly angels', admits one senior Argyll executive – but it was wildly exaggerated in the minds of the Guinness senior executives. 'Mounting a successful bear market operation in the middle of a takeover bid is very difficult,' says a leading merchant banker. 'I've never seen it achieved. It is about the most dangerous tactic you can employ.'

In the classic bear market operation, shares are sold that the seller does not actually have, but hopes to buy back at a lower price. The difference between the selling price and the buying price is his profit. But if the price rises – and the other side could well decide to push it up just at the wrong moment – then losses are disproportionately large.

This was the tactic that Saunders and his team were convinced they had to counter at all costs. As one participant in the support operation, Gerald Ronson, explained later: 'It was, in effect, as I understood it, designed as a legitimate corrective to the tactics of the other side.' Olivier Roux, in a letter written by the (then) Guinness solicitors Kingsley Napley based on several interviews with Roux (Roux later refuted parts of the letter, which he never signed, after it was published in the *Sunday Times*), said: 'Argyll began to employ strange tactics in order to affect the market price of Guinness – for example, by giving late orders to jobbers and selling the shares late at night.'

Saunders himself, in his interviews with us, also many times mentioned the tactics of the other side with distaste. Whether he genuinely believed it, or whether it was his own private justification for what was developing as part of Guinness's bid strategy, is impossible to say. He later stated that there never was a strategy relating to a support operation. He now paints a picture very different from the one seen from the outside at the time: of a bid operation, employing nobody but the best, but hastily put together; of an enormous workload on him as chief executive, in running the business, integrating Bell's, dealing with the OFT, the Scottish lobby, and so much else. Everyone involved mentions the large number of groups working separately and without central control. 'Maybe it was because there were so many people involved, all dealing with different things, that the cohesion of the structure broke down and lead into the dilemmas that were created,' said a Guinness director, deeply involved in the operation, later. The bankers and the advisers increasingly did their own thing, keeping Roux loosely informed. The Saunders defence against the wave of criticism of him is that he was simply not able to control it, that all his shortcomings as a financial man were now exposed, and that he simply left it to the highly paid professionals. Others, however, blame Saunders, accusing him of something more serious than neglect, although he himself denies any wrong-doing. The full details await the inspectors' report and the many court cases that are being put in train at the time of writing.

What we do know is that the tactics which were to put Guinness in so much trouble began within days of the battle opening. That same week, one of Britain's richest men was asked for help. Gerald Ronson is probably a billionaire; he is owner of Heron International, a private company which had become Britain's biggest independent petrol retailer by the 1970s, and has diversified substantially since then. Ronson, born in 1939 in Paddington, north London, is the grandson of Russian emigrants who fled the pogroms in the early part of the century. His father was a useful amateur light-heavyweight in the 1930s, but his real skill was furniture-making. Gerald started in the family business after leaving school before he was 15, and discovered the property world in the mid-1950s when he and his father built a new factory for £100,000 and sold it immediately for £198,500 – more than they made in four years, working 13 hours a day and employing 350 people. His move into petrol stations provided him with cash flow, and allowed him to finance some major property developments, and move on into other trading activities: the HR Owen franchise for Rolls-Royce and many other businesses. Today he has property all over the world. Half his profits are made in the United States where he owns Pima Savings and Loan Association with assets of $2.2bn. Profits have risen for 30 years in a row – and early in 1986, when he received his approach from the Guinness camp, Ronson's empire made profits of £40m a year. A chunk of that came from one of his favourite activities: buying and selling shares. Ronson loved to be involved where the stock market action was, and was close to most of the big players.

It was late on Wednesday evening, 22 January, that a visitor arrived at Ronson's Hampstead home. Tony Parnes was a man who often dropped in – he lived round the corner – and the two knew each other well. Parnes had been Ronson's personal stockbroker for years, and had been involved with many of the billionaire's more spectacular market coups. Parnes was to become one of the central characters in the Guinness support operation that was now under way. He was ideally suited to the job. Known as 'The Animal', Tony Parnes had prospered mightily during the stock market boom of the 1980s. In the early 1970s, he had some doubtful clients, notably Gerald Caplan who fled Britain after stealing millions from his company London & County. But by the 1980s, by which stage he was an associate of the stockbroking firm Alexanders Laing & Cruickshank, Parnes numbered many of the leading players as his clients: besides Ronson, there were Robert Maxwell, Sir Philip Harris (occasionally), and Ephraim Margulies, the flamboyant chairman of S&W Berisford. For 15 years Parnes had been one of the most colourful stockbrokers on the London scene, bustling with ideas and energy, working all hours, involving himself in every deal he could find. In 1968 he moved house, boasting that his new place had cost him nearly £5m – more than Ronson's house, in which the billionaire had lived for 20 years with his wife Gail and their growing family of daughters, was worth. The offspring of a Jewish ragtrade family, he is a cousin of Larry Parnes, the impresario behind the 1960s rock stars Tommy Steel and Billy Fury.

That evening he had a deal to put to Ronson, as he invariably did have: Guinness reckoned its shares were going to come under pressure from the Argyll camp, he explained. There were signs they were already selling short in the market. 'It was explained to me that the general opinion (which I must say I shared) was that it was in Distillers' as well as Guinness's best interests that the bid should succeed,' said Ronson later in a letter he wrote to the new Guinness chairman, Sir Norman Macfarlane,* almost exactly a year later. 'I understood that with the approval of the Guinness senior management (and Ernest Saunders) in particular – whose skill and integrity were always regarded as of the highest) efforts were being made to support the Guinness share price by persuading Guinness's friends to buy in the market.' (Saunders strongly denies this.)

Ronson agreed to invest an initial £10m supporting Guinness shares. But it was not done purely out of friendship. 'I was told that in the event that Heron suffered any loss it would be covered by Guinness. This did not seem to me at the time to be in any sense unusual or sinister, particularly as it was public knowledge that Distillers itself had agreed to cover the expenses of Guinness in rescuing it from the Argyll bid.'

The words 'unusual or sinister' are the key here. Ronson was implying that he, and others, were often asked for similar support – and indemnified against loss when they gave it. Ronson of course had been involved on the edge, and sometimes centrally, in many of the bids of recent years. He himself had lost out to the Australian Robert Holmes à Court in bidding for Associated Communications Corporations, Lord Grade's former ATV group; he had been tested by Hanson in bidding for the stores groups UDS. He had almost made a run on Burmah Oil, but had pulled back when the price took off, and the story leaked. He had at one stage seriously thought of taking over Woolworth, but decided against that too, on the grounds that there would have had to be many redundancies. He might have done it, he explained, but just that very week Israeli prime minister Menachem Begin sent planes to bomb Beirut, and there was an ugly anti-Jewish backlash around the world. Ronson, for all his apparent self-confidence and brusque, no-nonsense manner is an intensely private man, and would not subject his family to the risk of adverse publicity.

His letter confirmed what many suspected: there was a well-oiled machine which those in the know could tap and use to support their shares. In this case, however, it went further. The first £10m was peanuts. More, much more, was needed. Parnes came back again and

---

*Macfarlane succeeded Saunders after Saunders had been sacked by the Guinness board.

again to Ronson. By 3 April, in the closing stages of the bid, Ronson had increased his investment in Guinness shares to £25m. But he was now demanding a higher price. 'It was by then agreed that in the event of the Guinness bid being successful we would receive a success fee of £5m. These arrangements were expressly confirmed to me by Mr Saunders. In due course our invoices were rendered in the total funds mentioned . . . and these were paid,' he wrote to Macfarlane. Saunders insisted he had nothing to do with the arrangement, claiming the dealings with Ronson were carried out by Roux.

Ronson later repaid £5.8m, £5m for his success fee and £800,000 loss on his share purchases, apologising profusely for ever stepping into it. 'I am very upset to have been involved, albeit in good faith, in these transactions in support of the Guinness endeavour.' By that stage he was not speaking to Parnes, whom he blamed for getting him into it. At a dinner party, given by Sir Philip Harris for the 18th birthday of his son Martin, Ronson insisted on sitting at a different table from Parnes, whom he shunned all night. Ronson was stunned by the turn of events. By that stage, he admitted, he fully appreciated 'the implications of our role in the affair'. He should never, he added, 'have succumbed to the request for support'.

Ronson's contrition, although genuine, has to be set against the size of his fee. '£5m for doing what?' asked a merchant banker, appalled by what happened. 'He couldn't lose any money – he already had an indemnity. He was in effect agreeing to hold the shares for a period of time. As a straightforward banking proposition he would be entitled to a fee of, say, £50,000 for that. What did he consider he was doing in order to get a fee of £5m?'

Ronson was only a small part of it. Parnes himself received a fee of £3m for what he claimed was 'key advice'. It had, he said, been negotiated by two Guinness directors, but he refused to name them. The money was paid to a Swiss company, Consultants et Investissement, again not exactly a usual feature of a straightforward operation. However, the Guinness financial machinery, not aware of the bigger picture, dealt with it perfectly properly, even charging value added tax on it. (In all, it was reckoned that the government may have received £3.8m out of the 'special' fees that Guinness paid out in this period.)

Parnes, in a statement issued in January 1987, insisted the fees 'reflected the true value of his service to the company. In no sense did the fee represent monies paid as an indemnity against movements in share prices.' So what did he do for it? Parnes, according to a spokesman on his behalf, 'was involved in putting blocks of shares together for a number of his clients'. His fees, however, related to the 'technical' advice he gave on strategy and tactics during the closing stages of the bid. By that stage, given the level of the fees, Guinness must have been the best advised company in corporate history.

Parnes was just part of the network which helped Guinness in those crucial few weeks. He was a director of a company called J. Lyons Chamberlayne which was the private company of yet another central character, Sir Jack Lyons. Aged 71, Lyons was a friend of the Saunders. He and his wife Roslyn helped Ernest and Carole Saunders act as hosts to the Queen and Prince Philip at the Barbican when Guinness, after the Distillers takeover, sponsored Leonard Bernstein conducting the music of Leonard Bernstein. Lyons was also a London director of Bain & Co., the consultancy business which supplied Guinness with so many of its kept people, including Olivier Roux. His connections were considerable: on 7 January, 1987, he entertained the prime minister, Mrs Thatcher, to lunch with a glittering list of guests. Only a few days later he was admitting he, too, had accepted hefty fees during the bid – for 'valuable advisory services rendered to Guinness'. Within hours, Bain asked him to quit.

Already another Parnes client had admitted he, too, had received a special fee. Ephraim Margulies, one of the most successful commodity dealers in London, was involved by Tom Ward. Margulies later explained, in a letter to Macfarlane dated 22 January, 1987, that during the bid, the chief executive of S & W Barisford American subsidiary was introduced to Ward 'with whom he discussed proposed co-operation between our two companies in relation to international trade, and in particular the provision by us of a stand-by facility for the purpose of conducting counter-trade and barter transactions on your behalf'. Margulies insisted the arrangement was perfectly innocent, and essentially involved agreeing to buy £50m of Guinness/Distillers products over a period of three years 'for dealings in countries where we can arrange barter transactions or where you might otherwise have difficulty in obtaining payment'.

But in return the Berisford subsidiary, Erlanger & Co., received a fee in advance of £1,495,000. The invoice was marked 'Work in connection with the acquisition of Distillers'. Margulies insisted that this meant only that it was in connection with 'services we are to provide related to Distillers' products and therefore arose by reason of your acquisition of that company'. He understood, he added, 'that the wording was suggested by Guinness and I regret that an invoice in these terms was issued'. He, like Ronson, offered to pay it back – and Guinness accepted the offer.

Margulies had shown his support in another way: another American subsidiary, Berisford Capital Corporation, bought 2.8m Guinness shares during the bid. There was no idemnity, and Margulies insisted that the subsidiary had bought them 'on its own initiative'.

On 3 March, 1986, the Distillers bid was moving into its final stages. Guinness issued its formal offer, which became fully operative on 21 March when the Monopolies Commission issues had finally been settled. That was the day Gulliver decided to increase his bid, putting him well ahead of the Guinness offer, and Gulliver at that point had every hope of winning.

The Argyll camp now waited for Guinness to come back with a still higher offer; without it, they believed Guinness would drop out of the running. Guinness, however, astonished everyone by doing nothing. One of the Argyll advisers recalled later: 'It appeared confident that its share price alone would carry the day: a belief for which at that time there seemed to be no justification.'

That Monday afternoon Guinness shares stood at 281p. By Friday they were 311p; the following week they added another 14p. The Argyll share price by contrast was stuck fast, although the food sector of which it had previously been a star performer, was moving ahead rapidly. Only in April did Argyll finally get out of the rut, and its own shares began to rise, but it was too late: Guinness was well ahead. Guinness shares peaked at 353p just at the climax of the bid. Later in 1986 they slid all the way back to 280p again.

In those last weeks, the scale of the operation seems to have been extraordinary. But even in these last days, after nearly three months of open battle, there is little evidence to suggest there was any mastermind behind it. 'In my view it was a hotchpotch,' said a Guinness director who was not party to the operation, and only learned about it afterwards. 'They didn't move from a great plan. It was a question of them saying, "Now who can we get to help us?" You could see them saying, "Now come on, Gerald, we need some help here."'

That accords with the accounts of others. Olivier Roux talked about everyone being 'dead tired' at the height of the bid, and agreeing to things they only half understood. He himself was later appalled by the way it all got out of hand. 'I got onto a fast train and it was bloody difficult to step off,' he told a fellow director apologetically. Even so, he remained Saunders' closest ally throughout – he and Ward. Suggestions that Saunders and Roux had the ability and knowledge to hold the support operation together are dismissed by other Guinness executives. 'I cannot believe that they could organise all that,' said another Guinness director after hearing the list of fees Guinness had secretly paid for support and special advice in those final weeks.

That list seemed to go on and on. The board found invoices for just over £25m which could not easily be explained – and had not been accounted for as part of the costs of the bid. Besides the Ronson, Lyons, Parnes and Margulies fees, there was £5.2m paid to a Jersey-based company, Marketing and Acquisitions Consultants Ltd. This was Tom Ward's fee, which would later be the subject of the first litigation as Guinness demanded it back. Guinness sued both Ward and Saunders over this payment. In February 1987 Saunders wrote to the inspector to inform them that over £3m of this money had been transferred by Ward to a Swiss bank account held by Saunders. His explanation was that Ward in May 1986 had asked him could he borrow a Swiss bank account, as he needed one and did not have one. Saunders said he had inherited one from his father, and used it only to keep a few bonds he had inherited with it. He gave Ward the details and only months later, when he was catching up on his personal affairs while on holiday in August, did he discover the money was still there. He rang Ward to remove it to another account. Guinness in court dropped suggestions that Saunders personally had benefited from this money.

There was £254,000 to an Austrian bank which denied any illegality. There was another £3m to an unknown Swiss company, and nearly £2m to a Dutch-Antilles company called Rudani Corp. There was also an extra £1.65m paid to Morgan Grenfell. Another untraced company got £1.94m. Some of these, like Ronson and Margulies, have now come forward and explained their role; others have denied any involvement. Still others remain to be uncovered from the shadows of overseas companies.

This list however is only part of what went on. There was much more. The Zurich-based Bank Leu, headed by Dr Arthur Fuerer, appointed to the board by Saunders, admitted it held £50m of Guinness money on deposit, and in turn held nearly 5 per cent of Guinness' shares. According to a letter from Sir Norman Macfarlane to Guinness shareholders on 16 January, 1987, these transactions had been carried out by Bank Leu 'on the strength of Guinness's agreement, signed on its behalf by Mr Ward or Mr Roux, to purchase the shares at cost plus carrying charges – an agreement which, at least as regards its own shares, Guinness could not lawfully have fulfilled'. Bank Leu had been a big buyer of Distillers shares during the bid, which it later converted into Guinness shares. (It sold them for £140m in May 1987.)

Then there was Meshulam 'Rik' Riklis, who was as important as anyone. Riklis, like so many of the others involved, is a larger than life character. An Israeli-American, he is married to the young actress Pia Zadora. He was one of the most controversial raiders on Wall Street during the 1970s as he built his company, and was known at one stage as 'the most frequently sued executive' in the United States. His company, the Rapid-American conglomerate, owns Schenley Industries which has distributed Dewar's whisky in the United States since 1936. Scotch distribution is a key business for Riklis – and when Gulliver first made his bid for Distillers, he became concerned. After the Argyll bid had been launched, Riklis turned up in London. There were rumours in the market that he was already a big buyer of Distillers shares. He arranged to see Argyll, and, according to Gulliver, hinted he might bid for Distillers himself. He asked about Gulliver's plans for Dewars, and left Gulliver with the impression that he would support his bid if he could have some guarantee for the Dewar's franchises. Riklis denies this. Riklis bought £30m worth of Distillers shares and £60m worth of Guinness shares – and ended up owning all rights to Dewar's label in the United States. In addition he had also captured the valuable Gordons Gin distribution, worth an estimated $20m a year. Again the man involved on the Guinness side was Tom Ward, whose Washington law firm, Ward, Lazarus, Crow and Cihlar, officially Guinness's American legal advisers at the time, recommended the deal with the objective, according to Sir Norman Macfarlane, 'of protecting the leading Scotch whisky brand in the US market from erosion by unauthorised imports'. Riklis's support for Guinness shares was at one stage so heavy that he went over the 5 per cent level at which a holding has to be declared – but only informed the authorities months afterwards, by which stage the scandal was breaking.

While all this was going on, Roger Seelig at Morgan Grenfell was working hard for his fees, moving faster and faster around the City, persuading clients, friends, institutions and the press that the Guinness bid was the one that should succeed. He was of course being helped by the brokers, Cazenove and Wood Mackenzie. 'They said they would do their best to find support for Guinness from their own friends, contacts, clients etc,' said the Roux letter prepared by Kingsley Napley (some of which he refuted).

Seelig's path took him across that of an old Morgan colleague, Lord (Patrick) Spens, now running the corporate finance department of a much smaller bank, Henry Ansbacher. As it happens Spens had no reason to love Guinness: he had acted for Bell's in the previous bid, and had emerged a poor second. But professional bankers, like lawyers, are used to changing sides. Seelig asked for help to support the Guinness share price, wondering if Ansbacher, as a principal, would buy some shares. This was fairly standard practice, and there would normally be a quid pro quo – in *his* next bid, Spens would ask Morgans to support his client. Spens consulted his chief executive Richard Fenhalls, who refused to have anything to do with it: emphatically he turned it down. Spens, however, without Fenhall's knowledge, then persuaded five institutional clients of Ansbacher to buy Guinness shares. The total amount involved was £7.5m. In the final days of the bid, however, with Guinness shares peaking, Spens indicated he wanted to sell the shares. Guinness was desperately anxious that he did not. Something had to be cobbled together quickly. It was Roux who apparently took the decision to deposit, interest free, the exact sterling equivalent of the cost of the shares. Seelig arranged for the deposit to be made. Guinness was later accused of using its own money to support its own share price. It was the revelation of this particular arrangement which cost Seelig and then Patrick Spens their jobs – both resigned, thereby ending the careers of two of the brightest minds in corporate finance.

All of the personalities used by Guinness for its support operation were in some way connected. It was like a giant web: Roux had brought in Parnes, who in turn had contacted Ronson. Lyons knew all of them, including Roux and Saunders. Parnes knew Margulies – who also knew the others. Fuerer was the chairman of Bank Leu and, in turn, from his Nestlé days, had contact with Tom Ward – who involved Margulies. Seelig also knew Ronson well – and of course he knew Spens. And so it went around and around, the figures getting bigger and bigger, and no single individual probably ever fully aware of the complete picture.

There is one man at the centre of the web who should not be left out: Ivan Boesky had taken a keen interest in the bid for Distillers from the beginning. He was in London promoting his book *Merger Mania* when the battle was in fill swing. But he had sent out feelers to Gulliver in the very early days, looking for a deal. He was already buying Distillers shares heavily, and sent an envoy to the Argyll camp proposing a deal. 'I never actually met him,' says Gulliver. 'This intermediary came to see us and said that Boesky would like to get close to us during the bid. In return he would buy Distillers shares and do everything he could to make sure we won. But I wasn't sure what his role would be. I saw no balance of advantage to us from talking to him.'

Gulliver's assessment was undoubtedly right. Boesky had no loyalty to any side, regardless of how they helped him and kept him 'informed'. His business was to trade shares at the highest price, and Gulliver knew as well as anybody that, if the wind changed at a vital moment, then Boesky would change with it.

Once Guinness entered the bidding, Boesky didn't bother Gulliver again. The web of connections was in full play: Boesky had played a decisive $70m role in Nestlé's bid for Carnation in 1984, hailed as one of his greatest strokes at the time (yet curiously not mentioned in his book *Merger Mania*). That of course involved Dr Fuerer, and his Washington friend Tom Ward. And so we're back to the circle again.

The full details of Boesky's involvement may have to await the report from the DTI inspectors. What we do know is that Boesky was a big buyer of both Distillers and Guinness shares. And it was later suggested that the quid pro quo for it was that Guinness make a major investment in a new Boesky fund set up at that time, although Saunders strongly denies it. Guinness duly invested $100m, just under the limit it would have to declare. The investment would become just part of other investments in the published accounts. Saunders did not consult his board about it at the time. Seelig swears that he never knew about a Boesky connection until it was revealed nearly a year later. He professed himself appalled – and looking at him that day, it was impossible to doubt it. Another investor in that same fund was Meshulam Riklis. Again the links were going around and around.

Against this scale of support, Gulliver slipped behind in those final few weeks of the bid in April 1986. He had to compete with still further elements: a dirty tricks campaign, run not by Guinness but by Distillers. As part of its defences, Distillers had hired a private detective to look at the private and public life of Gulliver. A man called Nick Vafiadis, the son of a Greek, who for years had floated on the edges of what was loosely termed 'the intelligence world', had been tracking back over Gulliver's career for weeks. The Argyll camp knew all about it – and him. He had turned up in New York to question a former Gulliver employee, Charles Walford, and had even offered him money. Walford secretly recorded the conversation and sent it to his old friend Gulliver.

'I could not see what useful information I could give him,' said Walford afterwards, 'and I decided I was interested to know who his paymaster was, so I gave him some time. He said that the information he gleaned would be heard in the Distillers' camp.' The fee suggested was a $1000 for the meeting and another $9000 if Gulliver lost the bid for Distillers.

Vafiadis does not seem to have discovered much about Gulliver that was helpful to his side. But, on 7 March, a public relations man working for Distillers leaked a document to several carefully selected journalists, including the *Wall Street Journal* and the *Sunday Times*. It contained a detail which a few months before or even a few weeks later would have been of no relevance whatsoever. It indicated that in his *Who's Who* entry, filled out by the individual himself, Gulliver listed his education as 'Glasgow and Harvard'. It turned out that it should have read 'Glasgow and Georgia Institute of Technology' – Gulliver had never actually studied at Harvard, except for the odd week as part of his Georgia Tech course. 'In the early days when I talked about it I discussed both Harvard and Georgia,' said Gulliver later. 'Georgia was less fashionable, obviously, and gradually it sank into the background.'

When the story broke that weekend in the *Sunday Times*, Gulliver received a wave of sympathy – but it may also have helped to untie one or two wavering institutions from him. We have talked to two who switched their allegiance, and decided to support the Guinness bid after this story appeared. 'If he could mislead about small things like that, he could mislead about bigger things too,' said one fund manager.

It was marginal, however, compared to Guinness's support operation. Argyll in the final weeks reckoned that Guinness had as much as £200m of its own funds out supporting its share price. At the last moment there was a further development, too. Warburgs had been part of the Argyll core underwriting group. It was the single biggest shareholder in Distillers, and its support in the final analysis could have been crucial. But in the final week, Warburgs decided that in the best interests of its investors (they were managed funds, not its own money) they should offer the shares to both camps. They gave Argyll and Guinness the option to buy the shares at a price above the market – which theoretically, according to the Panel rules, should have meant raising the bid to that level. The value of the highest offer at the time was Guinness's – the rise in its own share price had now driven the value of its share offer to 700p, 100p above its cash offer. Argyll was 50p a share behind on the paper offer, but 30p ahead on the cash offer.

'We couldn't raise the money,' says Gulliver. 'We needed another £72m. The shares were snapped up by Guinness.' The Takeover Panel has still to finish its investigation of this deal.

That was the end of the bid. Saunders and Guinness moved on to victory.

Only a tiny handful of close Guinness associates had any real idea of what had occurred. There were some suspicions and even unease among some of the professionals involved, but they kept them to themselves. Anyone with doubts had the chance to air them later that summer when a row erupted over Saunders' decision to appoint himself chairman as well as chief executive of the group, and ignore the promise to Sir Thomas Risk.

The Risk affair was a curious interlude in the Guinness scandal. The bid was already won, and nothing could reverse that. Saunders now rode higher than ever, commanding one of the largest companies in Britain. In five years he had achieved an astonishing amount, transforming the old family firm of Guinness beyond recognition, its market value now some 35 times what it was when he took it over. Guinness was in the super-league, a world power in the drinks world where size and brand names mattered. And yet . . . Saunders wanted still more. Essentially he wanted unfettered power at the enlarged company, and, within weeks of the bid, discovered that the man chosen to be chairman, his new Lord Iveagh in effect, had other ideas. Sir Thomas Risk, it turned out, had no intention of being a mere figurehead.

It was 17 May, a month after the end of the bid, before the first hint of trouble surfaced. Risk had gone on holiday in the immediate aftermath, and then Saunders went to the US. By mid-May the new management structure had not been put in place and Risk politely indicated a degree of impatience. Saunders asked him to fly to Washington. Within hours of his arrival, the two were at loggerheads. One of the key meetings occurred in Tom Ward's office, with Saunders, Vic Steel, the Guinness director now running most of the Distillers business, Ward and Risk present. Risk reminded Saunders of promises made to the Scottish lobby, and indicated he intended to have a considerable say in the running of the company. Saunders emerged convinced that he could not work with Risk, at least not on Risk's terms, whereby Risk would be an active and involved chairman.

The enmity between the two men simmered through the summer, and finally boiled over in mid-July when Saunders decided to appoint himself both chairman and chief executive. There would be no job for Risk. This decision, although relatively minor compared to the bid, still today works up extraordinary passions, and has tended to obscure the more critical issues. There was much talk of the 'sanctity of the bid document', although the actual bid document only mentioned Risk in the small print. The fracas brought to a head all the latent dislike that Saunders in his rapid climb had built up. When the news broke, Saunders ran into a wall of criticism from which his reputation never recovered, and from which he was still reeling when he finally left Guinness six months later. It began with his own merchant banker Christopher Reeves, who strongly argued against the move. In the

Bank of England, David Walker, the man in charge of industrial policy, expressed his disapproval when Saunders took his problem there. Soon the Governor himself joined in, and Saunders received censures from the Secretary of State for Scotland, Malcolm Rifkind, from the Stock Exchange, the Takeover Panel and just about every other body that had anything to say on the subject.

The issue, which for a time was presented as the greatest threat yet seen to the whole system of self-regulation in the City, eventually went to a shareholders meeting. Saunders received overwhelming support. In doing so, however, he had exhausted his City goodwill. Wood Mackenzie resigned, and Cazenove and Morgan Grenfell almost did. The knives were now out for him. Even so, he was surviving, and starting to recover again – until, on the morning of 1 December, exactly a year after Gulliver had formally opened hostilities, the Department of Trade inspectors arrived at his Portman Square Office.

The casualty list from then on was enormous: Saunders, Ward, Roux and Fuerer all departed or were asked to depart. Morgan Grenfell lost first Seelig, asked to resign, and then Christopher Reeves and Graham Walsh, probably the two most important men in the bank. Parnes was cast aside by Alexanders Laing & Cruickshank. Ronson appeared hurt behind a battery of lawyers, devastated by the public humiliations and the damage to his reputation. And there were many others.

And yet Saunders might still be there, enjoying his salary, his prestige and his health, had it not been for an event no-one could ever have foreseen. Remember that web – and the man at the centre of it all, Ivan F. Boesky? It was Boesky who threw the stone into the takeover pond, and the ripples have not stopped spreading yet.

CHAPTER TEN •

Fall of the House of Ivan

By the end of business on Wall Street on Friday, 14 November, 1986, arbitrageurs and traders were exhaustedly preparing to leave for what they felt had been a well-earned weekend rest. It had been one of the heaviest weeks yet in the whole takeover boom, which after a pause in the summer had erupted at yet new record levels. As they wearily tidied up their desks, few on Wall Street had any inkling that they would not see another week like it for many years – if ever. When the New York Stock Exchange closed for business that day, it was effectively pulling down the curtain on the end of the most extraordinary five years in American corporate history.

There was nothing special in the market that day to alert them. True, it had been frantically, almost desperately busy. The arbs had been hurt badly by the extraordinary moves of the 43-year-old Ronald Perelman, victor of a $1.8bn battle for the cosmetics company Revlon, and in recent weeks by far and away the most active of the raiders. In the past week, Perelman had staged three dazzling moves, each one catching the arbs unprepared. He had made a run on Transworld, the Hilton Hotels company, revealing that he and his partners had 14.8 per cent of it. Transworld which had already shed its Trans World Airline business – it was acquired by Carl Icahn – had that very morning emerged with its defence plan: a complex liquidation under which the Hilton hotels outside the United States would be spun off to a liquidating trust and the proceeds paid to shareholders. The remaining parts of the business would be sold. Perelman had also

242

surprised the arbs by accepting an offer from Salomon Brothers for his stake in CPC food group, causing the share price to plummet, and losing the arbs a lot of money. Perelman was unimpressed by the cries of 'greenmail' that greeted this move, and that Friday morning used his profit for another venture, his biggest and boldest yet: he made a $4bn bid for Gillette, the razor and consumer products company.

The mergers and acquisition divisions of the investment banks were also wrestling with a series of Perelman-scale bids: Carl Icahn was bidding $5bn for USX, the United States steel complex, once, when it was originally put together with a series of takeovers by J. Pierpont Morgan, the biggest corporation the world had ever seen, but now, like so many of the great giants of the past, just another target for the 1980s school of raiders. And Sir James Goldsmith had unleashed a $5bn bid for Goodyear, the tyre company.

There were plenty of rumours too: shares of Lockheed jumped another $8 a share, making a 20 per cent gain in two days, despite a denial from the company that it was having talks with Ford Motor. The arbs had moved on to other engineering stocks, such as Borg-Warner, the gear-box maker, where a 10 per cent holding had been disclosed.

The arbs were trying to get some of the losses back. But it had been a bad week for them. 'Oh God – I feel like a dog let loose on the freeway in the rush hour,' one arbitrageur moaned after the latest Perelman move caught him wrong-footed yet again.

But, as the janitors swept the debris from the trading floor of the New York Stock Exchange, it still seemed just a normal working day. In Washington, President Ronald Reagan was beginning to face up to the growing crisis over his secret US arms shipments to Iran. In London the news was that the UK inflation rate had held at 3 per cent, but the government gloomily admitted it would probably rise in coming months. In Canada, the rumour was that the Hong Kong Chinese businessman Li Ka-Shing might bid for Husky Oil.

The bombshell that would effectively end the takeover boom came in a discreet announcement put out after the market closed. It came from the offices of the SEC and revealed that Ivan Boesky, the king of the arbitrageurs and the man at the centre of almost every takeover for the past five years, had agreed to hand back $50m in illegal profits from insider dealing, pay a $50m penalty, and be barred for life from the securities industry. Boesky also agreed to plead guilty to a criminal charge which could send him to jail.

But most serious of all, from the point of view of the arb community and for all those who had dealt with Boesky over the years, the SEC that evening calmly announced that the 49-year-old arbitrageur had done some hard bargaining and, in return for leniency, had agreed to co-operate fully with the investigators. Over the weekend it became known that for at least six weeks Boesky had been walking into meetings wired up with a hidden tape recorder, and all his thousands of telephone calls had also been recorded. Those tapes were in the hands of the investigators.

The shock almost literally shook Wall Street. There had been nothing to equal it since the Great Crash of 1929. 'The repercussions will rock Wall Street for twenty years,' said one commentator that weekend. The arbitrage community, so much a part of the 1980s merger and acquisitions scene, seemed to have been dealt a death blow. Junk bonds, which only that morning had been set to finance Perelman's acquisition of Gillette, abruptly faced a doubtful future. Rumours swirled around Drexel Burnham, previously the most fashionable house in town. The raiders themselves, dependent on both junk bonds and the arbitrageurs, reeled, and within a week Sir James Goldsmith would drop out of his bid for Goodyear, quoting growing anti-takeover sentiment and blaming 'this ghastly Boesky affair'.

All around the world critics of takeovers seized upon the revelations. Senator William Proxmire, the Wisconsin Democrat who had just been appointed chairman of the Senate banking committee, and Howard Metzenbaum, the new chairman of the senate judiciary committee's antitrust subcommittee, both indicated that they believed that insider trading and junk bond-financed takeover activity were problems deserving urgent legislative activity. Proxmire said he did not want to kill takeovers altogether but in view of 'the latest occurrences and the problems of mounting corporate debt, there is a good case to make it harder'.

Sir James Goldsmith gloomily surveying the scene as he dropped out of Goodyear (albeit with a $90m profit for himself and partners), told the *Sunday Times* he had detected a change of mood in America. After Boesky, he said, 'we have now entered the post-Reagan period with the triple alliance of big business, big government and big unions fighting back'.

Ivan Boesky had been one of the central cogs in the whole takeover boom. As the risk arbitrage business had expanded – and it was the fastest-growing area of the financial services industry until Boesky's demise – so it had played a bigger and bigger role in takeovers. Boesky and his ilk provided essential liquidity to the raiders, in a sense lubricating the market, and freeing the flow of shares and cash which otherwise might have become clogged. Boesky was at his height during the oil bids, turning over a block of shares in Getty to Texaco for an estimated profit of $100m, and buying into Gulf when Boone Pickens made a run on that company. Not a bid went through either Wall Street or the City of London without Boesky examining, weighing and assessing every aspect of it, looking for every scrap of information and rumour he could get hold of, and invariably taking a position. He had become a legend. And now, so abruptly that few on that Friday evening could quite grasp the significance of it, he was gone.

For such a momentous event, the Boesky affair had a remarkably low-key beginning. In May 1985 in Caracas, Venezuela, someone – the person has never been identified – noticed something odd about the dealings of two employees, Carlos Zubillaga and Max Hofer, in the local office of Merrill Lynch, the world's largest stockbroker. Time after time they both seemed to be able to forecast major takeover bids about to happen in the United States – and were successfully buying and selling shares in the target companies. It obviously struck the unknown observer that the accuracy of their dealings could scarcely be explained away by coincidence, or just by good judgement. The two men never seemed to get it wrong. And they were recording increasingly handsome profits. In May the Merrill Lynch head office in New York received an anonymous letter from Caracas, accusing the two brokers of illegally dealing on inside information. The letter was routinely passed to the company's 'compliance' department, which is designed to make sure a company's employees stick to its own rules. The lawyers and experts there examined the details – and suddenly became interested.

The two men were summoned to New York and grilled carefully. Zubillaga cracked first. Yes, he admitted, he *had* been receiving tips. The source was a man called Brian Campbell whom he had met on a Merrill Lynch training course. Campbell had left the Merrill office some months before for another job, but his records were available. They were run through a computer, and revealed a pattern of dealings in his own personal account almost identical to that of the two Venezuelans. But where had Campbell been getting his inside information from? Further investigation showed that Campbell managed a customer account opened by the Bahamas branch of Bank Leu, one of the largest Swiss banks. This account was buying and selling shares in exactly the same pattern as Campbell and the two Venezuelans. Campbell had simply noticed the accuracy and prescience of the unnamed customer behind that account, and copied his dealings. And passed the information on to his friend Zubillaga in Caracas.

But who was behind the Bank Leu account? It was no longer strictly the business of the Merrill Lynch compliance officers. They had no hope of investigating a Swiss bank account, particularly one that was doubly protected by Swiss bank law and Bahamas law, both of which insist on secrecy. The compliance officers turned their files over to the SEC.

If it had happened a year previously, that would probably have been that. The SEC might have tried to follow it through but, with poor resources and few weapons to fight with, it would soon have given up. The insider trading out of Bank Leu would have gone on. But, as it happened, the SEC was in a receptive mood for such an investigation. The Reagan administration, despite its relaxed attitude to the broad thrust of the takeover trends, was becoming concerned by the abuses it was bringing with it. 'Insider trading' was increasingly a word heard well outside Wall Street, and it was starting to become something of an issue.

By another curious coincidence, the SEC's enforcement division had a new ambitious young chief. The previous head of the 600-strong squad of enforcement officers, John Fedders, an ex-university athlete star and Republican rising star, had just resigned after squalid revelations about his domestic life which emerged in a steamy divorce case which was a talking point in Washington for months. The man who replaced him was everything Fedders was not. Gary Lynch was a 33-year-old lawyer, from Middletown, NY, who had graduated from Duke University law school in 1975. After a brief stint with a Washington law firm, he joined the SEC in 1976 and soon established his reputation as one of the brightest investigators in the whole commission.

When the SEC's chairman John Shad appointed him to replace Fedders, the move was generally greeted favourably. 'He knows the takeover business better than any federal regulatory official,' said Edward Herlihy, a former SEC enforcement attorney, and now a partner in Wachtell, Lipton, the leading takeover lawyers. 'He understands the process; he knows the players, and he's bringing that perspective to bear.'

The SEC, at the time of Lynch's appointment, stood in low regard along Wall Street. He inherited a department whose officers were desperately overstretched and seemed to be no match for the sophisticated systems used by the yuppies on Wall Street to profit illegally from the takeover activity which was sweeping the country. A report by an American Bar Association task force said that the enforcement staff was probably too small 'for the commission to effectively discharge its statutory responsibilities'. Month after month the enforcement department had to pass up promising chances of prosecutions because of lack of resources. The New York Stock Exchange in the 1980s referred an average of 50 million documented cases a year of insider trading to the SEC; the National Association of Securities Dealers (NASD), the self-regulatory body of over-the-counter markets, sent another hundred. An average of only 200 a year was investigated, and that actually fell in 1985. 'The SEC is horribly overmatched by the bad guys in the marketplace,' Royce Grifin, the president of the North American Securities Administrators Association, a group of state regulators, told the *Wall Street Journal**. All across the board, the SEC seemed to be retreating under a hail of paperwork, unable to cope with its routine functions.

'Nowhere is this retreat more evident than in the SEC's beleaguered division of corporation finance,' said the *Wall Street Journal*. 'Its analysts are reviewing less than 1 per cent of the flood of 13-D reports on significant stock purchases.' Ten years before, all 13-D reports were checked. Richard Phillips, a Washington attorney who chaired the Bar Association committee on the regulation of the securities markets, remarked that he had never 'been more concerned about the adequacy of the SEC's resources to prevent fraud, promote full disclosure, and otherwise safeguard our securities markets'. He produced data which showed that over the previous decade, the volume of stock transactions in the United States had risen by more than 700 per cent; the number of people employed in the securities industry had risen 400 per cent; and the number of investment advisers had tripled from 1975 to 11,146 in 1985. Yet the SEC staff had actually shrunk in the Reagan years.

By June (when the file from Merrill Lynch landed on his desk) Lynch had already decided he had little hope of catching all insider traders. But if he could pick out just a handful, and nail them, that might stand as an effective example which would discourage the others.

The Merrill customer who used the Bank Leu branch in the Bahamas became known as 'Mr X'. As the months went by it became clear that 'Mr X' was not only still dealing, but getting it right time after time. This was somebody more than just another greedy little yuppie. This fish was much bigger.

Mr X's biggest deal to date had been in the spring of 1985. He bought 145,500 shares of American Natural Resources between 14 February and 1 March at an average price of $49.93 a share. On 1 March Coastal Crop announced a $60 a share bid – and Mr X sold out for a profit of $1.37m. Within weeks, Mr X had bought into another

*16 December, 1985.

bid stock: Nabisco. A fortnight later, Nabisco announced it was merging with R. J. Reynolds, and Mr X sold out for a profit of $2.7m.

Some of these deals were picked up by the computers at the New York Stock Exchange and at the National Association of Securities Dealers. These systems were relatively new, but by the mid-1980s America's stock exchange had in place a computerised monitoring system which noted any unusual trading activity – involving excessive price or volume swings – in stocks which were sensitive to pending announcements, either of results or of mergers. If the computer notices unusual trading, the stock exchange can ask for the individual brokers' records – and the brokers must give them up. Another more sophisticated computer system allows investigators to cross-check those unusual trades against a databank which contains information on 40,000 companies and 70,000 individuals. It can spot patterns and similarities: same names or clubs, or even the same old schools. The exchanges have no powers beyond their own members, and cannot subpoena outside witnesses or demand explanations from clients. But if they suspect insider trading they can – and do – pass the information on to the SEC. It was this system which first triggered interest in the dealings of a share tipster on the *Wall Street Journal* called Foster Winans, who was later convicted of insider dealings on the back of his column 'Heard on the Street'. It was to be invaluable in tracking the deals of Mr X.

For Lynch however, it was slow going. In November he found himself suddenly faced with a flurry of alleged insider trades, of wild buying on the back of rumours, and a rush of complaints. Mr X was only one of the investigations he was pursuing, and he warned that his investigations should be taken seriously, in a speech reiterating his avowed intention to 'get to the bottom of insider trading and professional rumour planting,' but Wall Street took little notice.

By early 1986, however, sentiment began to change, and the investigations took on a keener, harder edge. There was for instance the Santa Fe case, where a former director of Santa Fe International, a major oil services company, was charged with insider trading on his own stock. The case was significant, in that it marked the first case where a Swiss bank was persuaded to divulge information about its client to American investigators. The USA and Switzerland had in fact signed a treaty in 1982 agreeing mutual assistance on criminal matters. Under the treaty, Swiss banks agreed to waive their clients' rights to secrecy if there was any suspicion of illegal activities. In January 1986, a federal grand jury charged that the former director, Darius N. Keaton, and a Jordanian associate made a profit of $4.9m by trading Santa Fe stock and options just before Kuwait Petroleum announced a $2.2bn deal to buy the Californian group. The Jordanian, according to the indictment, had made the bulk of the profits: $4.5m of it. But Keaton had bought 10,000 Santa Fe shares for $233,000 under an alias through a Swiss bank, according to the indictment. The shares were $25 when Kuwait Petroleum made its bid of $51 a share. At the time of writing, Keaton is still awaiting trial.

To unmask and to prosecute Mr X, Lynch and his investigators had to get help from Bank Leu. They increasingly suspected that Mr X must have an accomplice inside the Bahamas bank who was dealing on the same information, except in much smaller amounts. They now knew their man had to be a senior executive at or near the top of one of the leading investment houses – and one who had close links with the arbitrage community.

When the investigators first approached the Bank Leu in August 1985, the Swiss bank was far from helpful. It fell back on the traditional defence of bank secrecy, and had clearly no intention of surrendering the information Lynch needed. It also pointed out that if it were to help, it would be subject to prosecution under the laws in the Bahamas which made it an offence to break bank secrecy. But in March 1986 the SEC investigators raised the pressure by subpoening the bank's records involving trading through the Bahamas bank in some 28 stocks that were subsequently involved in takeovers. It also threatened the bank, which has a branch in New York, with trouble with the regulators if it refused to help. The bank by that stage seems to have been cooperative, although Mr X, it later emerged, twice threatened to sue if it broke its own secrecy rules.

The Bank Leu later insisted it willingly cooperated because the type of insider trading the SEC was investigating 'has no place in our bank'. The same sentiment was echoed by Paul Adderley, the attorney general of the Bahamas, who stated that his country's bank secrecy laws were 'never intended to protect fraud, never intended to protect a thief'. Adderley promised the Swiss bank exemption from prosecution under its secrecy laws if it revealed the name of Mr X. In the second week of May the investigators learned that Mr X was attempting to move $10m from his Bank Leu account into the Caymen Islands branch of Morgan Grenfell. It was time for action. On 12 May, the Bank Leu's lawyers passed over a bundle of material which showed order tickets for stock purchases, telexes and wires and a detailed record of the dealings of Mr X. It also disclosed his name.

On Monday, 12 May, Dennis Levine, the 33-year-old star of Drexel Burnham's investment banking side, learned that marshals from the prosecutors office at the Justice Department wanted to see him. They had a warrant for his arrest. Levine's first instinct was to hide. 'Right after they sent the marshals to arrest him, he disappeared,' recalled Fred Joseph, the chief executive officer of Drexel Burnham, and Levine's boss.* 'He called in later and we told him, "That's dumb. You ought to turn yourself in immediately."' That evening Levine went to the office of US attorney Rudolph Giuliani. There he was instantly arrested, handcuffed and taken off to spend the night in the Metropolitan Correction Center in lower Manhattan. Mr X had been unmasked.

Levine's arrest was dramatic. It was as if a bomb had gone off in the financial community. 'His arrest has shocked Wall Street in a way that few recent events have,' said the *Wall Street Journal*. 'Who may be next is a topic of almost compulsive speculation.' The *Washington Post* expressed the same sentiment: 'Levine's arrest threw Wall Street into panic, not merely because of the case's size and gravity, but because the SEC's charges raised a plethora of unanswered – and frightening – questions. Was Levine acting alone or did he have accomplices?' As the details of the charges against Levine emerged there was soon no doubt whatsoever that he was part of a network which would in the end reach into many corners of Wall Street, and involve some of the biggest names of the takeover boom. 'With all the political pressure building, it was clear Gary Lynch was out to get somebody,' said one top securities lawyer.† 'But this is a real stunner, a grand slam home-run.'

The SEC claimed that Levine had illegally traded on inside information in 54 takeover situations over five-and-a-half years between June 1980 and December 1985. In 35 of them neither he nor any of his three employers over that period – he had worked at Smith Barney, Harris Upham, then at Lehman Brothers Kuhn Loeb and finally at Drexel, the house which had risen so dramatically on the back of the great takeover wave – were involved as investment bankers. In the days that followed this was seen as confirmation that Levine was just part of an information ring. A wave of fear swept along Wall Street when the investigators announced that, within two days of his arrest, Levine had agreed to co-operate. He had done a deal with the investigators. On 5 June Levine publicly dropped his protestations of innocence and pleaded guilty to one count of securities fraud for trading on the basis of inside information in the stock of Jewel Cos., which received a bid from American Stores in 1984. He also pleaded

*Manhattan Inc, August 1986.
† Business Week, 26 May, 1986.

guilty to two counts of tax evasion, and one count of perjury for misleading the SEC in an earlier investigation. Even on the guilty pleas, he still faced a maximum jail sentence of 20 years of imprisonment and $620,000 of fines. He had agreed to give the court $10.6m from his Bahamas account. He also issued a statement of contrition, saying he 'accepted the consequences of my conduct and have agreed to cooperate fully' with the US attorney Guiuliani and with the SEC.

There were reports over the next few days of messengers on Wall Street sporting buttons saying 'Who's next?' (they had pinched them from a beer promotion campaign). There was even the black joke that Levine had been sacked by Drexel instantly because he had *only* managed to make a profit of $10.6m on his insider information. But there were few jokes about Wall Street that week. 'The network of rumours overnight stopped humming and arbitrage activity got quiet – too quiet,' wrote a columnist in *Baron*'s, the favourite reading of most Wall Streeters. 'Perhaps most ominous of all, so a grizzled observer of the market scene pointed out the other day, Wall Street's endless supply of black humour, usually on tap for any disaster, abruptly dried up.'

It was in truth no laughing matter for an entire generation which lived on rumour and information which continually bordered on the inside and sometimes stretched over. Lynch had caught a big fish, but the affair would not stop there. Before it was finished, the reputation of Wall Street and of the whole financial system would be seriously damaged. Many promising young careers would end abruptly. An opinion poll taken that weekend showed that the majority of the American people believed that insider trading was rampant on Wall Street. It had become a major political issue.

The significance of Dennis Levine was that he was not just an ordinary yuppie in one of the lesser houses. He was one of the leading names in the fastest growing investment houses in the land. He earned more than $1m a year in salary and bonuses. He lived in a smart Park Lane apartment on Manhattan's Upper East Side, was married to his college sweetheart – who at the time of his arrest was pregnant with their second child – and he drove an $80,000 red Ferrari. Along Wall Street he was both liked and respected. His immediate boss at Drexel, David Kay, heaped praise on him, even after his arrest: 'He had star quality – that was immediately apparent. He could make things happen. This is a strange business, and it's sometimes hard to say just what it is that makes someone a huge success. But Dennis was flawless.'

Other legendary figures of the takeover world put in a good word for him. 'I always considered him one of the best and brightest among the young M&A people,' said Marty Lipton. Joe Flom of Skadden Arps had, like his friend and sparring partner Lipton, recommended him to Drexel. At Lehman Brothers, where Levine had worked until 1984, he had been seen as one of the main protégés of Peter Solomon, the powerful co-head of the mergers and acquisitions department, and even had an office next to Solomon's – an important accolade, not lightly given by Solomon. Lehman had paid him $400,000 a year and had been angry when he was poached by Drexel.

Levine had been involved at the centre of some of the leading takeover bids of the day: he was in charge of Coastal's bid for American Natural Resources, and had used that information for personal profit. He had also worked closely with Sir James Goldsmith in his bid for Crown Zellerbach, and later his arrest would trigger some old memories of his behaviour during that time: on 25 April, 1985, Levine was in a meeting with Sir James Goldsmith and Goldsmith's long-time associate, Roland Franklin, once one of the key executives of the (now defunct) London bank Keyser Ullmann. They were working out their strategy for the next stage of the bid for Crown Zellerbach, which was probably the toughest battle of Goldsmith's takeover career. Goldsmith suddenly disclosed that a competing bid for Crown Zellerbach was going to be withdrawn – which would mean the shares would immediately fall. Franklin later recalled that Levine 'went grey... We speculated that he had a number of shares... We suspected that he was anxious to get to his broker as quickly as possible.' Franklin was right: Levine had 100,000 Crown Zellerbach shares which he sold later that day for a profit of over $80,000.*

Why had he done it? Levine seemed to have everything he could possibly need, so why did he need to trade illegally on top of it all? That too was a question which would echo from Wall Street to the rest of America and beyond. There had been others of course in similar positions: Ilan Reich, 31, a brilliant young takeover lawyer at Wachtell Lipton, who apparently never collected anything from an insider trading scheme which wrecked his career. Or Ira B. Sokolow, 32, one of Shearson Lehman's most promising young takeover specialists earning $400,000, who collected $120,000 in cash for information he learned at his own investment bank. Or Robert Wilkis, a first vice president at E. F. Hutton who confessed to the SEC he had made $3.3m from illegal stock trades. As the list of insider trading charges grew longer, and as bright young men from the offices of lawyers, banks and broking houses were asked to account for their dealings,

*Wall Street Journal 22 May, 1986.

Wall Street coined a new phrase for it: Yuppie Scam.

But none of the yuppies was anything like as senior as Levine. As more details of his dealings dribbled out, Wall Street became even more amazed. He seemed to be at the centre of a ring of arbs, lawyers, and investment bankers. Between them they had inside information on a grand scale. As the profits had become larger, so they had widened the ring to take in bigger and bigger fish with better and better information.

Levine himself had gone to elaborate lengths to conceal his dealings. He made calls from phone boxes during his lunch hour, always using the name, according to the SEC, of 'Diamond', a name he also used when he travelled to Nassau. When he flew down, he never went direct, but would change planes up to half a dozen times on the way, but invariably try to get there and back on the same day. And he did have an accomplice, according to the SEC indictment: a Bank Leu official turned over to the investigators 28 typewritten 'cover stories' which he said Levine had helped to produce to hide his trail once he discovered the SEC was after him. They had, according to the official, been prepared by Bernard Meier, who worked in the Bahamas branch. It was, according to the SEC, Meier who received Levine's calls, and who then channelled the stock orders through two Panamanian companies to New York brokers.

The SEC released previously undisclosed evidence to support the charges of perjury and tax evasion. Information in any business has always commanded a premium, but never more so than in the great takeover game of the mid-1980s. 18 months before he was charged, and before even the Caracas letter had arrived at Merrill Lynch's New York offices, Levine had been questioned by the SEC about trading in the shares of Textron.

According to the new information now produced by the SEC, what happened was this: in 1984 Levine learned that Textron, a large Providence, Rhode Island-based conglomerate, was about to get a takeover bid. He instantly recognised in it an opportunity even more valuable than making an insider dealing profit – it could be used for another purpose, too. First, on 1 October, he bought 51,500 Textron shares through his Bahamas account. Then he told his boss at Lehman Bros, Stephen Waters, about it. On 4 October, 1984, Waters rang the chairman of Textron, B.F. Dolan. The company, he told Dolan, could be about to get a takeover bid. How about Lehman handling the defence? Dolan politely thanked him, and declined the offer. Then a week later Levine rang Dolan. He told him that he had more information (in fact he was simply dribbling out bit by bit what he already knew, in order to pretend to Dolan he was working on the situation). A group was accumulating Textron shares; to add spice, Levine threw in the most feared names of the day: they included, he said, Carl Icahn, Saul Steinberg, Victor Posner and Ivan Boesky. Dolan still declined. But Levine had no intention of giving up. His own statement said that 'Our objective was to be retained by Textron, and we provided them with information over a period of time to keep a dialogue going and to maintain continuity.'

Within a month the bid arrived. Chicago Pacific Corporation launched a $43 a share bid and the price of Textron shares soared. Levine sold, allegedly making a profit of $200,000 on that one deal. When the SEC enquired into dealings in Textron shares, Levine, still riding high at the time, was called to give testimony. How had he known about the bid? He had, he said, heard a rumour. Where? Levine then gave the SEC an elaborate explanation of how he had pieced together bits of information, hunches and guesswork.

I was in the reception area of Drexel Burnham in New York and overheard a conversation between two gentlemen. One gentleman was talking to the other and discussed the following: Lester Crown has a group together with approximately $300m equity and they need an additional billion-plus dollars to accomplish their objective. That although the economics of the transaction are attractive, Bankers Trust could be a problem and we should consider these guys and Citibank as alternatives.

I then overheard what I would characterise as garbled where they said something about a 13-D filing, the words 'Skadden Arps' and 'First Boston' and also 'fireworks in Rhode Island'.

From that he had worked out what was happening, he explained. After his arrest, Levine admitted this was false. But the story illustrates the fine border line between what is insider information, and what is informed guesswork. Men like Levine and Boesky have extraordinarily finely tuned antennae, and can read a great deal into even the tiniest of hints.

Levine both made a handsome capital profit and gave himself a leg up the corporation ladder. 'At Shearson Lehman, a unit of American Express Co, no-one produced it [inside information] like Mr Levine,' said the *Wall Street Journal*. 'The firm, officials say, loved him for it. They paid him more than $400,000 a year.'

But where had he really got his information from, in the Textron case? Shearson Lehman's general counsel David Hirshberg believed he had the answer to that. Levine, he said, heard about it from 'stock-market takeover speculators, known on Wall Street as arbitrageurs'.

In all the speculation about who Levine would incriminate as he cooperated with the investigators, there was one central group, and within that group one central character, who now became the main focus of attention. The comment that echoed most was made by a senior Wall Street figure. 'The whole arb community is next. Dennis Levine worked off the arb community and with the arb community. The investigative trail will lead to the arbs.'

And the leader of the arbs community was of course Ivan Boesky, now seemingly at the very height of his powers, dealing in bigger and bigger numbers, appearing on TV and at conferences to preach the gospel of the arbitrage business, the messenger of the new wave of corporate takeovers which was going to restore dynamism to flagging industries.

In the weeks that followed Levine's arrest there was almost feverish anticipation of Boesky's fate. Boesky, however, appeared unperturbed. He was less obvious in the market than he had been, but then he had a good excuse: he had published his book, *Merger Mania*, and was busily promoting it, making a whirlwind tour of Britain as well as America. It was an almost unreadable technical exposition of the arbitrage business, but the promotion was so heavy, and Boesky's name so hot, that it shot up the bestseller list. Every yuppie on Wall Street had a copy. There was some cynicism at the sub-title: 'Arbitrage; Wall Street's best kept money-making secret.' There was even more wry amusement at the final sentence in Boesky's dedication: 'May those who read my book gain some understanding of the opportunity which exists uniquely in this great land.'

As the weeks passed and there as no mention of Boesky in the SEC investigations, the speculation gradually died down. Lynch followed up his Levine success with a series of smaller fry. Wealthy young merger experts at Lazard Freres, Goldman Sachs and Shearson found themselves facing criminal indictments as the Yuppie Scam deepened.

In fact, although it would not be revealed for another five months Lynch had already netted Boesky. Levine had indeed implicated him within days of his arrest, and Boesky, like Levine, was cooperating. If Levine had been a big fish, then Boesky was a whale, and Lynch played him all through the summer and autumn.

Levine provided the crucial evidence against him without which, SEC officials admitted later, it would have been difficult to find the evidence to prosecute him. And without that, there would have been no deal with Boesky. According to the papers filed in the case, it was Levine who had first approached Boesky in February of 1985. The first few tips he gave him were free. But later Boesky agreed to give him 5 per cent of the profits he made on any stock purchase he made on his tips.

It was this kickback arrangement which would later seal Boesky's fate. The SEC focused on seven stocks in which Boesky had dealt on information received from Levine. The biggest were Nabisco, Houston Natural Gas and FMC Corporation; but they also included others on which Levine had already admitted to insider trading. Details on the indictment against Boesky shed further light on the way the whole system worked. The SEC now disclosed the names of two more of Levine's sources: Robert Wilkis, at one stage a young banker at Lazard Freres and later at E.F. Hutton, and Ira Sokolow, of Lehman Brothers. They passed information on activities in which their own houses were involved to Levine, who in turn passed it on to Boesky, while at the same time dealing in his own Bahamas account.

Day by day now there seemed to be fresh revelations, each one showing the network of insider dealings to have been even wider than suspected. As each new charge was brought, so the person plea-bargained, as Levine had done, and added the names of new people, who in turn did a deal with the SEC and implicated still others. Levine was the key which opened up the Pandora's box, but after Boesky the figures emerging from it were at the very heart of the Wall Street dealing system. Officials at the SEC baldly announced they were poised to penetrate for the first time the 'golden triangle', Wall Street parlance for the relationship between corporate raiders, arbitrageurs and investment banking houses. In the days that followed the whole investment community watched with almost dumb fascination as the list of big names subpoenaed increased by the hour. Carl Icahn, hero of so many raids, got his subpoena. Victor Posner, another of the legendary names in the takeover world, also received his subpoena from the SEC. So did the man who was arguably the most important influence in the whole of the 1980s takeover boom in the US: Mike Milken, the person who developed the junk bond market and propelled Drexel Burnham to the heights of the financial community. Milken had recently been the subject of a profile in *Forbes* Magazine which put his personal worth at $500m. Boyd Jeffries, chairman of Jeffries & Co., a major Los Angeles brokerage house, also received a summons from the SEC. Simply getting a subpoena did not, of course, automatically imply that the person was suspected of insider trading. But in the hothouse atmosphere that pervaded the investment community in the days that immediately followed the demise of Ivan Boesky, speculation and rumour abounded. How far would the insider trading scandal reach? Boesky after all had been involved at the centre of so many of the major bids. For at least six weeks he had been walking around wired for sound, recording all his telephone calls and his meetings. Those tapes were now with the investigators. And Boesky was under intense pressure to deliver names and evidence which would lead to successful prosecutions of others. Preferably names even bigger than his own. Would he involve some of the major raiders themselves? Boone Pickens? Perelman? Hanson? The rumours became so absurdly widespread that, at one stage in the week that followed, Sir Gordon White of Hanson issued a statement denying the rumours that were beginning to engulf him – Boesky had after all played a role in the battle for SCM. Innocent or not, everyone ran for cover.

For the previous five years, the ambience of the American and British financial markets had never been more favourable to the raiders. In the early 1970s, they had been social villains. Now – with some reservations of course – they were folk heroes, the Davids tackling the struggling old Goliaths, and with enormous nerve and verve, injecting new life into corporate America. With the arrest of Levine the warning signs had gone out, but after a pause the merger spree revived again. Boesky's arrest, however, altered the atmosphere dramatically. Now the raiders were fighting the social climate as well as the boards of their target companies. The odds turned against them. The pressure for new anti-takeover legislation became intense. 'I think that takeovers can perform a useful function,' said Senator William Proxmire a few days after the Boesky demise.* '... Icahn taking over TWA, many people feel, was a good change. He took some very painful actions, he discharged a lot of people but he saved a company. I think that corporate managements are too smug but the best cure for corporate management is to enforce our anti-trust laws and have some real competition.'

Proxmire also said: 'This insider/merger mania had plunged our corporations deeply into debt,' adding that since 1950 the average US corporation's debt servicing ratio had risen from 20 per cent to 509 per cent of pre-tax income. 'In some cases it just kills companies,' he added, singling out Unocal which had borrowed $4bn to fight off its unwelcome bidders. 'They have to pay $3m a day more just to service the debt.'

Now Proxmire had much more ammunition for his cause.

It [insider trading] is a real cancer in our market. It is very unfair because it means that people who have access to inside information have an enormous advantage over the others. We also want to follow up takeovers financed by junk bonds, because those are closely related.

Mr Boesky took advantage of the takeover situation to get in as an

*Interview with the *New York Times*, 2 December, 1986.

arbitrageur in the investment pool, if you will, and bid up the price of the stock. He would know, as an insider, when the pools were going to move so he could buy in advance. He would know when the pools were going to get out, so he could sell at the right time. He made an enormous amount on inside information – not on a matter of prudence or research or study but on the basis of having information he had stolen, in effect. We have to find out what we can do to stop that.

The SEC indictment against Boesky supported the senator's claim that the arbitrageur had made an 'enormous amount'. In seven stocks Boesky's profits amounted to $50m, all of them connected with Dennis Levine's information. There had been many more profitable deals, too, which the SEC set out to investigate. Boesky would fight a long rearguard action, trying to hang on to some of his once considerable fortune. But from now on his battle would be to stay out of jail.

The bid market took on a much more subdued and low-key atmosphere. Ron Perelman followed Goldsmith and pulled out of his bid for Gillette, taking with him a handsome greenmail profit. Icahn did the same with his huge bid for USX, the great American steel company. The market dried up almost overnight. The arbs were now almost out of it, nursing still greater wounds from Ivan Boesky's final act in the market: in the days before the SEC made its announcement about him, Boesky had used the one bit of insider information which he was entitled to hold and sold out of all the bid stocks he held in his portfolio. When the news of his SEC indictment finally came, the stocks crashed, creating even greater dismay in a community which was feeling battered and bruised.

By the end of 1986, the busiest and most traumatic year on record in the corporate takeover world, there were more sober voices asking whether the reaction had not gone too far, and whether in the new climate there would be no takeovers at all – even those which were clearly in the interests of the community. There were even those posing the theory that the SEC might have gone too far, and in hitting the complete arb community, almost closing down the junk bond market, and pursuing the yuppies into the lawyers and brokerage offices, it was in serious danger of damaging the entire market system, and ushering in another post-1929 style situation. The SEC however was unmoved: Gary Lynch had, against the odds and expectations, taken the fight against insider dealing right into the heart of the system and was winning. The general judgement was that, unless the investigation took on a McCarthyite element, it could do nothing but good.

By the time of Boesky's demise, Britain had its own insider scandal: a young Dennis Levine lookalike, Geoffrey Collier, the star of Morgan Grenfell's new securities business, had been accused of dealing on inside information and asked to resign. But that was soon overshadowed by a much more dramatic event. Boesky had not just talked about the Wall Street players. He also gave the investigators details about his dealings with Guinness, and his role in the bid for Distillers. That little bit of information was soon winging its way to the Department of Trade and Industry in London. And on 1 December, inspectors appointed by the DTI turned up at Guinness's headquarters at Portman Square, showed their credentials, and began taking away boxfulls of papers. The biggest takeover bid in City history was about to turn into the biggest City scandal anyone could ever remember.

CHAPTER ELEVEN

The Aftermath

The Boesky/Levine insider trading episode on Wall Street and the Guinness affair in London confirmed what was already happening in both markets: the takeover wave was subsiding.

Even before the scandals, the level of activity, particularly the number of hostile bids for major companies, was in decline. The takeover boom did not die away overnight, but well before the autumn it had become clear, in London particularly, that the astonishing spate of bids seen in the spring was not sustainable.

For one thing, if the Distillers/Imps scale of bid were to be the norm, there would soon be no companies left to bid for, and the bidders would be bidding for each other. Secondly, fund managers and private investors had made so much money out of investing in target companies before a bid that any potential target company was now becoming expensive. The stock markets around the world continued their longest-ever bull markets, and to bid for anything significant now required mega-bucks. The choicer targets had long gone, with Hanson and Owen Green moving well ahead of the pack in London, while Pickens, Goldsmith, Icahn, Jacobs and the others were either digesting what they already owned, or preparing to go up a notch for even bigger fish. What was left was very fully priced, not worth having, or could muster formidable defences. Target companies were now taking defensive action, livening themselves up, launching media campaigns, and paying large fees to merchant bankers to put in place defensive walls.

In Britain, public opinion did not turn hard against takeovers in the 1980s as it had done in the 1970s – at least not until BTR bid for Pilkington in November 1986. This was partly because the bidders were experienced enough to avoid the crude 'asset stripping' activities which had come to characterise the Slater era of a decade before; it was partly because the trade unions in the mid-1980s were a diminished force; but it was also because there was an ambivalence towards takeovers, with a widespread view, by no means shared by all, that maybe inefficient companies deserved to be taken over. There was, however, a discernible feeling that the takeover boom was running too fast, and that perhaps the *threat* of a bid, rather than the event itself, was enough to produce the desired improvements. This view was increasingly pervasive inside the City pension funds and insurance companies which made up the major holders of all stocks. They had been perfectly prepared to sell out Distillers to the highest bidder; there was never any serious City move to keep either Distillers or the Imperial Group independent. Later, however, attitudes began to change.

The first bid to encounter the new climate was Dixons for Woolworth. Dixons was a favourite City company, which had done wonderfully well from taking over Currys. Woolworth, by contrast, was still unproven under a new management, and the City institutions which had helped buy it out from the American parent five years earlier were sitting on handsome profits. When Dixons made its bid in the spring of 1986, there was little doubt in most observers' minds who was going to win. Yet somewhere in the middle of that campaign the mood shifted, not just over Woolworth, but probably over the whole of the bid scene. This is to take nothing away from the Woolworth management for a well-fought defensive campaign. But it may be that, if Dixons had made its move several months earlier, the Woolworth institutional shareholders would not have given their management the benefit of the doubt. Now they were more inclined to stick with existing management than they were to surrender control to a raider.

From that moment on, the odds moved against hostile bids. Yet in the corporate finance divisions of the City banks, focused as they were on the next bid targets, there was little recognition of this. In September and October of 1986, Morgan Grenfell was humming as loudly as ever and was by no means alone in working on bids. Other banks were at it, too; and indeed there would still be plenty of activity that autumn and winter.

But the first major casualty of the changed atmosphere was BTR's £1.2bn bid for Pilkington: it hit a wall of antipathy. Once again it was a Morgan Grenfell bid, but Morgan by now had a few problems. The aggressive tactics used to win Guinness, although not yet a major talking point, had left their mark. More noticeably, the insider trading scandal surrounding Geoffrey Collier, the man designed to play a senior role in taking the bank into Big Bang, had damaged its reputation. In the intangible way these things work in the City, Morgan was already identified as waning, no longer a 'comer' but a 'goer'. It had also recently become a fully quoted public company, and its shares, far from being the high fliers which would have raised its reputation, had gone into decline. Since a considerable number were held by the bank's own employees, this had done nothing for morale.

Sir Owen Green of BTR, as he opened hostilities for Pilkington, got the backwash of this. Green had decided, as he approached retiring age, to phase himself out, and this was to be his last major battle. After acquiring Thomas Tilling, he had not been a major player, and had contented himself with the purchase of Dunlop for just over £100m. He had not needed to do more. His company had thrived and his reputation stood high, on a par with Weinstock or Hanson. For a brief few months, before everything turned disastrously sour for him, Ernest Saunders, the victor of Distillers, was moving into that league too.

Luck is as important to the successful businessman as it ever was to a Napoleonic general. And Green's luck was out. Within days of launching his bid, the news about Ivan Boesky broke. Events which had nothing whatsoever to do with him or his bid were now racing to thwart him. In a straight fight under the conditions of a year earlier, he might have won Pilkington, although the glass company, its profits recovering rapidly and its years of research and investment paying off, would not have been an easy target. Within a matter of weeks he found that his bid had become a major political issue, a matter of minor embarrassment to the government but of serious embarrassment to the Secretary of State for Trade and Industry, Paul Channon. BTR suddenly found itself the subject of attacks from the Labour party, trade unions, the press, the City and even Conservative MPs.

The Guinness scandal had broken. Takeover bids were abruptly completely out of fashion.

In the first few days after the inspectors of the Department of Trade had arrived at Guinness on 1 December, the City was bewildered. What was going on? Insider trading was rife in Wall Street and in the City; so was it to do with that? There were charges that a senior man had been inside trading at Morgan Grenfell, Guinness's bank; was there a connection? There were rumours that the inspectors had been appointed on the strength of information passed on by the SEC in Washington; so was there a Boesky link?

The following day, Tuesday 2 December, Guinness held a board meeting, the first attended by the four new non-executive directors (a fifth, Ian Chapman, chairman of the publishing company William Collins, would join a few weeks later). Saunders was in the chair, and there was an expectant hush as they began. When business proceeded as normal, there was a stir of impatience and unease. Finally Sir David Plastow, the chairman of Vickers and one of the new directors, spoke up. Could Saunders enlighten the board as to why the inspectors were there? No, he had no idea. The others joined in, to press for some explanation. Saunders remained adamant. No, he couldn't even speculate; he could think of no reason why they should want to investigate Guinness. 'Chairman, can you think back and try to think of anything they might be interested in?' asked Plastow. Again a very definite, 'No'. One director suggested that it might be advisable to try to anticipate the areas in which the inspectors would be interested, and to begin preparing information and answers. Saunders firmly ruled that out, too.

There was even greater unease when Saunders went on to tell the new directors about Guinness's $100m investment in a Boesky fund. The others had been told about it back in July, but at that stage it had not assumed the relevance it had now, and they felt they had been given at best a partial explanation. Saunders elaborated on the reasons for the investment: Guinness's next bid would be in the United States, and Boesky was a big player there. Guinness wanted some influence with him, and wanted to position itself for a major leap. Again it was Plastow who asked the question on everyone's mind. 'Chairman, is there any link between this investment and Boesky's role in the bid?' It got what one director later described as 'an absolutely implacable denial'.

The meeting broke up, leaving both directors and the outside world still puzzled. By the weekend £360m had been wiped off the value of Guinness's market capitalisation. But by then there were a few straws in the wind. It did not seem to be about insider trading at all, at least in the conventional sense. The two inspectors, David Donaldson QC and Ian Watt, a chartered accountant, seemed to be primarily interested in the performance of Guinness shares in those last weeks of the Distillers bid.

In the weeks that followed, both Saunders and Olivier Roux retained, outwardly at least, their balance. 'The sang-froid of the leading players didn't show any distress until just before Christmas,' said a director afterwards, with just a trace of awe in his voice. Behind the scenes, however, both were feeling the strain.

To outsiders the relationship between Saunders and Roux had always seemed close; before Christmas it broke down. Roux consulted his own solicitors who advised him to tell the Guinness board and the inspectors all he knew.

By now the revelations were coming thick and fast. In the week before Christmas, the Boesky deal was announced by Guinness. Then a few days after the festivities came details of the arrangements made with Ansbacher. There was almost an element of farce as it became known that a cheque for £48,000, the dividend on the 2.15m Guinness shares bought for Ansbacher clients, went from bank to bank around the City, with no-one willing to claim it. Whoever admitted to owning those shares would be sucked into the worsening scandal and might even face charges under the Companies Act.

But it was no farce for Roger Seelig who had suggested that Ansbacher buy the shares at a key time in the bid – and had later suggested that Guinness deposit, interest free, a matching sum with Ansbacher when the bank considered selling them. For a few days the pressure shifted from Guinness to Morgan Grenfell. Just two days before the turn of the most momentous year in British takeover history, Morgan Grenfell announced that Roger Seelig had been asked to resign. He had, as the *Sunday Times* wrote that weekend, been 'pitched unceremoniously into the seething waters of the City's piranha pool'. Morgan's clear hope was that his departure would take the heat out of the Guinness affair. In fact it did the opposite. 'The betting in banking parlours is that the parade of victims has only just begun,' wrote Peter Wilsher in the *Sunday Times*.

On 4 January, which was a Sunday, the fate of Saunders as head of Guinness was finally sealed. Olivier Roux made a long statement to Guinness's solicitors. He told of the £25m of fees which Guinness had paid out to support its share price; he put down what he knew of the arrangements made by Ward, by Seelig, by himself – and by Saunders. Again and again he insisted that Saunders had full or partial knowledge of most of the arrangements (Saunders later strongly denied this). It was one of the most devastating indictments ever made of a company chairman by his own finance director.

A weaker man might have accepted the inevitable at that point. Saunders, however, still tried to brave it through. As the Roux document was circulated among directors even the Guinness family stepped back from Saunders. He was increasingly isolated on the board, with the (now) five executive directors appalled by what was being uncovered, and only Ward, Fuehrer and several of the executive directors ostensibly standing by him.

On Friday, 9 January, the directors were summoned for a late evening board meeting. Each was given a copy of the Roux letter. Saunders at the last moment tried to bar Roux himself from the meeting, but the non-executive directors over-rode him. The meeting that followed was extraordinary by any standards. One director described how Saunders sat at one end of the table and Roux at the other. The young Frenchman, visibly upset but fully in control, went through the items, each one seemingly more damaging that the previous one. At the other end Saunders solemnly denied knowing about each one in turn. Finally Saunders was asked to leave while the others considered his fate. When he was called back he was given the verdict: he would be asked to stand aside until the DTI investigation was completed. After what they had just heard, everyone in that room that evening must have known that he would never come back – except for Saunders himself. Later that evening he confided his intention to clear his name – and make a triumphant return. He still sounded cheerful and confident.

Events, already moving at breakneck speed, now speeded up. In the weeks that followed Guinness released a full list of those who had received the £25m in fees. Roux circulated a note indicating that the cost of the bid had not just been £100m, as he had told the shareholders' meeting back in September, but £180m. It became known that the auditors Price Waterhouse were already questioning those fees in November. Gerald Ronson released a statement detailing his role, and repaid £5.8m. Ephraim Margulies similarly explained his involvement, insisting it was perfectly innocent. Sir Jack Lyons now agreed to co-operate with the inspectors in explaining why he had received fees of nearly £1m. Guinness asked Ward and Fuehrer to resign, and formally sacked Saunders, electing Sir Norman Macfarlane to the position of chairman.

Saunders later denied any knowledge of wrong-doing. 'I have spent a number of years at considerable personal and family cost building Guinness into one of the leading British companies and I am determined to see all the true facts emerge, and those responsible for any wrong-doing brought to account, whatever steps are necessary to achieve this.' In a letter to Guinness shareholders in May 1987 he added that he had no knowledge of or part in 'any *unlawful* share support operations or any other unlawful transactions.'

All this time speculation had grown that more heads had to roll at Morgan Grenfell. Seelig was openly insisting that, although he might have been the person heading the team, he did not act without support from his own bank. There were various times when he had been away during the bid battle, and his head of corporate finance, Graham

Walsh, had then taken over. He had kept Christopher Reeves himself informed of the major developments. He had to seek authority to commit Morgan's funds to the support operation – and he got it. 'You can't take a taxi without getting authority for it in this bank,' he said. 'Anyone who thinks I acted on my own must think I'm six feet taller than I am.'

Morgan set up a top-level internal enquiry into its own management structure in the hope of dampening down the speculation. But over the weekend of 11 January, speculation reached a peak. On that day the *Sunday Times* Business News forecast that both Reeves and Walsh would be forced to resign from Morgan. Morgan's chairman Lord Catto sent out a letter which, although careful not to dismiss the possibility of further resignations, tried to convey the impression that all was now well, although the shares, issued at 500p, had sunk as low as 360p and there was speculation that Morgan, the master of the takeover bid, was now a target itself. Catto, however, said he was confident that the bank would 'continue to prosper as one of London's leading merchant banks'.

It was not seen like that in Downing Street. The government was becoming seriously concerned by the tide of opinion running against it over the BTR bid for Pilkington. The Guinness scandal had spread into disturbing areas, including those identified as major Tory supporters. There seemed to be a pervasiveness about insider trading, support operations, and other City practices which many in the Thatcher government found both disturbing and politically threatening. The atmosphere was now influencing competition policy once again, and Channon was perceived as surrendering to it by referring a £700m bid for IC Gas by the Barclay brothers to the Monoplies Commission although the competition element was negligible. But, correctly in terms of competition policy, and against an enormous lobby which included Labour and Conservative MPs alike, Paul Channon now took the decision not to refer BTR's Pilkington bid. It brought a furore every bit as big, although short-lived, as the Westland affair a year earlier. The noise over Guinness and now Pilkington had reached the proportions which a government, running towards an election, could not ignore.

Exactly who took the decision that Morgan Grenfell should lose its chief executive is not known precisely. But there is a view, shared by senior Morgan executives and by some ministers, that it came directly from Mrs Thatcher herself. The initiative certainly did not come from inside Morgans. 'We would never have sent out a letter like that if we had the slightest inkling this was going to happen,' said a senior director afterwards. The Chancellor of the Exchequer, Nigel Lawson, later made no secret of his involvement, clearly outlining to the House of Commons the fact that he and the Governor of the Bank of England, Robin Leigh-Pemberton, took direct responsibility for changes at Morgan. But the insistence on instant action and change may have come from even higher than that. It had an immediate effect.

Through most of Monday and Tuesday morning Lord Catto, Morgan's chairman, was locked in talks in the Bank of England. His letter of reassurance was only just arriving at the homes of Morgan's shareholders, but now he was being told that unless major changes at the top were made, the Bank would take tough action of its own against Morgan. It had powers to suspend its banking licence and could, if it chose, effectively put Morgan out of business. That week it indicated it was prepared to do so – under orders from Downing Street. The Governor was not impressed with Morgan's own internal enquiry; nor was he placated by the resignation of Seelig for what Morgan described as 'breaches of established procedures and policies'. He and his deputy George Blunden pointed out that even if Morgan's senior executives had not approved or known of any illicit actions, they bore managerial responsibility for them.

By Tuesday lunchtime, the City was faced with its latest bombshell: Christopher Reeves, Morgan's chief executive and until a few weeks before probably the City's top merchant banker, resigned. So did Graham Walsh, a former director-general of the City's own watchdog committee, the Takeover Panel. Neither, as Morgan pointed out, was in any way involved in 'personal misconduct' over Guinness. But the two men, a Morgan statement went on, did accept that their management responsibility for Morgan's actions during the bid for Distillers left them no choice but to resign.

Within hours of that came another significant announcement: BTR abandoned its bid for Pilkington. Sir Owen Green denied his move had in any way been influenced by the political storm surrounding it, and pointed instead to the way Pilkington shares had climbed on the back of major new profit figures and forecasts. 'BTR's decision is a manifestation of the workings of the free market, whose judgment they may not always respect but whose verdict they will always accept,' said the company in an official statement. Sir Owen, 61, was not to have the crowning glory to his career after all. There was jubilation in St Helens, the Merseyside town where many of the Pilkington factories are based. 'It's the town that's won,' said the chairman of the town council. Perhaps it was. But there were those close to Green who blamed others. The Guinness scandal, Morgan's troubles, and the stage of the cycle of the takeover boom, had undone BTR. Pilkington's chairman, Anthony Pilkington, was nearer the mark when he said:

'This has pointed up a lot of problems with the present way of managing industry from the takeover point of view. It will change quite a number of people's views.' In reality those views had already changed. The boom was over.

There would soon be more casualties from the Guinness affair; Lord Spens resigned from Ansbacher, and the new management of Guinness was busy severing the connections Saunders had brought to it. Cazenove, brokers to Guinness during the bid, carried out its own internal enquiry, and concluded that it had behaved properly. Freshfields, the leading City lawyers who had advised Guinness during the bid, and are solicitors to the Bank of England, remained tight-lipped and removed from the scandals engulfing Guinness and its banking advisors.

The damage had at last been contained. But it had been severe. From now on the Guinness affair would move into the courts, as Guinness tried to recover some of its money. At the time of writing the inspectors are still uncovering new information and, from what we have seen so far, there is much more to come when their report finally appears. Criminal charges have already been brought before Saunders over the issue of destroying documents – which he strongly denies and intends vigorously to defend. There are many unanswered questions which must await the inspectors who have access to documents, papers and evidence not available to the rest of us.

But the Guinness takeover of Distillers stands as the bid that finally took all the City practices of aggressive banking, advertising and support operations to their logical extreme – and burst the bubble.

CHAPTER TWELVE

But Do They Work?

In the first week in April 1987 two events occurred which caused us to feel that we had come full circle in the writing of this book.

Until that point, our chapter on the battle of Harrods, although it raised so many of the issues we have discussed, stood aside from the central stream of takeover activity. There were many allegations connected with it, but they did not include insider trading and support operations, which with the Boesky and Guinness affairs had become the flavour of the day. For the two years that the Fayeds had owned House of Fraser, Tiny Rowland had kept up a continual stream of complaint to successive secretaries of state. Norman Tebbit, who was running the Department of Trade and Industry when the Fayeds' bid went through, replied tartly in June 1985 that

> The Al Fayeds gained control of House of Fraser by acquiring a majority of its shares. The shareholders who sold their shares (including Lonrho), not the Government, were responsible for the Al Fayeds' successful acquisition.

Leon Brittan, who succeeded Tebbit, had similarly fended off Rowland. Channon, for more than a year, did the same. But in April 1987, as the legal battles between the Fayeds and Lonrho escalated, Channon decided to call a halt; he appointed two inspectors to look in particular at the 'circumstances surrounding the acquisition of shares in House of Fraser plc in 1984 and 1985'. As the *Financial Times* commented the next day: 'At five o'clock on Thursday evening the longest running and most convoluted takeover battle in recent corporate history – a saga that has dominated the headlines for a decade – suddenly gained a whole new lease of life.' As with the investigation into Guinness, it will be some time before the inspectors report, so this book is written without the benefit of that report. But the takeover with which we started has reassumed centre stage.

The second event, which pulled the strands of our takeover story together even more unexpectedly, was that Tiny Rowland and Ernest Saunders became friends.

Even as Saunders was battling in court, Rowland himself was telling the world about his new found friendship. He released a copy of his latest letter to Paul Channon, written just two days before the decision to appoint the inspectors, which began: 'Yesterday I saw Ernest Saunders. What he says confirms that the manner in which senior officials of the Department of Trade have massaged the decisions of the Department is disgraceful.'

Rowland laid out his own version of events at Guinness, gleaned from his meeting with Saunders. 'Let me tell you what happened – just as if you didn't know!' he wrote to Channon.

When Guinness' bid for Distillers was referred, he said,

'Guinness's principal adviser, Thomas Ward, telephoned the head of the Monopolies Commission, Sir Godfray Le Quesne. Was there, he enquired, any way in which the refusal could be cancelled?'

They were astonished to hear Sir Godfray invite them to a private meeting to talk it over. Accompanied by John Swift, QC, who was most helpfully known to Sir Godfray, Ernest Saunders and Thomas Ward set off.

Sir Godfray told them he would assist them. It had never been done before, but the Guinness bid could be withdrawn, reframed, and presented again for approval, and he would help them to put a new collar on the same dog.

Sir Godfray, as dignified and unflustered as ever, ignored this slight on his unquestioned integrity.

That weekend Rowland said he might even offer Saunders a job in Europe where Lonrho was considering making an acquisition. 'I imagine there would be a lot of companies happy to have Mr Saunders working for them,' he said. 'As a marketing man he would be an excellent man to have. If he were cleared, then obviously I would be very happy to consider him.'

*

Saunders must have read this with considerable interest. At the time he was in Switzerland, his health only gradually improving from a sharp decline following his departure from Guinness. His wife Carole, who had initially borne the disastrous turn of fortunes remarkably well, was still in hospital after a severe breakdown. One of their sons had been involved in an accident and had nearly had his hand severed. April 1986 had found the Saunders family celebrating victory at Distillers; April 1987 found them practically friendless, and hospitalised, Saunders fighting on several legal fronts, his assets in Britain frozen. Seldom had there been a more dramatic change of fortunes.

Other events, too, have crowded in around the final writing of this book. There was no way to know until much later just how much of the merger frenzy of the past decade, particularly in the US, had been shot through with insider trading schemes. There were signs, yes; we had noted, along with others, the pattern of rising share prices in almost all bid stocks before the events. In March 1986 a London Stock Exchange official shook the City and the Conservative government when he claimed he had evidence of organised rings of professionals who were dealing on inside information through offshore accounts. 'Time and again our investigations have run up against a brick wall of an offshore company whose true ownership we cannot discover,' Michael Feltham of the Stock Exchange's surveillance department told the *Financial Times*. 'We can track down the insider deals which are done in this country, but the big fish go offshore.'

This was in the days just before Levine was uncloaked. Feltham painted a picture of organised groups of City professionals pooling their inside knowledge of takeover deals. Around 80 per cent of the suspected insider deals were purchases of shares in companies which received bids shortly afterwards at much higher prices. After the initial shock of Feltham's outburts, there was a strange silence. The Stock Exchange was reluctant to allow the *Sunday Times* to follow it through. But we turned up patterns of share price movements which supported his contention.

In 1985 there were 139 bids, almost all of them signalled by a sharp rise in the share price of the target company. The magazine *Acquisitions Monthly* revealed in March 1986 that the average rise in 100 mergers studied was 54 per cent during the six months before a bid, 39 per cent during the month before, and 25 per cent on the day before. In one case, a bid for the engineering group J.& H.B. Jackson, the price rose 89 per cent in the month before the bid. Arthur Bell, taken over by Guinness, featured: up 60 per cent in a month, and up from 160p to 192p in the four days before the bid (Saunders formally complained about it at the time, and brought forward the announcement of his bid).

The *Acquisitions Monthly* survey revealed even more startling statistics: of 35 bids which were contested, share price movements were particularly marked. They averaged 40 per cent the day before the bid, 55 per cent the month before, and 71 per cent during the six months before. Yet, until the Levine and Boesky affairs hit the headlines, there was no sign of the investigations being pursued with any vigour or determination. The Stock Exchange, which has its own investigative unit but no ability to prosecute, referred 93 cases of alleged insider trading to the Department of Trade and Industry in six years. Only five resulted in prosecutions, and three in convictions. There were of course substantial problems: insider trading is notoriously difficult to prove, and offshore accounts made it almost impossible to get the necessary evidence.

After Levine was arrested, insider trading, instead of being a minor if unpleasant side-effect of the merger boom, assumed great importance. Indeed, as events unfolded, it was sometimes tempting to make it the focus of this book. There are those who now argue that cheating was the catalyst that turned a cyclical and probably economically sound episode of corporate combinations into a wasteful flare-off of capital piracy. That is truer of the United States than it is of Britain, where it is still possible to perceive insider trading as a parasite on the otherwise healthy body of the takeover business, rather than a disease attacking the bone structure. Unfortunately, there are other parasites too – as we have seen over the Guinness affair. But, parallel with Guinness, ran the battle for Imperial Group, and we could argue that here is a contrasting example which is on the whole positive. Hanson fought and won against a hostile board, and proved that bids, however large and whatever the proposition, don't require Guinness-style tactics. There have been no nasty side-effects from the Imperial affair.

There are plenty of voices now bemoaning the sharp decline in business morality, as represented by the insider trading and Guinness scandals. That is an argument we will leave for others to resolve. But it is true that in the 1970s, at the height of the condemnation of Jim Slater and his acolytes, there were those who argued that the City was simply applying a 1970s morality to an activity which had been widespread until then. Insider trading has been part of the City since the South Sea Bubble. That does not make it any more acceptable – far from it. But there are great dangers in assuming that somehow, with

Big Bang and the appearance of so many new faces with different backgrounds on the financial stage, human nature has altered. It is safer to assume that the biggest takeover boom of all time brought with it the biggest temptations of all time. The point is to stop it happening again.

There have been thieves before. Wall Street has had its share of them, certainly. In the 1920s there was Samuel Insull and his utility trust, Charles Mitchel of National City Bank and even Richard Whitney, the president of the New York Stock Exchange in 1929. What marks out the current phase is another factor: never in Wall Street's history, perhaps never in America's history, have the supposed 'best and brightest' betrayed their trust with such monumental impact. And probably never before has there been such a public exposure of City and financial scandal in Britain.

'The worst part of all this is that these are the most tightly controlled markets in the world,' says Jules Kroll, the financial private investigator who has watched the phenomenon from both roles, the corporate insider and the investigator working without. In his listing of causes for the insider trading scandal, he notes the youth of many of the participants; the tremendous sums of money being dangled in front of recruits; and the changed nature of the financial services industry on Wall Street, especially the risk arbitrage business. 'Although the problems seem pervasive at the moment, the number of people involved in wrongdoing is a very small percentage of the number of people in the industry. Look at markets elsewhere and you find this kind of manipulation to be ingrained and institutionalised,' Kroll says.

These people were greedy. Ilan Reich, the Wachtell, Lipton mole for Dennis Levine, recalled how impressed he had been the first time he saw his seducer. The tailoring of his clothes and his self-assured manners attracted Reich. Later, Levine would peel back another side of the attitudes they had in common – the belief that the rest of the world were suckers. Others would stand in line and wait for their rewards; not Levine. It was what an unhappy man like Ilan Reich yearned to hear. There were other similarities in the personalities of most of the insider ring leaders.

Boesky was 49 at the time of his confessions. He was a lone ranger who had transformed the stuffy, mechanical world of arbitrage into a glamourous game. Dennis Levine was 33, but already the premier designer of company takeover schemes that were financed by high-risk junk bonds. After his arrest, Drexel Burnham hastily cut Levine's photograph out of its annual report and pasted in that of Martin Siegel who had been hired away from Kidder Peabody for $4m a year to clean up the firm's troubled mergers department. Then Siegel also fell.

Siegel's arrest jolted Wall Street the hardest. It was very public. There was no polite appointment to pick a subpoena and arrest warrant. The scenes of one of the ring members being led away, handcuffed and weeping, traumatised a community where integrity had once more been taken for granted.

What was striking to the observer was how different these men – Boesky, Levine, Siegel – now appeared from their former public images. Now they were shown to be false. What else had they been hiding?

Going over three years of notes of interviews for this book, we summoned back the images. Siegel was still at Kidder Peabody, where he had taken over the corporate finance division in his early 30s with orders to make it a major player. He was a handsome young man who was under a lot of pressure but who thrived on it. There were few clues to his personality in the largely functional, interchangeable offices that Wall Streeters keep. There were the little lucite squares which frame the various bond underwritings he had led. There was a tiny scorpion on another square, a gift from a grateful client for a successful defence.

Marty Siegel had it all. Good looks that had caused a *Business Week* profile to say that he could 'play the heartthrob in an old Greta Garbo movie', and a Harvard MBA (class of 1971) that was the intellectual talisman of corporate fortune. He had been a star on Wall Street since Gulf Western's failed 1972 bid to take over Great Atlantic and Pacific Tea. He had greatly impressed the likes of Lord King, chairman of British Airways and Babcock International, when he handled a Babcock bid in the US for him. But there was an adversarial streak to his conversations. It helped explain why he and his Kidder Peabody, mergers department had tried to stake out a reputation as the pre-eminent defence strategists while other houses were building their offence capabilities.

It's more exciting. We are not against takeovers as such, you have to understand that. What we say to a client faced with a bid it does not like, we say you don't have to take that offer. We can produce a better bid for your firm, or another bidder, or we can arrange it where you do not have to take bids at all. So the other side says, here we come. And we say, oh, no you don't. And we see who wins.

A game, nothing more?

Only in the sense that the best man wins. You have to remember what an impact you have on people's lives, the workers as well as the management.

There was more to it, Siegel argued. He hastened to add that he was opposed to greenmail and he wasn't sure just how solid the new kind of junk bonds were. There was something not right about it, not classy enough. The message came through that this was a man to whom class and honour and prestige counted as one.

But of course, all this time Marty Siegel was cheating. Later it would emerge that he had an arrangement with Boesky whereby he got a percentage of all the profits Boesky made on insider information he supplied to him. And, as the man centrally involved in many of the biggest bids raging, he had a great deal. At the end of the year they would meet on a park bench and Siegel would give Boesky a list of leaks. Siegel's reward, over $700,000 of it, was paid in used notes in suitcases which he kept under his bed and used to pay his day-to-day bills.

Ivan Boesky also talked one life and lived another with apparent ease. He used his humble beginnings as a counterpoint to convince others, if not himself, of how far he had come. He had a homily he would deliver to journalists about America and what it meant to be the son of a Russian immigrant, a son who had been poor and not at all well educated. There was a night law school degree and not much else propping up young Ivan Boesky when he took off to Wall Street to seek his fortune. The fortune was at first elusive. Boesky's early years as an arbitrage broker were marked by mistakes and failure. Ultimately he had to borrow money, $700,000 from his father-in-law, and go into business for himself. But, he would say, look at me now, look at what America will do for you if you play the game.

Yet he was cheating, too. Even as he was pushing away the dish of salted peanuts at the Harvard Club, he was cheating. Even as he was boasting of his skills as an odds-maker and risk-taker, he was deep into his scheme to buy information from Dennis Levine to give him confidential access to the top merger contests of our decade. And even as he was talking to us in the Savoy Hotel in London, he was completing some dubious deals with Guinness.

And Levine? Consider this version of himself furnished by his lawyers to the judge who sentenced him to two years in prison after noting publicly that Levine deserved at least ten years.

In the pre-sentencing memorandum filed on Levine's behalf, much was made of his low middle-class background in Queens, New York, his night school degrees and his general handicap and lack of the 'academic credentials and social advantages customarily required to enter – let alone succeed in – investment banking'.

In the memo one reads how young Dennis refused to join his father's construction business and how he slogged through an MBA degree at a second-rate local college. Some of the more maudlin exhibits were the rejection letters from the more than 60 Wall Street investment houses which had passed over Levine for recruits from more acceptable backgrounds. He had kept the letters for more than a decade.

'Dennis Levine had played by the rules of the game and he had lost,' the memo intones with just the slightest hint of menace yet to come.

In the end, one wearies of these men using their wounded psyches as a grievance. Who did they think they were fooling other than themselves? Are their pretensions to class and to excellence as poisonous to them as they are to us? Any first-year student of psychology knows that some emotional deprivations are so severe that some individuals never can be reassured of their own worth. Some of these use money as a way to count love, others use public success to bolster the darkened corners of their private hells. But these men and others who have followed them also have shown a disdain for the rest of us who live our ordinary lives having to trust one another because civilised life is otherwise impossible.

As Jules Kroll notes:

> There are so many major houses with a problem that it is hard to make a convincing argument for self-regulation. I doubt Wall Street will ever operate the same way again. And there is some question about whether the whole business built around risk arbitrage will exist.

Very few of these considerations occupied the minds of the participants in the takeover world two years ago. The world seemed a healthier and simpler place. Were there signs then that this takeover boom would culminate in the explosive way it eventually did? Possibly. But they were not easy to detect. There were certainly warnings. In the spring of 1983 *The Times* echoed some of them. Noting that the City was 'limbering up for another spate of takeover mania', it warned 'if it breaks, it will find Whitehall and even the Monopolies Commission in a state of total confusion over what our policy towards takeovers actually is, let alone what it ought to be.' The lack of a clear policy was not the major factor behind the abuses that have been thrown up since. But more thought and planning could have anticipated some of the worst abuses.

Under Mrs Thatcher, competition policy has been as variable, as conflicting and as subject to political pressure as it had been at any time before. Tiny Rowland could complain, with some justification, that he had been given three different decisons from three separate Monopolies Commission enquiries into his battle for House of Fraser: the first a 'yes, it is not against the public interest for you to be the dominant shareholder'; the second a 'no, Lonrho is expressly forbidden from taking over this treasured asset'; and the third 'yes, by all means go ahead and bid' – by which stage it was too late. Secretaries of state came and went with bewildering speed: Nott, Biffen and Cockfield in the first Thatcher government, then Parkinson, Tebbit, Brittan and Channon in the second, with Sir Alex Fletcher and Geoffrey Pattie respectively standing in for Parkinson and Tebbit when they were undergoing their problems.

There were times when competition policy was a shambles. The confusion which it reached under the reign of Lord Cockfield was epitomised by Charter Consolidated's bid for Anderson Strathclyde: four of the six commissioners ruled it would operate against the public interest and two, including the chairman Sir Godfray Le Quesne, disagreed. Cockfield himself was a shareholder in Charter and stood aside. His deputy, Peter Rees, accepted the minority report, the first time in 18 years of merger investigators that the Commission's advice had been rejected. Cockfield found himself the centre of a major parliamentary row, sitting brooding in the gallery while MPs severely criticised him. There was also widespread criticism a few months later when Cockfield, in response to considerable lobbying and a threat by the chief executive of Sotheby's to blow his brains out if the bid succeeded, referred an offer from two Americans to the Commission.

It was the middle of 1984 before Norman Tebbit, who had replaced Cecil Parkinson, produced the basis of a workable competition policy, based on the simple principle that competition should rule. If a takeover reduced competition, then the Commission should look at it. If there was no effect on competition, then it should be left to the marketplace to resolve. It was a far from perfect policy, but it had the merit, at least as interpreted by Tebbit and, with less enthusiasm, by Leon Brittan, of consistency and predictability. But (as we saw with the manner in which both the Imperial and the Distillers situations were first referred and then taken out of the Commission again) there was – and still is – a marked inconsistency and confusion. We have seen how helpless was the City Takeover Panel when James Gulliver complained to it about the activities of Guinness, and how subject it was to lobbying and pressure of the type Morgan Grenfell was so good at.

The plain truth is that the authorities, both statutory and self-regulatory, which have had the task of monitoring and controlling the excesses of the takeover business have not performed well in Britain during this time. Again some haunting echoes come back as we look through the notes of early interviews. Here is Roger Seelig, sitting at a polished old mahogany table inside Morgan Grenfell, talking about the City Panel:

> What we've done is destroy the clarity of the general principles and strength and decisiveness of the authority of the directorate. And I think the thing has lost public respect and the respect of the practitioners. It's got buried in its own bureaucracy. Competition policy requires going back to the simple clarity of general principles that people can understand and then the strong enforcement, and decisive enforcement, of those principles by a respected practitioner who is going to take a firm line. I think it worked extremely well in the early days, and it's got muddled now.

Because of the growing complexity of bids?

> I actually think it's a reflection of the people running it, although you can't say that or they get cross. The Panel itself would argue that it's a consequence of the increased aggression of people like me. I don't think that's actually fair. We get very frustrated when we don't think the rules are rational. I don't think we're incapable of following the general principles. I think there is still – and this is a bit medieval if you like – but there's still a tremendous degree of chivalry and the code of war under which we practitioners can operate.

He pauses, then goes on reflectively (this was 1986):

> After all, I've got to live with these people for the next ten years. I can't actually play that badly. Talk to Graham [Walsh] about it. I fear that by maintaining statutes and turning it into a legislative thing it will actually worsen it, because once you do that then it will really be like income tax, I mean you'll stick to the letter of the text and not feel obligated to do anything more, whereas the general principles were really much more effective because they were expressing a spirit.

The Panel of course still has no statutory powers, but it was then, as it is now, a City debating point. Seelig would probably argue now that it never gave any clear guidance on the extent to which merchant banks could go in supporting a bidder's share price. What happened at Guinness was simply an extension of common practice, frowned on perhaps, but never firmly ruled out.

Merger policy was not any better organised in Washington. The US

Justice Department had signalled that the new administration in the White House meant not only that government agencies were to get out of business regulation, but that corporate combinations and reorganisations were to be construed liberally. There was special concern about the American banking industry which was being outstripped by investment banks and securities brokers on Wall Street and nearly every other kind of financial institution which competed internationally. It was believed at the time that the less Washington interfered with the reshaping of the capital markets, the better off everyone would be.

Not everyone believed it, to be sure. Felix Rohatyn, the Lazard Freres chief and a legend in the business, looked at the rush to finance the merger boom and concluded; 'All this frenzy may be good for investment bankers now, but it's not good for the country or investment bankers in the long run. We seem to be living in a 1920s Jazz Age atmosphere.'

Or listen to Dr Henry Kaufman, a senior partner at Salomon Brothers and indisputely Wall Street's leading forecaster:

> The target companies of today's takeover bids invariably are firms that are cash-rich or which own assets which currently are undervalued but which can be turned into cash. This is because we are in the midst of a crisis of credit, the lack of capital to continue to grow. And it is this which threatens not just the United States or Britain but the entire complex web of economic relationships that we call the free world. We are drowning in debt.

In an examination of the web of law firms being drawn into the merger mania on Wall Street, the *American Lawyer* spotted another force for distorting the process: 'a bunch of brainless 30-year-old kids who will do anything for a quick buck because their goddam jobs depend on beating the Standard and Poor every week or every month'. This element is less serious in London, but is still a serious worry to more thoughtful observers who have noted a tendency for numbers of institutions to sell out, regardless of the longer-term considerations, at key times in bid situations in the hope of maximising profits. The fact that a tiny group, usually no more than 20, fund managers in the City of London can decide the fate of a great concern, with all its employees, customer relationships, position in the community and all the rest of it, is always a disturbing thought. In reality there are brakes and public opinion does count – witness the BTR/Pilkington case. But they can't always be relied on.

Do takeovers work? Do they help the economy, by picking off the inefficient companies and kicking others into life? Are the raiders good for the business community, in the same way that the wolf packs keep the great caribou herds healthy by attacking the sick and the lame? Should we encourage them or try to slow them down? In this book we have focused more on the abuses than on the healthy bids, and on the personalities of the principal players than on the wider issues.

In November 1985 Louis Lowenstein and James Cofee, two professors at Columbia's Centre for Law and Economic Studies, organised what was the first systematic look at the merger frenzy by leading academicians in the law and business disciplines. Not surprisingly, attention was paid to the question of whether takeovers benefited the shareholders of the respective suitor and target firms. Less attention was paid at the time to the question of whether corporate raiders had a right, either legal or economic, to strip the assets of a conquered firm. As Professor Lowenstein noted at the time, much of the theoretical thinking that prevailed earlier in the decade considered takeovers as the cutting edge of an efficient marketplace.

> Under a widely held view, the prototype target company is relatively unprofitable . . . and excessively liquid such that a healthy change of control could only bring improved performance. It is all rather simple. This view relies on an aspect of the inefficient market hypothesis according to which the stock market is able to price securities so precisely in accordance with their actual value that the only significant opportunities to profit by a tender offer are those instances in which a bidder can hope for real gains by bringing in better management.

This is a point one hears over and over again in the study of merger doctrines. It is the marketplace which decided what a share is worth. But does it really? Even in an honest marketplace, one without cheating, does the market, or even a detailed analysis prepared by an investment bank at great expense, properly measure value? Remember Sir Gordon White of Hanson, and how he valued SCM? He barely read the formal reports he had been given by his advisers. He relied on what he called 'gut feeling'. And the result? He paid $1bn for SCM, including costs. Within months he had sold off about a third of the business – and recouped his full $1bn. The buyers of their subsidiaries, including ICI, are happy. What remains should make a profit of $170m, more than SCM ever made before. 'I could sell it tomorrow for $1.7bn,' said White. That would be pure profit, all in the space of a year. He won't sell it of course. But it is an indication of how much the academics can miss in their studies; and also says something about the value of investment bankers. It says even more about the efficiency of the market.

Lowenstein himself elaborated on the point.

The stock market is not nearly as efficient as we would like it to be. In any event, it is only efficient as a secondary or trading market, and that is quite different from efficiency in pricing for intrinsic value to a bidder for control. Accordingly, tender offers are often a process of indiscriminate and random selection, rather than a process of pruning out the deadwood.

Of course tender offers (particularly of the kind favoured by Boone Pickens or Carl Icahn which offer all cash for the first 50 per cent and junk bonds 'valued' at an equal sum for the latecomers) are an American phenomenon. But the same principle holds in Britain.

There are now available enough statistical data on mergers to show that predatory takeovers on the whole do not work – that they are, on average, not good for both the companies and the shareholders on both sides of the bid. Studies by management consultants McKinsey, and by Kidder Peabody, and by a host of academic institutions, have reached a similarity of conclusions in spite of widely different methods and data bases.

Even the most favourably constructed studies have concluded almost uniformly that hostile mergers typically had a neutral or negative effect on company profitability. From the point of view of what a takeover bid means to the various shareholder groups, the data appear even more gloomy. Of course, shareholders of a target firm do better in a takeover battle which increases their share price. But what about the shareholders of the aggressor firm? The results are not good. According to a consensus of studies, suitor shareholders see appreciation in the value of *their* shares after a successful takeover raid only one time in three. In the other 66 per cent of the confrontations studied the successful suitor firm's shares either remain unmoved or actually plunged in value in the months following the consummation of the deal.

Indeed there is only one study that we could find by Harvard's Michael Jensen – a pro-mergers economist – which presents evidence showing that share prices of both suitor and target firms rise at about the time the merger takes place.

Few practitioners either in London or New York have much interest in academic studies. And our experience suggests that there are many factors which cannot be measured. Gordon White, although arguing that there are more winners than losers in the merger business, adds:

I am not for a moment suggesting that all takeovers are beneficial. Some are ill-conceived and do not live up to their promises – either in greater efficency or financial saving. Successful acquisitions require skills and these are, frankly, not very well distributed among British industrial management.

White is right. 'Companies like Hanson and BTR have established that one of the most profitable businesses in Britain today is the acquisiton of insufficiently profitable businesses,' said John Kay, then director of the Institute of Fiscal Studies. But most British studies have shown these are the exception rather than the rule. Professor Julian Franks of the London Business School has studied 3,000 companies involved in takeovers over 30 years. His conclusion is that the return to shareholders, measured as a combination of share price movement and dividend payments, is lower than it was before. These returns still on average beat the market as a whole, but Franks holds that they are less than they might have been if the mergers had not taken place.

Another leading British academic, Geoff Meeks, a Cambridge economist, has been studying mergers for 20 years, consistently producing the same result. He recently analysed more than 200 mergers and compared profitability of the companies involved before and after merger. He found there was a decline in profit performance after the bid. 'The experience of mergers has been on average to dilute performance,' said Professor Franks and Meeks supports him.

Epilogue

On 19 October 1987 world stock markets suffered one of the worst days in their history. Rising fears over the level of the American budget deficit, a collapsing dollar, high interest rates and the growing realization that share prices everywhere were over-anticipating the advance of corporate earnings led to a bout of selling even greater than on Black Tuesday on Wall Street in 1929. It had begun in New York the previous week after a set of disastrous US trade figures, but over the weekend the Far Eastern and then the European markets crashed. When Wall Street opened for business that Monday morning, everyone feared share prices were going to topple. No one, however, was prepared for what did happen: the Dow Jones fell 500 points, by far and away the worst day in its history. The bull market, which had lasted for thirteen years in London and five years in most markets around the world, had come to an end.

For five years the bull market had been fuelled by a record level of bid activity, but even before the Great Crash, hostile bids were becoming rarer. Now activity dried to a trickle. Within a week, there was just one hostile bid in the whole of the London market: an improbable offer for Sir Terence Conran's Storehouse Group from the tiny Benlox company, which started off at over £2 billion but with the fall in the stock markets was now only worth around half that. In the US the pattern was much the same, with the raiders, notably Boone Pickens, Carl Icahn and Ron Perelman, running for cover. Sir James Goldsmith had already done so, the most successful anticipant of the bear market in America. The boom was well and truly over, and the latest – and greatest – bid cycle had fully run its course.

There was still much unfinished business, however, which will linger on for several years yet. Apart from the fact that the full effects, good, bad and indifferent, of all the bids that were made in this period will take up to a decade to emerge, the more visible and damaging side was the enforcement effect. Laws had been broken on both sides of the Atlantic, and not all the infringements had been swept under the carpet. In the US, Gary Lynch and the SEC were still moving forward in their battle against insider trading; Dennis Levine was behind bars and Ivan Boesky, more than a year after he first agreed to co-operate, was still providing evidence about alleged insider trading on many battles that he had been involved in.

The week of the crash had been preceded by a series of events which had reminded the British financial world of the consequences of just one little bit of Boesky evidence. New York had seen its wave of arrests for insider trading a year earlier, with some of the greatest stars of the mergers and acquisitions business led off in handcuffs, tears streaming down their faces. Now it was London's turn.

Superintendent Richard Botwright, a senior officer in Scotland Yard's Fraud Squad, was put on alert within days of the DTI investigation of Guinness starting on 1 December 1986. He should stand ready, he was told, to begin serious investigations if and when the DTI inspectors turned up something they reckoned might be criminal. He waited five months, his only source of information on the investigations coming from the newspapers, fretting impatiently all the while.

Then at the beginning of May 1987 he was ordered into action: he should put together a squad to begin work straight away. The DTI inspectors had enough evidence, it was now believed, to justify a full criminal investigation. It was to be no small affair: Botwright assembled a team of seventeen officers for the job, an unprecedented number for an investigation of this kind. The members of his team were no ordinary 'Constable Plods': Botwright chose detective chief inspector John Wooton as his deputy, and between them they picked the best of the hard core of experienced fraud squad investigators, with a proven record in supplying the good detective work, persistence, attention to detail and sheer man hours the inquiry was going to require. It would be the largest fraud inquiry ever mounted in Britain.

They began work just as Margaret Thatcher called an election, one where the opposition had hoped to score points over the issue of corruption in the City and the number of rich capitalists, some of them

Tory supporters, who had become involved in the widening Guinness affair. In the event, however, financial scandals and Guinness scarcely featured in the election campaign: the arrest and charges against Ernest Saunders early in May saw to that. There were reports of an unnamed cabinet minister warning that unless 'we get the handcuffs on quick', financial scandals and insider trading were going to be a serious embarrassment to the government in the election. Now government ministers could and did plead that the matter was *sub judice*, and if pressed further could point to the Saunders arrest and the jailing of the insider trader Geoffrey Collier. Action was being taken against financial abuse, alleged or proven, arising from the takeover boom and the rise in share prices; what more was there to talk about? The subject as an election issue sputtered and died in the first week of the campaign.

Botwright soon found that he did not have to start empty-handed. The DTI inspectors had been at work since December and had interviewed at length many of those involved in the Guinness scandal. The inspectors in many ways have much greater powers than ordinary policemen: witnesses have no right of silence before them, and if a person refuses to co-operate fully they can move quickly to bring charges of contempt. Anyone caught lying to the inspectors can be charged with perjury. The police of course have no such powers, and in a criminal investigation most interviewees are advised by their lawyers to say as little as possible.

In the Guinness case, the major participants had talked for hours, and had provided documents, letters, share certificates and much else. They were also anxious to blame each other for their involvement, so evidence had mounted all the faster. Botwright, early in the investigation, took the same approach that Gary Lynch did: he would concentrate on the principals involved, ignore, at least for the moment, the minor figures, with the object of being able to bring the big fish to court as soon as possible. Previous investigations by the fraud squad had ranged so wide that efforts had become diffused, and years had passed before charges could be brought – by which stage everyone had lost interest and the deterrent factor had disappeared.

He arranged to have on call a team of specialists to help him through the labyrinthine paperwork involved in the case; lawyers, chartered accountants, bankers and brokers all stood by with advice. Within weeks the papers were beginning to pile up, and months into the case a visit to the cramped offices on the twelfth floor of Greenway House, just behind Holborn police station where Botwright operated from, revealed documents stacked to the ceiling.

Technically Botwright had no direct access to the DTI papers, but nonetheless they were soon dribbling onto his desk via the office of the Director of Public Prosecutions. Guinness also provided him with large wodges of paper, particularly the details of the £25 million of 'special fees' that had been paid out in the closing stages of the bid in return for support of its share price. Botwright focused his efforts on the names on that list.

In the first week in May Saunders made his first appearance in court, neatly in time for the election according to cynics, but all part of the procedure according to Scotland Yard. But those who thought the investigation would die away with the successful return of Mrs Thatcher soon learned differently. Early in October Tony Parnes, the stockbroker who had originally persuaded Gerald Ronson to become involved, stepped off an Air France flight in Los Angeles with his wife and young children, and was arrested. He was taken to Terminal Island, a tough federal prison thirty miles south of Los Angeles and Botwright began extradition proceedings to bring him back to Britain to face charges of false accounting. At the time of writing the proceedings are still in progress.

A week later there was an even more dramatic arrest. A team from Botwright's Metropolitan Police squad appeared without warning at the home of Sir Jack Lyons. His house and offices were searched, and the 71-year-old millionaire was taken back to Holborn and charged with nine counts of theft of £3.25 million, forgery and false accounting. He appeared in Bow Street court the next day to be charged.

Five days later there was a further startling development: Gerald Ronson, one of Britain's richest men, was about to fly out of Britain on his own G3 jet for Japan and elsewhere, as he often did in the course of his busy life. Instead he was invited to appear at Botwright's office. It was not just for a friendly chat, or even further inquiries: he was arrested and charged with eight offences, including theft of £5.8 million (which he had already repaid to Guinness). He too turned up at Bow Street magistrates court to take his turn behind the prostitutes, shoplifters, burglars and the usual riff-raff who passed through the court daily, and was formally charged. As with Lyons, he was remanded on £500,000 bail, and his passport was taken away.

Botwright was not finished yet, not by a long way. Late on Thursday evening, 15 October, Roger Seelig, the man hired by Ernest Saunders on the basis that he was the best takeover man in the whole merchant banking fraternity, was arrested. The next day he too made the now familiar journey to Bow Street to face twelve charges, seven of which related to the fees charged by his bank, Morgan Grenfell. He was remanded on bail of £500,000 and two sureties of £250,000 were stood by his friends Sir Terence Conran and Paul Hamlyn, the publisher.

And Saunders all this while? The once proud, aloof chairman and chief executive of Guinness was now a depressed and sad figure. His world had changed dramatically in a year, not least his private life. In the early months of 1987 his health had suffered considerably, and he came close to a major heart attack. His country house at Penn, in Buckinghamshire, was continually surrounded by reporters and photographers, and every day seemed to bring a new revelation at Guinness. His wife Carole, who stood by him loyally, had finally broken under the stress and strain and suffered a mental breakdown. A great sense of tragedy descended over what had once been a happy family home, probably affecting Saunders more deeply than anything in his business life. They sold the house in Penn, but Saunders could not transfer his share of the proceeds out of the country after Guinness brought an action against him. Claiming to be desperately short of money, he took Carole to a clinic in Switzerland, and then to their ski chalet at Les Diablerets, near Gstaad, a relic from their days at Vevey when he worked for Nestlé. Guinness, when it dismissed him, had cut off all salary and pension payments to him, so he had no source of income. His legal fees were mounting by the day, and although he had been comfortably off before his dismissal, Saunders all his life had worked for a salary which he spent on bringing up and educating his family, and on a good life. He had saved little. His house in France had a mortgage on it, and soon, according to his own account, the only property he had left was his ski chalet. From Switzerland he continually travelled back to London, living in a house lent by a friend, and going into the West End each day by the London underground to see his lawyers. He talked to the inspectors for many hours, explaining his role and actions in the Distillers battle, and these interviews too had, via the DPP's office, filtered on to Botwright's desk.

Saunders was not left out of the charges that week. On the same day that Ronson was arrested, Saunders appeared at Bow Street to face a battery of new charges: thirty-seven in all, relating to the Guinness takeover of Distillers. Ten of the charges alleged theft, in the same way they did against Ronson, Lyons and others. That incensed Saunders. 'The mere idea of charges that involve the word stealing – that is, in the vernacular, putting a hand in the till and taking out any of the Guinness money – is absolutely appalling and absolutely untrue. I have stolen nothing. I *have* nothing. I have absolutely nothing to hide. My conscience is clear.'

That evening Saunders staged an impromptu little press conference in a colourless, rented room in the Waldorf Hotel. It was a miserable, wet, evening, and the proceedings were equally bleak. Accompanied by his 21-year-old son James, a law student, Saunders explained how he was the victim of events. 'This portrayal of me in a class of world tycoons with riches all over the world and yachts is crazy', he said. He was now asking friends to pay his legal fees, and if that failed, he was in big financial trouble. Tiny Rowland had already stood half his bail of £500,000 for him, and he was asking others to help. 'I can see myself becoming a millionaire in debt terms,' he said, echoing the famous phrase of Jim Slater who once described himself as a 'minus-millionaire'. The next day Saunders flew back to Lausanne, and collapsed in the same clinic as his wife, now suffering her second breakdown.

Botwright meanwhile got back to preparing the paperwork for a series of new arrests; and for a 'big bang' trial in which all those charged would appear in court at the same time. He also flew to New York for detailed conversations with Ivan Boesky, who talked about many of the other bids he had been involved in. At the time of writing Botwright is still negotiating for Boesky to appear as a witness in the cases against those charged with offences in the Guinness scandal.

The market crash destroyed or seriously damaged the reputations – and the fortunes – of some of the most astute practitioners of the takeover art. Robert Holmes à Court was caught flat-footed with a 10 per cent stake in Texaco, where a Texas court had just upheld the Pennzoil claim for damages resulting from the takeover battle of two years before, a 30 per cent stake in Australia's biggest company, BHP, 15 per cent of Standard Chartered Bank which had just fought off an unwelcome bid from Lloyds Bank, 8.2 per cent of Sears PLC, and even a 5.2 per cent stake in Morgan Grenfell, now trying desperately to keep its independence after the damage from the Guinness affair. Holmes à Court had been Australia's richest man with his bewildering series of share purchases and bids, and appeared to be on the verge of putting together a major international conglomerate when the dams burst. Now all his skills were devoted to juggling his assets and his debts in a fight to stay alive. In a single day, Holmes à Court lost $500 million, and the shares of his Bell Resources fell by 80 per cent in a month as the worst of the world crash hit Australia harder than any other market. Rupert Murdoch's family holding in News Corporation dropped by nearly $1 billion in two weeks, but unlike Holmes à Court his cash flow handsomely exceeded his debt payments, and within weeks Murdoch was back in the takeover market, snapping up companies which had become cheaper with the market fall.

There were some who had seen it coming. Donald Trump, the American real estate and casino tycoon, and Laurence Tisch, the head of CBS, both claimed to have got out in time. Lord Hanson and Sir Gordon White ended up well placed too, with over $1.2 billion in cash in their balance sheet and a portfolio of companies well equipped to stand a recession. With the market fall they doubled their efforts to find the next target that would push them even higher up the ladder: by the end of 1987 Hanson PLC was the sixth biggest company in Britain and in the top sixty in the US.

Sir James Goldsmith however was ahead of all of them.

Joseph Kennedy, father of President John Kennedy, used to tell the story of how he saved his fortune in October 1929. He was having his shoes polished on Wall Street when the shoeshine boy began telling him about the stocks he had bought. Kennedy decided that a market where even shoeshine boys were giving tips was no place for him, and he sold out. Goldsmith in the summer of 1987 formed the same view. Although his share of the profits made by his investor group in their raid of Goodyear came to $42 million, Goldsmith, in the wake of the Boesky affair, decided the bid boom was over. He would still however make a run on Pan Am, but when that failed too he decided that something more than the bid boom had come to an end. Starting early in 1987 he began to sell off all his shareholdings, liquidating all the strategic holdings he had built in companies he had considered bidding for. He closed down his office in New York which he used for the purpose of running his takeovers and by October he had $500 million in cash in his Liechtenstein holding company, and his personal fortune at the end of his successful run of takeovers was put at $1.2 billion. He is by no means finished as a bidder however: when the time is ripe, he will be back, he says. In the meantime 'like the scorpion in La Fontaine's fable, I may be tempted to sting, even if it's not in my best interest, just because I like to sting,' he said.

Some final thoughts

At the end of the day, the transatlantic case of insider traders and of cheating and fraud came to dominate our consideration of the corporate takeover phenomena of the 1980s. We had from the outset accepted some level of information sharing among City and Wall Street financial forces as both inevitable and not necessarily all that evil. It was a given fact among the individuals we interviewed that every major takeover personality had his own network of informants between Beverly Hills and the Square Mile and that the informal flow of rumours, facts and educated guesses would vary in quality and accuracy and thereby put insiders at almost the same disadvantage as the first-time buyer. Almost.

There was no way to know just how driven some of the major merger contests in the US were by the insiders themselves, or the extent to which, as in the case of Guinness, how far the rules would be bent in the pursuit of winning at any cost. How many companies were 'put into play' by men who falsely pretended to the fiduciary trust of the shareholders and company managers who hired them? How many bids were decided by support operations of the kind that Guinness used, albeit just on the right side of the law? It would be hard even now to assess the true economic damage of a single betrayal – say of Unocal's 1985 takeover defence against T. Boone Pickens, or of the defeat of James Gulliver's bid for Distillers – let alone to calculate the billions of pounds of wealth that were squandered over the last decade.

James Gulliver has been realistic and philosophical enough to get on with his life and his career. But think for a moment how he might feel: he believed, with some justification, that he and his team provided a better alternative management to the old Distillers board. There is every indication that enough Distillers shareholders agreed with him to have given him control. In the absence of Guinness, even with all the false starts and early problems, Distillers would be owned by Argyll today, and Gulliver would head up one of the great drinks companies of the world. Instead, as we know, Guinness did enter the bidding, the Distillers board supported it – a point often forgotten, particularly by an Edinburgh financial fraternity now trying to persuade itself it never wanted anything to do with Ernest Saunders – but still only won by resorting to a support operation involving some of the leading figures of the financial community. Despite the demise of Saunders and many of his board, the bid can never be undone; Gulliver, however well he does elsewhere, will always be the man who lost the bid battle, and the company he created with his colleagues Alastair Grant and David Webster, has developed in a different direction with the takeover of Safeway supermarkets. Gulliver has since left the company, and Grant has taken over as chairman. Guinness, now under new and unblemished management, still owns Distilliers, which means that, despite everything, it has come out ahead.

In the US meanwhile there is a growing frustration about the inability to bring the malefactors to book. Justice is seen to be very definitely delayed, if not denied. A just resolution of the various cases may be harder to come by than was first assumed when, on 14 November 1986, it was revealed that Ivan Boesky had not only confessed to widespread insider dealings himself, but that he and Dennis Levine and a still-to-be-disclosed group of other Wall Street heavyweights had been systematically bilking the merger game out of millions of dollars for some years. The notion at the time was that because

Levine and Boesky had confessed, the round-up of the rest of the gang would take just a matter of months. It has not worked out that way.

Nor has Boesky made any secret of the fact that what he did in the Guinness case, he also did in some other British bids. We don't yet know which ones, but Superintendant Botwright and his colleagues seem to feel they have enough on their plate with Guinness without taking on more. How far do they want – or will they be allowed – to extend their investigation? And given the damage caused to the City by the Guinness affair, how many more scandals can the system take? The cynics, unhappy even now with the pace of the investigations, point out that they have slowed with the market crash. Confidence in the securities market is a delicate flower, which can only withstand so many shocks, it is argued. Yet how can there be confidence in the markets if there is also widespread cheating?

While Levine is winding up his prison term at this writing, and Boesky's sentence is a more recent development, most of the insiders on Wall Street are still outside the confines of the justice system. Indeed with each passing month it appears that the US government prosecutors have their work cut out for them if they expect juries of average citizens to pass on the convoluted financial schemes and to pierce through the pettifog of defence lawyers and thereby sort out the guilty from the victims.

Insider trading is no longer quite so prevalent, but that may be a factor more of the low level of hostile bid activity than of a new sense of integrity. It may even be that the insiders have learned a trick or two about hiding it better. It is still noticeable, particularly in Britain, that share prices still tend to rise in anticipation of a bid. Someone, somewhere, is still taking advantage of confidential information to profit.

The sentencing of Levine and Boesky has satisfied no one; certainly not the malefactors themselves nor, increasingly, the prosecutors who made the leniency deals in exchange for evidence, nor the judges who are bound by those deals, and certainly not the public at large.

Part of this dissatisfaction lies with the nature of the crime and the criminals but part also lies with a change in public attitudes toward the recent reliance of prosecutors on super-grasses who exchange evidence not otherwise obtainable by investigators for light sentences for themselves.

Dating from before the Watergate trials of the 1970s American prosecutors had become increasingly dependent on plea bargaining witnesses to crack the increasingly complex webs of fraud that white-collar criminals and organized crime organizations were using to mask their felonies. But juries have reacted to tame witnesses and 'sting' operations by demanding corroborating evidence and by showing a willingness to turn defendants loose without it.

One of the hallmarks of this more recent jury resistance is the distrust that focuses on government witnesses who are accused of the same crimes as the defendant, but whose pleas and co-operation have resulted in freedom or drastically reduced prison terms. The worry that these individuals would be willing to perjure themselves, to tailor their information to prosecution needs, is not without foundation.

So no one is happy with the deals struck between Dennis Levine, Ivan Boesky and the US District Attorney Rudolph Giuliani in New York. Levine and Boesky may well feel that if they had remained obdurate, even in the face of the evidence against them, it would have been years before government prosecutors could have brought a firm case against them to a jury; even than the result would be in doubt.

Nor are the prosecutors and investigators from the SEC happy with their own deal any more. Levine, now counting the months to the time he becomes eligible for parole, is no longer a co-operative witness.

Worse, there is a growing feeling that Boesky, despite his co-operation in grassing on others, including Guinness, pulled a skilful flim-flam on the government itself. His record $100 million in returned profits and penalties turned out to be partly in assets of his Cumbria investment trust which netted only $30.7 million on the open market. In the meantime Boesky was able to unravel his own positions in the stock market, netting millions more, and to sell off other properties and sequester other millions beyond reach either of the government or of his creditors. The $900 million invested in his Ivan Boesky limited partnership (including the $100 million put in by Guinness) may never be returned to creditors.

Ominously, the other men named by Boesky and Levine at Kidder Peabody and other firms, have shown little visible terror at the accusations. The paper trial of evidence needed to corroborate the testimony of the two confessed villains will have to be very clear indeed before a lay jury will act.

As for the takeover trend itself, during 1987 the hostile bid was replaced by divestitures and spin-offs, partly a result of the merger activity in the first place, but also a part of the major restructuring which is taking place, particularly in the US. According to Roger Miller of Salomon Brothers, there is hardly a major corporation in the US which has not recently undertaken, or at least seriously considered, some form of reorganization. There are leveraged buy-outs by the score, the most spectacular being the buy-out of GAF by its chief executive officer, Sam Heyman, for $2.3 billion.

There have been some highly successful foreign bids in the US too, the most notable being the $566 million takeover of J. Walter Thompson, the so-called 'university of advertising' by Martin Sorrell, the former finance director of Saatchi & Saatchi; or the takeover of Manpower for $1.34 billion by Tony Berry's Blue Arrow to make it the biggest employment agency business in the world. And some failures: Robert Maxwell made a $1.7 billion bid for Harcourt, Brace, Jovanovich, pushing that company into a massive restructuring and an increase in the share value received by its shareholders from the $44 offered by Maxwell to $54 created by a leveraged recapitalization. Harcourt then embarked on a programme of having to sell off some of its operations to reduce the debt it had taken on. Maxwell remained one of the most active bidders all the way through 1987, and reacted to the October market crash by launching a $500 million buying spree, ranging from a US printing company to the bid for Watford football club.

Maxwell however is the exception. Most of the takeover players have remained quiet. Boone Pickens and his partners are content to play for small stakes. Carl Icahn, who personified the corporate raider whose focus was solely on the share price and not the underlying corporation, got a kind of rough justice in 1986 when he ended up in control of the ailing airline Trans World Airways Inc. against his better judgement. To his credit, Icahn has buckled down to the unenviable task of turning TWA around and may prove a better manager than many of the air transport experts who hooted at him earlier.

The good news is that Washington's alarm about takeovers, which threatened to translate into draconian legislation that would have killed off all kinds of mergers, the friendly with the hostile, the good with the pernicious, has abated. The Congress has been distracted by other things, budget deficits, taxes and the like. The slow work of securities reform, new tender offer legislation and other less dramatic improvements probably now will not take place until after the 1988 elections.

In Britain yet another Secretary of State for Trade and Industry, Lord Young, has taken over since the June election and has returned to the Tebbit principles of letting competition decide. In his first few months he was delivered two nasties: Rupert Murdoch's agreed takeover of the Today newspaper (from Tiny Rowland) and the British Airways bid for British Caledonian. The former one went through without referral; the latter was referred but the Monopolies Commission moved fast to complete its report in the promised four months. In both cases, Young has emerged well, but there are more testing times ahead for his competition policy.

So in the final analysis, the debate over takeovers is left where we began it, still unresolved, or more optimistically, resolving itself with the passing of time and with the ability of the market and its participants to adjust to their own self interests.

Ivan Fallon, Kent.
James Srodes, Washington D.C.

December, 1987.

Index

John Adair
Effective Leadership £3.99

THE FULLY REVISED AND UPDATED GUIDE TO DEVELOPING
LEADERSHIP SKILLS

Some people are born leaders, some people become leaders, and some have
leadership thrust upon them. The art of good leadership is highly prized, and
demands a keen ability to appraise, understand and inspire both colleagues
and subordinates.

EFFECTIVE LEADERSHIP is carefully structured to ensure a steady, easily
acquired insight into leadership skills, helping you to:

* understand leadership – what you have to be, know and do

* develop leadership abilities – defining the task, planning, briefing, controlling,
setting an example

* grow as a leader – making certain your organisation encourages leaders to
emerge

With EFFECTIVE LEADERSHIP, John Adair has provided an invigorating book
that reflects his vivid experiences as a worker, researcher and teacher, making
it the ideal passport to the development of leadership.

William Kay
Tycoons £2.95

Where they came from and how they made it

'I remember our bank sneering at Habitat when it started. They thought it was here today and gone tomorrow . . .' Sir Terence Conran

How do tycoons like Robert Maxwell and Sir Terence Conran make their fortunes? When did they decide to start out on their own? How did they begin? What attracted them to the competitive, exciting world of business. And what keeps them at it long after they've made more money than they could spend in several lifetimes? Do *you* have what it takes?

In this highly stimulating and above all instructive analysis of what makes top tycoons tick, William Kay, City Editor of *The Times*, charts the careers of thirteen of Britain's most successful entrepeneurs. In far greater depth than ever before, they explain to Kay how they got going, they reveal the secrets behind their continuing success, and they offer priceless advice to every aspiring tycoon who wants to take the plunge.

'In business, if you are persistent you normally arrive. It's the old tortoise and hare story. You don't have to be supergood . . .' Noel Lister, MFI

John Winkler
Pricing For Results £3.95
How to set, present, discount and negotiate prices

Bad pricing decisions can ruin the sales prospects of any product, as countless businesses have discovered. John Winkler has used his unique appreciation of the pricing mechanism to win many commercial battles. In *Pricing for Results*, he shows how to win the price war.

Effective pricing skills are crucial in the industrial, consumer and service sectors of any country. The Winkler approach can thus be commended to all finance and sales directors/managers, key account negotiators, general managers and students of marketing.

The Winkler formula explains:

- How to SET prices
- How to PRESENT prices
- How to DISCOUNT prices
- How to NEGOTIATE prices

Pan Management Guides

For busy executives who want to acquire quickly essential new management skills to develop their careers

Pan Management Guides will give today's hard-pressed executives and those who run their own businesses a more thorough grounding in essential management skills, sufficient to enable them to run their departments or businesses more effectively and successfully.

Pan Management Guides are written by authors who combine practical international experience of their subject with deep background knowledge. Each book in the series covers one crucial area of modern business so that a complete library of vital information can be built.

Pan Management Guides are down-to-earth and uncluttered, designed to enable you to quickly absorb only the facts that matter.

Books in the series:

Advertising and PR £2.95
Company Accounts £2.95
Essential Law £3.95
Financial Management £3.95
Industrial Relations £2.95
Information Technology £3.95
Management Accounting £2.95
The Management of Business £3.95
Marketing £2.95
Personnel Management £2.95
Production and Operations Management £2.95